PART 2

Paper 2.4

Financial Management and Control

REVISION SERIES

Official Publisher

◆ **FOULKS***lynch*

3119/F02

British Library Cataloguing-in-Publication Data

A catalogue record for this book is available from the British Library.

Published by Foulks Lynch Ltd
Number 4
The Griffin Centre
Staines Road
Feltham
Middlesex
TW14 0HS

ISBN 0 7483 5311 9

© Foulks Lynch Ltd, 2002

Printed in Great Britain by Antony Rowe Ltd, Chippenham, Wiltshire

Acknowledgements

The past ACCA examination questions are the copyright of the Association of Chartered Certified Accountants. The answers to the questions from June 1994 onwards are the answers produced by the examiners themselves and are the copyright of the Association of Chartered Certified Accountants. The answers to the questions prior to June 1994 have been produced by Foulks Lynch Ltd.

We are grateful to the Chartered Institute of Management Accountants and the Institute of Chartered Accountants in England and Wales for permission to reproduce past examination questions. The answers have been prepared by Foulks Lynch Ltd.

Contents

Standard costing and variance analysis

Examiner plus – the examiner's official answers

Budgeting, budgetary control and decision-making

Examiner plus – the examiner's official answers

Scenario-based questions

Examiner plus – the examiner's official answers

Preface – How to use this book

The 2002 edition of the ACCA Revision Series, published for the June and December 2002 examinations, contains a wealth of features designed to make your prospects of passing the exams even brighter.

We have taken the opportunity with the introduction of the new syllabus to reorganise this book. All the practice questions are organised by key syllabus topic categories. This will help you see at a glance a range of questions relevant to each syllabus area to date, topic by topic. The Pilot Paper, December 2001 exam and the previous two years' exams (where relevant) have been cross-referenced to the syllabus category in the contents pages.

Key features

1   Examiner plus

This book includes a wide selection of questions from relevant past ACCA exams including the 2001 Pilot Paper and December exam, the first of the new syllabus examinations. In addition, there are full, up-to-date answers, many of which have been prepared by examiners. Where relevant under the new syllabus, the last two years' exams have also been included as full examinations in an 'old syllabus examinations' section.

2   Key answer tips

An important feature in this Revision Series is the inclusion of key answer tips for all practice questions.

For each question we have highlighted the most important part of the answer and displayed it as the key answer tip. This will ensure that you focus on the essential part of the question and will help you give the best possible answer.

3   Examination technique

It is very important that you are prepared before sitting the examination. This section provides practical advice on sitting the examination and valuable guidance on examination technique, such as how to approach a question and write an answer plan.

4   The Revision Series also contains the following features:

- The syllabus and format of the examination.

- An analysis of past exams from June 1997 to June 2001 (where relevant), and the new syllabus Pilot Paper and December 2001 examination.

- Examination technique and general revision guidance – an essential guide to ensure that you approach and prepare for the examinations correctly.

- Key revision topics.

- Essential update notes (where appropriate) to bring you up-to-date for new examinable documents and inform you of any changes to important legislation.

- Practice questions and answers grouped by syllabus topic – a substantial bank of questions and answers in this book.

- The Pilot Paper and December 2001 examination paper.

- Formulae and tables where appropriate.

Section 1

SYLLABUS AND EXAMINATION FORMAT

◆ **FOULKS***lynch*

Format of the examination

The examination is a three-hour paper in two sections:

		Number of marks
Section A	One compulsory scenario-based questions	50
Section B	Choice of 2 from 4 questions (25 marks each)	50
		100

Financial management issues will always, but not exclusively, be examined in Section A. Most of the Section B questions will contain a mix of computation and discursive elements although it is intended that at least one question will be entirely discursive. The balance between computation and discursive elements will remain largely constant from one examination to the next.

Present value and annuity tables will be provided in the examination.

Syllabus content

1 Financial management objectives

(a) The nature, purpose and scope of financial management.

(b) The relationship between financial management, management accounting and financial accounting.

(c) The relationship of financial objectives and organisational strategy.

(d) Problems of multiple stakeholders in financial management and the consequent multiple objectives.

(e) Objectives (financial and otherwise) in not-for-profit organisations.

2 The financial management environment

(a) Financial intermediation and credit creation.

(b) Money and capital markets

    (i) Domestic and international
    (ii) Stock markets (both major markets and small firm markets).

(c) The Efficient Markets Hypothesis.

(d) Rates of interest and yield curves.

(e) The impact of fiscal and monetary policy on business.

(f) Regulation of business (for example, pricing restrictions, green policies and corporate governance).

3   Management of working capital

(a)   The nature and scope of working capital management.

(b)   Funding requirements for working capital.

(c)   Working capital needs of different types of business.

(d)   The relationship of working capital management to business solvency.

(e)   Management of stock, debtors, short-term funds, cash, overdrafts and creditors.

(f)   Techniques of working capital management (including, inter alia, ratio analysis, EOQ, JIT, credit evaluation, terms of credit, cash discounts, factoring and invoice discounting, debtors cycles, efficient short term fund investing, cash forecasting and budgets, Miller-Orr models, basic foreign exchange methods, probabilities and risk assessment, terms of trade with creditors).

4   Sources of finance

(a)   Sources and relative costs (including issue costs) of various types of finance and their suitability to different circumstances and organisations (large and small, listed and unlisted) including:

    (i)   access to funds and the nature of business risk

    (ii)   the nature and importance of internally generated funds

    (iii)   capital markets (types of share capital, new issues, rights issues, loan capital, convertibles, warrants)

    (iv)   the effect of dividend policy on financing needs

    (v)   bank finance (short, medium and long term, including leasing)

    (vi)   trade credit

    (vii)   government sources: grants, regional and national aid schemes and tax incentives.

    (viii)   problems of small company financing (collateral, maturity funding gap, risk)

    (ix)   problems of companies with low initial earnings (R&D, Internet, and other high-technology businesses)

    (x)   venture capital and financial sources particularly suited to the small company

    (xi)   international money and capital markets, including an introduction to international banking and the finance of foreign trade.

(b)   Requirements of finance (for what purpose, how much and for how long) in relation to business operational and strategic objectives.

(c)   The importance of the choice of capital structure: equity versus debt and basic analysis of the term profile of funds.

(d)   Financial gearing and other key financial ratios and analysis of their significance to the organisation.

(e)   Appropriate sources of finance, taking into account:

    (i)   cost of finance

    (ii)   timing of cash payments

    (iii)   effect on gearing and other ratios

    (iv)   effect on company's existing investors.

5   Capital expenditure and investment

(a)   Appraisal of domestic capital investment opportunities for profit and non-profit making organisations through the use of appropriate methods and techniques:

    (i)   the risk return relationship

    (ii)   return on capital employed

    (iii)   payback

    (iv)   internal rate of return

    (v)   net present value

    (vi)   single and multi-period capital rationing

    (vii)   lease or buy decisions

    (viii)   asset replacement.

Including (in categories (i)-(viii)) the effects of taxation, inflation, risk and uncertainty (probabilities, decision trees, sensitivity analysis, simulation).

6   Costing systems

(a)   The purpose of costing as an aid to planning, monitoring and control of business activity.

(b)   Information requirements of different approaches.

(c)   Costing information requirements and limitations in not-for-profit organisations.

(d)   Behavioural implications of different costing approaches including performance evaluation.

(e)   Implications of costing approaches for profit reporting, the pricing of products and internal activities/ services.

(f)   The role of costing systems in performance evaluation and decision-making.

7   Costing techniques

(a)   Allocating/apportioning costs through the use of appropriate techniques:

    (i)   absorption, marginal and opportunity cost approaches to the accumulation of costs for specific orders (job, batch, contract) or operations (process, service)

    (ii)   activity based costing; use of cost drivers and activities

    (iii)   life cycle costing

    (iv)   target costing.

8   Standard costing and variance analysis

(a)   Standard costing:

    (i)   determination of standards

    (ii)   identification and calculation of sales variances (including quantity and mix), cost variances (including mix and yield); absorption and marginal approaches

    (iii)   significance and relevance of variances

    (iv)   operating statements

    (v)   interpretation and relevance of variance calculations to business performance.

◇ FOULKS*lynch*

(b)   Planning and operational variances.

(c)   Behavioural implications of standard costing and variance reporting.

9   Budgeting and budgetary control

(a)   Objectives of budgetary planning and control systems including aspects of behavioural implications.

(b)   Evaluation of budgetary systems such as fixed and flexible, zero based and incremental, periodic, continuous and activity based.

(c)   Development, implementation and coordination of budgeting systems: functional, subsidiary and master/ principal budgets (including cash budgeting); budget review.

(d)   Calculation and cause of variances as aids to controlling performance.

(e)   Quantitative aids to budgeting and the concepts of correlation, basic time series analysis (seasonality) and forecasting; use of computer-based models.

(f)   Implications of costing systems on profit reporting.

(g)   Behavioural implications of budgeting and budgetary control.

Section 2
ANALYSIS OF PAST PAPERS

Below is an analysis of the old paper 8 **Managerial Finance** exams (June 1997 to June 2001), on which paper 2.4 is broadly based, and the Pilot Paper plus the December 2001 paper under the new syllabus.

Topics	J97	D97	J98	D98	J99	D99	J00	D00	J01	Pilot Paper 2001	D01
Financial management objectives											2 O
The financial management environment			3 O					2 O			
Ratio analysis	1 □		2 ●						1 ■	2 O	
Management of working capital	1 3 ■ ●	1 □		3 O	2 O	1 □	3 O		3 O	1 □	4 O
Money and capital			1 ■					3 O			
Sources of finance and gearing		2 ●	1 □	2 3 O ●	3 O		1 □		1 3 □ ●	2 O	3 O
Dividend policy		2 ●					1 ■	3 O			
Project financing	1 □						1 □				
Investment appraisal	2 3 O O	3 O	2 O	1 □	1 □	2 O		1 □	2 3 O	3 O	1 □
Costing systems: not for profit organisations											5 O
Capital rationing						3 O	2 O		3 ●		
Management accountant's role			4 O			6 ●			4 O		
Performance evaluation	6 ●										
Decision-making (including pricing)		6 O	6 O	4 O	6 O	5 O			3 ●		
Process costing							5 O				
Absorption/marginal/activity based costing	4 5 ● O	4 O					6 O	4 O		5 O	3 5 O O
Service department costing	6 ●										
Standard costing & variance analysis	4 O	5		6 O O	5 O	4 O		4 6 O O	5 O	4 O	
Budgeting	5 6 ● O		5 O	5 O	4 O	4 6 ● O	4 O	5 O	6 O	1 □	
Forecasting/statistical techniques	5 ●					1 ■		6 1 ● □			

Key
The number refers to the number of the question where this topic was examined in the exam.
Topics forming the whole or a substantial part of a question:
□   Compulsory O   Optional
Topics forming a non-substantial part of a question
■   Compulsory ●   Optional

◆ FOULKS*lynch*

Section 3

GENERAL REVISION GUIDANCE

Planning your revision

What is revision?

Revision is the process by which you remind yourself of the material you have studied during your course, clarify any problem areas and bring your knowledge to a state where you can retrieve it and present it in a way that will satisfy the examiners.

Revision is not a substitute for hard work earlier in the course. The syllabus for this paper is too large to be hastily 'crammed' a week or so before the examination. You should think of your revision as the final stage in your study of any topic. It can only be effective if you have already completed earlier stages.

Ideally, you should begin your revision shortly after you begin an examination course. At the end of every week and at the end of every month, you should review the topics you have covered. If you constantly consolidate your work and integrate revision into your normal pattern of study, you should find that the final period of revision - and the examination itself - is much less daunting.

If you are reading this revision text while you are still working through your course, we strongly suggest that you begin now to review the earlier work you did for this paper. Remember, the more times you return to a topic, the more confident you will become with it.

The main purpose of this book, however, is to help you to make the best use of the last few weeks before the examination. In this section, we offer some suggestions for effective planning of your final revision and discuss some revision techniques that you may find helpful.

Planning your time

Most candidates find themselves in the position where they have less time than they would like to revise, particularly if they are taking several papers at one diet. The majority of people must balance their study with conflicting demands from work, family or other commitments.

It is impossible to give hard and fast rules about the amount of revision you should do. You should aim to start your final revision at least four weeks before your examination. If you finish your course work earlier than this, you would be well advised to take full advantage of the extra time available to you. The number of hours you spend revising each week will depend on many factors, including the number of papers you are sitting. You should probably aim to do a minimum of about six to eight hours a week for each paper.

In order to make best use of the revision time that you have, it is worth spending a little of it at the planning stage. We suggest that you begin by asking yourself two questions:

- How much time do I have available for revision?
- What do I need to cover during my revision?

Once you have answered these questions, you should be able to draw up a detailed timetable. We will now consider these questions in more detail.

How much time do I have available for revision?

Many people find it helpful to work out a regular weekly pattern for their revision. We suggest you use the time planning chart provided to do this. Your aim should be to construct a timetable that is sustainable over a period of several weeks.

Time planning chart

	Monday	Tuesday	Wednesday	Thursday	Friday	Saturday	Sunday
00.00							
01.00							
02.00							
03.00							
04.00							
05.00							
06.00							
07.00							
08.00							
09.00							
10.00							
11.00							
12.00							
13.00							
14.00							
15.00							
16.00							
17.00							
18.00							
19.00							
20.00							
21.00							
22.00							
23.00							

1   First, block out all the time that is **definitely unavailable** for revision. This will include the hours when you normally sleep, the time you are at work and any other regular and clear commitments.

2   Think about **other people's claims on your time**. If you have a family, or friends whom you see regularly, you may want to discuss your plans with them. People are likely to be flexible in the demands they make on you in the run-up to your examinations, especially if they are aware that you have considered their needs as well as your own. If you consult the individuals who are affected by your plans, you may find that they are surprisingly supportive; instead of being resentful of the extra time you are spending studying.

3   Next, give some thought to the times of day when you **work most effectively**. This differs very much from individual to individual. Some people can concentrate first thing in the morning. Others work best in the early evening, or last thing at night. Some people find their day-to-day work so demanding that they are unable to do anything extra during the week, but must concentrate their study time at weekends. Mark the times when you feel you could do your best work on the timetable. It is extremely important to acknowledge your personal preferences here. If you ignore them, you may devise a timetable that is completely unrealistic and which you will not be able to adhere to.

4   Consider your **other commitments**. Everybody has certain tasks, from doing the washing to walking the dog, which must be performed on a regular basis. These tasks may not have to be done at a particular time, but you should consider them when planning your schedule. You may be able to find more convenient times to get these jobs done, or be able to persuade other people to help you with them.

5   Now mark some time for **relaxation**. If your timetable is to be sustainable, it must include some time for you to build up your reserves. If your normal week does not include any regular physical activity, make sure that you include some in your revision timetable. A couple of hours spent in a sports centre or swimming pool each week will probably enhance your ability to concentrate.

◆ FOULKS*lynch*

6   Your timetable should now be taking shape. You can probably see obvious study sessions emerging. It is not advisable to work for too long at any one session. Most people find that they can only really concentrate for one or two hours at a time. If your study sessions are longer than this, you should split them up.

What do I need to cover during my revision?

Most candidates are more confident about some parts of the syllabus than others. Before you begin your revision, it is important to have an overview of where your strengths and weaknesses lie.

One way to do this is to take a sheet of paper and divide it into three columns. Mark the columns:

OK   Marginal   Not OK

or use similar headings to indicate how confident you are with a topic. Then go through the syllabus (reprinted in Section 1) and list the topics under the appropriate headings. Alternatively, you could use the list of key topics in Section 5 of this book to compile your overview. You might also find it useful to skim through the introductions or summaries to the textbook or workbooks you have used in your course. These should remind you of parts of the course that you found particularly easy or difficult at the time. You could also use some of the exercises and questions in the workbooks or textbooks, or some of the questions in this book, as a diagnostic aid to discover the areas where you need to work hardest.

It is also important to be aware which areas of the syllabus are so central to the subject that they are likely to be examined in every diet, and which are more obscure, and not likely to come up so frequently. Your textbooks, workbooks and lecture notes will help you here, and Section 2 of this book contains an analysis of past papers. Remember, the examiner will be looking for broad coverage of the syllabus. There is no point in knowing one or two topics in exhaustive detail if you do so at the expense of the rest of the course.

Writing your revision timetable

You now have the information you need to write your timetable. You know how many weeks you have available, and the approximate amount of time that is available in each week.

You should stop all serious revision 48 hours before your examination. After this point, you may want to look back at your notes to refresh your memory, but you should not attempt to revise any new topics. A clear and rested brain is worth more than any extra facts you could memorise in this period.

Make one copy of this chart for each week you have available for revision.

Using your time planning chart, write in the times of your various study sessions during the week.

In the lower part of the chart, write in the topics that you will cover in each of these sessions.

Example of a revision timetable

Revision timetable Week beginning:							
	Monday	Tuesday	Wednesday	Thursday	Friday	Saturday	Sunday
Study sessions							
Topics							

Some revision techniques

There should be two elements in your revision. You must **look back** to the work you have covered in the course and **look forward** to the examination. The techniques you use should reflect these two aspects of revision.

Revision should not be boring. It is useful to try a variety of techniques. You probably already have some revision techniques of your own and you may also like to try some of the techniques suggested here, if they are new to you. However, do not waste time with methods of revision that are not effective for you.

- Go through your lecture notes, textbook or workbooks and use a highlighter pen to mark important points.

- Produce a new set of summarised notes. This can be a useful way of re-absorbing information, but you must be careful to keep your notes concise, or you may find that you are simply reproducing work you have done before. It is helpful to use a different format for your notes.

- Make a collection of key words that remind you of the essential concepts of a topic.

- Reduce your notes to a set of key facts and definitions that you must memorise. Write them on cards that you can keep with you all the time.

- When you come across areas which you were unsure about first time around, rework relevant questions in your course materials, then study the answers in great detail.

- If there are isolated topics that you feel are completely beyond you, identify exactly what it is that you cannot understand and find someone (such as a lecturer or recent graduate) who can explain these points to you.

- Practise as many exam standard questions as you can. The best way to do this is to work to time, under exam conditions. You should always resist looking at the answer until you have finished.

- If you have come to rely on a computer in your day-to-day work, you may have got out of the habit of writing at speed. It is well worth reviving this skill before you sit down in the examination hall: it is something you will need.

- If you have a plentiful supply of relevant questions, you could use them to practise planning answers, and then compare your notes with the answers provided. This is not a substitute for writing full answers, but can be helpful additional practice.

- Go back to questions you have already worked on during the course. This time, complete them under exam conditions, paying special attention to the layout and organisation of your answers. Then compare them in detail with the suggested answers and think about the ways in which your answer differs. This is a useful way of 'fine tuning' your technique.

- During your revision period, do make a conscious effort to identify situations that illustrate concepts and ideas that may arise in the examination. These situations could come from your own work, or from reading the business pages of the quality press. This technique will give you a new perspective on your studies and could also provide material that you can use in the examination.

- Read good newspapers and professional journals, especially the ACCA students' newsletter, the Student Accountant. The articles will keep you up-to-date and the examiners' reports on previous sittings will give you an advantage in the exam.

Additional revision aids

To help with your revision, and in addition to the Revision Series, Foulks Lynch has prepared two other resource series:

- Lynchpins - these pocket-sized books complement the Textbooks by providing a distillation of the core information necessary to pass the paper and include illustrations, examples, focal points and space for your own notes
- Tracks audio tapes - designed to be used throughout your course as well as during revision, these user-friendly audio tapes are fully integrated with other ACCA publications and include chapter and topic summaries and highlight key points of the syllabus.

Section 4

EXAMINATION TECHNIQUES

The examination

This section is divided into two parts. The first part considers the practicalities of sitting the examination. If you have taken other ACCA examinations recently, you may find that everything here is familiar to you. The second part discusses some examination techniques that you may find useful.

On the day of your exam

What to take with you

You should make sure that you have:

- your ACCA registration card
- your ACCA registration docket.

You may also take to your desk:

- pens and pencils
- a ruler
- a calculator
- charting template and geometrical instruments
- eraser and correction fluid.

You are not allowed to take rough paper into the examination.

If you take any last-minute notes with you to the examination hall, make sure these are not on your person. You should keep notes or books in your bag or briefcase, which you will be asked to leave at the side of the examination hall.

Although most examination halls will have a clock, it is advisable to wear a watch, just in case your view is obscured.

If your calculator is solar-powered, make sure it works in artificial light. Some examination halls are not particularly well lit. If you use a battery-powered calculator, take some spare batteries with you. For obvious reasons, you may not use a calculator that has a graphic/word display memory. Calculators with printout facilities are not allowed because they could disturb other candidates.

Getting there

You should arrange to arrive at the examination hall at least half an hour before the examination is due to start. If the hall is a large one, the invigilator will start filling the hall half an hour before the starting time.

Make absolutely sure that you know how to get to the examination hall and how long it will take you. Check on parking or public transport. Leave yourself enough time so that you will not be anxious if the journey takes a little longer than you anticipated. Many people like to make a practice trip the day before their first examination.

At the examination hall

Examination halls differ greatly in size. Some only hold about ten candidates. Others can sit many hundreds of people. You may find that more than one examination is being taken at the hall at the same time, so don't panic if you hear people discussing a completely different subject from the one you have revised.

While you are waiting to go in, do not be put off by other people talking about how well, or badly, they have prepared for the examination.
You will be told when to come into the examination hall. The desks are numbered. (Your number will be on your examination docket.) You will be asked to leave any bags at the side of the hall.

Inside the hall, the atmosphere will be extremely formal. The invigilator has certain things that he or she must tell candidates, often using a particular form of words. Listen carefully, in case there are any unexpected changes to the arrangements.

On your desk you will see a question paper and an answer booklet in which to write your answers. You will be told when to turn over the paper.

During the examination

You will have to leave your examination paper and answer booklet in the hall at the end of the examination. It is quite acceptable to write on your examination paper if it helps you to think about the questions. However, all workings should be in your answers. You may write any plans and notes in your answer booklet, as long as you cross them out afterwards.

If you require a new answer booklet, put your hand up and a supervisor will come and bring you one.

At various times during the examination, you will be told how much time you have left.

You should not need to leave the examination hall until the examination is finished. Put up your hand if you need to go to the toilet, and a supervisor will accompany you. If you feel unwell, put up your hand, and someone will come to your assistance. If you simply get up and walk out of the hall, you will not be allowed to re-enter.

Before you finish, you must fill in the required information on the front of your answer booklet.

Examination techniques

Your general strategy

You should spend the first few minutes of the examination reading the paper. Where you have a choice of question, decide which questions you will do. You must divide the time you spend on questions in proportion to the marks on offer. Do not be tempted to spend more time on a question you know a lot about, or one that you find particularly difficult. If a question has more than one part, you must complete each part.

On every question, the first marks are the easiest to gain. Even if things go wrong with your timing and you do not have time to complete a question properly, you will probably gain some marks by making a start.

Spend the last five minutes reading through your answers and making any additions or corrections.

You may answer written questions in any order you like. Some people start with their best question, to help them relax. Another strategy is to begin with your second best question, so that you are working even more effectively when you reach the question you are most confident about.

Once you have embarked on a question, you should try to stay with it, and not let your mind stray to other questions on the paper. You can only concentrate on one thing at once. However, if you get completely stuck with a question, leave space in your answer book and return to it later.

Answering the question

All examiners say that the most frequent reason for failure in examinations, apart from basic lack of knowledge, is candidates' unwillingness to answer the question that the examiner has asked. A great many people include every scrap of knowledge they have on a topic, just in case it is relevant. **Stick to the question and tailor your answer to what you are asked. Pay particular attention to the verbs in the question.**

You should be particularly suspicious if you come across a question that appears to be almost identical to one that you have practised during your revision. It probably isn't! Wishful thinking makes many people see the question they would like to see on the paper, not the one that is actually there.

Read a question at least twice before you begin your answer to ensure you focus on precisely what is required. Underline key words on the question paper, if it helps focus your mind on what is required. Look closely at the mark allocation and how many components there are to each question. You must ensure that you answer all components relative to their mark allocation. For essay questions, take a little time to plan your answer before starting to write. This will help you identify and concentrate on the main points that need to be covered in your answer.

If you do not understand what a question is asking, state your assumptions. Even if you do not answer in precisely the way the examiner hoped, you may be given some credit, if your assumptions are reasonable. Include clear definitions of important terms and concepts, and where necessary, include examples and cases to illustrate your answer.

Presentation

You should do everything you can to make things easy for the marker. Although you will not be marked on your handwriting, the marker will find it easier to identify the points you have made if your answers are legible. The same applies to spelling and grammar. Use blue or black ink. The marker will be using red or green.

Use the margin to identify clearly which question, or part of a question, you are answering.

Start each answer on a new page. The order in which you answer the questions does not matter, but if a question has several parts, these parts should appear in the correct order in your answer book.

If there is the slightest doubt when an answer continues on another page, indicate to the marker that he or she must turn over. It is irritating for a marker to think he or she has reached the end of an answer, only to turn the page and find that the answer continues.

Use columnar layouts for computations. This will help you to avoid mistakes, and is easier to follow.

Use headings and numbered sentences if they help to show the structure of your answer. However, do not write your answers in one-word note form.

It is a good idea to make a rough plan of an answer before you begin to write. Do this in your answer booklet, but make sure you cross it out neatly afterwards. The marker needs to be clear whether he or she is looking at your rough notes, or the answer itself.

Multiple-choice questions

Don't treat these as an easy option – students often gain low marks on this section because they rush them.

Read the questions carefully and work through any calculations required. If you don't know the answer, first eliminate those options you know are incorrect and see if the answer is then obvious. If you are still unsure, make a note and come back to the question later. When returning to the question, if you are still unsure, guess – at least you will have some chance of getting the mark; if you leave a blank, you won't have any chance.

Computations

Before you begin a computation, you may find it helpful to jot down the stages you will go through. Cross out these notes afterwards.

It is essential to include all your workings and to indicate where they fit in to your answer. It is important that the marker can see where you got the figures in your answer from. Even if you make mistakes in your computations, you will be given credit for using a principle correctly, if it is clear from your workings and the structure of your answer.

If you spot an arithmetical error early in your answer that has implications for figures later in your answer, it may not be worth spending a lot of time reworking your computation.

If you are asked to comment or make recommendations on a computation, you must do so. There are important marks to be gained here. Even if your computation contains mistakes, you may still gain marks if your reasoning is correct.

Many computational questions require the use of a standard format: company profit and loss account, balance sheet and cash flow statement for example. Be sure you know these formats fluently before the examination and use the layouts that you see in the answers given in this book and in model answers. A clear layout will help you avoid errors and will impress the marker. Show workings, but don't overdo things by presenting ledger accounts for every item in a balance sheet question, as some candidates still do.

Essay questions

You must plan an essay before you start writing. One technique is to quickly jot down any ideas that you think are relevant. Re-read the question and cross out any points in your notes that are not relevant. Then number your points. Remember to cross out your plan afterwards.

Your essay should have a clear structure. It should contain a brief introduction, a main section and a conclusion. Do not waste time by restating the question at the start of your essay.

Break your essay up into paragraphs. Use sub-headings and numbered sentences if they help show the structure of your answer.

Be concise. It is better to write a little about a lot of different points than a great deal about one or two points.

The examiner will be looking for evidence that you have understood the syllabus and can apply your knowledge in new situations. You will also be expected to give opinions and make judgements. These should be based on reasoned and logical arguments. You must also explain any concepts used – imagine the examiner as an intelligent layperson.

Case studies

To write a good case study, first identify the area in which there is a problem, outline the main principles/theories you are going to use to answer the question, and then apply the principles/theories to the case.

When applying the principles, first outline the facts of the case problem in relation to principles/theories you are using. Be careful only to include relevant points and then reach a conclusion, and – if asked for – recommendation(s). If you can, compare the facts to real-life examples – this may gain you additional marks in the exam.

Reports, memos and other documents

Some questions ask you to present your answer in the form of a report or a memo or other document. It is important that you use the correct format - there are easy marks to be gained here. Adopt the format used in sample questions, or use the format you are familiar with in your day-to-day work, as long as it contains all the essential elements.

You should also consider the audience for any document you are writing. How much do they know about the subject? What kind of information and recommendations are required? The examiner will be looking for evidence that you can present your ideas in an appropriate form.

Section 5

KEY REVISION TOPICS

◈ FOULKS*lynch*

The aim of this section, which is based on the official ACCA study guide, is to provide you with a checklist of key information relating to this Paper. You should use it as a reminder of topics to be revised rather than as a summary of all you need to know. Aim to revise as many topics as possible because many of the questions in the exam draw on material from more than one section of the syllabus. You will get more out of this section if you read through Section 3, General Revision Guidance, first.

1   The economic environment I

Macroeconomic objectives

Monetary, inflation and exchange rate policy
- macroeconomic policy targets
- how government economic policy may affect planning and decision-making in business
- the role of fiscal, monetary, interest rate and exchange rate policy.

Fiscal policy

- the main tools of fiscal policy
- how public expenditure is financed and the meaning of PSBR
- how PSBR and taxation policy interact with other economic indicators
- implications of fiscal policy for business.

2   The economic environment II

- monetary policy
- influences on inflation and exchange rates, including the impact of interest rates
- implications of monetary, inflation and exchange rate policy for business.

Aspects of government intervention and regulation

- competition policy
- official aid intervention
- Green policies
- examples of government intervention and regulation.

3   The nature and scope of financial management

- relationship between financial management, management accounting and financial accounting
- financial objectives for private sector companies in the context of organisational objectives
- social and non-financial objectives in private sector companies and their financial implications
- objectives (financial and otherwise) in not-for-profit organisations and the extent to which they differ from private sector companies
- the problems of multiple stakeholders in financial management and the consequent multiple objectives and scope for conflict.

4   The financial management framework

- financial intermediaries
- commercial banks as providers of funds (including the creation of credit)
- risk-return trade-off
- international money and capital markets
- functions of a stock market and corporate bond market
- types of security in terms of the risk-return trade-off
- Efficient Markets Hypothesis and its broad implications for corporate policy and financial management
- Separation Theorem
- functions of and links between the money and capital markets.

5   Management of working capital I

General issues

- nature and scope of working capital management
- distinction between cash flow and profits
- requirement for effective working capital management
- relationship between working capital management and business solvency
- working capital needs of different types of business.

Management of stock

- stock ratios
- role of stock in the working capital cycle
- tools and techniques of stock management
- results of stock management techniques.

6   Management of working capital II

Management of creditors

- role of creditors in the working capital cycle
- availability of credit and the role of the guarantee
- risks of taking increased credit and buying under extended credit terms
- how methods of paying suppliers may influence cash flows of both parties
- managing overseas accounts payable
- creditor ratios
- tools and techniques of creditor management
- results of creditor management techniques.

Management of debtors

- role of debtors in the working capital cycle
- how the credit-worthiness of customers may be assessed
- balance of risks and costs of customer default against the profitability of marginal business
- factoring and invoice discounting
- settlement discounts
- managing overseas accounts receivable
- debtor ratios
- tools and techniques of debtor management
- results of debtor management techniques.

7   Management of working capital III

Management of cash

- role of cash in the working capital cycle
- calculation of optimal cash balances
- functions of and benefits from centralised cash control and Treasury Management
- cash ratios
- tools and techniques of cash management
- results of cash management techniques.

8   Sources of finance I: small and medium sized enterprises (SMEs)

- financing in terms of the risk/return trade-off
- requirements for finance of SMEs (purpose, how much, how long)
- the financing problems for small businesses - funding gap, maturity gap and inadequate security
- role of risk and the lack of information on small companies in the explanation of the problems of SME financing
- the role of information provision provided by financial statements
- particular financing problems of low-earning/high growth companies
- response of government agencies and financial institutions to the SME financing problem

- other measures taken to ease the financial problems of SMEs such as trade creditors, factoring, leasing, hire purchase, AIM listing, business angels and venture capital
- how capital structure decisions in SMEs may differ from larger organisations
- appropriate sources of finance for SMEs
- appropriate ratios.

9   Sources of finance II: equity financing

- how a company may obtain a stock market listing
- how stock markets operate, including AIM
- requirements of stock market investors in terms of returns on investment
- appropriate financial ratios (e.g. EPS, PE, yield, etc.)
- dividend valuation model, including the growth adjustment
- importance of internally generated funds
- advantages and disadvantages of rights issues
- the price of rights
- purpose and impact of a bonus issue, scrip dividends and stock splits.

10   Sources of finance III: debt and near-debt financing

- features of different types of preference shares and the reasons for their issue
- features of different types of long-term straight debt and the reasons for their issue
- features of convertible debt and warrants and the reasons for their issue
- the reasons for the choice of financing between preference shares, debt and near-debt instruments in terms of the risk/return trade-off
- effect on EPS of conversion and option rights
- international debt markets and the financing of foreign trade
- appropriate ratios.

11   Sources of finance IV: the capital structure decision

- level of financial gearing
- operational and financial gearing
- effects of gearing on the value of shares, company risk and required return
- how a company may determine its capital structure in terms of interest charges, dividends, risk and redemption requirements
- role of short-term financing in the capital structure decision
- relationship between the management of working capital and the long-term capital structure decision
- appropriate ratios.

12   Investment decisions

- capital and revenue expenditure
- fixed asset investment and working capital investment
- impact of investment projects on financial statements
- payback and its usefulness as a measure of investment worth
- ROCE and its usefulness as a measure of investment worth.

13   Investment appraisal using DCF methods

- importance of the time value of money and the role of the cost of capital in appraising investments
- identification of relevant cash flows of potential investments
- NPV and IRR measures of investment worth
- superiority of DCF methods over payback and ROCE
- merits of IRR and NPV
- application of DCF methods to asset replacement decisions.

14   Project appraisal allowing for inflation and taxation

Inflation

- relationship between inflation and interest rates, distinction between real and nominal rates
- distinction between general inflation and specific price increases and their impact on cash flows
- capital investment projects evaluated on a real terms basis
- capital investment projects evaluated on a nominal terms basis.

Taxation

- effect of capital allowances and Corporation Tax on project cash flows
- profitability of capital investment projects on a post-tax basis.

15   Project appraisal allowing for risk

- risk and uncertainty
- sources of risk affecting project profitability
- sensitivity of project NPV to changes in key variables
- probability approach to calculating expected NPV of a project and the associated standard deviation
- decision tree analysis in project appraisal situations
- role of simulation in generating a probability distribution for the NPV of a project
- risk reduction strategies for projects
- usefulness of risk assessment methods.

16   Capital rationing

- hard and soft capital rationing
- profitability index techniques for single period divisible projects
- project evaluation involving single and multi-period capital rationing.

17   Leasing decisions

- operating and finance leases
- DCF methods for projects involving buy or lease problems
- relative advantages and disadvantages of different types of lease
- impact of leasing on company gearing.

18   Costing systems: context and framework

- nature and scope of management accounting and the role of costing in meeting the needs of management
- purpose of costing as an aid to planning, monitoring and controlling business activity
- influence of different costing approaches on cost accumulation and profit reporting
- costing information requirements and limitations in not-for-profit organisations
- implications of different costing approaches for performance evaluation
- role of costing systems in decision-making.

19   Cost accumulation I

- requirement to allocate overheads
- absorption and marginal costing
- reconciliation of the resulting profits/losses from absorption and marginal costing
- opportunity and activity based costing
- impact of life cycle costing on cost accumulation
- target costing methods
- interaction between life cycle and target costing
- advantages and disadvantages of the different costing approaches.

20   Cost accumulation II

- appropriate cost accumulation methods for problems of job, batch and contract costing
- appropriate cost accumulation methods for problems of process costing
- statements which value losses in process and work in progress
- costing joint products and process costing statements which account for by-products
- appropriate cost accumulation methods for problems of service costing
- difficulties of service costing in the not-for-profit sector
- difficulties in identifying relevant and accurate costs.

21   Standard costing I

- uses of standard costs and methods by which they are derived and subsequently reviewed
- capacity limitations when setting standards
- types of standard (ideal, attainable, current and basic) and their behavioural implications
- basic labour, material, overhead (variable and fixed) and sales variances, including problems of labour idle time
- reasons for variances
- appropriate management action arising from the variances identified.

22   Standard costing II

- reconciliations using operating statements which:
  - reconcile budgeted and actual profit figures, and/or
  - reconcile the actual sales less the standard cost of sales with the actual profit
- operational and planning variances
- how absorption and marginal approaches can be used in standard costing
- mix and yield variances for materials
- mix and quantity variances for sales
- an understanding of the inter-relationships between variances
- reasons for variances
- appropriate management action arising from the variances identified.

23   Budgetary planning and control I

- purposes of budgetary planning and control systems
- planning and control cycle, and the control process
- implications of controllability for responsibility reporting
- budget preparation timetable
- functional, subsidiary and master budgets, including cash budgeting
- processes involved with the development and implementation of budgets
- process of participation in budget setting and how this can address motivational problems.

24   Budgetary planning and control II

- fixed and flexible budgets and evaluation of the resulting variances
- preparation of flexed budgets when standard fixed overhead absorption is employed
- behavioural implications of budgetary control and performance evaluation, including participation in budget setting.

25   Budgetary planning and control III

- main features of zero based budgeting systems
- areas/organisations in which zero based budgeting may be applied
- incremental budgeting and its differences from zero based budgeting
- periodic and continuous budgeting systems.

26   Quantitative aids to budgeting

- techniques of:
  - least squares regression
  - scatter diagrams and correlation
  - forecasting with least squares regression
  - time series to identify trends and seasonality
  - forecasting with time series
- evaluation of the results of quantitative aids.

27   Costs and decision-making

- relevant and non-relevant costs
- limiting factor analysis
- make or buy problems, shutdown decisions, additional shift decisions and overtime, accepting or rejecting special orders, and further processing
- cost-volume-profit analysis
- different product pricing approaches.

Section 6

PRACTICE QUESTIONS

Financial management objectives and environment

1 Company objectives

(a) Justify and criticise the usual assumption made in financial management literature that the objective of a company is to maximise the wealth of the shareholders. (Do not consider how this wealth is to be measured.)

(15 marks)

(b) Outline other goals that companies claim to follow, and explain why these might be adopted in preference to the maximisation of shareholder wealth. **(10 marks)**

(Total: 25 marks)

2 Cleevemoor Water Authority

(a) The Cleevemoor Water Authority was privatised in 20W8, to become Northern Water plc (NW). Apart from political considerations, a major motive for the privatisation was to allow access for NW to private sector supplies of finance. During the 20W0s, central government controls on capital expenditure had resulted in relatively low levels of investment, so that considerable investment was required to enable the company to meet more stringent water quality regulations. When privatised, it was valued by the merchant bankers advising on the issue at £100 million and was floated in the form of 100 million ordinary shares (par value 50p), sold fully-paid for £1 each. The shares reached a premium of 60% on the first day of stock market trading.

Required:

In what ways might you expect the objectives of an organisation like Cleevemoor/NW to alter following transfer from public to private ownership? **(5 marks)**

(b) Selected *bi-annual* data from NW's accounts are provided below relating to its first six years of operation as a private sector concern. Also shown, for comparison, are the *pro forma* data as included in the privatisation documents. The *pro forma* accounts are notional accounts prepared to show the operating and financial performance of the company in its last year under public ownership as if it had applied private sector accounting conventions. They also incorporate a dividend payment based on the dividend policy declared in the prospectus.

The activities of privatised utilities are scrutinised by a regulatory body which restricts the extent to which prices can be increased. The demand for water in the area served by NW has risen over time at a steady 2% per annum, largely reflecting demographic trends.

Key financial and operating data for year ending 31 December (£m)

	20W8 (pro forma)	20X0 (actual)	20X2 (actual)	20X4 (actual)
Turnover	450	480	540	620
Operating profit	26	35	55	75
Taxation	5	6	8	10
Profit after tax	21	29	47	65
Dividends	7	10	15	20
Total assets	100	119	151	191
Capital expenditure	20	30	60	75
Wage bill	100	98	90	86
Directors' emoluments	0.8	2.0	2.3	3.0
Employees (number)	12,000	11,800	10,500	10,000
P/E ratio (average)	–	7.0	8.0	7.5
Retail Price Index	100	102	105	109

Required:

Using the data provided, assess the extent to which NW has met the interests of the following groups of stakeholders in its first six years as a privatised enterprise:

(i)   shareholders   **(5 marks)**

(ii)   consumers   **(2 marks)**

(iii)   the workforce   **(4 marks)**

(iv)   the government, through NW's contribution to the achievement of macro-economic policies of price stability and economic growth.   **(4 marks)**

If relevant, suggest what other data would be helpful in forming a more balanced view.   **(5 marks)**

(Total: 25 marks)

(ACCA Dec 95)

3   Non-profit

Management accounting in profit-seeking organisations may be different from that which could apply in non-profit-seeking organisations.

Required:

(a)   Briefly outline the role of a management accountant using a profit-seeking organisation as a setting.   **(6 marks)**

(b)   Contrast the main features of a non-profit-seeking organisation, with one that is profit-seeking, which makes management accounting in this environment different.   **(6 marks)**

(c)   Discuss how a management accountant may respond to the challenge of providing appropriate information in a non-profit-seeking organisation.   **(8 marks)**

(Total: 20 marks)

(ACCA June 98)

4   Objectives

(a)   'Managers and owners of businesses may not have the same objectives.' Explain this statement, illustrating your answer with examples of possible conflicts of interest.   **(7 marks)**

(b)   In what respects can it be argued, that companies need to exercise corporate social responsibility?   **(7 marks)**

(c)   Explain the meaning of the term 'Value for Money' in relation to the management of publicly owned services/utilities.   **(6 marks)**

(Total: 20 marks)

(ACCA Dec 99)

Management of working capital

5   Hexicon plc

(a)   Give reasons, with a brief explanation, why the net present value (NPV) method of investment appraisal is thought to be superior to other approaches.   **(5 marks)**

(b)   Hexicon plc manufactures and markets automatic washing machines. Among the many hundreds of components which it purchases each year from external suppliers for assembling into the finished article are drive belts, of which it uses 40,000 units pa. It is considering converting its purchasing, delivery and stock control of this item to a just-in-time system. This will raise the number of orders placed but lower the administrative and other costs of placing and receiving orders. If successful, this will provide the model for switching most of its inwards supplies on to this system. Details of actual and expected ordering and carrying costs are given in the table below.

				Actual	*Proposed*
O	=	Ordering cost per order		£100	£25
P	=	Purchase cost per item		£2.50	£2.50
I	=	Inventory holding cost (as a percentage			
		of the purchase cost)		20%	20%

To implement the new arrangements will require 'one-off' reorganisation costs estimated at £4,000 which will be treated as a revenue item for tax purposes. The rate of corporation tax is 33% and Hexicon can obtain finance at 12%. The effective life span of the Determine new system can be assumed to be eight years.

Required:

(i)   Determine the effect of the new system on the economic order quantity (EOQ).

(ii)   Determine whether the new system is worthwhile in financial terms.

Note: EOQ is given by $Q = \sqrt{\dfrac{2 \times D \times O}{I \times P}}$ where D = demand, or usage.   **(10 marks)**

(c)   **You are required** to briefly explain the nature and objectives of JIT purchasing agreements concluded between components users and suppliers.   **(5 marks)**

(Total: 20 marks)

(ACCA Pilot Paper)

6   Ripley plc

(a)   The Treasurer of Ripley plc is contemplating a change in financial policy. At present, Ripley's balance sheet shows that fixed assets are of equal magnitude to the amount of long-term debt and equity financing. It is proposed to take advantage of a recent fall in interest rates by replacing the long-term debt capital with an overdraft. In addition, the Treasurer wants to speed up debtor collection by offering early payment discounts to customers and to slow down the rate of payment to creditors.

As his assistant, you are required to write a brief memorandum to other Board members explaining the rationales of the old and new policies and pin-pointing the factors to be considered in making such a switch of policy.

(6 marks)

(b)   Bramham plc, which currently has negligible cash holdings, expects to have to make a series of cash payments (P) of £1.5m over the forthcoming year. These will become due at a steady rate. It has two alternative ways of meeting this liability.

Firstly, it can make periodic sales from existing holdings of short-term securities. According to Bramham's financial advisers, the most likely average percentage rate of return (i) on these securities is 12% over the forthcoming year, although this estimate is highly uncertain. Whenever Bramham sells securities, it incurs a transaction fee (T) of £25, and places the proceeds on short-term deposit at 5% per annum interest until needed. The following formula specifies the optimal amount of cash raised (Q) for each sale of securities:

$$Q = \sqrt{\dfrac{2 \times P \times T}{i}}$$

The second policy involves taking a secured loan for the full £1.5m over one year at an interest rate of 14% based on the initial balance of the loan. The lender also imposes a flat arrangement fee of £5,000, which could be met out of existing balances. The sum borrowed would be placed in a notice deposit at 9% and drawn down at no cost as and when required.

Bramham's Treasurer believes that cash balances will be run down at an even rate throughout the year.

Required:

Advise Bramham as to the most beneficial cash management policy.

Note: ignore tax and the time value of money in your answer.   **(9 marks)**

(c)   Discuss the limitations of the model of cash management used in part (b).   **(5 marks)**

(Total: 20 marks)

(ACCA Dec 96)

7   PCB plc

PCB plc manufacture printed circuit boards for use in pocket calculators. Since 20X5 business has been expanding very rapidly, and the company has now encountered a liquidity problem, as illustrated by the most recent balance sheets reproduced below:

PCB company balance sheets

	As at 30 November 20X8 £	As at 30 November 20X7 £
Fixed assets	308,000	264,000
Current assets		
Stock	220,000	95,000
Debtors	210,000	108,000
Cash	Nil	1,750
	430,000	204,750
Current liabilities		
Bank	158,000	41,250
Trade creditors	205,000	82,500
Net current assets	67,000	81,000
Capital and reserves		
Issued share capital	18,000	18,000
Reserves	357,000	327,000
Equity		
Shareholders' funds	375,000	345,000

Other information

(i)   Sales for the year to 30 November 20X7 were £1·7 million, yielding a gross profit of £330,000, and a net profit before tax of £82,000.

(ii)   The corporation tax rate is 30%.

(iii)   For the year ending 30 November 20X7, dividends of £35,000 were paid out.

(iv)   At the beginning of the year to 30 November 20X8 the company bought some new manufacturing equipment and recruited six more sales staff.

(v)   Sales for the year to 30 November 20X8 were £3 million, with a gross profit of £450,000, and net profit before tax of £60,000.

(vi)   Dividends payable for the year to 30 November 20X8 amount to £12,000.

Required:

(a)   Illustrating your answer with figures taken from the question, explain why it is not unusual for manufacturing companies to face a cash shortage when sales are expanding very rapidly.   **(4 marks)**

(b)   Explain why PCB plc has not increased its net profit, despite the large increase in sales between 20X7 and 20X8.   **(4 marks)**

(c)   How has the mix of funding used by PCB changed between the two years, and what are the implications of such changes in terms of investor and creditor risks?   **(6 marks)**

◆ FOULKS*lynch*

(d)   Suggest ways in which PCB might seek to resolve its current funding problems, and avoid the risks associated with over-trading.

(6 marks)
(Total: 20 marks)
(ACCA Dec 98)

8   Fenton Security plc

Fenton Security plc are manufacturers and wholesalers of locks and household security fittings. Over the last twelve months the company has encountered increasing problems with late payment by debtors.

The last twelve months of credit sales of £67.5 million show an increase of 10% over the previous year, but the company's overdraft, on which it is charged 12% p.a. has also increased (by £1.8 million) over the last year. The company is concerned to reduce its working capital requirements by reducing the debtor collection period.

Fenton's management accountant has extracted an aged debtors profile which is shown below:

% of Total debtor payments (by value)	Average Collection Period
5	30
28	45
10	60
30	75
16	90
11	120

Bad debts currently stand at £2 million per annum.

Fenton is considering the introduction of early settlement discounts. The current invoicing terms require payment to be made within 30 days of the date of issue of the invoice. The management accountant has suggested that a 1% discount be offered to all customers who comply with these payment terms, and he estimates that 50% of total payments (by value) would be on these terms (an average settlement period of 30 days for these payments can be assumed). The discount scheme would be expected to be taken up by customers who already pay in 75 days or less.

As an alternative way of reducing the debtors figure, Fenton could use a with recourse debt collection service, which has quoted a price of 1% of sales receipts. It is estimated that using the service will have the effect of reducing debtor days by 20 and eliminating 50% of bad debts.

Required:

(a)   Calculate the change in working capital requirements and bad debts which would result from:

(i)   the introduction of the early settlement discounts
(ii)   the use of the debt collection service

and recommend which (if either) policy should be adopted by Fenton. Your answer should clearly show all workings.   **(10 marks)**

(b)   There are a number of methods that can be adopted to assess the credit-worthiness of a potential credit customer. Describe and comment upon two such methods that Fenton could adopt to help reduce the current level of bad debts.   **(5 marks)**

(c)   Explain the term 'invoice discounting' and the pros and cons of its use as a way of improving cash flow.

(5 marks)
(Total: 20 marks)
(ACCA June 99)

Sources of finance

9 Newsam plc

Newsam plc is a quoted company which produces a range of branded products all of which are well-established in their respective markets, although overall sales have grown by an average of only 2% per annum over the past decade. It is now December 20X4. The board of directors is concerned about the company's level of financial gearing, which although not high by industry standards, is near to breaching the covenants attaching to its 15% debenture issue, made in 20W2 (12 years ago) at a time of high market interest rates. Issued in order to finance the acquisition of the premises on which it is secured, the debenture is repayable at par value of £100 per unit of stock at any time during the period 20X4 –20X7.

There are two covenants attaching to the debenture, which state:

'At no time shall the ratio of debt capital to shareholders' funds exceed 50%. The company shall also maintain a prudent level of liquidity, defined as a current ratio at no time outside the range of the industry average (as published by the corporate credit analysts, Creditex), plus or minus 20%.'

Newsam's most recent set of accounts is shown in summarised form below. The buildings have been depreciated since 20W2 at 4% per annum, and most of the machinery is only two or three years old, having been purchased mainly via a bank overdraft. The interest rate payable on the bank overdraft is currently 9%. The finance director argues that Newsam should take advantage of historically low interest rates on the European money markets by issuing a medium-term Eurodollar bond at 5%. The dollar is currently selling at a premium of about 1% on the three-month forward market.

Newsam's ordinary shares currently sell at a P/E ratio of 14, and look unattractive compared to comparable companies in the sector which exhibit an average P/E ratio of 18. According to the latest published credit assessment by Creditex, the average current ratio for the industry is 1.35.

The debentures currently sell in the market at £15 above par.

The summarised financial accounts for Newsam plc for the year ending 30 June 20X4 are as follows:

Balance sheet as at 30 June 20X4

Assets employed	£m	£m	£m
Fixed (net)			
Land			5.0
Premises			4.0
Machinery and vehicles			11.0
			20.0
Current			
Stocks	2.5		
Debtors	4.0		
Cash	0.5		
		7.0	
Current liabilities			
Creditors	(4.0)		
Bank overdraft	(3.0)		
		(7.0)	
Net current assets			0.0
Total assets less current liabilities			20.0
Long-term creditors			
15% Debentures 20X4 – 20X7			(5.0)
Net assets			15.0
Financed by			
Ordinary shares (25p par value)			5.0
Reserves			10.0
Shareholders' funds			15.0

Profit and loss account extracts for the year ended 30 June 20X4

	£m
Sales	28.00
Cost of sales	(20.00)
Administration and distribution costs	(5.00)
Operating profit	3.00
Interest payable	(1.00)
Profit before tax	2.00
Taxation	(0.66)
Profit after tax	1.34
Dividend	(0.70)
Retained profit	0.64

Required:

(a)   Calculate appropriate gearing ratios for Newsam plc using:

   (i)   book values; and
   (ii)   market values.   **(4 marks)**

(b)   Assess how close Newsam plc is to breaching the debenture covenants.   **(4 marks)**

(c)   Discuss whether Newsam plc's gearing is in any sense 'dangerous'.   **(5 marks)**

(d)   Discuss what financial policies Newsam plc might adopt:

   (i)   in order to lower its capital gearing; and
   (ii)   to improve its interest cover.   **(12 marks)**
                                                                                                           (Total: 25 marks)
                                                                                                               (ACCA Dec 94)

10   Collingham plc

Collingham plc produces electronic measuring instruments for medical research. It has recorded strong and consistent growth during the past 10 years since its present team of managers bought it out from a large multinational corporation. They are now contemplating obtaining a stock market listing.

Collingham's accounting statements for the last financial year are summarised below. Fixed assets, including freehold land and premises, are shown at historic cost net of depreciation. The debenture is redeemable in two years although early redemption without penalty is permissible.

Profit and loss account for the year ended 31 December 20X4

	£m
Turnover	80.0
Cost of sales	(70.0)
Operating profit	10.0
Interest charges	(3.0)
Pre-tax profit	7.0
Corporation tax (after capital allowances)	(1.0)
Profits attributable to ordinary shareholders	6.0
Dividends	(0.5)
Retained earnings	5.5

◇ FOULKSlynch

Balance sheet as at 31 December 20X4

	£m	£m	£m
Assets employed			
Fixed:			
Land and premises		10.0	
Machinery		20.0	
			30.0
Current:			
Stocks	10.0		
Debtors	10.0		
Cash	3.0		
		23.0	
Current liabilities:			
Trade creditors	(15.0)		
Bank overdraft	(5.0)		
		(20.0)	
Net current assets			3.0
Total assets less current liabilities			33.0
14% Debenture			(5.0)
Net assets			28.0
Financed by:			
Issued share capital (par value 50p)			
Voting shares			2.0
Non-voting 'A' shares			2.0
Profit and loss account			24.0
Shareholders' funds			28.0

The following information is also available regarding key financial indicators for Collingham's industry.

Return on (long-term) capital employed	22% (pre-tax)
Return on equity	14% (post-tax)
Operating profit margin	10%
Current ratio	1.8:1
Acid-test	1.1:1
Gearing (total debt equity)	18%
Interest cover	5.2
Dividend cover	2.6
P/E ratio	13:1

Required:

(a)   Briefly explain why companies like Collingham seek stock market listings.   **(4 marks)**

(b)   Discuss the performance and financial health of Collingham in relation to that of the industry as a whole.   **(8 marks)**

(c)   In what ways would you advise Collingham:

(i)   to restructure its balance sheet *prior* to flotation   **(5 marks)**
(ii)   to change its financial policy *following* flotation?   **(3 marks)**

(Total: 20 marks)
(ACCA June 95)

◈ FOULKS*lynch*

11   Burnsall plc

Burnsall plc is a listed company which manufactures and distributes leisurewear under the brand name Paraffin. It made sales of 10 million units world-wide at an average wholesale price of £10 per unit during its last financial year ending at 30 June 20X5. In 20X5/20X6, it is planning to introduce a new brand, Meths, which will be sold at a lower unit price to more price-sensitive market segments. Allowing for negative effects on existing sales of Paraffin, the introduction of the new brand is expected to raise total sales value by 20%.

To support greater sales activity, it is expected that additional financing, both capital and working, will be required. Burnsall expects to make capital expenditures of £20m in 20X5/20X6, partly to replace worn-out equipment but largely to support sales expansion. You may assume that, except for taxation, all current assets and current liabilities will vary directly in line with sales.

Burnsall's summarised balance sheet for the financial year ending 30 June 20X5 shows the following:

Assets employed	£m	£m	£m
Fixed (net)			120
Current			
Stocks	16		
Debtors	23		
Cash	6		
		45	
Current liabilities			
Corporation tax payable	(5)		
Trade creditors	(18)		
		(23)	
Net current assets			22
Long-term debt at 12%			(20)
Net assets			122
Financed by			
Ordinary shares (50p par value)			60
Reserves			62
Shareholders' funds			122

Burnsall's profit before interest and tax in 20X4/X5 was 16% of sales, after deducting depreciation of £5m. The depreciation charge for 20X5/X6 is expected to rise to £9m. Corporation tax is levied at 33%, paid with a one-year delay. Burnsall has an established distribution policy of raising dividends by 10% pa. In 20X4/X5, it paid dividends of £5m net.

You have been approached to advise on the extra financing required to support the sales expansion. Company policy is to avoid cash balances falling below 6% of sales.

Required:

(a)   By projecting its financial statements, calculate how much additional *external* finance Burnsall must raise.

Notes

(1)   It is not necessary to present your projection in FRS 1 format.
(2)   You may ignore advance corporation tax in your answer.
(3)   You may assume that all depreciation provisions qualify for tax relief.   **(8 marks)**

(b)   Evaluate the respective merits of *four* possible external long-term financing options open to Burnsall.**(12 marks)**
(Total: 20 marks)
(ACCA Dec 95)

12   Phoenix plc

Phoenix plc, which manufactures building products, experienced a sharp increase in pre-tax profits from the £25m level in 20X5–20X6 to £40m in 20X6–20X7 as the economy emerged from recession, and demand for new houses increased. The increase in profits has been entirely due to volume expansion, with margins remaining static. It still has substantial excess capacity and therefore no pressing need to invest, apart from routine replacements.

In the past, Phoenix has followed a rather conservative financial policy, with restricted dividend payouts and relatively low borrowing levels. It now faces the issue of how to utilise an unexpectedly sizeable cash surplus. Directors have made two main suggestions. One is to redeem the £10m 7% secured loan stock issued to finance a capacity increase several years previously, the other is to increase the dividend payment by the same amount.

Phoenix's present capital structure is shown below:

	£m
Issued share capital (25p par value)	70
Reserves	130
Creditors falling due after more than one year:	
7% secured loan stock 20X7	10

Further information

(i)   Phoenix has not used an overdraft during the two years.
(ii)   The rate of corporate tax is 33%.
(iii)   The dividend paid by Phoenix in 20X5–20X6 was 1.50 pence per share.
(iv)   Sector averages currently stand as follows:

dividend cover	2.6 times
gearing (long-term debt/equity)	45%
interest cover	6.5 times

Required:

(a)   Calculate the dividend payout ratios and dividend covers for both 20X5–20X6 and for the reporting year 20X6–20X7, if the dividend is raised as proposed.   **(6 marks)**

(b)   You have recently been hired to work as a financial strategist for Phoenix, reporting to the finance director. Using the information provided, write a report to your superior, which identifies and discusses the relative merits of the two proposals for utilising the cash surplus.   **(14 marks)**
                                                                                                                                   (Total: 20 marks)
                                                                                                                                   (ACCA Dec 97)

13   Jeronimo plc

Jeronimo plc currently has 5 million ordinary shares in issue, which have a market value of £1.60 each. The company wishes to raise finance for a major investment project by means of a rights issue, and is proposing to issue shares on the basis of 1 for 5 at a price of £1.30 each.

James Brown currently owns 10,000 shares in Jeronimo plc and is seeking advice on whether or not to take up the proposed rights.

Required:

(a)   Explain the difference between a rights issue and a scrip issue. Your answer should include comment on the reasons why companies make such issues and the effect of the issues on private investors.   **(6 marks)**

(b)   Calculate:

(i)   the theoretical value of James Brown's shareholding if he takes up his rights; and
(ii)   the theoretical value of James Brown's rights if he chooses to sell them.   **(4 marks)**

(c)   Using only the information given below, and applying the dividend growth model formula, calculate the required return on equity for an investor in Jeronimo plc.

> **Jeronimo plc:**
> Current share price: £1.60
> Number of shares in issue: 5 million
> Current earnings: £1.5 million
> Dividend Paid (Pence per share):
> 20X5: 8
> 20X6: 9
> 20X7: 11
> 20X8: 11
> 20X9: 12

The formula for the dividend growth model is as follows: $R = \left(\dfrac{D_1}{MV} + g \right) \times 100$ **(4 marks)**

Where R = Percentage required return on equity

(d)   If the stock market is believed to operate with a strong level of efficiency, what effect might this have on the behaviour of the finance directors of publicly quoted companies?   **(6 marks)**
          (Total: 20 marks)
          (ACCA June 99)

Capital expenditure and investment

14   Howden plc

(a)   Explain how inflation affects the rate of return required on an investment project, and the distinction between a real and a nominal (or 'money terms') approach to the evaluation of an investment project under inflation.
          (6 marks)

(b)   Howden plc is contemplating investment in an additional production line to produce its range of compact discs. A market research study, undertaken by a well-known firm of consultants, has revealed scope to sell an additional output of 400,000 units pa. The study cost £0.1 m but the account has not yet been settled.

The price and cost structure of a typical disc (net of royalties), is as follows:

	£	£
Price per unit		12.00
Costs per unit of output		
Material cost per unit	1.50	
Direct labour cost per unit	0.50	
Variable overhead cost per unit	0.50	
Fixed overhead cost per unit	1.50	
		(4.00)
Profit		8.00

The fixed overhead represents an apportionment of central administrative and marketing costs. These are expected to rise in total by £500,000 pa as a result of undertaking this project. The production line is expected to operate for five years and require a total cash outlay of £11m, including £0.5m of materials stocks. The equipment will have a residual value of £2m. Because the company is moving towards a JIT stock management policy, it is expected that this project will involve steadily reducing working capital needs, expected to decline at about 3% pa by volume. The production line will be accommodated in a presently empty building for which an offer of £2m has recently been received from another company. If the building is retained, it is expected that property price inflation will increase its value to £3m after five years.

While the precise rates of price and cost inflation are uncertain, economists in Howden's corporate planning department make the following forecasts for the average annual rates of inflation relevant to the project:

Retail Price Index	6% pa
Disc prices	5% pa
Material prices	3% pa
Direct labour wage rates	7% pa
Variable overhead costs	7% pa
Other overhead costs	5% pa

Note: you may ignore taxes and capital allowances in this question.

Required:

Given that Howden's shareholders require a real return of 8.5% for projects of this degree of risk, assess the financial viability of this proposal.   **(13 marks)**

(c)   Briefly discuss how inflation may complicate the analysis of business financial decisions   **(6 marks)**

(Total: 25 marks)

(ACCA Dec 94)

15   Filtrex plc

(a)   Distinguish between 'hard' and 'soft' capital rationing, explaining why a company may deliberately choose to restrict its capital expenditure.   **(6 marks)**

(b)   Filtrex plc is a medium-sized, all equity-financed, unquoted company which specialises in the development and production of water- and air-filtering devices to reduce the emission of effluents. Its small but ingenious R & D team has recently made a technological breakthrough which has revealed a number of attractive investment opportunities. It has applied for patents to protect its rights in all these areas. However, it lacks the financial resources required to exploit all of these projects, whose required outlays and post-tax NPVs are listed in the table below. Filtrex's managers consider that delaying any of these projects would seriously undermine their profitability, as competitors bring forward their own new developments. All projects are thought to have a similar degree of risk.

Project	Required outlay £	NPV £
A	150,000	65,000
B	120,000	50,000
C	200,000	80,000
D	80,000	30,000
E	400,000	120,000

The NPVs have been calculated using as a discount rate the 18% post-tax rate of return which Filtrex requires for risky R & D ventures. The maximum amount available for this type of investment is £400,000, corresponding to Filtrex's present cash balances, built up over several years' profitable trading. Projects A and C are mutually exclusive and no project can be sub-divided. Any unused capital will either remain invested in short-term deposits or used to purchase marketable securities, both of which offer a return well below 18% post-tax.

Required:

(i)   Advise Filtrex plc, using suitable supporting calculations, which combination of projects should be undertaken in the best interests of shareholders.

(ii)   Suggest what further information might be obtained to assist a fuller analysis.   **(12 marks)**

(c)   Explain how, apart from delaying projects, Filtrex plc could manage to exploit more of these opportunities.

(7 marks)

(Total: 25 marks)

(ACCA Dec 94)

16   Armcliff Ltd

Armcliff Ltd is a division of Shevin plc which requires each of its divisions to achieve a rate of return on capital employed of at least 10% pa. For this purpose, capital employed is defined as fixed capital and investment in stocks. This rate of return is also applied as a hurdle rate for new investment projects. Divisions have limited borrowing powers and all capital projects are centrally funded.

The following is an extract from Armcliff's divisional accounts:

Profit and loss account for the year ended 31 December 20X4

	£m
Turnover	120
Cost of sales	(100)
Operating profit	20

Assets employed as at 31 December 20X4

	£m	£m
Fixed (net)		75
Current assets (including stocks £25m)	45	
Current liabilities	(32)	
		13
Net capital employed		88

Armcliff's production engineers wish to invest in a new computer-controlled press. The equipment cost is £14m. The residual value is expected to be £2m after four years operation, when the equipment will be shipped to a customer in South America.

The new machine is capable of improving the quality of the existing product and also of producing a higher volume. The firm's marketing team is confident of selling the increased volume by extending the credit period. The expected additional sales are:

Year 1	2,000,000 units
Year 2	1,800,000 units
Year 3	1,600,000 units
Year 4	1,600,000 units

Sales volume is expected to fall over time due to emerging competitive pressures. Competition will also necessitate a reduction in price by £0.5 each year from the £5 per unit proposed in the first year. Operating costs are expected to be steady at £1 per unit, and allocation of overheads (none of which are affected by the new project) by the central finance department is set at £0.75 per unit.

Higher production levels will require additional investment in stocks of £0.5m, which would be held at this level until the final stages of operation of the project. Customers at present settle accounts after 90 days on average.

Required:

(a) Determine whether the proposed capital investment is attractive to Armcliff, using the average rate of return on capital method, as defined as average profit-to-average capital employed, ignoring debtors and creditors.

Note: Ignore taxes.   (10 marks)

(b) (i) Suggest *three* problems which arise with the use of the average return method for appraising new investment.   (3 marks)

(ii) In view of the problems associated with the ARR method, why do companies continue to use it in project appraisal?   (3 marks)

(c) Briefly discuss the dangers of offering more generous credit, and suggest ways of assessing customers' creditworthiness.   (9 marks)
(Total: 25 marks)
(*ACCA June 95*)

17   Burley plc

(a)   Burley plc, a manufacturer of building products, mainly supplies the wholesale trade. It has recently suffered falling demand due to economic recession, and thus has spare capacity. It now perceives an opportunity to produce designer ceramic tiles for the home improvement market. It has already paid £0.5m for development expenditure, market research and a feasibility study.

The initial analysis reveals scope for selling 150,000 boxes per annum over a five-year period at a price of £20 per box. Estimated operating costs, largely based on experience, are as follows:

Cost per box of tiles (£) (at today's prices):

Material cost	8.00
Direct labour	2.00
Variable overhead	1.50
Fixed overhead (allocated)	1.50
Distribution, etc.	2.00

Production can take place in existing facilities although initial re-design and set-up costs would be £2m after allowing for all relevant tax reliefs. Returns from the project would be taxed at 33%.

Burley's shareholders require a nominal return of 14% per annum after tax, which includes allowance for generally expected inflation of 5.5% per annum. It can be assumed that all operating cash flows occur at year-ends.

Required:

Assess the financial desirability of this venture in *real* terms, finding both the Net Present Value and the Internal Rate of Return (to the nearest 1%) offered by the project.

Note: Assume no tax delay.   **(7 marks)**

(b)   Briefly explain the purpose of sensitivity analysis in relation to project appraisal, indicating the drawbacks with this procedure.   **(6 marks)**

(c)   Determine the values of

(i)   price
(ii)   volume

at which the project's NPV becomes zero.

Discuss your results, suggesting appropriate management action.   **(7 marks)**
                                                                                         (Total: 20 marks)
                                                                                         (ACCA Dec 96)

18   Deighton plc

You are the chief accountant of Deighton plc, which manufactures a wide range of building and plumbing fittings. It has recently taken over a smaller unquoted competitor, Linton Ltd. Deighton is currently checking through various documents at Linton's head office, including a number of investment appraisals. One of these, a recently rejected application involving an outlay on equipment of £900,000, is reproduced below. It was rejected because it failed to offer Linton's target return on investment of 25% (average profit-to-initial investment outlay). Closer inspection reveals several errors in the appraisal.

Evaluation of profitability of proposed project NT17
(all values in current year prices)

Item (£'000)	0	1	2	3	4
Sales		1,400	1,600	1,800	1,000
Materials		(400)	(450)	(500)	(250)
Direct labour		(400)	(450)	(500)	(250)
Overheads		(100)	(100)	(100)	(100)
Interest		(120)	(120)	(120)	(120)
Depreciation		(225)	(225)	(225)	(225)
Profit pre-tax		155	255	355	55
Tax at 33%		(51)	(84)	(117)	(18)
Post-tax profit		104	171	238	37

Outlay

Stock	(100)
Equipment	(900)
Market research	(200)
	(1,200)

$$Rate\ of\ return = \frac{Average\ profit}{Investment} = \frac{£138}{£1,200} = 11.5\%$$

You discover the following further details:

1   Linton's policy was to finance both working capital and fixed investment by a bank overdraft. A 12% interest rate applied at the time of the evaluation.

2   A 25% writing down allowance (WDA) on a reducing balance basis is offered for new investment. Linton's profits are sufficient to utilise fully this allowance throughout the project.

3   Corporate tax is paid a year in arrears.

4   Of the overhead charge, about half reflects absorption of existing overhead costs.

5   The market research was actually undertaken to investigate two proposals, the other project also having been rejected. The total bill for all this research has already been paid.

6   Deighton itself requires a nominal return on new projects of 20% after taxes, is currently ungeared and has no plans to use any debt finance in the future.

Required:

Write a report to the finance director in which you:

(a)   identify the mistakes made in Linton's evaluation   **(10 marks)**

(b)   restate the investment appraisal in terms of the post-tax net present value to Deighton, recommending whether the project should be undertaken or not.   **(15 marks)**
(Total: 25 marks)
(ACCA June 97)

19   Chromex plc

Chromex plc manufactures bicycles for the UK and European markets, and has made a bid of £150 million to take over Bexell plc, their main UK competitor, which is also active in the German market. Chromex currently supplies 24% of the UK market and Bexell has a 10% share of the same market.

Chromex anticipates labour savings of £700,000 per year, created by more efficient production and distribution facilities, if the take-over is completed. In addition, the company intends to sell off surplus land and buildings with a balance sheet value of £15 million, acquired in the course of the take-over.

Total UK bicycle sales for 20X7 were £400 million. For the year ended 31 December 20X7, Bexell reported an operating profit of £10 million, compared with a figure of £55 million for Chromex. In calculating profits, Bexell included a depreciation charge of £0.5 million.

Note: the take-over is regarded by Chromex in the same way as any other investment, and is appraised accordingly.

Required:

(a)   Assuming that the bid is accepted by Bexell, calculate the payback period (pre-tax) for the investment, if the land and buildings are immediately sold for £5 million less than the balance sheet valuation, and Bexell's sales figures remain static.   **(3 marks)**

(b)   Chromex has also appraised the investment in Bexell by calculating the present value of the company's future expected cash flows. What additional information to that required in (a) would have been necessary?   **(5 marks)**

(c)   Explain how and why the UK government might seek to intervene in the take-over bid for Bexell.   **(6 marks)**

(d)   Suggest four ratios, which Chromex might usefully compute in order to compare the financial performance of Bexell with that of companies in the same manufacturing sector. You should include in your answer a justification of your choice of ratios. Briefly explain why it is important to base a comparison on companies in the same sector.   **(6 marks)**
(Total: 20 marks)
(ACCA June 98)

20   Prime Printing plc

(a)   Explain the cash flow characteristics of a finance lease, and compare it with the use of a bank loan or cash held on short-term deposit. Your answer should include some comment on the significance of a company's anticipated tax position on lease versus buy decisions.   **(10 marks)**

(b)   Prime Printing plc has the opportunity to replace one of its pieces of printing equipment. The new machine, costing £120,000, is expected to lead to operating savings of £50,000 per annum and have an economic life of five years. The company's after tax cost of capital for the investment is estimated at 15%, and operating cash flows are taxed at a rate of 30%, one year in arrears.

The company is trying to decide whether to fund the acquisition of the machine via a five-year bank loan, at an annual interest rate of 13%, with the principal repayable at the end of the five-year period. As an alternative, the machine could be acquired using a finance lease, at a cost of £28,000 p.a. for five years, payable in advance. The machine would have zero scrap value at the end of five years.

Note: due to its current tax position, the company is unable to utilise any capital allowances on the purchase until year one.

Required:

Assuming that writing-down allowances of 25% p.a. are available on a reducing balance basis, recommend, with reasons, whether Prime Printing should replace the machine, and if so whether it should buy or lease.   **(15 marks)**
(Total: 25 marks)
(ACCA Dec 98)

21   Benland plc

Benland plc manufacture and fit a variety of children's playground equipment. The company at present purchases the rubber particles used in the playground surfacing from an outside supplier, but is considering investing in equipment which would process and shred used vehicle tyres to produce equivalent rubber particles. One tonne of purchased particles is saved per tonne of tyres processed. Disposal of used tyres is becoming an environmental problem, and Benland believes that it could charge £40 per tonne to garages/tyre distributors wishing to dispose of their old tyres. This price would be 20 per cent lower than the cost of the landfill sites currently being used, and so Benland believes that it would face no risk or shortage of supply of what would be a key raw material for the business. The price charged by Benland for tyre disposal (£40 per tonne) remains fixed for the next five years.

The cost to Benland of purchased particles is £3·50 per tonne for each of the next five years, and the price has been contractually guaranteed. If the contract is terminated within the next two years, Benland will be charged an immediate termination penalty of £100,000 which will not be allowed as a tax deductible expense.

The machine required to process the tyres will cost £1·06 million, and it is estimated that at the end of year five the machine will have a second-hand value of £120,000 before selling costs of £5,000.

Sales of the playground surfacing which uses rubber particles are forecast to be £1.2 million in year one, rising by 10% per year until year five but prices will remain constant. The new equipment will result in Benland incurring additional maintenance costs of £43,000 per year.

80,000 tonnes of tyres need to be processed in order to meet the raw material requirement for the forecast sales in year one. Processing costs are estimated at £37 per tonne (excluding additional depreciation and maintenance).

Benland is subject to corporation tax at a rate of 33%, payable one year in arrears. Capital expenditure is eligible for 25% allowances on a reducing balance basis, and sales proceeds of assets are subject to tax. Benland has sufficient profits to fully utilise all available capital allowances.

Required:

(a)   Using 12% as the after-tax discount rate, advise Benland on the desirability of purchasing the tyre processing equipment.   **(12 marks)**

(b)   Discuss which cash flows are most important in determining the outcome of the proposed investment and how Benland might seek to minimise the risk of large changes in predicted cash flows.   **(8 marks)**

(Total: 20 marks)

(ACCA Dec 99)

Costing systems and techniques (including decision making)

22   A polytechnic

A polytechnic offers a range of degree courses. The polytechnic organisation structure consists of three faculties each with a number of teaching departments. In addition, there is a polytechnic administrative/management function and a central services function.

The following cost information is available for the year ended 30 June 20X7:

(1)   **Occupancy costs**

Total £1,500,000. Such costs are apportioned on the basis of area used which is:

	Square feet
Faculties	7,500
Teaching departments	20,000
Administration/management	7,000
Central services	3,000

(2)   **Administration/management costs**

Direct costs: £1,775,000
Indirect costs: an apportionment of occupancy costs.

Direct and indirect costs are charged to degree courses on a percentage basis.

(3)   Faculty costs

Direct costs: £700,000.
Indirect costs: an apportionment of occupancy costs and central service costs.

Direct and indirect costs are charged to teaching departments.

(4)   **Teaching departments**

Direct costs: £5,525,000.
Indirect costs: an apportionment of occupancy costs and central service costs plus all faculty costs.

Direct and indirect costs are charged to degree courses on a percentage basis.

(5)   **Central services**

Direct costs: £1,000,000.
Indirect costs: an apportionment of occupancy costs.

Direct and indirect costs of central services have in previous years been charged to users on a percentage basis. A study has now been completed which has estimated what user areas would have paid external suppliers for the same services on an individual basis. For the year ended 30 June 20X7, the apportionment of the central services cost is to be recalculated in a manner which recognises the cost savings achieved by using the central services facilities instead of using external service companies. This is to be done by apportioning the overall savings to user areas in proportion to their share of the estimated external costs.

The estimated external costs of service provision are as follows:

	£'000
Faculties	240
Teaching departments	800
Degree courses:	
Business studies	32
Mechanical engineering	48
Catering studies	32
All other degrees	448
	1,600

(6)   Additional data relating to the degree courses are as follows:

	Business Studies	Mechanical Engineering	Catering Studies
Number of graduates	80	50	120
Apportioned costs (as % of totals)			
Teaching departments	3%	2.5%	7%
Administration/management	2.5%	5%	4%

Central services are to be apportioned as detailed in (5) above.

The total number of graduates from the polytechnic in the year to 30 June 20X7 was 2,500.

Required:

(a)   Prepare a flow diagram which shows the apportionment of costs to user areas. No values need be shown.

(3 marks)

(b)   Calculate the average cost per graduate, for the year ended 30 June 20X7, for the polytechnic and for each of the degrees in business studies, mechanical engineering and catering studies, showing all relevant cost analysis.

(13 marks)

(c)   Suggest reasons for any differences in the average cost per graduate from one degree to another, and discuss briefly the relevance of such information to the polytechnic management.   **(4 marks)**

(Total: 20 marks)
(ACCA June 88)

23   Amazon plc

Amazon plc manufactures two types of industrial sealant by passing materials through two consecutive processes. The results of operating the two processes during the previous month are shown below:

Process 1

Costs incurred (£):

Materials 7,000 kg @ £0.50 per kg	3,500	
Labour and overheads	4,340	

Output (kg):

Transferred to Process 2		6,430
Defective production		570

Process 2

Costs incurred (£):

Labour and overheads	12,129	

Output (kg):

Type E sealant		2,000
Type F sealant		4,000
By-product		430

It is considered normal for 10% of the total output from process 1 to be defective and all defective output is sold as scrap at £0.40 kg. Losses are not expected in process 2.

There was no work in process at the beginning or end of the month and no opening stocks of sealants.

Sales of the month's output from Process 2 were:

Type E sealant	1,100 kg
Type F sealant	3,200 kg
By-product	430 kg

The remainder of the output from Process 2 was in stock at the end of the month.

The selling prices of the products are: Type E sealant £7 per kg and Type F sealant £2.50 per kg. No additional costs are incurred on either of the two main products after the second process. The by-product is sold for £1.80 per kg after being sterilised, at a cost of £0.30 per kg, in a subsequent process. The operating costs of process 2 are reduced by the net income receivable from sales of the by-product.

Required:

(a)   Calculate, for the previous month, the cost of the output transferred from process 1 into process 2 and the net cost or saving arising from any abnormal losses or gains in process 1.   **(6 marks)**

(b)   Calculate the value of the closing stock of each sealant and the profit earned by each sealant during the previous month using the following method of apportioning costs to joint products:

    (i)   according to weight of output
    (ii)   according to market value of output.   **(10 marks)**

(c)   Consider whether apportioning process costs to joint products is useful. Briefly illustrate with examples from your answer to (b) above.   **(4 marks)**
                                              (Total: 20 marks)

24   Miozip Co

The Miozip Co operates an absorption costing system which incorporates a factory-wide overhead absorption rate per direct labour hour. For 20X0 and 20X1 this rate was £2.10 per hour. The fixed factory overhead for 20X1 was £600,000 and this would have been fully absorbed if the company had operated at full capacity, which is estimated at 400,000 direct labour hours. Unfortunately, only 200,000 hours were worked in that year so that the overhead was seriously under-absorbed. Fixed factory overheads are expected to be unchanged in 20X2 and 20X3.

The outcome for 20X1 was a loss of £70,000 and the management believed that a major cause of this loss was the low overhead absorption rate which had led the company to quote selling prices which were uneconomic.

For 20X2 the overhead absorption rate was increased to £3.60 per direct labour hour and selling prices were raised in line with the established pricing procedures which involve adding a profit mark-up of 50% onto the full factory cost of the company's products. The new selling prices were also charged on the stock of finished goods held at the beginning of 20X2. In December 20X2 the company's accountant prepared an estimated profit and loss account for 20X2 and a budgeted profit and loss account for 20X3. Although sales were considered to be depressed in 20X1, they were even lower in 20X2 but, nevertheless, it seems that the company will make a profit for that year. A worrying feature of the estimated accounts is the high level of finished goods stock held and the 20X3 budget provides for a reduction in the stock level at 31 December 20X3 to the (physical) level which obtained at 1 January 20X1. Budgeted sales for 20X3 are set at the 20X2 sales level.

The summarised profit statements for the three years to 31 December 20X3 are as follows:

Summarised profit and loss accounts

	Actual 20X1 £	Actual 20X1 £	Estimated 20X2 £	Estimated 20X2 £	Budgeted 20X3 £	Budgeted 20X3 £
Sales revenue		1,350,000		1,316,250		1,316,250
Opening stock of finished goods	100,000		200,000		357,500	
Factory cost of production	1,000,000		975,000		650,000	
	1,100,000		1,175,000		1,007,500	
Less: Closing stock of finished goods	200,000		357,500		130,000	
Factory cost of goods sold		900,000		817,500		877,500
		450,000		498,750		438,750
Less: Factory overhead under-absorbed		300,000		150,000		300,000
		150,000		348,750		138,750
Administrative and financial costs		220,000		220,000		220,000
Profit/(loss)		(70,000)		128,750		(81,250)

Required:

(a)   Write a short report to the board of Miozip explaining why the budgeted income for 20X3 is so different from that of 20X2 when the sales revenue is the same for both years.   **(5 marks)**

(b)   Restate the profit and loss account for 20X1, the estimated profit and loss account for 20X2 and the budgeted profit and loss account for 20X3 using marginal factory cost for stock valuation purposes.   **(7 marks)**

(c)   Comment on the problems which may follow from a decision to increase the overhead absorption rate in conditions when cost plus pricing is used and overhead is currently under-absorbed.   **(3 marks)**

(d)   Explain why the majority of businesses use full costing systems whilst most management accounting theorists favour marginal costing.   **(5 marks)**

Note: assume in your answers to this question that the value of the £ and the efficiency of the company have been constant over the period under review.   **(Total: 20 marks)**
(ACCA Dec 82)

25   Your company

Your company will shortly be completing its acquisition of a small manufacturing company which is engaged in producing a range of products via a number of processes. The production side of that company is well established. However, its cost and management accounting function is not so well developed. This type of multi-process production system is new to your company.

Required:

Prepare a report for management which clearly explains the problems associated with process costing, and which looks particularly at:

–   the treatment of overheads;
–   valuation problems;
–   normal and abnormal gains and losses.

(Total: 25 marks)
(ACCA Dec 94)

26   Brunti plc

The following budgeted information relates to Brunti plc for the forthcoming period:

	Products		
	XYI	*YZT*	*ABW*
	('000)	('000)	('000)
Sales and production (units)	50	40	30
	£	£	£
Selling price(per unit)	45	95	73
Prime cost (per unit)	32	84	65
	Hours	*Hours*	*Hours*
Machine department (machine hours per unit)	2	5	4
Assembly department (direct labour hours per unit)	7	3	2

Overheads allocated and apportioned to production departments (including service cost centre costs) were to be recovered in product costs as follows:

Machine department at £1.20 per machine hour
Assembly department at £0.825 per direct labour hour

You ascertain that the above overheads could be re-analysed into 'cost pools' as follows:

Cost pool	*£'000*	*Cost driver*	*Quantity for the period*
Machining services	357	Machined hours	420,000
Assembly services	318	Direct labour hours	530,000
Set up costs	26	Set ups	520
Order processing	156	Customer orders	32,000
Purchasing	84	Suppliers' orders	11,200
	941		

You have also been provided with the following estimates for the period:

	Products		
	XYI	*YZT*	*ABW*
Number of set-ups	120	200	200
Customer orders	8,000	8,000	16,000
Suppliers' orders	3,000	4,000	4,200

Required:

(a)   Prepare and present profit statements using:

    (i)   conventional absorption costing; and   **(5 marks)**
    (ii)   activity-based costing.   **(10 marks)**

(b)   Comment on why activity-based costing is considered to present a fairer valuation of the product cost per unit.

                (5 marks)
                (Total: 20 marks)
                (ACCA June 95)

27   ABC plc

ABC plc, a group operating retail stores, is compiling its budget statements for 20X8. In this exercise revenues and costs at each store A, B and C are predicted. Additionally, all central costs of warehousing and a head office are allocated across the three stores in order to arrive at a total cost and net profit of each store operation.

In earlier years the central costs were allocated in total based on the total sales value of each store. But as a result of dissatisfaction expressed by some store managers alternative methods are to be evaluated.

The predicted results before any re-allocation of central costs are as follows:

	A £'000	B £'000	C £'000
Sales	5,000	4,000	3,000
Costs of sales	2,800	2,300	1,900
Gross margin	2,200	1,700	1,100
Local operating expenses			
Variable	660	730	310
Fixed	700	600	500
Operating profit	840	370	290

The central costs which are to be allocated are:

	£'000
Warehouse costs:	
Depreciation	100
Storage	80
Operating and despatch	120
Delivery	300
Head office:	
Salaries	200
Advertising	80
Establishment	120
Total	1,000

The management accountant has carried out discussions with staff at all locations in order to identify more suitable 'cost drivers' of some of the central costs. So far the following has been revealed.

	A	B	C
Number of despatches	550	450	520
Total delivery distances			
(thousand miles)	70	50	90
Storage space occupied (%)	40	30	30

1   An analysis of senior management time revealed that 10% of their time was devoted to warehouse issues with the remainder shared equally between the three stores.

2   It was agreed that the only basis on which to allocate the advertising costs was sales revenue.

3   Establishment costs were mainly occupancy costs of senior management.

This analysis has been carried out against a background of developments in the company, for example, automated warehousing and greater integration with suppliers.

Required:

(a)   As the management accountant prepare a report for the management of the group which:

   (i)   computes the budgeted net profit of each store based on the *sales value* allocation base originally adopted *and* explains 'cost driver', 'volume' and 'complexity' issues in relation to cost allocation commenting on the possible implications of the dissatisfaction expressed   **(7 marks)**

   (ii)   computes the budgeted net profit of each store using the additional information provided, discusses the extent to which an improvement has been achieved in the information on the costs and profitability of running the stores and comments on the results.   **(14 marks)**

(b)   Explain briefly how regression analysis and coefficient of determination (r^2) could be used in confirming the delivery mileage allocation method used in (a) above.   **(4 marks)**
                                                                                                 (Total: 25 marks)
                                                                                                 (ACCA June 97)

28   EXE and WYE

A firm manufactures two products, EXE and WYE, in departments dedicated exclusively to them. There are also three service departments, stores, maintenance and administration. No stocks are held as the products deteriorate rapidly.

Direct costs of the products, which are variable in the context of the whole business, are identified to each department. The step-wise apportionment of service department costs to the manufacturing departments is based on estimates of the usage of the service provided. These are expressed as percentages and assumed to be reliable over the current capacity range. The general factory overheads of £3.6m, which are fixed, are apportioned based on floor space occupied. The company establishes product costs based on budgeted volume and marks up these costs by 25% in order to set target selling prices.

Extracts from the budgets for 20X8 are provided below:

				Annual volume (units)	
				EXE	*WYE*
Max capacity				200,000	100,000
Budget				150,000	70,000

	EXE	WYE	Stores	Maintenance	Admin
Costs (£m)					
Material	1.8	0.7	0.1	0.1	
Other variable	0.8	0.5	0.1	0.2	0.2
Departmental usage (%)					
Maintenance	50	25	25		
Administration	40	30	20	10	
Stores	60	40			
Floor space (sq m)					
	640	480	240	80	160

Required:

Workings may be £'000 with unit prices to the nearest penny.

(a)   Calculate the budgeted selling price of one unit of EXE and WYE based on the usual mark up.   **(6 marks)**

(b)   Discuss how the company may respond to each of the following independent events, which represent additional business opportunities:

(i)   an enquiry from an overseas customer for 3,000 units only of WYE where a price of £35 per unit is offered

(ii)   an enquiry for 50,000 units of WYE to be supplied in full at regular intervals during 20X8 at a price which is equivalent to full cost plus 10%.

In both cases support your discussion with calculations and comment on any assumptions or matters on which you would seek clarification.   **(13 marks)**

(c)   Explain the implications of preparing product full costs based on maximum capacity rather than annual budget volume.   **(6 marks)**
(Total: 25 marks)
(ACCA Dec 97)

29   Rayman Company

Rayman Company produces three chemical products, J1X, J2Y and B1Z. Raw materials are processed in a single plant to produce two intermediate products, J1 and J2, in fixed proportions. There is no market for these two intermediate products. J1 is processed further through process X to yield the product J1X, product J2 is converted into J2Y by a separate finishing process Y. The Y finishing process produces both J2Y and a waste material, B1, which has no market value. The Rayman Company can convert B1, after additional processing through process Z, into a saleable by-product, B1Z. The company can sell as much B1Z as it can produce at a price of £1.50 per kg.

At normal levels of production and sales, 600,000 kg of the common input material are processed each month. There are 440,000 kg and 110,000 kg respectively, of the intermediate products J1 and J2, produced from this level of input. After the separate finishing processes, fixed proportions of J1X, J2Y and B1Z emerge, as shown below with current market prices (all losses are normal losses):

Product	Quantity kg	Market Price per kg
J1X	400,000	£2.425
J2Y	100,000	£4.50
B1Z	10,000	£1.50

At these normal volumes, materials and processing costs are as follows:

	Common Plant Facility	Separate Finishing Processes		
		X	Y	Z
	£000	£000	£000	£000
Direct materials	320	110	15	1.0
Direct labour	150	225	90	5.5
Variable overhead	30	50	25	0.5
Fixed overhead	50	25	5	3.0
Total	550	410	135	10.0

Selling and administrative costs are entirely fixed and cannot be traced to any of the three products.

Required:

(a) Draw a diagram which shows the flow of these products, through the processes, label the diagram and show the quantities involved in normal operation.   **(3 marks)**

(b) Calculate the *cost per unit* of the finished products J1X and J2Y and the *total manufacturing profit*, for the month, attributed to each product assuming all joint costs are allocated based on:

    (i)   physical units   **(3 marks)**
    (ii)   net realisable value   **(5 marks)**

    and comment briefly on the two methods.   **(3 marks)**

    Note: All losses are normal losses.

(c) A new customer has approached Rayman wishing to purchase 10,000 kg of J2Y for £4·00 per kg. This is extra to the present level of business indicated above.

    Advise the management how they may respond to this approach by:

    (i)   developing a financial evaluation of the offer   **(6 marks)**
    (ii)   clarifying any assumptions and further questions which may apply.   **(5 marks)**
                                                                    (Total: 25 marks)
                                                                 (ACCA June 98)

30   Zorro Company

The Zorro Company manufactures a line of four related products in a single factory which is currently operating below capacity. Annual sales and costs of the products are shown below:

	W £000	X £000	Y £000	Z £000	Total £000
Sales	2,000	2,500	1,000	500	6,000
Factory cost of sales:					
materials	300	400	200	40	940
labour	500	600	400	100	1,600
overhead	600	800	500	100	2,000
	1,400	1,800	1,100	240	4,540
Gross margin	600	700	(100)	260	1,460
Selling overhead	300	375	150	75	900
Operating profit/(loss)	300	325	(250)	185	560

The factory overheads costs allocated to products are based on predetermined overhead rates of which 40% is estimated to be variable at the current operating volume. Selling overheads are applied to products based on 15% of sales value, the variable component of this is approximately 5% of sales.

The loss being reported in the above table against product Y is indicative of recent results and has led the management to consider its withdrawal. It is estimated that if product Y were to be withdrawn a saving of fixed factory and selling costs of £100,000 would occur.

Required:

(a) On financial grounds should Y be withdrawn? Briefly explain and qualify your answer.   **(9 marks)**

(b) The chief executive has said that he believes in the long run a product that does not cover its costs should not be retained.

    (i)   Is it conceivable that in the long run it might be profitable to keep Y in the product line?
    (ii)   In what circumstances would it be appropriate to consider dropping product Y?   **(6 marks)**

(c)   Following some further enquiries it is established that:

-    Product Z may in some cases be a substitute for Y. If Y were to be withdrawn, sales of Z would increase by £300,000.

-    Products W and Y are complementary. Twenty per cent of Y is sold in conjunction with W. These customers would not be able to substitute Z for Y and would be likely to move to other companies for their supplies if product Y is dropped. As a consequence sales of W would drop by 10% if Y were to be withdrawn completely. Product Y could however be retained as a service to these specific product W customers only, in which case the increased sales of Z, mentioned above, would still apply.

-    The saving of fixed costs achieved by the complete withdrawal of product Y would still be £100,000. If product Y was to be retained as a service to product W customers only the saving in fixed factory and selling costs would be £50,000.

Required:

In the light of this new information, should product Y be continued, withdrawn completely, or continued as a service only to the specific customers for product W? Briefly explain your answer.   **(10 marks)**

(Total: 25 marks)

(ACCA Dec 98)

31   Holiday Company

A holiday company offers a range of package holidays abroad. The management are examining the viability of three types of holiday for the coming season.

An analysis of costs and revenues of each of the holiday packages is shown below:

		Sports Holiday		*Culture Holiday*		*Special Interest Holiday*
Maximum Number of Customers	100		100		100	
	£	£	£	£	£	£
Total Revenue (100 customers)		42,000		48,000		30,000
Costs: (100 customers)						
Air Travel	8,100		8,400		7,800	
Hotel and Meals	16,800		19,800		7,200	
Local Courier	1,500		1,500		1,750	
Other customer costs and office overheads	10,560		11,880		6,180	
Commission	6,300		4,800		6,000	
		43,260		46,380		28,930
Profit/(Loss)		(1,260)		1,620		1,070

Past experience has shown that the average number of places taken up on the holidays, as a percentage of the maximum number of customers, will be 70% on sports, 80% on culture and 60% on special interest holidays.

The costs of the local couriers will not change irrespective of the number of customers. The costs of air travel are also fixed and are based on a block booking of seats for the season. The booking with the airline has already been confirmed. Contracts for the couriers have not yet been signed.

All accommodation costs are variable with the number of customers. The commission is proportional to the price of the holiday.

The other customer costs and office overheads, in the table above, are allocated over all the company's different package holidays. They are semi-variable costs and an analysis of these costs for the last three years relating to all holidays is as follows:

	Total number of customers	Total customer costs and office overheads £
20X6	10,000	900,000
20X7	12,000	990,000
20X8	15,000	1,125,000

The effects of exchange rates and inflation may be ignored.

Required:

(a)   Analyse the costs and revenues into a form more suitable to an assessment of the short-term viability of each holiday. Calculate one possible break-even number of customers required for each holiday.

   Note: Your analysis should be presented showing, where appropriate, costs and revenues per customer.

   (10 marks)

(b)   Identify clearly the shortcomings of the original analysis, explain your preferred analysis and interpret the results.   **(10 marks)**

(Total: 20 marks)

(ACCA June 99)

32   Plastic tools

A small company is engaged in the production of plastic tools for the garden.

Sub-totals on the spreadsheet of budgeted overheads for a year reveal the following:

	Moulding Department	Finishing Department	General Factory Overhead
Variable overhead £'000	1,600	500	1,050
Fixed overhead £'000	2,500	850	1,750
Budgeted activity			
Machine hours ('000)	800	600	
Practical capacity			
Machine hours ('000)	1,200	800	

For the purposes of reallocation of general factory overhead it is agreed that the variable overheads accrue in line with the machine hours worked in each department. General factory fixed overhead is to be reallocated on the basis of the practical machine hour capacity of the two departments.

It has been a long-standing company practice to establish selling prices by applying a mark-up on full manufacturing cost of between 25% and 35%.

A possible price is sought for one new product which is in a final development stage. The total market for this product is estimated at 200,000 units per annum. Market research indicates that the company could expect to obtain and hold about 10% of the market. It is hoped the product will offer some improvement over competitors' products, which are currently marketed at between £90 and £100 each.

The product development department have determined that the direct material content is £9 per unit. Each unit of the product will take two labour hours (four machine hours) in the moulding department and three labour hours (three machine hours) in finishing. Hourly labour rates are £5.00 and £5.50 respectively.

Management estimate that the annual fixed costs which would be specifically incurred in relation to the product are: supervision £20,000, depreciation of a recently acquired machine £120,000 and advertising £27,000. It may be assumed that these costs are included in the budget given above. Given the state of development of this new product, management do not consider it necessary to make revisions, to the budgeted activity levels given above, for any possible extra machine hours involved in its manufacture.

Required:

(a)   Briefly explain the role of costs in pricing.   **(6 marks)**

(b)   Prepare full cost and marginal cost information which may help with the pricing decision.   **(9 marks)**

(c)   Comment on the cost information and suggest a price range which should be considered.   **(5 marks)**
                                                                          (Total: 20 marks)
                                                                          (ACCA Dec 99)

Standard costing and variance analysis

33   Material variances

A company makes a product using two materials, X and Y, in the production process. A system of standard costing and variance analysis is in operation. The standard material requirement per tonne of mixed output is 60% material X at £30 per tonne and 40% material Y at £45 per tonne, with a standard yield of 90%.

The following information has been gathered for the three months January to March:

	January	*February*	*March*
Output achieved (tonnes)	810	765	900
Actual material input:			
X (tonnes)	540	480	700
Y (tonnes)	360	360	360
Actual material cost (X plus Y) (£)	32,400	31,560	38,600

The actual price per tonne of material Y throughout the January to March period was £45.

Required:

(a)   Prepare material variance summaries for each of January, February and March which include yield and mix variances in total plus usage and price variances for each material and in total.   **(15 marks)**

(b)   Prepare comments for management on each variance including variance trend.   **(6 marks)**

(c)   Discuss the relevance of the variances calculated above in the light of the following additional information. The company has an agreement to purchase 360 tonnes of material Y each month and the perishable nature of the material means that it must be used in the month of purchase and additional supplies in excess of 360 tonnes per month are not available.   **(4 marks)**
                                                                          (Total: 25 marks)
                                                                          (ACCA June 91)

34   Perseus Co Ltd

The Perseus Co Ltd a medium sized company, produces a single product in its one overseas factory. For control purposes, a standard costing system was recently introduced and is now in operation.

The standards set for the month of May were as follows:

Production and sales	16,000 units
Selling price (per unit)	£140

Materials

Material 007	6 kilos per unit at £12.25 per kilo
Material XL90	3 kilos per unit at £3.20 per kilo

Labour

4.5 hours per unit at £8.40 per hour

Overheads (all fixed)
£86,400 per month. They are not absorbed into the product costs.

The actual data for the month of May, is as follows.

Produced 15,400 units which were sold at £138.25 each.

Materials

Used 98,560 kilos of material 007 at a total cost of £1,256,640 and used 42,350 kilos of material XL90 at a total cost of £132,979.

Labour

Paid an actual rate of £8.65 per hour to the labour force. The total amount paid out, amounted to £612,766.

Overheads (all fixed)

£96,840

Required:

(a)   Prepare a standard costing profit statement, and a profit statement based on actual figures for the month of May.

(6 marks)

(b)   Prepare a statement of the variances which reconciles the actual with the standard profit or loss figure.

(9 marks)

(c)   Explain briefly the possible reasons for inter-relationships between material variances and labour variances.

(5 marks)
(Total: 20 marks)
(ACCA June 94)

35   Acca-chem Co plc

Acca-chem Co plc manufacture a single product, product W, and have provided you with the following information which relates to the period which has just ended:

Standard cost per batch of product W

Materials		*Kilos*	*Price per kilo* £	*Total* £
	F	15	4	60
	G	12	3	36
	H	8	6	48
		35		144
Less:	Standard loss	(3)		
	Standard yield	32		

Labour		*Hours*	*Rate per hour* £	£
Department P		4	10	40
Department Q		2	6	12
				196

Budgeted sales for the period are 4,096 kilos at £16 per kilo. There were no budgeted opening or closing stocks of product W.

The actual materials and labour used for 120 batches were:

Materials		Kilos	Price per kilo £	Total £
	F	1,680	4.25	7,140
	G	1,650	2.80	4,620
	H	870	6.40	5,568
		4,200		17,328
Less: Actual loss		(552)		
Actual yield		3,648		

Labour	Hours	Rate per hour £	
Department P	600	10.60	6,360
Department Q	270	5.60	1,512
			25,200

All of the production of W was sold during the period for £16.75 per kilo.

Required:

(a)   Calculate the following material variances:

      (i)   price
      (ii)   usage
      (iii)   mix
      (iv)   yield.   **(6 marks)**

(b)   Prepare an analysis of the material mix and price variances for each of the materials used.   **(4 marks)**

(c)   Calculate the following labour variances:

      (i)   cost
      (ii)   efficiency
      (iii)   rate

      for each of the production departments.   **(6 marks)**

(d)   Calculate the sales variances.   **(4 marks)**

(e)   Comment on your findings to help explain what has happened to the yield variance.   **(5 marks)**
                                                              (Total: 25 marks)
                                                               (ACCA Dec 95)

36   Component RYX

A manufacturing company has provided you with the following data which relates to component RYX, for the period which has just ended:

	Budget	Actual
Number of labour hours	8,400	7,980
Production units	1,200	1,100
Overhead cost (all fixed)	£22,260	£25,536

Overheads are absorbed at a rate per standard labour hour.

Required:

(a) (i) Calculate the fixed production overhead cost variance and the following subsidiary variances:

-    expenditure
-    efficiency
-    capacity

(ii) Provide a summary statement of these four variances.   **(7 marks)**

(b) Briefly discuss the possible reasons why adverse fixed production overhead expenditure, efficiency and capacity variances occur.   **(10 marks)**

(c) Briefly discuss two examples of inter-relationships between the fixed production overhead efficiency variances and the material and labour variances.   **(3 marks)**
                                                                        (Total: 20 marks)
                                                                        (ACCA Dec 96)

37   Alpha

A UK site of a chemical company has a number of semi-automated plants which specialise in individual products. One product, Alpha, has an annual budgeted volume of 240,000kg for which equal amounts of production and sales are planned in each of 12 reporting periods. The budgeted/standard manufacturing and selling costs for period 1 are shown below:

	Per kg £	Total P1 £
Manufacturing		
Material	3.50	70,000
Labour and variable overhead	2.50	50,000
Fixed overhead		100,000
Total manufacturing cost		220,000
Variable selling overhead	1.50	30,000
Fixed selling overhead		40,000
		70,000

1   The standard selling price is £17 per kg.
2   Variable selling overheads are incurred in proportion to units sold.
3   Manufacturing overheads are recovered based on the budgeted volume levels.

For reporting purposes and identifying stock values the company operates a standard absorption costing system. For P1 the production was 18,400kg, however sales amounted to only 12,400kg.

In order to undertake some basic sales and marketing planning the accountant analyses costs into variable and fixed elements in order to compute the break-even point and profits at various sales volumes. The sales manager had calculated the break-even point as 14,737kg and for 12,400kg sales he predicts a loss. He was mildly surprised therefore to see the profit statement which was produced for the period to reveal a small profit as follows:

Product Alpha
Profit Statement P1

Production	18,400 kg		
Sales	12,400 kg		
		£	£
Sales		208,800	
Manufacturing costs			
Standard cost of sales			
12,400 × £11		136,400	
Add Manufacturing variances			
Volume		8,000	
All other expenditure		5,500	
		149,900	
Actual selling overheads			
Variable		17,500	
Fixed		38,300	
			205,700
Actual net profit			3,100

Required:

(a) Analyse the budgeted costs into fixed and variable elements and calculate both the break-even point and the budgeted profit/loss based on the actual kg sold where a marginal cost system is in use. **(3 marks)**

(b) (i) Demonstrate how the value of the manufacturing volume variance has been computed and briefly explain its significance. **(5 marks)**

(ii) Calculate the variances which apply to the variable and fixed selling overheads. **(3 marks)**

(c) Reconcile the profit/loss from (a) above with the actual net profit given in the question showing all relevant variances. Briefly explain how a profit is revealed when a loss was anticipated by the sales manager. **(9 marks)**
(Total: 20 marks)
(ACCA June 97)

38   Hairdressing

A company operates a number of hairdressing establishments which are managed on a franchise arrangement. The franchisor offers support using a PC package which deals with profit budgeting and control information.

Budget extracts of one franchisee for November 20X7 are shown below analysed by male and female clients. For the purposes of budget projections average revenue rates are used. At the month end these are compared with the average monthly rates actually achieved using variance analysis. Sales price, sales quantity, sales mix and cost variances are routinely produced in order to compare the budget and actual results.

Staff working in this business are paid on a commission basis in order to act as an incentive to attract and retain clients. The labour rate variance is based on the commission payments, any basic pay is part of the monthly fixed cost.

Budget

	Male	Female
Clients	4,000	1,000
Average revenue	£	£
(per client)	7.5	18.0
Average commission		
(per client)	3.0	10.0
Total monthly fixed cost		£20,000

Actual result

	Male	Female
Clients	2,000	2,000
	£	£
Average revenue (per client)	8.0	20.0
Average commission (per client)	3.5	11.0
Total monthly fixed cost	£24,000	

Required:

(a)   Reconcile the budgeted and actual profit for November by calculating appropriate price, quantity, mix and cost variances, presenting the information in good form. You should adopt a contribution style, with mix variances based on units (i.e. clients).   **(10 marks)**

(b)   Write a short memorandum to the manager of the business commenting on the result in (a) above   **(4 marks)**

(c)   Comment on the limitations associated with generating sales variances as in (a) above.   **(6 marks)**
(Total: 20 marks)
(ACCA Dec 97)

39   Information source

A major information source within many businesses is a system of standard costing and variance analysis.

Required:

(a)   Describe briefly four purposes of a system of standard costing.   **(4 marks)**

(b)   Explain three different levels of performance which may be incorporated into a system of standard costing and comment on how these may relate to the purposes set out in (a) above.   **(6 marks)**

(c)   Comment on whether standard costing applies in both manufacturing and service businesses and how it may be affected by modern initiatives of continuous performance improvement and cost reduction.   **(4 marks)**

(d)   A standard costing system enables variances for direct costs, variable and fixed overheads to be extracted. Identify and briefly discuss some of the complexities and practical problems in calculation which may limit the usefulness of those variances.   **(6 marks)**
(Total: 20 marks)
(ACCA Dec 98)

40   Performance meeting

As a recently appointed assistant management accountant you are attending a monthly performance meeting. You have with you a statement of monthly actual costs, a summary of cost variances and other pieces of information you have managed to collect, as shown below:

	£
Actual cost of direct material purchased and used	62,700
Actual direct wages paid	97,350
Variable overheads incurred	19,500
Fixed overheads incurred	106,500
The variances from standard cost were:	
Direct material price variance	5,700 Adv.
Direct material usage variance	3,000 Fav.
Direct labour rate variance	1,650 Fav.
Direct labour efficiency variance	9,000 Fav.
Variable overhead variance	1,500 Adv.
Fixed overhead expenditure variance	1,500 Adv.
Fixed overhead volume variance	15,000 Adv.

The actual wage rate paid for the period was £8.85 per hour. It takes three standard hours to produce one unit of the finished product.

The single direct material used in the period cost 30p per kg above the standard price. Five kg of raw material input is allowed for as standard for one unit of output.

All figures relate to the single product which is manufactured at the plant. There were no stocks at the beginning or end of the accounting period. Variable and fixed overhead absorption rates are based on standard hours produced.

Managers from various functions have brought to the meeting measures which they have collected for their own areas of responsibility. In order to demonstrate the link between the accounting values and their measures you decide to work from the variances to confirm some of them.

Required:

(a)   The formula for the calculation of the labour cost variance is:

$$(SH \times SR) - (AH \times AR)$$

Provide formulae for the calculation of the labour rate variance and labour efficiency variance using similar notation to that above. Demonstrate how they will sum to the labour cost variance given above.   **(2 marks)**

(b)   Using variance formulae, such as those above, or otherwise, determine:

    (i)   the actual number of direct labour hours worked
    (ii)   the standard rate of pay per direct labour hour
    (iii)   the standard hours of production
    (iv)   the actual production in units
    (v)   the actual quantity of direct material consumed
    (vi)   the actual price paid for the direct material (per kg)
    (vii)   the standard direct material usage in kg for the actual number of units produced.   **(10 marks)**

(c)   From (b) above and any other calculations which may be appropriate, compute the standard cost per unit of finished product. Show separately standard prices and standard quantities for each element of cost.   **(4 marks)**

(d)   Briefly interpret the overhead variances given in the question.   **(4 marks)**
                                (Total: 20 marks)
                                (ACCA June 99)

41   Food manufacturer

A food manufacturer specialises in the production of frozen cakes and sweet products, selling mainly to supermarkets. The following monthly budget applies to one of its products.

Original Budget

	£000	£000
Sales		1,000
Costs:		
Ingredients	400	
Labour and energy	100	
Fixed overheads	300	
	——	
		800
		——
Profit		200
		——

For the ingredients, a standard quantity of 5 kg per pack is required; a standard price of 40p per kg applies in the original budget.

Considerable attention has been given to increasing the market share of this product whilst attempting to maintain its profitability. Consequently, since the preparation of the budget the management team implemented some changes to the manufacture and sale of this product. These changes were as follows:

(i)   The product was budgeted to sell for £5.00 per pack but, to promote sales, a price reduction on all sales to £4.50 per pack was made.

(ii)   The supplier of ingredients was changed and this secured a price reduction to 37.5p per kg on all ingredient supplies in return for a long-term contract.

(iii)   The method of working was changed in order to reduce the direct labour and energy costs which are regarded as variable.

All of the above changes applied for the whole of the month just ended and are reflected in the actual results shown below. The management intend, however, to use the original budget, for both cost and volume, as a reference point until the effect of the changes has been evaluated.

The following actual results have just been reported for the month:

Actual Results

	£000	£000
Sales		1,080
Costs:		
Ingredients	520	
Labour and energy	110	
Fixed overheads	340	
		970
Profit		110

Required:

(a)   Prepare a flexible budget (for the actual quantity sold in the month just ended) based on the original budgeted unit costs and selling price.   **(3 marks)**

(b)   Using variances, reconcile the original budget profit with the actual profit. You should use a contribution approach to variance analysis.   **(9 marks)**

(c)   Provide a commentary on the variances you have produced. Within this commentary refer to possible interrelationships between the variances and how the level of fixed overheads may be reduced.   **(8 marks)**
    (Total: 20 marks)
    (ACCA Dec 99)

Budgeting, budgetary control and decision-making

42   Cepheus Transport Co Ltd

Cepheus Transport Co Ltd currently does around 60% of its work for its holding company and the remainder for a small number of local manufacturers. It operates from a garage and warehouse complex located close to an airport and within two hours drive of the nearest seaport.

Their management accounting information is very limited and what they do have is shown below for the quarter which has just ended:

Type of vehicle	Type F	Type P	Type U	
Number of vehicles owned	8	4	7	
Mileage	*Miles*	*Miles*	*Miles*	
Holding company work	26,000	8,120	12,080	
Work for other companies	14,600	7,400	12,400	*Total*

Revenue	£	£	£	£
From holding company	47,450	13,601	14,798	75,849
From other companies	46,720	19,573	23,560	89,853
	94,170	33,174	38,358	165,702

Operating costs	£	£	£	£
Fuel (diesel at £2 per gallon)	4,368	1,404	1,752	7,524
Drivers' wages				
Fixed	12,800	6,000	10,500	29,300
Variable	7,200	1,625	3,750	12,575
Overtime premium	1,200	250	500	1,950
Other operating costs and maintenance costs	4,415	2,371	2,604	9,390
Fixed costs of vehicles (including insurance etc.)	3,850	2,142	2,881	8,873
*Depreciation	9,000	3,000	4,000	16,000
	42,833	16,792	25,987	85,612

* Depreciation is charged at 20% of cost per annum, taking a full year's depreciation in the year of purchase and none in the year of sale.

The company's administrative costs, garage and warehouse rent and other fixed overheads amounted to £58,220.

Edith Cepheus, the chief executive, has assured you that this data is quite typical and that to date the company has not experienced any violent fluctuations in trading conditions.

Required:

Prepare a report for submission to Mrs Cepheus in which, from the limited supply of data available, you:

(a)   evaluate and comment on current performance, and   **(10 marks)**

(b)   explain how the company can improve its recording system to assist them with planning, control and decision-making.   **(10 marks)**
(Total: 20 marks)
(ACCA June 94)

43   Flexible budgeting

You have been provided with the following operating statement which represents an attempt to compare the actual performance for the quarter which has just ended with the budget:

	Budget	Actual	Variance
Number of units sold ('000)	640	720	80
	£'000	£'000	£'000
Sales	1,024	1,071	47
Cost of sales (all variable)			
Materials	168	144	
Labour	240	288	
Overheads	32	36	
	440	468	(28)

Fixed labour cost	100	94	6
Selling and distribution costs			
Fixed	72	83	(11)
Variable	144	153	(9)
Administration costs			
Fixed	184	176	8
Variable	48	54	(6)
	548	560	(12)
Net profit	36	43	7

Required:

(a)   Using a flexible budgeting approach, re-draft the operating statement so as to provide a more realistic indication of the variances, and comment briefly on the possible reasons (other than inflation) why they have occurred.

(12 marks)

(b)   Explain why the original operating statement was of little use to management.   **(2 marks)**

(c)   Discuss the problems associated with the forecasting of figures which are to be used in flexible budgeting.

(6 marks)
(Total: 20 marks)
(ACCA June 95)

44   Sychwedd plc

Sychwedd plc manufacture and sell three products R, S, and T which make use of two machine groups, 1 and 2. The budget for period 1, the first quarter of their next accounting year, includes the following information:

	Machine Group	
Fixed overhead absorption rates:	*1*	*2*
Rate per machine hour	£10.00	£11.20

	Product R	*Product S*	*Product T*
Sales (kilos)	12,000	25,000	40,000
	£	£	£
Sales	120,000	250,000	360,000
Variable costs	73,560	164,250	284,400
Fixed overheads	19,752	38,300	42,400
Budgeted net profit	26,688	47,450	33,200

For the second quarter (period 2), it is estimated that the budgeted machine hours and direct labour hours needed to produce 1,000 kilos of each of the products are:

	Machine Group	
Machine hours	1	2
Product		
R	75	80
S	30	110
T	50	50

Direct labour hours

Product

R	30	40
S	10	50
T	20	20

Budgeted fixed overheads
(to be absorbed using a machine
hour rate)   £40,800   £68,365

**Budgeted variable labour and
overheads,** rate per direct
labour hour   £7.50   £8.50

	Product R	Product S	Product T
Budgeted material costs per 1,000 kilos	£4,508	£5,096	£6,125
Expected sales (kilos)	10,000	25,000	50,000
Planned price changes			
Compared with period 1	10% increase	no change	no change

A sales commission of 4% of the sales value will be paid.

There are no budgeted opening or closing stocks i.e., all production is expected to be sold.

Required:

(a)   Compute the machine hour rate for each machine group for period 2.   **(4 marks)**

(b)   Calculate the budgeted contribution and net profit for each of the three products for period 2.   **(12 marks)**

(c)   Assuming that the sales trend shown over the two periods is forecast to continue, comment briefly on the figures
        and advise management accordingly.   **(9 marks)**
                                                                                       (Total: 25 marks)
                                                                                        (ACCA June 96)

45   Rolling budgets

A company operates a system of quarterly rolling budgets. Budgets for the next three quarters have been prepared. The
figures below reflect the likely cost behaviour of each element of cost. Quarter four is being developed based on these
budgets and other information available.

Budget Quarters 1 to 3

	Q1 (000)	Q2 (000)	Q3 (000)
Activity:			
Sales (units)	18	34	30
Production (units)	20	40	30
Costs:	£000	£000	£000
Direct Materials	50	100	75
Production labour	180	280	230
Factory Overheads (excluding indirect labour)	170	200	185
Administration	30	30	30
Selling and Distribution	29	37	35

In the current planning stage for quarter four, flexible budgets are to be developed for low, most likely and high sales
volumes (38,000, 44,000 and 50,000 units respectively). The company wishes to have a closing stock (end of quarter
four) equal to the opening stock for quarter one. Management will therefore adjust the production levels to fall in line
with this policy.

Cost structures as for quarters one to three will apply to quarter four except that:

(i)   raw material prices are expected to rise by 10%

(ii)   production labour rates will increase by 2.5%. However, management have declared that all labour rate increases must be matched by increased efficiency so that labour costs (both total fixed and variable per unit) are unaltered.

(iii)   a quarterly bonus payment, of 50% of the variable labour cost per unit, will apply for all production above 40,000 units.

(iv)   fixed factory overheads and fixed selling and distribution expenses will rise by 5%.

The expected selling price per unit is £18. Stock is valued at full factory cost of £13 per unit. This has been established using absorption principles and based on long run cost and capacity predictions. Small fluctuations in cost prices or volumes will not cause this unit cost to be amended.

Required:

(a)   Explain what is meant by a 'rolling budget' and what additional benefit may be claimed for this compared to the annual style of budget.   **(4 marks)**

(b)   Summarise the variable cost per unit and the total fixed cost, for each cost heading, that will apply to quarter four, for production below 40,000 units.   **(6 marks)**

(c)   Prepare detailed flexed budget profit statements for quarter four under the separate assumptions of low, most likely and high levels of sales and corresponding production volumes.   **(8 marks)**

(d)   Produce in *summary form only* a statement of the likely change in profit for quarter four if management change their policy on stock levels so as to manufacture the same volume as the forecast sales for the quarter. Comment on the reason for the profit change and how this might motivate management regarding production levels in the future.   **(7 marks)**
                                                                                                          (Total: 25 marks)
                                                                                                          (ACCA June 98)

46   Budget compilation

A product manager has responsibility for a single product and is in the process of submitting data to be compiled into budgets for 20X9. The manager has performance targets set in relation to sales volume, profitability levels and a target cash surplus from the product.

Shown below are the agreed budgeted sales for the product for December 20X8 to May 20X9.

	Dec	Jan	Feb	Mar	April	May
Units	14,000	16,000	22,000	17,000	20,000	24,000

The company policy is that, at each month end, the closing stock of finished goods should be 25% of the following month's forecast sales and the stock of raw material should be sufficient for 10% of the following month's production. Stock levels currently conform to this policy. One unit of raw material makes one unit of finished stock, there is no wastage.

Raw material purchases are paid for during the month following the month of purchase. All other expenses are paid for as incurred. All sales are made on credit and the company expects cash receipts for 50% of sales in the month of sale and 50% in the following month.

The company operates an absorption costing system which is computed on a monthly basis. That is, in addition to direct costs it recovers each month's fixed and variable manufacturing overhead expenses in product costs using the budgeted production and budgeted expenditure in the month to establish an absorption rate. This cost is used to place a value on the stock holding. Opening stock is valued at the unit cost which was established in the previous month. At 1 January 20X9 finished stock should be assumed at £40 per unit. A flow of cost based on FIFO is assumed.

Sales are made at a price of £58 per unit.

Estimated costs to be used in the budget preparation for the product are:

Manufacturing costs:
material	£10.00 per unit produced
variable overhead and labour	£16.00 per unit produced
Fixed overhead costs	£210,000 per month
(including depreciation of £54,000 per month)	

Selling costs:
Variable	£7.00 per unit sold
Fixed	£164,000 per month

Required:

(a)   Compute the monthly budgeted production and material purchases for January to March 20X9.   **(6 marks)**

(b)   Prepare a budgeted profit and loss account and a statement of cash receipts and payments for January 20X9.
(10 marks)

(c)   Explain briefly the implications of the company's treatment of fixed manufacturing overheads compared to a predetermined overhead rate prepared annually.   **(4 marks)**

(d)   The preparation of budget data may be assisted by the use of a time series. Explain what a time series is and the various components which comprise one.   **(5 marks)**
(Total: 25 marks)
(ACCA Dec 98)

47   Budget behaviour

For many organisations in both the private and public sectors the annual budget is the basis of much internal management information. When preparing and using budgets, however, management and the accountant must be aware of their behavioural implications.

Required:

(a)   Briefly discuss four purposes of budgets.   **(8 marks)**

(b)   Explain the behavioural factors which should be borne in mind and the difficulties of applying them in the process of budgeting and budgetary control.   **(12 marks)**
(Total: 20 marks)
(ACCA June 99)

48   Planning and control

Accounting information plays a major part in the planning and control activities of any organisation. Often these planning and control activities, in which budgets feature prominently, are undertaken within a structure known as responsibility accounting.

Required:

(a)   Briefly explain responsibility accounting and describe three potential difficulties with operating a system of responsibility accounting.   **(6 marks)**

(b)   Explain 'feedback' and 'feed-forward' in the context of budgetary control. Present a simple diagram to illustrate each.   **(7 marks)**

(c)   Typical purposes of budgets are:

(i)   resource allocation
(ii)   authorisation
(iii)   control.

Explain each of these giving an example from the setting of a non-profit organisation.   **(7 marks)**
(Total: 20 marks)
(ACCA Dec 99)

Scenario-based questions

49   Manray plc

Manray plc manufactures and distributes automatic security lighting systems, which are purchased primarily by households, but also by business customers. When formed, some dozen years ago, Manray issued four million 25p ordinary shares, and one million £1 nominal 8% cumulative preference shares. Although Manray still relies on a single product, this has been modified numerous times in order to remain abreast of competitors. It is now contemplating investment in computer-controlled manufacturing technology which will further improve the product. It will also significantly alter the cost structure by raising fixed costs by £400,000 but lowering variable cost by £10 per unit, as a result of increased automation.

The improvement in the quality of the product is also expected to raise annual sales by 10,000 units, with no price change. Despite the volume increase, there is expected to be no increase in working capital requirements due to the introduction of a JIT system of stock control. In the trading period ended 31 March 20X3, Manray sold 80,000 units largely to edge-of-town DIY outlets, at a price of £35 per unit.

The new production facility will be financed by borrowing £3m from its present bankers, who currently provide overdraft facilities. The interest rate will be variable, but is initially set at 10% pa. £1m of the loan will be used to repay the existing overdraft. The loan itself will be repaid in three equal instalments, every two years over the anticipated lifetime of the equipment. If the equipment is purchased in the very near future, the company can begin to claim capital allowances against taxation liability. (Tax is paid a year in arrears.) At present, these operate on a **straight-line basis** over four years. The equipment is not expected to have any resale value.

Exhibit 1 shows Manray's profit and loss account for the year ended 31 March 20X3.

Exhibit 1

		£'000
Sales		2,800
Less: Variable expenses	1,600	
Fixed expenses	250	
		1,850
Operating profit		950
Less: Interest payable		150
Taxable profit		800
Less: Corporation tax*: at 33%		264
Profit after tax		536
Less: Preference dividend		80
Profit available for ordinary shareholders		456
Less: Dividend		228
Retained profit		228

* *Note:* a full tax charge was payable, there being no depreciation allowances available for the year in question.

Required:

(a)   Using a 15% discount rate, determine whether the project is worthwhile, taking account of corporation tax and the depreciation allowance.   **(12 marks)**

(b)   Calculate the change in earnings per share if Manray introduces the new production facility at once.   **(6 marks)**

(c)   Explain the term 'operating gearing', and illustrate your answer using data relating to Manray.   **(7 marks)**

(d)   Determine the break-even volumes for Manray, both before and after the introduction of the new facility.   **(5 marks)**

(e)   One of Manray's directors argues that the proposed method of finance over-exposes Manray to increases in interest rates. What macro-economic factors might be expected to cause increases in interest rates? What difficulties might such an increase cause?   **(10 marks)**
(Total: 40 marks)
(ACCA Pilot Paper)

50   Netherby plc

Netherby plc manufactures a range of camping and leisure equipment, including tents. It is currently experiencing severe quality control problems at its existing fully-depreciated factory in the south of England. These difficulties threaten to undermine its reputation for producing high quality products. It has recently been approached by the European Bank for Reconstruction and Development, on behalf of a tent manufacturer in Hungary, which is seeking a UK-based trading partner which will import and distribute its tents. Such a switch would involve shutting down the existing manufacturing operation in the UK and converting it into a distribution depot. The estimated exceptional restructuring costs of £5m would be tax-allowable, but would exert serious strains on cash flow.

Importing, rather than manufacturing tents appears inherently profitable as the buying-in price, when converted into sterling, is less than the present production cost. In addition, Netherby considers that the Hungarian product would result in increased sales, as the existing retail distributors seem impressed with the quality of the samples which they have been shown. It is estimated that for a five-year contract, the annual cash flow benefit would be around £2m pa before tax.

However, the financing of the closure and restructuring costs would involve careful consideration of the financing options. Some directors argue that dividends could be reduced as several competing companies have already done a similar thing, while other directors argue for a rights issue. Alternatively, the project could be financed by an issue of long-term loan stock at a fixed rate of 12%.

The most recent balance sheet shows £5m of issued share capital (par value 50p), while the market price per share is currently £3. A leading security analyst has recently described Netherby's gearing ratio as 'adventurous'. Profit-after-tax in the year just ended was £15m and dividends of £10m were paid.

The rate of corporation tax is 33%, payable with a one-year delay. Netherby's reporting year coincides with the calendar year and the factory will be closed at the year-end. Closure costs would be incurred shortly before deliveries of the imported product began, and sufficient stocks will be on hand to overcome any initial supply problems. Netherby considers that it should earn a return on new investment projects of 15% pa net of all taxes.

Required:

(a)   Is the closure of the existing factory financially worthwhile for Netherby?   **(7 marks)**

(b)   Explain what is meant when the capital market is said to be information-efficient in a semi-strong form.

      If the stock market is semi-strong efficient and without considering the method of finance, calculate the likely impact of acceptance and announcement of the details of this project to the market on Netherby's share price.
           (6 marks)

(c)   Advise the Netherby board as to the relative merits of a rights issue rather than a cut in dividends to finance this project.   **(8 marks)**

(d)   Explain why a rights issue generally results in a fall in the market price of shares.

      If a rights issue is undertaken, calculate the resulting impact on the existing share price of issue prices of £1 per share and £2 per share, respectively. (You may ignore issue costs.)   **(7 marks)**

(e)   Assuming the restructuring proposal meets expectations, assess the impact of the project on earnings per share if it is financed by a rights issue at an offer price of £2 per share, and loan stock, respectively.   **(4 marks)**

      (Again, you may ignore issue costs.)

(f)   Briefly consider the main operating risks connected with the investment project, and how Netherby might attempt to allow for these.   **(8 marks)**

(Total: 40 marks)
(ACCA June 94)

51   Bardsey plc

Bardsey plc operates a chain of city centre furniture stores, specialising in high quality items. It is 60% owned by the original family founders. Its sales over the past decade have never grown faster than 5% in any one year, even falling during a recent recession. No growth is expected from existing operations in the next few years despite continuing to offer generous credit to customers.

In order to achieve faster growth, it is considering the development of a number of 'out of town' sites, adjacent to giant supermarkets and DIY stores. During 20X7, this would involve a capital outlay of £50m plus additional working capital requirements of £20m in order to finance stock-building. In recent years, Bardsey's capital expenditure, mainly store refurbishments and vehicle replacements, and averaging around £10m per annum, has been financed entirely from cash flow. This category of investment will continue at about the same level in 20X7. Bardsey's fixed assets were revalued two years ago.

Bardsey's accounting statements for the last financial year are summarised in Exhibit A, and Exhibit B gives information on key financial indicators for the stores sector as a whole (listed companies only).

Bardsey's debentures currently sell on the stock market at £130 per £100 nominal. The current bank base rate is 8%, and economists expect interest rates in general to fall over the next few years. The stock market currently applies a price: earnings ratio of 11:1 to Bardsey's shares.

Required:

As Bardsey's chief accountant, you are instructed to:

(a)   Calculate Bardsey's expected net cash flow in 20X7 without the investment, assuming no changes in the level of net working capital.   **(5 marks)**

(*Note:* a statement in FRS 1 format is not required.)

(b)   Prepare a report, containing suitable reservations about the use of ratio analysis, which compares Bardsey's financial performance and health with the stores sector as a whole.   **(15 marks)**

(c)   Advise the board of Bardsey as to how the proposed investment programme might be financed. You should refer to possible economic reasons why interest rates may fall, and to the possible implications for Bardsey's financing decision.   **(12 marks)**

(d)   Suggest other possible uses of the increasing cash balances if Bardsey rejects the proposed investment.

(8 marks)
(Total: 40 marks)
(ACCA June 97)

Exhibit A: Bardsey's financial statements
Profit and loss account for the year ended 31 December 20X6

	£m
Turnover	150.0
Cost of sales*	(90.0)
Operating profit	60.0
Interest charges	(15.0)
Pre-tax profit	45.0
Corporation tax	(12.0)
Profits after tax	33.0
Dividends proposed	(20.0)
Retained earnings	13.0

Balance sheet as at 31 December 20X6

Assets employed	£m	£m	£m
Fixed (net):			
Land and premises		200	
Fixtures and fittings		50	
Vehicles		50	
		——	300
Current:			
Stocks	60		
Debtors	100		
Cash	40		
	——	200	
Current liabilities:			
Trade creditors	(85)		
Dividends payable	(20)		
Tax payable	(12)		
		(117)	
Net current assets		——	
			83
			——
Total assets less current liabilities			383
15% Debentures 20Z0-20Z2			(100)
			——
Net assets			283
			——
Financed by:			
Issued share capital (par value 25p):			100
Revaluation reserve			60
Profit and loss account			123
			——
Shareholders' funds			283
			——

* This includes depreciation of £8m

Exhibit B: Selected ratios for the stores sector

Return on (long-term) capital employed	14.3% (pre-tax)
Return on equity	15.3% (post-tax)
Operating profit margin	26.2%
Fixed asset turnover (sales/fixed assets)	1.2 times
Stock period	180 days
Debtor days	132 days
Gearing (total debt/equity)	42%
Interest cover	3.2 times
Dividend cover	2.1 times
P/E ratio	15:1

52   Marton Ltd

Marton Ltd produces a range of specialised components, supplying a wide range of UK and overseas customers, all on credit terms. 20% of UK turnover is sold to one firm. Having used generous credit policies to encourage past growth, Marton now has to finance a substantial overdraft and is concerned about its liquidity. Marton borrows from its bank at 13% per annum interest. No further sales growth in volume or value terms is planned for the next year.

In order to speed up collection from UK customers, Marton is considering two alternative policies.

Option one

Factoring on a with-recourse, service only basis, the factor administering and collecting payment from Marton's UK customers. This is expected to generate administrative savings of £200,000 per annum and to lower the average debtor collection period by 15 days. The factor will make a service charge of 1% of Marton's UK turnover and also provide credit insurance facilities for an annual premium of £80,000.

◈ FOULKS*lynch*

Option two

Offering discounts to UK customers who settle their accounts early. The amount of the discount will depend on speed of payment as follows:

Payment within 10 days of despatch of invoices: 3%
Payment within 20 days of despatch of invoices: 1.5%

It is estimated that UK customers representing 20% and 30% of Marton's sales respectively will take up these offers, the remainder continuing to take their present credit period.

Another opportunity arises to engage in a just-in-time stock delivery arrangement with the main UK customer, which normally takes 90 days to settle accounts with Marton. This involves borrowing £0·5m on overdraft to invest in dedicated handling and transport equipment. This would be depreciated over five years on a straight-line basis. The customer is uninterested in the early payment discount but would be prepared to settle after 60 days and to pay a premium of 5% over the present price in exchange for guarantees regarding product quality and delivery. Marton judges the probability of failing to meet these guarantees in any one year at 5%. Failure would trigger a penalty payment of 10% of the value of total sales to this customer (including the premium).

In addition, Marton is concerned about the risk of its overseas earnings. All overseas customers pay in US dollars and Marton does not hedge currency risk, invoicing at the prevailing spot rate, which is currently US$ 1·45:£1. It is considering the use of an overseas factor and also hedging its US dollar income on the forward market. Its bank has offered to buy all of its dollar earnings at a fixed rate of US$1.55:£1. Marton's advisers estimate the following chances of various dollar/sterling rates of exchange:

US Dollars per £	Probability
1.60	0.1
1.50	0.2
1.45	0.4
1.40	0.2
1.30	0.1

Extracts from Marton's most recent accounts are given below.

	(£'000)	(£'000)
Sales (all on credit)		
Home	20,000	
Export	5,000	
		25,000
Cost of sales		(17,000)
Operating profit		8,000
Current assets:		
Stock	2,500	
Debtors*	4,500	
Cash	–	

*There are no overseas debtors at the year-end.

Note: taxes and inflation can be ignored in this question.

Required:

(a)   Calculate the relative costs and benefits in terms of annual profit before tax of each of the two proposed methods of reducing domestic debtors, and recommend the most financially advantageous policy. Comment on your results.   **(14 marks)**

(b)   Calculate the improvement in profits before tax to be expected in the first trading year after entering into the JIT arrangement. Comment on your results.   **(8 marks)**

(c)   Suggest the benefits Marton might expect to derive from a JIT agreement in addition to the benefits specified in the question.   **(6 marks)**

(d)   Briefly outline the services provided by an overseas factor.   **(4 marks)**

(e)   (i)   Calculate the maximum loss which Marton can sustain through movements in the dollar/sterling exchange rate if it does not hedge overseas sales.   **(2 marks)**

(ii)   Calculate the maximum opportunity cost of selling dollar earnings forward at US$ 1.55:£1.   **(2 marks)**

(iii)   Briefly discuss whether Marton should hedge its foreign currency risk.   **(4 marks)**

(Total: 40 marks)
(ACCA Dec 97)

53   Stadium Eats

Stadium Eats is a themed football (soccer) restaurant, seating 150 people, which was set up four years ago by a partnership of two graduate caterers. The restaurant has proved very popular, and sales are now (20X8) averaging £8,500 per week for the 50 weeks of the year that the restaurant is open. The average spend per customer is £15 per head on Saturdays and Sundays, and £12 per head on weekdays. The gross profit margin is 20% and the operating profit margin is 11%.

Stadium Eats is now facing the problem of having to turn customers away on Saturdays and Sundays, as demand is starting to exceed the capacity. Customers are finding that they are needing to place bookings around eight weeks ahead in order to be certain of getting a table at the required time on these days.

In order to overcome the capacity problem, and expand the business further, Stadium Eats are planning to open a second restaurant. They have already identified a suitable site, and drawn up a simple forecast profit and loss account for the new outlet for the first year of trading and an end of year balance sheet. The forecasts are *loosely* based on the revenues and costs of the existing outlet, and are detailed below.

Profit and Loss Account forecast for the year ended 30 June 20X9

	£'000
Sales	600
Operating Profit	135
Interest Payable	18
Profit Before Tax	117
Taxation	35
Profit After Tax	82

Notes

(1)   In calculating operating profit, the two owners have not allowed for any salary costs for themselves, as they already draw a salary of £22,000 each from the existing business.

(2)   The new restaurant will be able to seat 180 people, and will be open 50 weeks of the year.

(3)   The tax rate is assumed to be 30%.

(4)   After tax profit is shared equally between the two partners, but will be wholly re-invested in the business. To date, the partners have made no drawings other than the salaries indicated above.

(5)   The current cash balance in the existing business amounts to £45,000, and it is expected that £25,000 of this will be required for refurbishment of the premises for the new restaurant.

(6)   The two partners will own equal shares in the new concern.

Forecast Balance Sheet as at 30 June 20X9

	£'000	£'000
Assets employed		
Fixed (net)		
Premises		280
Fixtures and fittings		75
		355
Current		
Food stocks	3	
Debtors	7	
Cash	18	
		28
Current liabilities		
Creditors	12	
Net current assets		16
Total assets less current liabilities		371
Long-term creditors		195
Net assets		176
Financed by:		
Ordinary shares (25p nominal)		94
Profit & loss account		82
		176

Notes

(1)   The long-term creditors would be made up of bank loans and a mortgage against the premises. The mortgage outstanding at 30 June 20X9 would be £184,000 and the balance of the long-term creditors represents a bank loan at 10% interest (fixed rate). The loan would be repaid in monthly instalments, and the balance cleared by June 2004.

(2)   Stadium Eats is currently run as a partnership, but it is intended that the new restaurant will be operated as a private limited company.

(3)   In order to raise the cash for their equity investment in the new venture, the two partners would need to raise loans totalling £75,000 against their own homes. They have been assured that the loans will be available but are a little concerned at the risk that they may be taking in borrowing so much to invest in a new business.

Required:

(a)   State and explain any reservations that you may have regarding the figures in the forecast profit and loss account, and draft a revised version, adjusted to take account of your criticisms.   **(10 marks)**

(b)   A bank may be concerned about the level of gearing in a business which has applied for additional loan finance. Explain the meaning of the term capital gearing, and why a lender/investor should be wary of further borrowing when gearing is already high.   **(10 marks)**

(c)   Calculate and comment on the level of gearing based on the 20X9 Forecast Balance Sheet. (Note that this excludes the proposed £75,000 personal loans for the new restaurant).   **(4 marks)**

◈ **FOULKS**lynch

(d)   Given that Stadium Eats are already operating successfully, what other sources of long-term finance might be available to the new business?   **(8 marks)**

(e)   An accountant has advised the partners that it might be best for them to combine the two restaurants under the umbrella of a single company, and seek a flotation on AIM in five year's time.

Explain the role of AIM within the financial markets, and identify the factors to be considered in seeking a stock market quotation.   **(8 marks)**
(Total: 40 marks)
(ACCA June 98)

54   Buntam plc

You are an accountant with a practice, which includes a large proportion of individual clients who often ask for information about traded investments. You have extracted the following data from a leading financial newspaper.

(i)

Stock	Price	P/E ratio	Dividend yield (% gross)
Buntam plc	160p	20	5
Zellus plc	270p	15	3.33

(ii)   Earnings and dividend data for Crazy Games plc are given below:

	20X3	20X4	20X5	20X6	20X7
EPS	5p	6p	7p	10p	12p
Div. per share (gross)	3p	3p	3.5p	5p	5.5p

The estimated before tax return on equity required by investors in Crazy Games plc is 20%.

(iii)   The gross yield to redemption on gilts are as follows:

Treasury 8.5% 20Y0	7.00%
Exchequer 10.5% 20Y5	6.70%
Treasury 8% 20Z5	6.53%

Required:

Draft a report for circulation to your private clients which explains:

(a)   the factors to be taken into account (including risks and returns) when considering the purchase of different types of traded investments   **(6 marks)**

(b)   the role of financial intermediaries, and their usefulness to the private investor   **(8 marks)**

(c)   the meaning and the relevance to the investor of each of the following:

(i)   Gross dividend (pence per share)
(ii)   EPS
(iii)   Dividend cover

Your answer should include calculation of, and comment upon, the gross dividends, EPS and dividend cover for Buntam plc and Zellus plc, based on the information given above.   **(12 marks)**

(d)   how to estimate the market value of a share

Illustrate your answer by reference to the data in (ii) on Crazy Games plc, using the information to calculate the market value of 1,000 shares in the company.   **(5 marks)**

(e)   the shape of the yield curve for gilts, based upon the information given in (iii) above, which you should use to construct the curve   **(4 marks)**

(f)   the meaning of the term 'gilts' and the relevance of yield curves to the private investor.   **(5 marks)**
(Total: 40 marks)
(ACCA Dec 98)

55   The Independent Film Co

The Independent Film Company plc is a film distribution company which purchases distribution rights on films from small independent producers, and sells the films on to cinema chains for national and international screening. In recent years the company has found it difficult to source sufficient films to maintain profitability. In response to the problem, the Independent Film Company has decided to invest in commissioning and producing films in its own right. In order to gain the expertise for this venture, the Independent Film Company is considering purchasing an existing filmmaking concern, at a cost of £400,000. The main difficulty that is anticipated for the business is the increasing uncertainty as to the potential success/failure rate of independently produced films. Many cinema chains are adopting a policy of only buying films from large international film companies, as they believe that the market for independent films is very limited and specialist in nature. The Independent Film Company is prepared for the fact that they are likely to have more films that fail than that succeed, but believe that the proposed film production business will nonetheless be profitable.

Using data collected from the existing distribution business and discussions with industry experts, they have produced cost and revenue forecasts for the five years of operation of the proposed investment. The company aims to complete the production of three films per year. The after tax cost of capital for the company is estimated to be 14%.

Year 1 sales for the new business are uncertain, but expected to be in the range of £4–10 million. Probability estimates for different forecast values are as follows:

Sales (£ million)	Probability
4	0.2
5	0.4
7	0.3
10	0.1

Sales are expected to grow at an annual rate of 5%.

Anticipated costs related to the new business are as follows:

Cost Type	£'000
Purchase of film-making company	400
Annual legal and professional costs	20
Annual lease rental (office equipment)	12
Studio and set hire (per film)	180
Camera/specialist equipment hire (per film)	40
Technical staff wages (per film)	520
Screenplay (per film)	50
Actors' salaries (per film)	700
Costumes and wardrobe hire (per film)	60
Set design and painting (per film)	150
Annual non-production staff wages	60

Additional information:

(1)   No capital allowances are available.

(2)   Tax is payable one year in arrears, at a rate of 33% and full use can be made of tax refunds as they fall due.

(3)   Staff wages (technical and non-production staff) and actors' salaries, are expected to rise by 10% per annum.

(4)   Studio hire costs will be subject to an increase of 30% in Year 3.

(5)   Screenplay costs per film are expected to rise by 15% per annum due to a shortage of skilled writers.

◈ FOULKS*lynch*

(6)   The new business will occupy office accommodation which has to date been let out for an annual rent of £20,000. Demand for such accommodation is buoyant and the company anticipates no problems in finding future tenants at the same annual rent.

(7)   A market research survey into the potential for the film production business cost £25,000.

Required:

(a)   Using DCF analysis, calculate the expected Net Present Value of the proposed investment. (Workings should be rounded to the nearest £'000.)   **(15 marks)**

(b)   Outline the main limitations of using expected values when making investment decisions.   **(6 marks)**

(c)   In addition to the possible purchase of the filmmaking business, the company has two other investment opportunities, the details of which are given below:

Post-Tax Cash Flows, £'000

	Year 0	Year 1	Year 2	Year 3	Year 4	Year 5	Year 6
Investment X	(200)	200	200	150	100	100	100
Investment Y	(100)	80	80	40	40	40	40

The Independent Film Company has a total of £400,000 available for capital investment in the current year. No project can be invested in more than once.

Required:

(i)   Define the term 'profitability index', and briefly explain how it may be used when a company faces a problem of capital rationing in any single accounting period.   **(4 marks)**

(ii)   Calculate the profitability index for each of the investment projects available to the Independent Film Company, i.e. purchase of the film production company, Investment X and Investment Y, and outline the optimal investment strategy. Assume that all of the projects are indivisible.   **(6 marks)**

(iii)   Explain the limitations of using a profitability index in a situation where there is capital rationing.
                                                                                                              (4 marks)
(d)   Briefly explain how the tax treatment of capital purchases can affect an investment decision.   **(5 marks)**
                                                                                                      (Total: 40 marks)
                                                                                                      (ACCA June 99)

56   Sprinter plc

Sprinter plc is a UK based company which produces 'designer' watches targeted at the youth market. UK sales in 20X7 equalled £6.5 million, which represented an average growth of 8% p.a. since 20X5. 20X8 sales are estimated to have grown by 12% per annum to date, and this growth rate is expected to continue until December 20X9. The company also exports its watches to Canada, the USA and Japan, invoicing foreign customers in their local currency. (Assume Sprinter's policy is to hold sterling prices constant.) The company has traditionally hedged its foreign currency exposure by the use of forward contracts, but is now considering abandoning their use, in the light of the exchange rate forecasts shown in Exhibit B.

The Managing Director is concerned at Sprinter's apparent increasing dependence on UK sales, but the Finance Director has assured him that it is probably a consequence of exchange rate movements and the relative strength of sterling. The Finance Director has also suggested that UK sales may in any case be preferable because they shorten the working capital cycle of the business.

Exhibit A shows the geographic breakdown of Sprinter's sales for the period 20X5–20X9. Exhibit B lists the average mid-point exchange rates for relevant currencies. Exhibit C contains information extracted from the annual report and accounts of Sprinter plc for the year ended 31 December 20X7.

Exhibit A: Geographic sales breakdown: based on sterling value

Country	20X5	20X6	20X7	20X8 (estimate)	20X9 (forecast)
UK	40%	50%	70%	65%	60%
USA	25%	25%	15%	15%	20%
Japan	25%	19%	10%	14%	12%
Canada	10%	6%	5%	6%	8%
TOTAL	100%	100%	100%	100%	100%

Exhibit B: Mid-point exchange rates

Rate	20X5	20X6	20X7	20X8 (estimate)	20X9 (forecast)
US $/£	1.55	1.58	1.64	1.62	1.59
Japanese Yen/£	185.65	190.50	209.75	196.83	188.30
Canadian $/£	2.20	2.29	2.34	2.29	2.20

Exhibit C: Information extracted from the accounts of Sprinter plc for the year ended 31 December 20X7

		Total	UK only
Stocks:	Raw materials	£1,404,000	£812,500
	WIP	£980,000	£568,750
	Finished goods	£1,120,000	£650,000
Purchases		£6,720,000	£3,900,000
Cost of goods sold		£8,130,000	£5,525,000
Sales		£9,290,000	£6,500,000
Debtors		£3,221,000	£1,300,000
Trade creditors		£773,300	£448,000

Assume 365 days per working year.
The average cost of capital for Sprinter is 12%.

Required:

(a)   Calculate the forecast sterling value of total sales for each of 20X8 and 20X9. Your answer should be in £ million, rounded to two decimal places.   **(4 marks)**

(b)   Calculate the sterling and yen value of sales to Japan for the period 20X5–20X9. Your answer should be rounded to two decimal places.   **(6 marks)**

(c)   Using the sales figures that you have computed in (b), comment on whether the Finance Director's view on exchange rates is an adequate explanation of trends in sales to Japan.   **(8 marks)**

(d)   Briefly explain how forward contracts may be used to hedge foreign exchange exposure.   **(2 marks)**

(e)   Calculate the length of the working capital cycle in respect of

(i)   UK sales, and
(ii)   total sales (worldwide).   **(8 marks)**

(f)   Why is the working capital cycle longer for total sales than for UK sales?   **(6 marks)**

(g)   Calculate and comment upon the profit impact of the longer working capital cycle associated with foreign sales.   **(6 marks)**
(Total: 40 marks)
(ACCA Dec 99)

◇ **FOULKS**lynch

Section 7

ANSWERS TO PRACTICE QUESTIONS

Financial management objectives and environment

1 Company objectives

Key answer tips

In part (a), note that you are asked to *justify* and *criticise* the assumption given – ensure that you answer clearly addresses both these requirements. First state why the maximisation of shareholder wealth is an important consideration in financial management decision making, then go on to discuss why it may not be the only objective set by businesses.

In part (b), try to structure your answer, using some sort of general categorisation of objectives, such as the four given in the following answer. Give specific examples for each category, and then move onto the discussion as to why they may be preferred.

(a)   Financial management is concerned with making decisions about the provisions and use of a firm's finances. A rational approach to decision-making necessitates a fairly clear idea of what the objectives of the decision maker are or, more importantly, of what are the objectives of those on behalf of whom the decisions are being made.

There is little agreement in the literature as to what objectives of firms are or even what they ought to be. However, most financial management textbooks make the assumption that the objective of a limited company is to maximise the wealth of its shareholders. This assumption is normally justified in terms of classical economic theory. In a market economy firms that achieve the highest returns for their investors will be the firms that are providing customers with what they require. In turn these companies, because they provide high returns to investors, will also find it easiest to raise new finance. Hence the so-called 'invisible hand' theory will ensure optimal resource allocation and this should automatically maximise the overall economic welfare of the nation.

This argument can be criticised on several grounds. Firstly it ignores market imperfections. For example it might not be in the public interest to allow monopolies to maximise profits. Secondly it ignores social needs like health, police, defence etc.

From a more practical point of view directors have a legal duty to run the company on behalf of their shareholders. This however begs the question as to what do shareholders actually require from firms.

Another justification from the individual firm's point of view is to argue that it is in competition with other firms for further capital and it therefore needs to provide returns at least as good as the competition. If it does not it will lose the support of existing shareholders and will find it difficult to raise funds in the future, as well as being vulnerable to potential take-over bids.

Against the traditional and 'legal' view that the firm is run in order to maximise the wealth of ordinary shareholders, there is an alternative view that the firm is a coalition of different groups: equity shareholders, preference shareholders and lenders, employees, customers and suppliers. Each of these groups must be paid a minimum 'return' to encourage them to participate in the firm. Any excess wealth created by the firm should be and is the subject of bargaining between these groups.

At first sight this seems an easy way out of the 'objectives' problem. The directors of a company could say 'Let's just make the profits first, then we'll argue about who gets them at a later stage'. In other words, maximising profits leads to the largest pool of benefits to be distributed among the participants in the bargaining process. However, it does imply that all such participants must value profits in the same way and that they are all willing to take the same risks.

In fact the real risk position and the attitude to risk of ordinary shareholders, loan creditors and employees are likely to be very different. For instance, a shareholder who has a diversified portfolio is likely not to be so worried by the bankruptcy of one of his companies as will an employee of that company, or a supplier whose main customer is that company. The problem of risk is one major reason why there cannot be a single simple objective which is common to all companies.

(b)   Separate from the problem of which goal a company ought to pursue are the questions of which goals companies claim to pursue and which goals they actually pursue. Many objectives are quoted by large companies and sometimes are included in their annual accounts. Examples are:

- to produce an adequate return for shareholders
- to grow and survive autonomously
- to improve productivity
- to give the highest quality service to customers
- to maintain a contented workforce
- to be technical leaders in their field
- to be market leaders
- to acknowledge their social responsibilities.

Some of these stated objectives are probably a form of public relations exercise. At any rate, it is possible to classify most of them into four categories which are related to profitability:

(i)   pure profitability goals e.g. adequate return for shareholders
(ii)   'surrogate' goals of profitability e.g. improving productivity, happy workforce
(iii)   constraints on profitability e.g. acknowledging social responsibilities, no pollution, etc
(iv)   'dysfunctional' goals.

The last category is goals which should not be followed because they do not benefit in the long run. Examples here include the pursuit of market leadership at any cost, even profitability. This may arise because management assumes that high sales equal high profits which is not necessarily so.

In practice the goals which a company actually pursues are affected to a large extent by the management. As a last resort, the directors may always be removed by the shareholders or the shareholders could vote for a take-over bid, but in large companies individual shareholders lack voting power and information. These companies can, therefore, be dominated by the management.

There are two levels of argument here. Firstly, if the management do attempt to maximise profits, then they are in a much more powerful position to decide how the profits are 'carved up' than are the shareholders.

Secondly, the management may actually be seeking 'prestige' goals rather than profit maximisation. Such goals might include growth for its own sake, including empire building or maximising turnover for its own sake, or becoming leaders in the technical field for no reason other than general prestige. Such goals are usually 'dysfunctional'.

The dominance of management depends on individual shareholders having no real voting power, and in this respect institutions have usually preferred to sell their shares rather than interfere with the management of companies. There is some evidence, however, that they are now taking a more active role in major company decisions.

From all that has been said above, it appears that each company should have its own unique decision model. For example, it is possible to construct models where the objective is to maximise profit subject to first fulfilling the target levels of other goals. However, it is not possible to develop the general theory of financial management very far without making an initial simplifying assumption about objectives. The objective of maximising the wealth of equity shareholders seems the least objectionable.

2   Cleevemoor Water Authority

Key answer tips

In part (a), as you are asked to discuss how objectives may change following privatisation, it makes sense to start your answer with a discussion of what they would have been whilst the organisation was still in the public sector. This then gives a framework for the alternations that follow. Note that these objectives won't necessarily all change radically on privatisation, they may just change in priority.

In part (b) use the marks allocated to each part to decide on the depth needed to your answer. For each, decide what factors they would be principally concerned with. You then need to review the data given to ascertain the extent to which these can be measured and assessed. For example, the investment objectives of shareholders should be familiar to you - a balance between income and growth. Whilst income is quite easily evaluated by looking at the dividend stream, capital growth requires some computations involving P/E ratios and EPS. You should have a good working knowledge of these fundamental equity measures.

Parts (ii) and (iii) need less technical knowledge and more practical application, but again use the data wherever you can to illustrate points made.

Part (iv) requires a reasonable grasp of economic principles, particularly relating to economic growth - the ways in which the economy as a whole can benefit from the investment, efficiency and tax payments of the company.

(a)   The main function of public enterprise is to serve the public interest – in the case of a water undertaking, it would be responsible for ensuring a safe and reliable supply of water to households at an affordable price which would also require close attention to control of operating and distribution costs. Prior to privatisation, UK public enterprises were also expected to achieve a target rate of return on capital which struck a balance between the going rate in the private sector and the long-term perspective involved in such operations. The authority would also have faced political constraints on achieving its objectives in the form of pressure to keep water charges down and also periodic restrictions on capital expenditure.

One problem faced by such enterprises was their inability to generate the funds necessary to finance the levels of investment required to maintain water supplies of acceptable quality.

Once privatised, NW would be required to generate returns for shareholders at least as great as comparable enterprises of equivalent risk. Moreover, it would be expected to generate a stream of steadily rising dividends to satisfy its institutional investors with their relatively predictable stream of liabilities.

Any capital committed to fixed investment would have to achieve efficiency in the use of resources and to achieve the level of returns required by the stock market. In the UK, it is alleged that there is an over-concern with short-term results, both to satisfy existing investors and to preserve the stock market rating of the company. Although this may safeguard future supplies of capital, it has militated against infrastructure projects and activities such as R & D, which generate their greatest returns in the more distant future.

(b)   (i)   **Shareholders**

In financial theory, companies are supposed to maximise the wealth of shareholders, as measured by the stock market value of the equity. In the absence of perfect information, it is not possible to measure the relationship between achieved shareholder wealth and the outright maximum. However, good indicators of the benefits received by shareholders are the returns they obtain in the form of dividend payments and share price appreciation.

Dividends

The pro forma dividend was 7p and by 20X4 the dividend per share had grown by 186% to 20p, an average annual growth of around 19%. The pro forma payout ratio was 33%, falling to 31% by 20X4. The pro forma EPS was 21p rising by 210% to 65p, an average annual increase of nearly 21%. This suggests that the company wishes to align dividend increases to increases in EPS over time.

Share price

The flotation price was £1, rising to £1.60 on the first day of dealing. By 20X0, the EPS had become 29p. Given a P/E ratio of 7, this implies a market price of 203p per share. By 20X4, the EPS had risen to 65p, and with a P/E ratio of 7.5, this corresponds to a market price of 488p. Compared to the close of first-day's dealings, the growth rate was 205% (a little over 20% as an annual average) and over the period 20X0 – 20X4, the growth was 140% (an annual average of about 25%).

Although information about returns in the market in general and those enjoyed by shareholders of comparable companies are not available to act as a yardstick, these figures suggest considerable increases in shareholders' wealth, and at a rate substantially above the increase in the Retail Price Index (RPI).

(ii)   **Consumers**

Although NW's ability to raise prices is ostensibly restrained by the industry regulator, turnover has risen by 38% over the period, an annual average of 5.5%. This is above the rate of inflation over this period (about 2% pa) and also above the trend rate of increase in demand (also 2% pa). This suggests relatively weak regulation, perhaps reflecting the industry's alleged need to earn profits in order to invest, or perhaps that NW has diversified into other, unregulated activities which can sustain higher rates of product price inflation.

However, before accusing NW of exploiting the consumer, one would have to examine whether it did lay down new investment, and also how productive it had been, especially using indicators like purity and reliability of water supply.

(iii)   **Workforce**

Numbers employed have fallen from 12,000 to 10,000 i.e. 17%. The average remuneration has risen from £8,333 to £8,600, a mere 1% in nominal terms but about minus 8% in real terms, after allowing for the 9% inflation in retail prices over this period.

Average remuneration 20W8	=	£100m/12,000
	=	£8,333
Average remuneration 20X4	=	£86m/10,000
	=	£8,600

This represents an increase of about 3.2% over 6 years. The equivalent annual rate is about 0.53% (1% rounded up).

This suggests a worsening of returns to the labour force, although a shift in the skill mix away from skilled workers and/or a change in conditions of employment away from full-time towards part-time and contract working might explain the figures recorded. Certainly, the efficiency of the labour force as measured by sales per employee (up from £37,500 to £62,000 – an increase of 65%) has outstripped movements in pay. However, apparently greater labour efficiency could be due to product price inflation and/or the impact of new investment.

The directors, however, seem to have benefited greatly. It is not stated whether the number of directors has increased, but as a group, their emoluments have trebled. Arguably, this might have been necessary to bring hitherto depressed levels of public sector rewards into line with remuneration elsewhere in the private sector in order to retain competent executives. Conversely, the actual remuneration may be understated as it does not appear to include non-salary items such as share options, which would presumably be very valuable given the share price appreciation that has occurred over this period.

(iv)   **Macro-economic objectives**

There are numerous indicators whereby NW's contribution to the achievement of macro-economic policies can be assessed. Among these are the following.

(1)   *Price stability*

–   *Via its pricing policy.* As noted NW's revenues have risen by 38% in nominal terms and 29% in real terms. This questions the company's degree of responsibility in cooperating with the government's anti-inflationary policy.

–   *Via its pay policy.* There is evidence that NW has held down rates of pay, but if this has not been reflected in a restrained pricing policy, then the benefits accrue to shareholders rather than to society at large. Moreover, the rapid increase in directors' emoluments is hardly anti-inflationary, providing signals to the labour force which are likely to sour industrial relations.

(2)   *Economic growth*

–   *Via its capital expenditure.* Higher profitability has been implicitly condoned by the regulator in order to allow NW to generate funds for new investment. This appears to have been achieved. Capital expenditure has nearly quadrupled. As well as benefiting the industry itself, this will have provided multiplier effects on the rest of the economy to the extent that equipment has been domestically-sourced.

–   *Via efficiency improvements.* It is not possible to calculate non-financial indicators of efficiency, but there are clear signs of enhanced financial performance. The sharp increase in sales per employee has been noted. In addition, the return on capital as measured by operating profit to total assets has moved steadily upward as follows:

20W8	*20X0*	*20X2*	*20X4*
26%	29%	36%	39%

3   Non-profit

Key answer tips

Focus your answer around the roles of planning, control and decision-making – but don't forget to distinguish your answer in (b) from that of (a). Note that (b) also asks for the features of a non-profit organisation. For part (c) you would find that the three Es are a good starting point for setting out the aims.

(a)   A major objective of a profit-seeking organisation is profit maximisation, this tends to influence the provision of management accounting information. The role of the management accountant (MA) involves the provision of information which directly or indirectly supports the achievement of this objective. Management accounting is a decision-making, planning and control facilitating activity. The management accounting system must provide information to enable managers to allocate scarce resources in the most efficient manner. Some writers subdivide the role of the MA into at least three distinct areas, stock valuation and product costing, decision-making, planning and control.

Stock valuation and product costing involves the generation of a manufacturing cost of a product for the purposes of the preparation of periodic profit and loss accounts. This may be extended to the preparation of a full product cost as an input to the pricing deliberations of a management team. In a profit seeking service organisation there is no requirement to value stock but the average cost of a service may still be generated.

Accounting for decision-making involves the identification of costs and revenues associated with alternative courses of action so that their relative profitability may be ascertained. This may focus, for example, on the relevant costs and benefits concerned with a particular decision, the profit implications of a change in volume, or a trade-off between volumes and price.

Accounting for planning and control is concerned with the creation and use of systems in the organisation to establish responsibilities for particular outcomes and commit the resources to be devoted to achieve the outcomes especially profit. These are often contained within the organisation's budget, consisting of statements of organisational intent of both a financial and a non-financial nature.

An alternative perspective on the role of the MA that is often quoted is that of 'score-keeping, problem solving and attention directing'. These are not dissimilar to the areas mentioned above in that costing and the ascertainment of profit of a company, or department of it, is like keeping a score. Problems solving is the arrangement of information to enable managers to choose between alternative courses of action – i.e. decision-making. Attention directing involves ensuring that activities are in line with management's intentions, or particularly, where this is not the case, to be alerted to cases which are at variance to plan – planning and control.

Whilst either of the above groups of activities describe the traditional role of the MA or management accounting department, this is not exhaustive. For example, with increasing competitive situations for many companies the MA should be concerned with looking outward rather than inward, that is, looking at competitors costs and the competitive position of his/her company. Likewise, rather than concern with merely short-term decision-making planning and control, a longer-term perspective may be appropriate involving, for example, lifecycle costing. These and other aspects can be grouped under a heading of strategic management accounting which, whilst not diminishing the importance of the traditional role is becoming an increasingly important part of the role of a management accountant.

(b)   There are some general similarities between profit-seeking organisations (PSOs) and non-profit organisations (NPOs) but some important differences which will be outlined below.

By definition there are no profit objectives for NPOs; they do not exist to maximise, or optimise, profits over any period, unlike PSOs for whom periodic profit is an important statistic. The absence of a profit motive may imply the absence of a profit measure. A PSO can compare expenses and revenues to produce profit, a 'guide' to the success of the organisation. This same implication cannot be drawn from a comparison made for an NPO. It may only mean, in the latter case, that the NPO has spent an amount related to that which was allocated or funded. That is, some goods, or more likely services, have been provided for a predetermined cost. It says nothing about the adequacy of that provision or the efficiency with which it was provided. This will be expanded upon below.

That NPOs usually provide services rather than products adds further complexities. It is more difficult to measure in convenient quantitative and aggregate terms the amount of service provided and therefore make judgements about the adequacy of any costs involved. This is a complication when planning how much should be spent and in control when the adequacy of achievement, for a particular outlay, is assessed. It is exacerbated further by the difficulty of measuring the quality of the service provided.

In the non-profit environment there is a reduced role for market forces. A PSO is influenced and can take signals from the choice exercised by consumers. For NPOs no direct alternative may exist, or if it does comparison is confused by measurement and judgement issues caused by the not-for-profit and service dimensions mentioned above.

(c)   The MA must endeavour to provide information which demonstrates the provision of value for money by the NPO. Value for money is a focus on, and regularly monitoring through performance indicators of, economy, efficiency and effectiveness. In a little more detail this implies:

- Economy in the acquisition of resources of the right quality and the right type for the right price.

- Efficiency in the use of resources i.e. the appropriate quantity of inputs are used to attain a given level of output.

- Effectiveness, the outputs achieved should be those that enable the organisation to achieve its pre-stated general objectives in all areas of delivering the service.

In the context of the earlier discussion the MA is required to provide information to assist in decision-making, planning and control. Decision-making involves selecting between competing alternatives. In this a statement of the costs of each alternative needs to be set out and these inputs must be compared with the benefits achieved or outputs. The latter are the more problematic and often involve a description and some approximate financial or non-financial measure of achievement. The outcomes for various competing alternatives can then be compared. This process, called cost-benefit analysis, is not easy because the features involved may not be easily aggregated or compared directly. It is also influenced by a high degree of subjective judgement and opinion, for example consider having to make a choice between spending for educational or medical purposes or judging the quality of service in different settings.

Planning and control involves the production of periodic budgets and the use of feedback to monitor actual attainment. In NPOs, budgets often identify a 'spending limit'. They are the decisions taken (as above) but codified in terms of organisation structure, responsibilities and timescale. The technique of zero based budgeting or a variation, priority based budgeting may be employed in order to help with the preparation of budgets and to systematise the choice between alternative spending categories or spending levels. Along with the authority to spend contained in the budget should be a statement of the expected outcomes to be achieved by the spending. This should be supplemented by regular reports of actual achievements against those required often using non-financial performance measures.

The MA should support management with a diverse range of statistics beyond the immediate objectives and achievements of the organisation. This will include information on other organisations and regions or other ways of achieving objectives. A maximum ingenuity is required to produce information in NPOs in order to overcome some of the difficulties and complexities involved. Some not-for-profit organisations are undertaking various forms of 'privatisation', creating 'artificial' markets or requiring compulsory competitive tendering in some areas of operation. These are further ways to attempt to obtain value for money in the non-profit environment. It is likely to increase the competitive element but it is unlikely to simplify the role of the MA in non-profit organisations.

4   Objectives

Key answer tips

Start part (a) with a general explanation of the different perspectives of managers and owners, which can lead to conflicts of interest. Then try to think of as many different examples of conflicts, each covering a different aspect – risk attitude, personal wealth, status etc.

In part (b), it helps to start with an explanation of the term corporate social responsibility (if only to focus your mind on what it is you're supposed to be talking about). Think of the parties involved, and to what extent a company has to have regard for their well-being. The framework for your discussion in (c) should be the three Es, but remember to direct your explanations towards the management of publicly owned services/utilities.

(a)   It may be argued that managers and owners of a business may not have the same interests because of the divorce between ownership and control. In many organisations, the shareholders will have very little influence over the day to day operations and management of a business. Managers will be aware of the need to seek to maximise the wealth of their shareholders, but at the same time they may be equally concerned to serve their own needs/interests.

For example, shareholders may be highly risk averse, looking only for one reasonable and steady income from their investment. By contrast, a manager may by nature be more of a risk taker, because he considers that his career may progress faster if he is successful in the risks taken. In such a scenario, if the manager follows his instincts in selecting business opportunities, then the shareholders' objectives are not being met. The reverse situation may be equally true, whereby shareholders believe that management are excessively cautious in their selection of business opportunities, but management are wary of taking risks as they wish to avoid any large-scale losses which might threaten their personal position. In both instances there is a gulf between the objectives of the managers and owners.

Another example of where objectives might conflict is in the case of mergers and take-overs. If a company has been reporting poor results, and becomes the victim of a take-over bid, the shareholders are likely to be pleased as they will see an increase in the value of their investment. In contrast, the managers of the victim company may well be very unhappy, as they sense the risk of redundancy.

Williamson suggested that many of the aims of managers actually work in direct conflict with those of owners, because managers look for perquisites and self-aggrandisement, which add to company costs. Shareholders may be happy if managers owned Ford Mondeos for the company cars. The managers may well seek to have Mercedes instead! Similarly, having a large office and many staff to supervise is good for a manager's self esteem, but they may not be essential to the efficient running of the business: owners may be better off without them.

One key area where owner-manager objectives may conflict is in terms of the time horizon used to judge success. Owners are often looking long-term in setting their objectives, whereas a manager may need to have short-term successes in order to further his/her career prospects.

(b)   Corporate social responsibility can be defined in a number of ways, but the term refers, in general, to the ways in which a privately owned company needs to be aware of and respect the needs of the wider community. The responsibility to shareholders is reasonably clearly defined and monitored by the financial markets and company reporting systems. Corporate responsibilities to customers, employees, and the community at large are less likely defined.

A company may be regarded as having responsibilities to its customers in terms of providing them with a quality product, at an appropriate price, which is supplied in a timely and efficient manner. The duty to the general public involves a responsibility not to endanger the public in any way, to respect the environment, and to support the local community where possible. Social responsibility also extends to creditors, who should expect to be paid accurately and promptly. In the UK there have been calls for legislation to restrict the period of credit which can be claimed from small companies.

National and local government are also affected by the activities of businesses and hence come under the remit of areas of social responsibility. Companies have a duty to pay their taxes as due, and comply with national and local laws e.g. planning/health and safety regulations. Lastly companies have a responsibility to take care of their employees, ensuring a safe working environment, and paying fair wages.

In conclusion it is no longer sufficient for a company to think that it need only serve the interests of its shareholders. It is now regarded as good practice to look to the needs of the broader stakeholder group, and so take on a wider social responsibility.

(c)   At its simplest, 'Value for Money' (VFM) means getting the best possible service at the least possible cost. Public services are funded by the taxpayers and in seeking value for money, the needs of the taxpayer are being served, insofar as resources are being used in the best manner to provide essential services.

It is important to note that VFM does not mean lowest cost per se: it assesses cost in relation to the service provided. Three aspects of VFM are of relevance: efficiency, economy and effectiveness. Efficiency relates to the level of output generated by a given input. Reducing the input : output ratio is an indication of increased efficiency. Economy measures the cost of obtaining the required quality of inputs needed to produce the service. The aim is to acquire the necessary inputs at the lowest possible cost. Effectiveness measures the extent to which the service meets its declared objectives. For example, a refuse collection service is only effective if it meets its target of, say, weekly collections from domestic premises. The service is economic if it is able to minimise the cost per weekly collection, and not suffer from wasted use of resources. The service is increasing its efficiency if it is able to raise the number of collections per vehicle per week.

Management of working capital

5   Hexicon plc

Key answer tips

Part (a) is standard textbook material. For five marks, you should give at least five reasons, and don't forget a brief explanation: "it uses cash flows" will not get the full marks available. As the question mentions other approaches, you should structure your answer around direct comparisons with alternative methods of investment appraisal.

In part (b) you are applying the familiar EOQ model in the context of a change to a just-in-time system. To answer both parts, you need to assess the "before" and "after" positions, evaluating the changes between the two. Note that the question includes information on tax and discount rates, so you are clearly intended to take account of both of these in your evaluation (particularly in the light of part (a)). You should be prepared for the examiner to include various syllabus areas and techniques within one question. Part (c) first requires an explanation of JIT agreements ("the nature of") and then a discussion as to the reasons for such agreements ("the objectives of").

(a)   The following reasons may be cited for using the net present value (NPV) method of investment appraisal:

   (i)   Compared to accounting rate of return (ARR), it discounts real cash flows as opposed to accounting profits which are affected by non-cash items.

   (ii)   Compared to measuring internal rate of return (IRR), the NPV method only gives one solution. In some circumstances, (when there are a number of outflows occurring at different times), multiple IRR solutions are possible.

   (iii)   Compared to the payback method, NPV considers all of the cash flows of a project.

   (iv)   By using a discount rate it measures the opportunity cost of the money invested by a person in a project.

   (v)   The interest rate used can be increased/decreased depending upon the level of perceived risk in the investment.

   (vi)   The NPV of a project can be shown to be equal to the increase in the value of shareholder's equity in the company. Thus the method is consistent with the objective of shareholder wealth maximisation.

(b)   (i)   The present EOQ is $\sqrt{\dfrac{2 \times £100 \times 40,000}{20\% \times £2.50}} = 4,000$ units/order

           The revised EOQ $= \sqrt{\dfrac{2 \times £25 \times 40,000}{20\% \times £2.50}} = 2,000$ units/order

           From this it can be seen that the EOQ is halved.

   (ii)   The number of orders has increased from (40,000/4,000) 10 orders to (40,000/2,000) 20 orders; however, ordering costs are reduced by:

           $(10 \times £100) - (20 \times £25) = £500$ per annum

           Average stocks have also reduced from $\dfrac{4,000}{2}$ (2,000 units) to $\dfrac{2,000}{2}$ (1,000 units). Consequently carrying costs have reduced by $20\% \times £2.50 \times 1,000 = £500$ per annum.

           Total inventory costs are thereby reduced by £1,000 per annum.

           Assuming that Hexicon plc pays tax in the same year as it earns profits the present value of the proposal is found by comparing the outflow cost with the discounted after tax savings over the eight-year life of the proposal (using a 12% discount rate).

Discounted savings: £

£1,000 × 67% (1 – tax rate) × 12% annuity factor - 8 years   = £670 × 4.968   =   3,329

Cost of reorganisation (tax deductible)   = £4,000 × 67% (1 – tax rate) = (2,680)

Net benefit   649

As the present value of the proposal is positive it is worthwhile.

(c)   The main objective of Just In Time (JIT) purchasing is to match the delivery of components from suppliers to their usage in production. If this is achieved there are significant benefits to be gained by both the supplier and the customer.

The customer is likely to use only one supplier for each component and to build up a relationship with the supplier which encourages communication thus enabling the supplier to benefit from advanced production planning and economies of scale. To enhance this relationship the customer makes a long-term commitment to future orders.

The supplier guarantees to deliver goods of an appropriate quality in accordance with an agreed delivery schedule. The benefit to the customer is thereby a reduction (or elimination) of stockholding and significant cost savings. These arise in both holding costs and also in materials handling, because goods are transferred directly from goods inwards to production.

6   Ripley plc

Key answer tips

For part (a) you have 6 marks to discuss three separate requirements - two explanations and a discussion of further factors. None can be covered in great depth (and you really need to look at the changes as a whole rather than individually) but you do need to bring out the contrast between the safer but possibly expensive 'matching' policy with the higher risk, more actively managed 'aggressive' policy.

You need to think carefully in part (b) about your approach before launching into computations here. It is a situation that is in many ways analogous to the optimum stock policy problem, and the formula given is the equivalent of the EOQ formula. The approach is to compare the two options on an annual cost basis.

The first option is to use the company's existing stocks of securities to meet the payments, by realising regular "optimal" amounts. This method incurs transaction costs, partly offset by short-term interest earned on the cash whilst it held, and loses interest from the securities realised.

The second option leaves the existing securities intact and meets the payments from a loan. The associated costs are the arrangement fee and the loan interest (again, partially offset by short-term interest earned on cash whilst it is held) - but no interest is lost from the securities.

Having worked through the numbers, don't forget that the aim is to advise - and you should consider other factors in addition to the cost comparison.

In part (c) you should recognise the model as the equivalent of the EOQ formula used in stock management. The limitations are thus the same, with appropriate translations of terms and costs.

(a)   **Memo to:**   Ripley plc Main Board
         From: An Accountant
         Subject: Alternative Financial Strategies

The present policy is termed a 'matching' financial policy. This attempts to match the maturity of financial liabilities to the lifetime of the assets acquired with this finance. It involves financing long-term assets with long-term finance such as equity or loan stock and financing short-term assets with short-term finance such as trade credit or bank overdrafts. This avoids the potential wastefulness of over-capitalisation whereby short-term assets are purchased with long-term finance i.e. the company having to service finance not continuously invested in income-earning assets. It also avoids the dangers of under-capitalisation which entails exposure to finance being withdrawn when the company is not easily able to liquidate its assets. In practice, some short-term assets may be regarded as permanent and it may be thought sensible to finance these by long-term finance and the fluctuating remainder by short-term finance.

The proposed policy is an 'aggressive policy' which involves far heavier reliance on short-term finance, thus attempting to minimise long-term financing costs. This requires very careful manipulation of the relationship between creditors and debtors (maximising trade creditors and minimising debtors), and highly efficient stock control and cash management. While it may offer financial savings, it exposes the company to the risk of illiquidity and hence possible failure to meet financial obligations. In addition, it involves greater exposure to interest rate risk. The company should be mindful of the inverse relationship between interest rate changes and the value of its assets and liabilities.

Before embarking on such an aggressive policy, the Board should consider the following factors:

- How good are we at forecasting cash inflows and outflows? How volatile is our net cash flow? Is there any seasonal pattern evident?

- How efficiently do we manage our cash balances? Do we ever have excessive cash holdings which can be reduced by careful and active management?

- Do we have suitable information systems to provide early warnings of illiquidity?

- Do we have any holdings of marketable securities that can be realised if we run into unexpected liquidity problems?

- How liquid are our fixed assets? Can any of these be converted into cash without unduly disrupting productive operations?

- Do we have any unused long- or short-term credit lines? These may have to be utilised if we meet liquidity problems.

- How will the stock market perceive our switch towards a more aggressive and less liquid financial policy?

(b)   To determine the net benefits of each policy, both cash costs and opportunity costs have to be considered.

First, consider the cash management costs expected from each policy over the course of the forthcoming year.

Policy 1 Selling securities

The cash transaction costs are partly offset by small interest earnings on the average cash balance held.
Transactions costs:

£

Optimal proceeds per sale: $Q = \sqrt{\dfrac{2 \times £1.5m \times £25}{0.12}} = £25,000$

No of sales	= £1.5m/£25,000	= 60	
Transaction costs	= 60 × £25	=	1,500
Average cash balances:	= £25,000/2	= £12,500	

Interest on short-term deposits:
Average cash balance × 5%	= £12,500 × 5%	=	(625)

Total management costs   875

Policy 2 Secured loan facility

Assuming an even run-down in cash balances:

Interest charges	= £1.5m × 14%	=	210,000

Offsetting interest receipts:

$(= \text{average balance} \times 9\%) \qquad = \dfrac{£1.5m}{2} \times 9\% \qquad\qquad = \qquad (67,500)$

Arrangement fee:		=	5,000

Total management costs   147,500

Hence, the policy of periodic security sales appears greatly superior in cost terms by [£147,500 - £875] = £146,625. However, this simple comparison ignores the income likely to be received from the portfolio of securities under each policy. By taking the secured loan, the company preserves intact its expected returns of [12% × £1.5m = £180,000] from the portfolio. Conversely, making periodic sales from the portfolio during the year lowers the returns to: [average holding of securities × 12%] = £1.5m/2 × 12% = £90,000.

The net benefits from the two policies can be shown thus:

			£
Security sales			
Income from portfolio	£90,000		
Net management costs	(£875)	Net income	89,125
Loan alternative			
Income from portfolio	£180,000		
Net management costs	(£147,500)	Net income	32,500
		Difference	56,625

The policy of periodic security sales thus offers greater benefits. However, it is necessary to consider also the company's net worth position at the end of the year ahead. By relying on security sales, the company would avoid the need to repay a loan at the end of the year, but, against this, will have no holdings of securities to fall back on. Moreover, the capital value of this portfolio is uncertain, due to exposure to variation in the return from the portfolio. For example, if money market rates rose over the year, the capital value of the portfolio would probably fall, although the extent of the decrease in value would depend on the nearness to maturity of the securities.

(c)   Some limitations of the simple cash inventory model are:

- It assumes a steady run-down in cash holdings between successive security sales. In reality, the pattern of cash holdings is likely to be far more erratic, with exceptional demands for cash punctuated by periods of excessive liquidity. However, the period between sales is short enough and the transaction cost low enough to allow flexibility in cash management.

- It allows for no buffer stock of cash. In reality, security sales are unlikely to be made when cash balances drop to zero, but when they fall to a level deemed to be the safe minimum.

- It uses a 'highly uncertain' estimate of the return from the portfolio. Bramham should investigate the implications of assuming alternative (higher and lower) rates, and perhaps determine a 'break-even rate' at which the two policies are equally attractive. In this example, the actual rate would have to be well above 12% to achieve this result.

- There may be economies in bulk-selling of securities, although exploiting these would increase the holding cost.

7   PCB plc

Key answer tips

In parts (a) and (b) the distinct questions to be answered here are 'if our sales are increasing so quickly, why are we (a) running out of cash all the time and (b) making less profits?' Whilst the wording of the requirement in (a) allows for a certain amount of general discussion of factors leading to over-trading, both parts must primarily focus on the information provided by the data given relating to PCB plc. Don't be afraid to state the obvious – e.g. the absolute/relative changes in key figures from one year to the next.

Part (c) is a two-part question - analysis and comment. First identify the changes in funding, then address the implications for both shareholders and creditors. If you are going to use ratios, e.g. gearing, make sure you say something sensible about what they show, or you will gain no marks.

In part (d), having identified the problems of PCB, you are now being asked to advise on ways to overcome them. The main aspect to be considered is the raising of further long term finance, which will help both the funding problems and the shortage of working capital. If you discuss the possibility of introducing tighter working capital control policies, you should try to quantify the effects of this. This ensures you are talking about significant amounts and it is therefore a worthwhile point to make.

(a) Manufacturing companies usually sell their products on credit. This means that increasing sales leads to a need for greater working capital in order to finance the higher levels of debtors, stock, and staff employed in sales.

PCB have seen their sales increase by 76% over 12 months, and the effect of this has been a need to increase their fixed asset base, as well as invest in more current assets. Between 20X7 and 20X8, the company has increased its fixed asset investments by £44,000 and its current assets by £225,250. The asset increase may well be more than is required to service the higher sales levels. These investments appear to have been paid for by a massive increase in both trade creditors and short-term bank borrowing. Bank borrowing has increased almost four-fold, whilst trade creditors have increased by almost 150%. This means that the company has run out of cash to pay for creditors, and is seeking to resolve the crisis by higher short-term borrowings.

The cash crisis faced by PCB is not unusual, as banks may often increase overdraft limits when companies have a full order book. It is also true that as the earnings from the increased sales feed through into the profit and loss account, the cash crisis should be eased.

(b) Extra sales do not always yield significantly higher profits and extra cash-flow in the short-term, because of the extra investment needed to facilitate the sales increase. The figures show that PCB has been forced to meet higher costs and perhaps sell at reduced prices in order to realise the extra sales, and profits (gross and net) have been hit. The gross profit margin has reduced from 19.4% to 15%. At the same time, the depreciation charge will rise because of new equipment having been purchased, and the wages bill will also be higher because of the new staff. The company will have to meet increased interest payments on its very large overdraft/short-term borrowings. As a result, and as the figures show, the company's net profits have actually fallen between 20X7 and 20X8, despite the higher sales. The net margin has fallen from 4.8% to just 2%; it could be difficult for the company to survive in the longer term when it earns such slim margins.

(c) As already indicated in (a) the company has become increasingly dependent on short-term borrowing from trade creditors and the bank in order to continue trading. Trade credit is a useful source of funding as it frequently does not incur an interest charge. The company may, however, risk forfeiting the goodwill of its suppliers if it takes excessively long periods of time to pay its debts. The ratio of bank loans: equity capital equals 1:8.4 approximately in 20X7. By 20X8 this ratio had fallen to 1:2.4. The company's balance of funding is moving away from the use of equity as the prime source, to increased dependence on short-term debt.

It is not wise for a company to fund large-scale long-term increases in its trading volume out of short-term funding. The company needs to match long-term investments with long-term finance. Furthermore, as net profit falls, the equity investor will see a drop in the return to equity, accompanied by an increase in equity risk. The higher risk comes from the fall in profit after interest, and the possibility that the lines of short-term credit may dry up for PCB, and they may be forced to cease trading.

Creditor risk is clearly increased, as the company is now committed to a level of short-term borrowing (£363,000) which exceeds its fixed asset base (£308,000). Creditors have no means of obtaining security against any loans (except against debtors). It seems very unlikely that any further credit would be made available to PCB.

(d) PCB needs to re-organise the funding of its business in a way which reduces its exposure to short-term debt. This could be done either by converting the short-term bank loan into a long-term debenture/loan or by increasing the equity investment in the business.

Conversion of the loan would not alter the overall level of financial gearing within the business, and so there would remain some high risks for both equity investors and creditors. Increasing the equity investment is the better alternative. The issued share capital is low, given the current level of sales. If current shareholders were to invest another £50,000, and the bulk of the short-term bank borrowings were re-arranged as a long-term loan, the balance sheet would look much healthier.

At the same time, PCB could look carefully at its current levels of working capital, and aim to reduce the level of stock and debtors as a means of releasing capital. In 20X7 debtor and stock levels stood at 6.4% and 5.6% of sales value respectively. If the 20X7 levels were maintained, the company's investment in these two current assets in 20X8 could be reduced from £430,000 to £360,000, a saving of £70,000. The cash freed up by tighter working capital controls may then provide sufficient capital to pay for further sales expansion in the future without the need to look for additional outside funding.

The risk of over-trading arises when a company has insufficient working capital to service the volume of business. PCB would appear to have exhausted its sources of working capital, and any further increases in sales would therefore place the company under a great cash strain. By re-organising its financing, and increasing the long-term equity investment, PCB could regain access to additional short-term borrowing, and so avoid the risk of over-trading.

8   Fenton Security plc

Key answer tips

Part (a) requires you to calculate *changes*, so it makes sense to set up the benchmark position first, i.e. the *current* funding and bad debts position. Once you have established this, you need to superimpose the new conditions for the new alternative policies and assess the impact. As the main problem with high levels of debtors is the cost of funding them, it makes sense to include this cost as part of your assessment.

Parts (b) and (c) should be very familiar to you, and offer a chance of high marks, provided your answers are given in the context of the given scenario, particularly in (b).

(a)   *Current Position*

Average collection period:
$= [(0.05 \times 30) + (0.28 \times 45) + (0.1 \times 60) + (0.3 \times 75) + (0.16 \times 90) + (0.11 \times 120)] = 70.2$ days

Working capital required to fund these collections can be calculated as:
$(70.2/365 \times £67.5$ million$) = £12.982$ million

Bad debt provision $= £2.0$ million

| Total current funding required | $= (£12.982$ million $\times 0.12) + £2.0$ million |
| | $= £3.558$ million |

(i)   Using early settlement discounts:

Revised Position
New sales value is £67.16 million

Average collection period	$= 59.9$ days
i.e. reduction	$= (0.28 \times 15) + (0.1 \times 30) + (0.07 \times 45)$
	$= 10.35$ days
New collection period	$= 70.2 - 10.35$ days $= 59.9$ days
Reduction in working capital	$= £1.962$ million
Reduction in overdraft costs at 12% per year	$= £235,440$
Cost of the discount	$= 50\% \times 1\% \times £67.5$ million
	$= £337,500$

Bad debts are assumed to remain unchanged.

Conclude: It is not worthwhile to offer the discount as the associated costs exceed the savings which would be generated.

(ii) Cost of debt collection service at 1% sales receipts	$= £655,000$
Reduction in debtor days	$= 20/365 \times £65.5$ million
	$= £3.589$ million
Interest saving at 12%	$= £430,685$
Savings from elimination of bad debts	$= 0.5 \times £2.0$ million
	$= £1.0$ million
Total savings	$= £1.430$ million

Conclude: The total savings far exceed the cost of the debt collection service, and so its use is recommended. The main reason for this is the huge reduction in bad debts, which alone generates in excess of £1 million of savings. Fenton should therefore choose to use the debt collection service.

(b)   There are a number of ways in which Fenton Security plc could ensure that customers are subjected to tighter credit appraisal checks before goods are supplied. The list below is indicative but not exhaustive, and includes significantly more detail than would be expected of examination candidates:

Bank and Trade References
It is customary to request a customer to give permission for a banker's reference to be sought, and also to name two to three current suppliers who may be willing to provide trade references. The difficulty associated with both of these types of reference is that they cannot be relied upon as confirmation that a customer is creditworthy. A bank is unlikely to give a customer a bad reference, and the customer is not going to name trade suppliers with which they have a bad payment record.

Trade Sources of Information
Within, for example, the credit card industry, it is not uncommon for information on an individual's credit rating to be shared. In similar vein, within the industrial sector, companies may share data on key customers in relation to their credit worthiness and debt records. Asking competitors if they are willing to share knowledge about a potential customer can help in establishing credit limits.

Credit Reference Agencies
A number of organisations e.g. Dun & Bradstreet and Standard & Poor provide credit scores and ratings for companies. These may take the form of a simple rating from AAA to CCC, or a more detailed report.

Credit Scoring
If Fenton Security already has extensive sales records, it may be possible to use those records to compile a credit scoring system. Credit scoring works by specifying the characteristics known to be associated with good/bad debts, and allocating customers a score based on their particular characteristic profile. Credit scoring is commonly used in retailing when determining the credit limits to be granted to personal customers, but the same principles can readily be applied to commercial customers.

(c)   Invoice discounting is a technique which can be used to raise finance against debtors. Invoice discounting works as follows: A company issues an invoice to a customer and sends a copy invoice to the discount company, which then makes a payment against the invoice and takes responsibility for collecting the debt from the customer. The amount of the payment will vary, but is very rarely 100% of the invoice value. The balance of money due is paid across to the selling company when the discount company has received full payment for the customer. The arrangement has the effect of allowing the selling company to collect its debts in early, so reducing the working capital requirement of the business, and improving the cash flow.

The price that is paid for the service is usually set at a fixed percentage monthly rate e.g. 1% of the value of invoices discounted. Even though the process operates "with recourse", companies will often find that they are only able to discount the invoices of customers with high credit ratings, who are therefore reliable debtors. This means that not all invoices can be funded, and the risk of bad debts remains. The extent to which companies may find that using invoice discounting does improve the cash flow is therefore dependent upon the credit profile of customers, and their bad debt record. The discounting is most advantageous (in cash flow terms) for companies which are selling to customers with high credit ratings and a good payment record.

Sources of finance

9   Newsam plc

Key answer tips

When faced with the imprecise information, such as the definition of gearing to be used in part (a), you should either state your assumption and work on that, or, if you have time, give alternatives, as in the answer below.

In (b), slightly more is needed for 3 marks than simply "close" or "not close", and this gives an opportunity to briefly discuss the dependence upon the exact definition of gearing. To answer part (c), you should structure your answer around the potential "dangers" of high gearing levels, and the extent to which Newsam appears to be exposed to them.

In (c)(i), first think how gearing can be lowered – by lowering debt, or increasing equity. Then think of ways to achieve these. In (ii) the only practical way to improve interest cover is to lower interest charges, either by reducing the debt itself, or refinancing to lower the interest rate. Here, make sure you incorporate the information given by the examiner in the question as regards other interest rates available.

(a)   The covenant does not give a precise measure of gearing in so far as it fails to stipulate whether short-term debt should be included in the calculation. It seems prudent to consider gearing measures with and without the bank overdraft.

(i)   **Using book values**

$$\frac{\text{Long - term debt}}{\text{Shareholders' funds}} = £5m/£15m = 33\% \qquad \frac{\text{Total debt}}{\text{Shareholders' funds}} = £8m/£15m = 53\%$$

(ii)   **Using market values**

The market value of the debentures	=	$1.15 \times £5m = £5.75m$
The price of the ordinary shares	=	P/E ratio × Earnings per share
	=	$14 \times \dfrac{\text{Profit after tax}}{\text{Number of shares}}$
	=	$14 \times \dfrac{£1.34m}{20m} = 14 \times 6.7p = 94p$
Market value of equity	=	$20m \times 94p = £18.8m$

The gearing ratios are:

$$\frac{\text{Long - term debt}}{\text{Shareholders' funds}} = \frac{£5.75m}{£18.8m} = 31\% \qquad \frac{\text{Total debt}}{\text{Shareholders' funds}} = \frac{£8.75m}{£18.8m} = 47\%$$

(b)   It would seem that, in terms of its borrowing, Newsam has already breached the covenant if a combination of book values and total debt is used, while it is very near to doing so if the market value base is used in conjunction with total indebtedness. It could be argued that short-term creditors also constitute part of Newsam's indebtedness, inclusion of which would increase the gearing measures, but as they are covered by cash and debtors, they have been excluded.

Regarding the liquidity stipulation, at present, Newsam's current ratio is precisely one, compared to a permissible range of (1.35 × 0.8) to (1.35 × 1.2) i.e. 1.08 to 1.62. It seems, therefore, that Newsam is also breaching the liquidity requirement in the covenant and will have to take steps to improve its liquidity, especially as the quick ratio is only £4.5m/£7m = 0.64 (although no industry standard is given).

(c)   Financial gearing exposes the company to the risk of inability to meet required interest payments, should the company's profitability falter. If the creditors decide to demand repayment of their capital, the company faces the problem of liquidating assets, and possibly, the whole enterprise, in order to meet these claims. Hence, the first consideration is the degree of safety implied by the firm's interest cover, the ratio of profit before tax and interest to interest payable, in the light of the stability of the firm's sales and profits.

Interest cover is £3m/£1m = 3 times, which might appear low to some analysts, but if the firm's operations are stable, this may be tolerable. In the case of Newsam, although sales growth has been sluggish, its products are branded and well-established, and probably not subject to wide fluctuations. This seems a safe cover.

The second consideration is the value of the firm's assets in relation to the debt capital. In the first instance, the ability to repay the debentures is critical, but if debenture holders demanded repayment, it is inconceivable that Newsam's bankers would not call in the overdraft. Hence, Newsam's ability to repay *all* its debt needs to be assessed.

At book values, fixed assets appear in the accounts at £20m. Whether Newsam could actually achieve this figure in a forced sale is questionable, although it is possible that the value of the land and premises on the open market might exceed their historic cost values. The current state of the property market is important in this respect.

The final consideration is the action which Newsam's debenture holders are empowered to take in the event of breach of covenant, and, more pertinently, what they are *expected* to do in the circumstances. Newsam is likely to have some idea of their probable reaction as precautionary discussions are likely to have taken place already.

(d)   (i)   To lower its gearing ratio, Newsam could adopt a number of policies as follows.

Revalue its fixed assets

It is possible that a revaluation could reveal a surplus, but this is likely to be a purely cosmetic adjustment – unless the revaluation conveys information which is genuinely new to the market, the share price is unlikely to respond, despite an increase in the book value of assets.

Place a value on its brands

Again, this may be a purely cosmetic exercise, as the market will already have taken into account the value of these brands in setting the share price.

Tighten working capital management

The bank overdraft could be lowered by a more aggressive working capital management policy. For example, the debtor collection period could be shortened and/or the trade credit period lengthened. There does appear to be some scope regarding debtor days which currently stand at: $4/28 \times 365 = 52$ days which appears quite lengthy, although the trade credit period, currently: $4/20 \times 365 = 73$ days, already is excessively long and would give rise to fears over suppliers' reaction if any further delay was attempted.

The stock turnover at $20/2.5 = 8$ times (or 46 days) may look fairly long and capable of reduction, but overall, the working capital cycle at $(52 + 46) – 73 = 25$ days is quite rapid already.

It may be possible to achieve economies in this area but the scope appears limited.

Issue more shares

In theory, it should not matter when a rights issue is made, because the share price in an efficient market would always indicate the correct value of the shares, and the only market reaction would be the technical adjustment caused by earnings dilution when shares are sold at a discount. In reality, it is often difficult to convince a flat stock market of the positive reasons for a rights issue. In the present case, the announcement that a moderately performing and poorly-rated company like Newsam was planning to make a rights issue on a weak stock market merely in order to reduce indebtedness would be likely to induce a negative reaction.

This problem could possibly be eased if the company were able to make a placing of new shares with supportive financial institutions after persuading shareholders to forgo pre-emptive rights of purchase.

    (ii)   To raise the interest cover, Newsam could do the following:

Refinance the debenture with a bank overdraft

The interest saving, assuming no change in the total debt, would be: $(15\% – 9\%) \times £5m = £0.3m$. This would raise the interest cover to £3.0m/£0.7m = 4.3 times.

Refinance the debenture with a Eurodollar issue

On the face of it, this alternative appears to offer bigger interest savings – i.e. $(15\% – 5\%) \times £5m = £0.5m$, which would raise the interest cover to £3.0m/£0.5m = 6 times. However, aside from the issue costs likely to be involved, there are dangers here. The forward market quotation for the dollar suggests that the dollar will appreciate against sterling by 1% over three months, or about 4% over one year. Although it is possible that the dollar could actually depreciate, thus lowering the sterling value of the debt, the foreign exchange market consensus is for a dollar appreciation of sufficient magnitude to eliminate the interest differential between Eurobonds and an overdraft.

In addition, there are dangers in replacing long-term debt with short-term debt. For example, a bank overdraft is, in principle (if not always in practice), repayable on demand, nor is the bank obliged to extend overdraft facilities indefinitely, while the company is exposed to the risk of adverse interest rate movements over the duration of its short-term financing. Newsam must balance these risks and their consequences against the interest cost differential.

10 Collingham plc

Key answer tips

In part (a) this is quite a common requirement, and it is well worth having four or five reasons for seeking a listing up your sleeve. However, note that it is not enough simply to cite a reason, without supporting explanation/comment.

In part (b) your discussion should focus around a comparison of Collingham's ratios with those given for the industry of a whole. However, it is not good enough to simply list the two figures for each ratio with possibly a short comment for each. You need to try to draw an overall picture, by seeing how the ratios may be inter-related, and using any information given to you in the question. You can structure your discussion around profitability (indicating performance), liquidity and capital structure (both contributing to financial health).

It is somewhat debatable as to when possible changes may be made, so don't worry too much about the exact split between pre and post flotation in part (c). The restructuring of the balance sheet looks at how the results of past transactions can be shown in their best light. Remembering what you have just done in (b) should make you think about the possible improvement of ratios as well as just the absolute figures, and their presentation, on the balance sheet. Changes to policy will affect the value of future transactions. 'Value' could be said to be in the eye of the beholder, and after flotation the main change is the nature of the shareholder body. Being listed means that any policy that does not suit the company's investors will be immediately, and very publicly, reflected in depressed market prices. You should therefore think about the sort of policies for which institutional investors may be looking. There is also the regulatory point to be made concerning the enfranchising of the 'A' shares.

(a)   Seeking a quotation places many strains on a company, in particular, the need to provide more extensive information about its activities. However, the costs involved in doing this may seem worthwhile in order to pursue the following aims:

   (i)   *To obtain more capital to finance growth.* Companies which apply for a market listing are often fast-growing firms which have exhausted their usual supplies of capital. Typically, they rely on retained earnings and borrowing, often on a short-term basis. A quotation opens up access to a wider pool of investors. For example, large financial institutions are more willing to invest in quoted companies whose shares are considerably more marketable than those of unlisted enterprises.

   Companies with a listing are often perceived to be financially stronger and hence may enjoy better credit ratings, enabling them to borrow at more favourable interest rates.

   (ii)   *To allow owners to realise their assets.* After several years of successful operation, many company founders own considerable wealth on paper. They may wish to liquidify some of their holdings to fund other business ventures or simply for personal reasons, even at the cost of relinquishing some measure of voting power. Most flotations allow existing shareholders to release some of their equity as well as raising new capital.

   (iii)   *To make the shares more marketable.* Existing owners may not wish to sell out at present, or to the degree that a flotation may require. A quotation, effected by means of a Stock Exchange introduction, is a device for establishing a market in the equity of a company, allowing owners to realise their wealth as and when they wish.

   (iv)   *To enable payment of managers by stock options.* The offer to senior managers of payment partially in the form of stock options may provide powerful incentives to improve performance.

   (v)   *To facilitate growth by acquisition.* Companies whose ordinary shares are traded on the stock market are more easily able to offer their own shares (or other traded securities, such as convertibles) in exchange for those of target companies whom they wish to acquire.

   (vi)   *To enhance the company's image.* A quotation gives an aura of financial respectability, which may encourage new business contracts. In addition, so long as the company performs well, it will receive free publicity when the financial press reports and discusses its results in future years.

(b)   The table below compares Collingham's ratios against the industry averages:

	Industry	Collingham		
Return on (long term) capital employed	22%	10/33	=	30.3%
Return on equity	14%	6/28	=	21.4%
Operating profit margin	10%	10/80	=	12.5%
Current ratio	1.8:1	23/20	=	1.15:1
Acid-test	1.1:1	13/20	=	0.65:1
Gearing (total debt/equity)	18%	10/28	=	35.7%
Interest cover	5.2	10/3	=	3.33 times
Dividend cover	2.6	6/0.5	=	12 times

Collingham's profitability, expressed both in terms of ROCE and ROE, compares favourably with the industry average. This may be inflated by the use of a historic cost base, in so far as assets have never been revalued. Although a revaluation might depress these ratios, the company appears attractive compared to its peers. The net profit margin of 12.5% is above that of the overall industry, suggesting a cost advantage, either in production or in operating a flat administrative structure. Alternatively, it may operate in a market niche where it is still exploiting first-comer advantages. In essence, it is this aspect which is likely to appeal to investors.

Set against the apparently strong profitability is the poor level of liquidity. Both the current and the acid-test ratios are well below the industry average, and suggest that the company should be demonstrating tighter working capital management. However, the stock turnover of $(10/70 \times 365) = 52$ days and the debtor days of $(10/80 \times 365) = 46$ days do not appear excessive, although industry averages are not given. It is possible that Collingham has recently been utilising liquid resources to finance fixed investment or to repay past borrowings.

Present borrowings are split equally between short-term and long-term, although the level of gearing is well above the market average. The debenture is due for repayment shortly which will exert further strains on liquidity, unless it can be re-financed. Should interest rates increase in the near future, Collingham is exposed to the risk of having to lock-in higher interest rates on a subsequent long-term loan or pay (perhaps temporarily) a higher interest rate on overdraft. The high gearing is reflected also in low interest cover, markedly below the industry average. In view of high gearing and poor liquidity, it is not surprising that the pay-out ratio is below 10%, although Collingham's managers would presumably prefer to link high retentions to the need to finance ongoing investment and growth rather than to protect liquidity.

(c)   It is common for companies in Collingham's position to attempt to 'strengthen' or to 'tidy up' their balance sheets in order to make the company appear more attractive to investors. Very often, this amounts to 'window dressing', and if the company were already listed, it would have little effect in an information-efficient market. However, for unlisted companies, about whom little is generally known, such devices can improve the financial profile of the company and enhance the prospects of a successful flotation.

(i)   Some changes in the balance sheet that Collingham might consider prior to flotation are as follows.

Revalue those fixed assets which now appear in the accounts at historic cost. The freehold land and premises are likely to be worth more at market values, although the effect of time on second-hand machinery values is more uncertain. If a surplus emerges, a revaluation reserve would be created, thus increasing the book value of shareholders' funds, and hence the net asset value per share. The disadvantage of this would be to lower the ROCE and the return on equity, although these are already well above the industry averages. Asset revaluation would also reduce the gearing ratio.

Dispose of any surplus assets in order to reduce gearing and/or to increase liquidity which is presently low, both absolutely, and also in relation to the industry.

Examine other ways to improve the liquidity position, by reducing stocks, speeding up debtor collection or slowing payment to suppliers, although it already appears to be a slow payer with a trade credit period of $(15/70 \times 365) = 78$ days.

Conduct a share split, because at the existing level of earnings per share, the shares promise to have a 'heavyweight' rating. Applying the industry P/E multiple of 13 to the current EPS of $(£6m/£4m \times 2) = 75p$, yields a share price of $(13 \times 75p) = £9.75$. While there is little evidence that a heavyweight rating is a deterrent to trading in already listed shares, it is likely that potential investors, certainly small-scale ones, will be deterred from subscribing to a highly-priced new issue. A one-for-one share split whereby the par value is reduced to 25p per share and the number of shares issued correspondingly doubles, would halve the share price, although other configurations are possible.

It will have to enfranchise the non-voting 'A' shares, because, under present Stock Exchange regulations, these are not permitted for companies newly entering the market.

(ii)   Following the flotation, Collingham would probably have to accept that a higher dividend pay-out is required to attract and retain the support of institutional investors. If it wishes to persist with a high level of internal financing, a compromise may be to make scrip issues of shares, especially if the share price remains on the 'heavy' side. Scrip issues are valued by the market because they usually portend higher earnings and dividends in the future.

Finally, if the company has not already done so, it might consider progressively lowering the gearing ratio. It might begin this by using part of the proceeds of the flotation to redeem the debenture early. However, it must avoid the impression that it requires a flotation primarily to repay past borrowings as that might cast doubts on the company's financial stability.

11   Burnsall plc

Key answer tips

In part (a) there are a number of clues to the approach needed here. First the requirement emphasises the word *external*, implying that some of the finance may be raised internally. How? by use of surplus cash arising from operations - you were guided to this by Note (1) that concerns FRS 1 i.e. cash flow statements. So the approach required is:

*   calculate the total finance needed (to cover a 20% increase in working capital, plus capital expenditure)

*   estimate the net cash inflow to be generated from next year's operations by converting profit information to cash flows, taking account of non-operating liabilities to be paid off from this year's balance sheet

*   deduce the shortfall of finance to be funded externally.

Even if you don't manage to sort out the cash flows exactly, setting out this approach up front will help to keep you on track and to convince the examiner you appreciate the nature of the problem.

In part (b) it is essential that you tailor your answer to the particular circumstances outlined in the question - it asks for the options open to Burnsall. Look back at the current long-term financing situation: equity - it is a listed company; debt - it already has some debt but at a reasonably low level. Just appreciating these basic facts will help to avoid making inappropriate, and thus time-wasting, suggestions. Note in particular that the examiner does not require:

*   discussions of the different methods of making public issues (and Burnsall is already listed)
*   discussion of short-term finance methods.
*   discussion of more than four options.

(a)   The company will need additional finance to fund both working and fixed capital needs.

As sales are expected to increase by 20%, and since working capital needs are expected to rise in line with sales, the predicted working capital needs will be 20% above the existing working capital level. Ignoring tax liability, this is:

$1.2 \times$ [Stock + Debtors + Cash − Trade creditors] = $1.2 \times$ [£16m + £23m + £6m − £18m]
= £32.4m, an increase of £5.4m

Together with the additional capital expenditures of £20m, the total funding requirement:

= [£5.4m + £20m]
= £25.4m

This funding requirement can be met partly by internal finance and partly by new external capital. The internal finance available will derive from depreciation provisions and retained earnings, after accounting for anticipated liabilities, such as taxation, that is, from cash flow.

Note that the profit margin on sales of £100m (£10 $\times$ 10m units) before interest and tax was 16% in 20X4/20X5. If depreciation of £5m for 20X4/20X5 is added back, this yields a cash flow cost of sales of £79m (ignoring movements in current assets/liabilities). No further adjustment for depreciation is required.

Using the same margin, and making a simple operating cash flow projection based on the accounts and other information provided:

Inflows	£m	£m
Sales in 20X5/20X6: (£10 × 10m units) + 20%	120.00	
Cost of sales before depreciation: (£79m + 20%)	(94.80)	
Operating cash flow		25.20
Outflows		
Tax liability for 20X4/20X5	(5.00)	
Interest payments: 12% × £20m	(2.40)	
Dividends: 1.1 × £5m	(5.50)	
		(12.90)
Net internal finance generated		12.30
Funding requirements		(25.40)
Net additional external finance required		(13.10)

(b) A wide variety of financing options is open to Burnsall including the following.

(i) Some new equipment could be leased via a long-term capital lease. Tax relief is available on rental payments, lowering the effective cost of using the equipment. Lessors may 'tailor' a leasing package to suit Burnsall's specific needs regarding timing of payments and provision of ancillary services. Alternatively, good quality property assets at present owned by Burnsall could be sold to a financial institution and their continued use secured via a leaseback arrangement, although this arrangement usually involves losing any capital appreciation of the assets.

(ii) If Burnsall's assets are of sufficient quality i.e. easily saleable, it may be possible to raise a mortgage secured on them. This enables retention of ownership.

(iii) Burnsall could make a debenture issue, interest on which would be tax-allowable. The present level of gearing (long-term debt to equity) is relatively low at £20m/£122m = 16%, Burnsall has no short-term debt apart from trade creditors and the Inland Revenue, and its interest cover is healthy at profit before tax and interest divided by interest charges = [16% × £100m]/[12% × £20m] = 6.7 times (even higher on a cash flow basis). It is likely that Burnsall could make a sizeable debt issue without unnerving the market. Any new debenture would be subordinate to the existing long-term debt and probably carry a higher interest rate.

(iv) An alternative to a debt issue is a rights issue of ordinary shares. Because rights issues are made at a discount to the existing market price, they result in lower EPS and thus market price, although if existing shareholders take up their allocations, neither their wealth nor their control is diluted. If the market approves of the intended use of funds, a capital gain may ensue, although the company and its advisers must carefully manage the issue regarding the declared reasons and its timing in order to avoid unsettling the market.

Note: only four sources are required for the answer, but other sources of finance may also be mentioned, such as the following.

(v) Burnsall could approach a venture capitalist such as 3i, which specialises in extending development capital to small-to-medium-sized firms. However, 3i may require an equity stake, and possibly insist on placing an appointee on the board of directors to monitor its interests.

(vi) Burnsall could utilise official sources of aid such as a regional development agency depending on its location, or perhaps the European Investment Bank.

12   Phoenix plc

Key answer tips

In part (a) the dividend payout ratio and dividend cover both relate the amount available for dividends (post-tax profits) to the amount actually paid - one is the inverse of the other. It is not clear whether the pre-tax profit figures given in the question are after interest or not - either assumption is fine.

In part (b) first, your answer must be in report format, with appropriate titles for writer and recipient, as indicated in the question. Second, it needs a good structure - introduction, main content, conclusion. Thirdly, it needs to focus on the two uses specified for the cash surplus, and fourthly it needs to incorporate the data given in the question where this supports or adds to the points being made. Try to take a commercial and practical view of the effect, say, of increasing dividends so substantially in the current economic environment and the particular circumstances of Phoenix.

(a)   **Payout ratios/Dividend cover**

In 20X5/20X6, the dividend was 1.50p per share, making a total payout of £70m × 4 × 1.50p = £4.2m. The profit after tax was:

	£
Operating profit	25.00
Interest	(0.70)
Taxable profit	24.30
Tax at 33%	(8.02)
Profit after tax	16.28

% Payout £4.20m/£16.28m = 26%
Dividend cover = 3.9 times

If the present cash balances are used to increase the dividend by £10m, making a total dividend of (£4.20m + £10m) = £14.20m, the figures will appear thus:

	£
Operating profit	40.00
Interest	(0.70)
Taxable profit	39.30
Tax at 33%	(12.97)
Profit after tax	26.33

% Payout £14.20m/£26.33m = 54%
Dividend cover = 1.9 times

This represents a substantial fall in dividend cover, from significantly above the sector average to well below it. Such an apparent shift in dividend policy is bound to provoke comment both from shareholders and also from the market in general.

(b)   **Report to:**   The Finance Director
       Subject: Utilisation of excess cash balances
       From: Financial Strategist

1   *Introduction*

Phoenix has built up significant cash balances over the past year as a result of exceptional growth in sales and profits as the economy has recovered from recession, sparking demand for the high quality building products in which we specialise. There are several possible uses for surplus cash balances such as investment in the short-term money market and acquisition of other companies. However, my remit is to consider only two such uses, firstly, an increase in dividends and secondly, early repayment of the long-term loan stock, repayable in 20Y7. This report will consider each of these in turn.

2   *Dividend increase*

The factors which will need to be considered and investigated are as follows.

(i)   *The preferences of our shareholders*. Many shareholders will have purchased Phoenix shares rather than those of competing companies with higher payouts not for dividend payments but for long-term capital growth. In the past, we have served their interests by restricting dividends and ploughing back profits into the business. We will need to consider how they are likely to respond to such a sharp shift in our distribution policy, albeit due to lack of investment opportunities.

(ii)   *Shareholders' tax position*. A major determinant of shareholders' preferences is their liability to tax. Some institutional shareholders enjoy tax advantages from distribution, while some private shareholders, perhaps the majority, prefer capital gains to dividends because of the tax advantages attaching to the former. This factor underlines the need to inspect our shareholder register and to consult with major shareholders.

(iii)   *Actual and expected liquidity*. Phoenix is highly liquid at present and there are no plans to engage in significant capital expenditures. However, it is prudent to examine our medium to long-term capital requirements to ascertain whether the monies concerned are best left on deposit so as to avoid having to mount a major capital-raising exercise in the future. By the same token, group cash flow forecasts will need examination to identify any major demands for cash of a non-capital nature e.g. closure costs, in the foreseeable future.

(iv)   *Loan covenants*. It is proposed to lower dividend cover significantly. Our lawyers will have to inspect the terms of our long-term loan outstanding to discover whether there are any restrictions on dividend payouts.

(v)   *Stock market reaction*. The proposal is to more than triple dividend payments. Clearly, this represents a major departure from past policy and raises several issues. Presumably, we will present this payment as a special dividend of the kind paid by certain UK utility companies in recent years to dampen any expectations of similar increases in the future. This would best be done by paying it at a different time to the regular dividend. However, this begs the tactical question of the extent to which the 'normal' final dividend should be raised. If the normal dividend is also raised significantly, this will signal directors' confidence in our ability to sustain future payments and thus exert pressure on the company to meet these expectations. Given that our earnings are cyclical and have recently been depressed, it is important that we settle on a dividend payout policy which we feel confident of maintaining through the various phases of the business cycle. The stock market tends to be unforgiving of companies which cut dividends.

3   *Repayment of the loan stock*

The factors which will need to be considered and investigated are as follows.

(i)   *Conditions of the loan*. Again, we must scrutinise the terms of the loan to ascertain whether early payment is permitted at all and whether it triggers any penalties.

(ii)   *The tax shield*. If we repay the loan, we will lose the benefit of the tax relief accorded to debt interest payments. Admittedly, the tax saving is not substantial. i.e. $33\% \times 7\% \times £10m = £0.23m$, but it is nevertheless worthwhile. Given our recent increase in profitability, and assuming this can be sustained, there is a strong case for increasing our gearing rather than reducing it, although this would be contrary to our traditional policy. Our capital gearing (Debt/Equity) is well below, and our interest cover is well above, current industry averages.

	Phoenix	Industry
Capital gearing	£10m/£200m* = 5%	45%
(*ignoring retentions for the current year)		
Interest cover	£40m/£0.7m = 57 times	6.5 times

(iii)   *Interest rate expectations*. If we need to borrow sometime in the future, we will lose if future interests rates exceed 7%, since we will have effectively replaced 7% debt by higher cost debt. The reverse argument also applies.

(iv)   *Reaction of the market.* When companies with high gearing levels and thus high levels of financial risk repay debt, there is usually a favourable effect on share price. Given our low level of gearing, it is doubtful that there would be any such benefit. Indeed, the effect could be adverse, if the market perceives the debt retirement as a signal of harder times ahead.

4   *Recommendation*

Subject to the conditions of the existing loan, if we believe that our profitability will remain buoyant, there is a strong case for raising the level of dividends and for increasing our level of financial gearing. The risks seem low, although we will need to consult our major shareholders in order to sound out their potential reactions.

13   Jeronimo plc

Key answer tips

In part (a) note there are three parts to this requirement - (1) the difference between the two types of issue, (2) why companies make rights issues and (3) the effect on private investors. Marks are allocated for each part - don't throw them away by overlooking any of them.

Part (b)(i) hinges around the computation of the theoretical ex-rights price, a fairly standard formula with which you should be familiar. The price at which the investor will sell the rights should be that which leaves him no worse off than if he had taken them up. Taking them up will give him a share worth £1.55, at a cost of £1.30, a net gain of £0.25. This is therefore the compensation he needs for selling the rights instead.

Part (c) – the dividend growth model is central to equity value theory, and you must be confident in using it. Here, growth is estimated from past dividends, and applied to the current dividend to estimate next year's.

Part (d) really tests your understanding of the *implications* of market efficiency, rather than simply the ability to regurgitate definitions.

(a)   A rights issue is a way of raising finance via the issue of shares to existing equity shareholders. In order to make such an issue, a company must have an authorised share capital which exceeds the issued share capital. Companies choose to make rights issues because of a need to raise long term finance, and a decision that such a method is the most cost effective or desirable. The finance raised may be used to fund any type of long term investment such as an acquisition, expansion of production facilities, or overseas investment. A scrip issue is an issue of shares for which no charge is made. The shares are issued free to existing shareholders, and may be called bonus or capitalisation issues.

The advantage of a rights issue made to existing investors, as opposed to an issue via public subscription, is that such investors are assumed to already have some level of commitment to the company. As such it may prove relatively easy to persuade them to buy shares, and certainly easier and less costly than making a public offering. It is, however, important for the company to explain the reason behind the share issue – what it is going to do with the cash raised. If an investor is to be persuaded to pay cash for additional shares, then it must be demonstrated that their newly invested cash will be used to earn returns at least equal to those they are currently receiving from their investment. If the return on capital is expected to decline in the company after the rights issue, then the issue is unlikely to be successful. As with any new share issue, it is common practice for a rights issue to be underwritten.

The individual investor in a company which is making a rights issue will be invited to take up or sell his/her rights. If the rights are taken up, then the investor will have to make a payment to the company equal to the price of the rights purchased. Alternatively, the investor may choose not to increase the scale of his investment, and sell the right on the open market. In an efficient market, the investor is no better nor no worse off because of choosing to sell his/her rights.

Scrip issues are often justified on the basis that there is a need to increase the number of shares in issue in order to bring down the price per share. It is often argued that the market "dislikes" shares which individually have a very high price, and by increasing the number of shares in issue, the unit share price can be diluted. This can be beneficial to shareholders because research evidence suggests that the drop in the unit share price is not as great as the proportionate change in the number of shares in issue. For example, if 10 million shares are in issue, and the current market price is £10 each, the market value of the equity is £100 million. If 10 million shares are now distributed via a scrip issue, one would expect the share price to drop to £5, leaving the overall equity value at £100 million. In practice, the lowering of the share price may make the shares more marketable, such that the post issue price settles at, say, £6. This results in an increase in the value of individual shareholdings, together with a rise in the total value of the equity. Individual investors may therefore experience some capital gain from a scrip issue.

◈ FOULKSlynch

When making a scrip issue, a company is converting some of the reserves into share capital, and the number of shares (fully paid up) to which an investor is entitled, will be expressed in relation to the current holding e.g. a 2 for 5 issue. As already suggested, although the private investor gains no theoretical advantage from this conversion of reserves, there may be a benefit in practice, because the shares are now more marketable.

(b) (i) Theoretical ex-rights value =

$$\frac{(\text{No. shares in issue} \times \text{market value}) + (\text{No. rights shares} \times \text{rights share price})}{\text{Total shares in issue post rights}}$$

$$= \frac{(5m \times £1.60) + (1m \times £1.30)}{6m}$$

$$= £1.55 \text{ per share}$$

After taking up the rights issue, James Brown will hold $10,000 + (0.2 \times 10,000) = 12,000$ shares. The theoretical value of the holding, at £1.55 per share is thus £18,600.

(ii) The value of the rights per share = Theoretical ex-rights price – Cost of taking up the rights

The value of the rights per share = £1.55 – £1.30
The value of the rights per share = £0.25 per share
If James Brown sells all of his rights to 2,000 shares, he will receive 2,000 x £0.25 = £500.

(c) Using the dividend growth formula:

$$R = \left(\frac{D_1}{MV} + g\right) \times 100$$

Where D_1 = Next year's dividend
g = Dividend growth rate
MV = Market price of share
R = Percentage required return

g = $(12/8)^{1/4} - 1$

= 0·1067 or 11%
D_1 = $12 \times 1·11$ pence
= 13·32 pence i.e. 13 pence

$$R = \left(\frac{13}{160} + 0.11\right) \times 100$$

$R = 19.125\%$

(d) In a strongly efficient market, finance directors will be alert to the fact that market prices are an accurate reflection of their company's financial prospects, and that if they behave in a manner which results in bad financial decisions, the share price will quickly fall to compensate for the worsening prospects.

This means that the effect of an efficient market on financial management is that it keeps managers alert to the consequences of their decisions. In an inefficient world, prices may take a while to adjust to reflect poor planning or control, but in a semi-strong or strong market environment this will not be true. It can thus be said that the efficient markets hypothesis encourages higher quality financial management. In a similar vein, it also serves to discourage the artificial manipulation of accounting information, as the truth will quickly be realised, and prices adjusted accordingly.

Capital expenditure and investment

14   Howden plc

Key answer tips

In part (a) the answer implies that it is possible to determine a 'real' rate of return which can then be adjusted in the light of estimated future rates of inflation. The most likely method of calculating a company's required rate of return will actually produce a 'money cost of capital'. To produce a 'real' cost of capital requires some tinkering with this initial calculation.

In part (b) a clear lay out will greatly assist both you and the marker. With projects of short time span, up to, say, five years, a horizontal tabulation is generally best. Where various annuities in real terms are inflating at different rates the best approach is to split them into single year flows and inflate each separately.
Note that in (c), the consideration is not limited to investment decisions – take care to read the requirements carefully.

(a)   Investors advance capital to companies expecting a reward for both the delay in waiting for their returns (time value of money) and also for the risks to which they expose their capital (risk premium). In addition, if prices in general are rising, shareholders require compensation for the erosion in the real value of their capital.

If, for example, in the absence of inflation, shareholders require a company to offer a return of 10%, the need to cover 5% price inflation will raise the overall required return to about 15%. If people in general expect a particular rate of inflation, the structure of interest rates in the capital market will adjust to incorporate these inflationary expectations. This is known as the 'Fisher effect'.

More precisely, the relationship between the real required return (r) and the nominal rate, (m), the rate which includes an allowance for inflation, is given by: $(1 + r) \times (1 + p) = (1 + m)$ where p is the expected rate of inflation.

It is essential when evaluating an investment project under inflation that future expected price level changes are treated in a consistent way. Companies may correctly allow for inflation in two ways each of which computes the real value of an investment project:

(i)   Inflate the future expected cash flows at the expected rate of inflation (allowing for inflation rates specific to the project) and discount at m, the fully-inflated rate – the 'money terms' approach.

(ii)   Strip out the inflation element from the market-determined rate and apply the resulting real rate of return, r, to the stream of cash flows expressed in today's or constant prices – the 'real terms' approach.

(b)   First, the relevant set-up cost needs identification. The offer of £2m for the building, if rejected, represents an opportunity lost, although this appears to be compensated by its predicted eventual resale value of £3m. The cost of the market research study has to be met irrespective of the decision to proceed with the project or not and is thus not relevant.

Secondly, incremental costs and revenues are identified. All other items are avoidable except the element of apportioned overhead, leaving the incremental overhead alone to include in the evaluation.

Thirdly, all items of incremental cash flow, including this additional overhead, must be adjusted for their respective rates of inflation. Because (with the exception of labour and variable overhead) the inflation rates differ, a disaggregated approach is required.

The appropriate discount rate is given by:

$$(1 + p) \times (1 + r) - 1 = m$$
$$= (1.06) \times (1.085) - 1$$
$$= 15\%$$

Assuming that the inflated costs and prices apply from and including the first year of operation, the cash-flow profile is as follows.

Cash flow profile	(£m)		Time			
Item	0	1	2	3	4	5
Equipment	(10.50)					2.00
Foregone sale of buildings	(2.00)					
Residual value of building						3.00
Working capital*	(0.50)					0.50
Revenue		5.04	5.29	5.56	5.83	6.13
Materials		(0.62)	(0.64)	(0.66)	(0.68)	(0.70)
Labour and variable overhead		(0.43)	(0.46)	(0.49)	(0.52)	(0.56)
Fixed overhead		(0.53)	(0.55)	(0.58)	(0.61)	(0.64)
Net cash flows	(13.00)	3.46	3.64	3.83	4.02	9.73
Present value at 15%	(13.00)	3.01	2.75	2.52	2.30	4.84

NPV = +£2.42m, therefore, the project appears to be acceptable.

However, the financial viability of the project depends quite heavily on the estimate of the residual value of the building and equipment.

Note: the working capital cash recovery towards the end of the project is approximately equal to the initial investment in stocks because the rate of material cost inflation tends to cancel out the JIT-induced reduction in volume, leading to roughly constant stock-holding in value terms throughout most of the project life-span.

(c)   In addition to the problems offered for investment appraisal such as forecasting the various rates of inflation relevant to the project, inflation poses a wider range of difficulties in a variety of business decision areas.

Inflation may pose a problem for businesses if it distorts the signals transmitted by the market. In the absence of inflation, the price system should translate the shifting patterns of consumer demand into price signals to which producers respond in order to plan current and future output levels. If demand for a product rises, the higher price indicates the desirability of switching existing production capacity to producing the goods or of laying down new capacity.

Under inflation, however, the producer may lose confidence that the correct signals are being transmitted, especially if the prices of goods and services inflate at different rates. He may thus be inclined to delay undertaking new investment. This applies particularly if price rises are unexpected and erratic.

Equally, it becomes more difficult to evaluate the performance of whole businesses and individual segments when prices are inflating. A poor operating performance may be masked by price inflation, especially if the price of the product sold is increasing at a rate faster than prices in general or if operating costs are inflating more slowly. The rate of return on capital achieved by a business is most usefully expressed in real terms by removing the effect on profits of generally rising prices (or better still, the effect of company-specific inflation). The capital base of the company should also be expressed in meaningful terms. A poor profit result may translate into a high ROI if the capital base is measured in historic terms. Unless these sorts of adjustment are made, inflation hinders the attempt to measure company performance on a consistent basis and thus can cloud the judgement of providers of capital in seeking out the most profitable areas for investment.

15   Filtrex plc

Key answer tips

The first parts of (a) are textbook definitions, leading into a discussion as to the circumstances under which soft capital rationing may arise. To get maximum marks, clearly split your response to this into separate points (reasons).

The sentence that dictates the approach to (b)(i) is "Project A and C are mutually exclusive and no project can be sub-divided." This rules out the pure NPV/£ invested key factor analysis approach, and some trial and error is needed. Take care not to overrun here – even if you don't arrive at the actual optimal solution, a well-argued, logical approach will gain most of the marks.

Part (c) requires some imaginative thinking; whilst raising further finance is an obvious possibility (and you should be specific about the various methods to get good marks) the examiner will reward any alternatives solutions, such as that given in the answer.

(a)   *Hard capital rationing* applies when a firm is restricted from undertaking all apparently worthwhile investment opportunities by factors external to the company, and over which it has no control. These factors may include government monetary restrictions and the general economic and financial climate, for example, a depressed stock market, precluding a rights issue of ordinary shares.

Soft capital rationing applies when a company decides to limit the amount of capital expenditure which it is prepared to authorise. The capital budget becomes a control variable, which the company may relax if it chooses. Segments of divisionalised companies often have their capital budgets imposed by the main board of directors.

A company may purposely curtail its capital expenditure for a number of reasons:

(i)   It may consider that it has insufficient depth of management expertise to exploit all available opportunities without jeopardising the success of both new and ongoing operations.

(ii)   It may be deliberate board policy to restrict the capital budget to concentrate managerial attention on generating the very best and most carefully thought out and analysed proposals. In this regard, self-imposed capital rationing may be an exercise in quality control.

(iii)   Many companies adopt the policy of restraining capital expenditure to the amounts which can be generated by internal resources i.e. retained earnings and depreciation provisions (or in reality, cash flow). This reluctance to use the external capital markets may be due to a risk-averse attitude to financial gearing, possibly because of the operating characteristics of the industry e.g. high operating gearing in a cyclical industry. Alternatively, it may be due to reluctance to issue equity in the form of a rights issue, for fear of diluting earnings, or in the case of an unlisted company, reluctance to seek a quotation owing to the time and expense involved and the dilution of ownership.

(b)   (i)   Assuming Filtrex wishes to maximise the wealth of its shareholders, it will seek the set of investment projects with the highest combined NPVs.

As a first approximation, it may examine the projects ranked according to their estimated NPVs, and select the projects with the highest NPVs, consistent with the budget limitation. However, this approach would confine the programme to project E alone, which apart from losing any benefits of diversification, is a solution which can be improved upon. This is because it overlooks the relationship between the NPV itself and the amount of capital required to yield the estimated NPV. Under capital rationing, it is often considered desirable to examine the productivity of each pound of scarce capital invested in the various projects. This information is given by the profitability index (PI). The ranking of the five projects according to their PIs is:

A	65/150	=	0.43
B	50/120	=	0.42
C	80/200	=	0.40
D	30/80	=	0.37
E	120/400	=	0.30

Moving down the ranking, Filtrex would select projects A and B, but then, due to the indivisibility problem, and also the fact that projects A and C are mutually exclusive, it would have to depart from the rankings and move down as far as D, where after the remaining project E is too demanding of capital. The selected programme of ABD would require an outlay of £350,000 and generate an NPV of £145,000. £50,000 of scarce capital would remain unspent and according to the stated policy, would be invested in short-term assets. Although of low risk, these offer a return less than the 18% required by shareholders. Consequently it might be preferable to return this unspent capital to shareholders in the form of a dividend or share repurchase, if shareholders are able to invest for higher returns in alternative activities. Perhaps, closer liaison with major shareholders is required to determine their preferences.

It is possible to improve on both of the previous selections by trial and error, in an attempt to utilise the whole of the capital budget. The optimal selection is BCD which offers a joint NPV of £160,000. However, even this result is suspect as it relies on evaluating the projects at the rate of return required in the absence of rationing, in this case, 18% post-tax. This neglects the impact of capital rationing on the cost of capital – if apparently worthwhile projects are rejected, there is an opportunity cost in the form of the returns otherwise obtainable on the rejected projects. Projects should be evaluated at the discount rate reflecting the rate of return on the best of the rejected projects. Unfortunately, until the evaluation and selection is made, this remains an unknown! Unless project indivisibility is a problem, ranking and selection using the internal rate of return (IRR) will yield the same solution – it would therefore be helpful to find the IRR for each project.

(ii) In addition to IRRs, other information which may aid the decision-maker might include the following.

    (1) Whether the rationing is likely to apply over the long-term, in which case,

    (2) The degree of postponability of projects should be more closely assessed i.e. whether a project can be postponed and the impact of postponement on its profitability. If projects can be postponed, it may be desirable for Filtrex to select projects in the base period offering a rapid return flow of cash in order to provide funds to enable investment in postponed projects in the next time period. In other words, it would be helpful to examine the cash flow profiles of these projects and hence their rates of payback.

    (3) The respective degrees of risk of these projects. It is implied that all projects have a similar degree of risk which is unlikely in practice, especially for the types of new product development planned by Filtrex. A capital-constrained company may use its limited access to finance to justify rejecting a high risk activity, especially if it is reliant on subsequent cash flows to finance postponed projects.

    (4) The likelihood of obtaining marginal supplies of finance and on what terms.

(c) There are two basic ways in which a company in Filtrex's position might still manage to exploit more projects. On one hand, it can involve other parties in the project, and on the other, it can resolve to seek outside capital.

Sharing the projects

(i) To the extent that some part of the project(s) still require further development e.g. design and market research, some of this work can be sub-contracted to specialist agencies, who may be able to perform the work at lower cost, or even to take payment out of the project cash flows.

(ii) The production and/or sale of the products can be licensed or franchised to another party, with Filtrex arranging to receive a royalty or a percentage of sales. This is particularly appropriate for overseas activities.

(iii) A joint venture could be mounted with a competitor, although for commercial reasons, it is often safer to arrange such alliances with companies outside the industry, or with overseas companies wishing to penetrate the UK market. Clearly, such an agreement would have to be carefully negotiated.

(iv) The patent rights to one or more products could be sold and the purchaser allowed to develop the projects.

Raising external finance

(i) A certain amount of marginal finance could be squeezed out of more intensive use of working capital, although this could be counter-productive e.g. reducing credit periods for customers may lose sales.

(ii) Some equipment could be leased.

(iii) If Filtrex has assets of sufficient quality, it may be possible to raise a mortgage or issue debentures secured on these assets.

(iv) Alternatively, good quality property assets could be sold to a financial institution and their continued use secured via a leaseback arrangement.

(v) Filtrex might approach official sources of aid such as a regional development agency, if relevant, or perhaps the European Investment Bank.

(vi) Filtrex might approach a venture capitalist such as 3i, which specialises in extending development capital to small-to-medium-sized firms. However, they may require an equity stake, and possibly insist on placing an appointee on the Board to monitor their interests.

(vii) Filtrex may decide to seek a Stock Exchange quotation, either on the main market or the AIM. However, this would be time-consuming and costly, and involve releasing a substantial part of the equity (less for the AIM) to a wider body of shareholders.

16   Armcliff Ltd

Key answer tips

In part (a) the first part of the data in the question relates to current operations - try to think why the examiner has given you this. The requirement is to determine whether the proposed project is attractive to *Armcliff* - not the parent company. Presumably what will make a project attractive to a division's management is one that will improve their current performance measure. Thus it is useful to know what the current level of ARR being achieved. This can then be compared with the project ARR.

Remember that the ARR is a financial accounting based measure - returns are in terms of accounting profits, and investments valued at balance sheet amounts - you must try to put all "relevant cost" principles to the back of your mind. Whilst there are various possible definitions of the ARR (a point that can be raised in (b)) here you are given precise directions, so make sure you follow them. Both average profits and average investment need to be ascertained

Don't forget to conclude by comparison with both current and required rates of return.

In part (b) the question requires you to show both theoretical and practical knowledge about investment appraisal methods. Your points must be made in sufficient depth to convince the examiner you actually understand the relevance of what you are saying. *Why is the use of accounting profits potentially a problem?*

In part (c), even though this is a examining a general area of credit management, try wherever you can to relate your points to the business in the question - it is stated that Armcliff intends to extend its credit to improve sales. Again make sure that you explain points enough to get the marks available, whilst still offering sufficient variety. Note that it is not enough simply to say that the advantages of APR is its simplicity. With spreadsheets, this is hardly going to be a consideration. Show instead that you appreciate that mangers are influenced by the methods used for their performance measurement - both internally and externally.

(a)   **Current return on capital employed**

= Operating profit/capital employed = £20m/(£75m + £25m) = £20m/£100m = 20%

Analysis of the project

Project capital requirements are £14m fixed capital plus £0.5m stocks. The annual depreciation charge (straight line) is:

(£14m – expected residual value of £2m)/4 = £3m pa

Profit profile (£m)

Year	1	2	3	4
Sales	$(5.00 \times 2m)$ = 10.00	$(4.50 \times 1.8m)$ = 8.10	$(4.00 \times 1.6m)$ = 6.40	$(3.50 \times 1.6m)$ = 5.60
Operating costs	(2.00)	(1.80)	(1.60)	(1.60)
Fixed costs	(1.50)	(1.35)	(1.20)	(1.20)
Depreciation	(3.00)	(3.00)	(3.00)	(3.00)
Profit	3.50	1.95	0.60	(0.20)

Capital employed (start-of-year):

Fixed	14.00	11.00	8.00	5.00
Stocks	0.50	0.50	0.50	0.50
Total capital employed	14.50	11.50	8.50	5.50

$$\text{Average rate of return} = \frac{\text{Average profit}}{\text{Average capital employed}} = \frac{£5.85/4}{£40.0/4} = \frac{£1.46}{£10.0} = 14.6\%$$

Note that if debtors were to be included in the definition of capital employed, this would reduce the calculated rate of return, while the inclusion of creditors would have an offsetting effect. However, using the ARR criterion as defined, the proposal has an expected return above the minimum stipulated by Shevin plc. It is unlikely that the managers of Armcliff will propose projects which offer a rate of return below the present 20% even where the expected return exceeds the minimum of 10%. To undertake projects with returns in this range will depress the overall divisional return and cast managerial performance in a weaker light.

However, it is unlikely that the senior managers of the Armcliff subsidiary would want to undertake the project.

(b)   (i)   The ARR can be expressed in a variety of ways, and is therefore susceptible to manipulation. Although the question specifies average profit to average capital employed, many other variants are possible e.g. average profit to initial capital, which would raise the computed rate of return.

It is also susceptible to variation in accounting policy by the same firm over time, or as between different firms at a point in time. For example, different methods of depreciation produce different profit figures and hence different rates of return.

Perhaps, most fundamentally, it is based on accounting profits expressed net of deduction for depreciation provisions, rather than cash flows. This effectively results in double-counting for the initial outlay i.e. the capital cost is allowed for twice over, both in the numerator of the ARR calculation and also in the denominator. This is likely to depress the measured profitability of a project and result in rejection of some worthwhile investment.

Finally, because it simply averages the profits, it makes no allowance for the timing of the returns from the project.

(ii)   The continuing use of the ARR method can by explained largely by its utilisation of balance sheet and profit-and-loss-account magnitudes familiar to managers, namely 'profit' and 'capital employed'. In addition, the impact of the project on a company's financial statements can also be specified. Return on capital employed is still the commonest way in which business unit performance is measured and evaluated, and is certainly the most visible to shareholders. It is thus not surprising that some managers may be happiest in expressing project attractiveness in the same terms in which their performance will be reported to shareholders, and according to which they will be evaluated and rewarded.

(c)   Armcliff intends to achieve a sales increase by extending its debtor collection period. This policy carries several dangers. It implies that credit will be extended to customers for whom credit is an important determinant of supplier selection, hinting at financial instability on their part. Consequently, the risk of later than expected, or even no payment, is likely to increase. Although losses due to default are limited to the incremental costs of making these sales rather than the invoiced value, Armcliff should recognise that there is an opportunity cost involved in tying up capital for lengthy periods. In addition, companies which are slow payers often attempt to claim discounts to which they are not entitled. Armcliff may then face the difficult choice between acquiescence to such demands versus rejection, in which case, it may lose repeat sales.

The creditworthiness of customers can be assessed in several ways as follows.

Analysis of accounting statements

In the case of companies which publish their annual accounts, or file them at Companies House, key financial ratios can be examined to assess their financial stability. However, these almost certainly will be provided in arrears and may not give a true indication of the companies' current situation. Some customers may be prepared to supply more up-to-date accounts directly to the seller, although these are unlikely to have been audited.

Analysis of credit reports

It may be possible to obtain detailed assessment of the creditworthiness of customers from other sources, such as their bankers, specialist credit assessment agencies such as Dun & Bradstreet, and from trade sources such as other companies who supply them. These assessments are likely to be more up-to-date than company accounts, but will inevitably be more subjective.

Previous experience

If the firm has supplied the customer in the past, its previous payment record will be available.

Cash-only trial period

If accounting and other data is sparse, and there is no previous trading record with the customer, the seller may offer a trial period over which cash is required, but if the payment record is acceptable (e.g. if the customer's cheques always clear quickly), further transactions may be conducted on credit.

Background information

General background information on the industry in which the customer operates will generate insights into the financial health of companies in that sector, and by implication, that of the customer. Many agencies supply such information, although it should only be used as a back-up to other assessments.

17   Burley plc

Key answer tips

In part (a), for the DCF techniques, you first need to identify the relevant cash flows, using the usual principles. These will include tax effects (with no delay, you are told to assume, and the capital allowance effects have already been accounted for). However, before discounting these for the NPV, you must adjust the discount rate as it is given as a nominal (or money) rate – i.e. incorporating inflation - and the cash flows and evaluation are in real terms, excluding inflation.

The simple annuity nature of the project means that the IRR can be estimated using annuity tables, rather than the less accurate interpolation formula. The latter is acceptable, but is more time consuming.

In part (b) your answer should start with an explanation of the aims and mechanics of sensitivity analysis, as applied to project appraisal. Then try to think of as many problems as you can with the procedure - the examiner was expecting at least 4. Think about how things may change/fluctuate in practice and whether the procedure can properly deal with these.

Part (c) requires an application of sensitivity analysis to two particular factors in your NPV computation. The basic approach is to go back to your computation, substitute a variable for the element now being varied, and find the value for which the NPV becomes 0. In order to comment sensibly on your results, it is more useful to evaluate the relative (%) change this represents. This will allow you to identify the more critical of the two factors, and your advice should focus around its management.

(a)   In a real-terms analysis, the real rate of return required by shareholders has to be used, is found as follows:

$$\frac{1 + \text{nominal rate}}{1 + \text{inflation rate}} - 1 = (1.14/1.055) - 1 = 8\%$$

The relevant operating costs per box, after removing the allocated overhead are $(8.00 + 2.00 + 1.50 + 2.00) = £13.50$. The costs of the initial research etc are not relevant as they are sunk. The set-up cost has already been adjusted for tax reliefs but the annual cash flows will be taxed at 33%.

The NPV of the project is given by:

$$\begin{aligned}
\text{NPV}(£) &= \text{[PV of after-tax cash inflows]} - \text{[set-up costs]} \\
&= 0.15\text{m} [20 - 13.50] (1 - 33\%) \text{ PVIFA}_{8.5} - 2\text{m} \\
&= 0.65\text{m} (3.993) - 2\text{m} \\
&= +2.6\text{m} - 2\text{m} \\
&= +0.6\text{m i.e.} + £0.6\text{m}
\end{aligned}$$

Hence, the project is attractive according to the NPV criterion.

The IRR is simply the discount rate, R, which generates a zero NPV i.e. the solution to the expression:

$$\text{NPV} = 0 = 0.65\text{m (PVIFA}_{R.5}) - 2\text{m}$$
whence $\text{PVIFA}_{R.5} = 2\text{m}/0.65 = 3.077$

To the nearest 1%, IRR = 19%. Since this exceeds the required return of 8% in real terms, the project is acceptable.

(b) A sensitivity analysis examines the impact of specified variations in key factors on the initially-calculated NPV. The starting point for a sensitivity analysis is the NPV using the 'most likely' value or 'best estimate' for each key variable. Taking the resulting 'base case' NPV as a reference point, the aim is to identify those factors which have the greatest impact on the profitability of the project if their realised values deviate from expectations. This intelligence signals to managers where they should arrange to focus resources in order to secure favourable outcomes.

Problems with sensitivity analysis include the following.

- It deals with changes in isolation, and tends to ignore interactions between variables. For example, advertising may alter the volume of output as well as influencing price, and price and volume are usually related.

- It assumes that specified changes persist throughout the project lifetime - e.g. a postulated 10% change in volume may be projected for each year of operation. In reality, variations in key factors tend to fluctuate randomly.

- It may reveal as critical, factors over which managers have no control, thus offering no guide to action. Nonetheless, it may still help to clarify the risks to which the project is exposed.

- It does not provide a decision rule e.g. it does not indicate the maximum acceptable levels of sensitivity.

- It gives no indication of the likelihood of the variations under consideration. Variations in a factor which are potentially devastating but have a minimal chance of occurring provide little cause for concern.

(c) The values for which NPV becomes zero are found by calculating the break-even values for the selected variables. Once determined, these give an indication of the sensitivity of the NPV to changes in these factors

    (i) *Price (P)*

$$
\begin{aligned}
\text{NPV} \quad &= \quad 0 \quad = \quad 0.15m\,[P - 13.50]\,(1 - 33\%)\,(PVIFA8,5) - 2m \\
\text{whence} \quad &= \quad 0 \quad = \quad [0.15mP - 2.025]\,(2.675) - 2m \\
& \quad 0 \quad = \quad 0.4P - 5.42m - 2m \\
& \quad 0.4P \quad = \quad 7.42m \\
& \quad P \quad = \quad £18.55m
\end{aligned}
$$

This means price can drop by [£20 – £18.55]/£20 = 7% from the level assumed in the initial evaluation without making the NPV negative.

    (ii) *Volume (V)*

Using a similar procedure:

$$
\begin{aligned}
\text{NPV} \quad &= \quad 0 \quad = \quad V[20 - 13.50]\,(1 - 33\%)\,(PVIFA8,5) - 2m \\
& \quad 0 \quad = \quad V\,[17.39m] - 2m \\
& \quad V \quad = \quad 2m/17.39m \\
& \quad \quad = \quad 115,000
\end{aligned}
$$

This means volume can drop by [150,000 - 115,000]/150,000 = 23% from the level assumed in the initial evaluation without making the NPV negative.

The results suggest that the NPV of the project is more sensitive to price variations than to changes in volume. Since price seems to be the more critical factor, management might plan to engage in price support measures like advertising and promotional expenditure. It might also attempt to obtain exclusive supply contracts with retailers, although these could violate competition regulations. Measures such as these are likely to be costly, in turn reducing the NPV of the project. It is possible that by making such adjustments, other variables become more critical, necessitating further analysis. At this stage, we might infer that, given the project has a positive NPV of £0.6m, Burley could afford to engage in promotional activity with a present value marginally below this amount over the lifetime of the project.

18   Deighton plc

Key answer tips

In part (a) Linton's evaluation is on the basis of an accounting based return on investment, and you are asked to identify the mistakes in the evaluation. The clues to the 'mistakes' lie in both the 'further details' given in the question, and the requirement of (b). The examiner was looking for an unfavourable comparison of the ROI with the theoretically sounder DCF approach, using the information to highlight differences re cash flows, timings, appraisal rates, time value etc. However, the examiner allowed the alternative approach of identifying mistakes in the calculation of the ROI itself.

Part (b) – a standard NPV requirement here, including tax and inflation (although, as the examiner says, cash flows and discount rate had already been adjusted for the latter, and thus it could be ignored). The layout of the question lends itself to a horizontal approach to tabulation of cash flows (a cash budget), although you can use whichever layout and order of workings you prefer, as long as it is clear. The tax effects of the individual WDA's can, for example, be incorporated within the main NPV computation. Make sure you conclude your computations with a written comment.

Note that where the examiner uses the word 'nominal' in this answer when describing discount rates, he means 'money cost of capital.

Report submitted to: Finance Director, Deighton plc

From:

Date:

Subject: Investment Project NT17

The above investment project was rejected by the former management of Linton Ltd, but it appears that the evaluation (attached) was flawed. This report identifies these flaws and re-evaluates the proposal which appears to be worthwhile. As the market opportunity is still open, I recommend acceptance of the project.

(a)   Mistakes by Linton

1   The initial investment in working capital should be offset by a working capital release in the final year, assuming a constant level of stock-holding until the last year.

2   The interest cost, although a cash outflow in reality, should be subsumed in the overall cost of capital. Linton's evaluation confused the investment decision with the financing decision. If the project were evaluated by the new owners, Deighton's required return of 20% would be the correct rate of discount (assuming no impact on Deighton's risk).

3   No scrap value was shown for either the old equipment, or the new machine at the end of four years.

4   Depreciation is not a cash outflow. By deducting the depreciation charge, Linton has double-counted for the capital cost.

5   However, the annual depreciation allowances (WDA) do affect the tax outflows. These were ignored.

6   No tax delay was allowed for.

7   The overhead charge was over-stated. Only half of the amount charged appears to be incremental.

8   The market research cost, whatever it relates to, is irrelevant i.e. it is sunk, unless a buyer could be found for the report.

(b)   In the following solution, the tax allowances in relation to the initial outlay on equipment are evaluated separately. (Other approaches are acceptable.)

The tax-adjusted cost of the capital expenditure can be found by deducting the present value of the tax savings generated by exploiting the writing-down allowance from the initial outlay. It is assumed that the available allowances can be set off against profits immediately i.e. beginning in the financial year in which the acquisition of the asset occurs. This yields five sets of WDAs as the project straddles five tax years. The solution assumes no scrap values.

Item (£'000)	0	1	2	3	4	5
			Year			
Allowance claimed at 25%	225	169	127	95	284	
Written-down value	675	506	379	284	0	
Tax saving at 33%		74	56	42	31	94
Discount factor at 20%		0.833	0.694	0.579	0.482	0.402
Present value		62	39	24	15	38

Present value of tax savings = £178,000

The effective cost of the equipment is:

[Nominal outlay   –   present value of tax savings] = [£900,000 - £178,000] = £722,000

The cash flow profile is as follows.

Item (£'000)	0	1	2	3	4	5
Equipment/scrap (net)	(722)				0	
Sales		1,400	1,600	1,800	1,000	
Materials		(400)	(450)	(500)	(250)	
Direct labour		(400)	(450)	(500)	(250)	
Inc overheads		(50)	(50)	(50)	(50)	
Operating cash flow		550	650	750	450	
Tax at 33%		-	(182)	(215)	(248)	(149)
Working capital	(100)				100	
Net cash flow	(822)	550	468	535	302	(149)
Discount factor at 20%		0.833	0.694	0.579	0.482	0.402
Present value	(822)	458	325	310	146	(60)

NPV = £357,000

Recommendation

Thus, the equipment purchase is acceptable and should be undertaken, although an analysis of its risk is also recommended.

19   Chromex plc

Key answer tips

Although there are various methods for calculating payback for part (a), they all use cash flows rather than profit, so your first job is to convert the operating profit figure given to a cash flow, as far as the information allows. You then have to decide whether to include the labour savings or not - if you decide not to, briefly explain why, so the examiner will know you haven't just ignored them.

In part (b) you may not have come across this sort of requirement before, but it offers some easy marks. Think of any NPV calculation you've done before and the information/data used - then see what is missing from the information you have here.

In part (c), even if you don't know much detail about the workings of the Monopolies and Mergers Commission, you should be able to give an outline of its purpose and what it may do. Note the role of the EU in this context.

In part (d), for 'financial performance' do not read solely 'profitability'. This is one aspect, certainly, but liquidity, gearing and shareholder returns are also important. Pick four ratios that cover this range, briefly explaining how they contribute to the evaluation. Note that the balance of the examiner's answer between the ratios and the commentary does not reflect the marking scheme, where only 1 mark is given for the latter. The discussion in the answer is, however, useful for future reference.

(a)   Payback period should be based on cash flows, that is, the cash generated from operations, and the capital invested by Chromex.

Profit differs from cash flow to the extent that depreciation has been charged in the accounts. The sum received from the sale of assets merely reduces the size of the capital investment.

This gives the following figures for the payback calculation (assuming that no further re-investment in plant is required):

Investment cost = £150 million – £10 million = £140 million

If the labour cost savings are ignored:
Annual cash flows from Bexell's operations post take over	= £10 million + £0.5 million
	= £10.5 million
Payback period (in years)	= 140/10.5
	= 13.33 years or 13 years 4 months

This is a conservative estimate in that it ignores the possible cash flow effects of the anticipated operating savings from reduced labour costs. If the savings are assumed to have a cash flow value of £700,000, this gives an adjusted figure for cash flow as follows:

Annual cash flow   = £10.5 million + £0.7 million
                          = £11.2 million

Payback period is therefore equal to:
140/11.2   = 12.5 years or 12 years and 6 months

The inclusion of the labour cost savings therefore reduces the payback period by 10 months.

(b)   Additional information required would include:

- specification of a time scale for the appraisal
- forecast cash flow details, year by year, for period specified in the time scale
- an estimate of the cost of capital for Bexell and the combined group
- a forecast of the realisable value of the investment at the end of the time period
- details of corporation tax rates, capital allowances and tax relief on debt finance
- forecast inflation rates, to facilitate calculation of an adjusted NPV.

(c)   The government might seek to intervene in the take-over bid because of fears that the market share of the combined group would constitute a monopoly, which would not be in the interests of UK consumers. The case might thus be referred to the Competition Commission for further investigation. The Commission investigates all such take-overs in relation to their anticipated effect on the 'public interest'. For example, the Commission may take the view that the take-over reduces the level of choice available to buyers of bicycles in the UK to an unacceptable level. In such instances it has the power to request changes in the terms of a deal, in order to protect the public interest. Historical evidence suggests that when the Competition Commission's predecessor, the Monopolies and Mergers Commission, became involved in reviewing a bid or merger proposal, it is frequently the case that the bid is delayed, sometimes for several years.

The UK government may also intervene, because it is required to do so in order to enforce EU regulations on fair competition. The European Union sets its own rules for maintenance of free competition, and the control of monopoly power, which are then enforceable throughout the whole of the Union.

(d)   A great number of ratios might be suitable for this purpose, depending on the specific type of financial performance which is being compared. Amongst those suitable for such a purpose are as follows.

- Return on equity
- Asset turnover (by classes of asset type)
- Gross/net profit margins
- Stock days
- Debtor days
- Interest cover
- Dividend cover
- Financial gearing
- Operating gearing
- P/E ratio

The ratios selected can be justified on the grounds that they measure the key determinants of financial performance, namely:

(1)   the company's profit performance (gross and net profit margins) and the returns it offers its investors (ROE & P/E ratio).

(2)   liquidity, which will affect its ability to continue trading: stock/debtor days and dividend and interest cover

(3)   capital structure and level of business risk: financial and operating gearing.

A comparison, which is to be used to assess the relative performance of a particular company, should be based on data from companies in the same sector, because other businesses in other sectors may have different production systems, operating technology and sources of finance. As a result, the average rates of return, the scale of operations, and the risks of a business will vary from sector to sector. For example, a retail bank may face very high fixed costs, as it has a large branch network to support. In contrast, a franchised restaurant chain will have very low fixed costs, because fixed assets are owned by the franchisees and not the main company. In such cases, judgement on the relative levels of operating gearing in the two businesses would be impossible, because of the variation in the cost structures. Similarly, the risks of operating a shoe factory are fundamentally different from those of a chemical plant, and so the financial ratios generated by each operation will differ widely.

At the same time it is useful to compare ratios with firms of differing sizes (in the one sector) because market dynamics and profitability may well be linked to the scale of a company's operations. For example, in some product markets larger companies may report higher net profit margins as a result of being able to exploit scale economies in production or distribution, or the benefits of vertical integration. By contrast, in other markets, specialisation and niche marketing may increase margins. Comparing ratios amongst companies of differing sizes facilitates some analysis of the factors, which can add to profit.

20   Prime Printing plc

Key answer tips

In part (a) take care not to be too general - you are being asked to explain the cash flow characteristics of the three options, so go through each saying what cash flows will arise, and when. The tax aspect of each can be included as you go through, or it can be discussed at the end.

Part (b) is a fairly standard lease or buy problem, also incorporating the investment decision. The most important principle here is the separation of the two decisions. The investment decision uses operating cash flows (cash savings) and capital cash flows (purchase cost/scrap proceeds of machine), with related tax effects (additional tax arising from savings and tax savings from capital allowances). These are discounted at the company's cost of capital. The finance decision concentrates on the cash flows you have discussed in (a), which are discounted at the post-tax cost of borrowing. Note that you can either include the tax savings from capital allowances as a direct benefit of the buy option, or as an opportunity cost of the lease option (but not both!). Don't forget to summarise your results and recommendations in words at the end. There are a number of different ways of calculating the comparative cost of the lease versus purchase, but all methods yield the same result. You will not be disadvantaged by the use of a specific method of approach.

(a)   A finance lease is usually arranged via a finance house, with the intention of providing a business with the funding to acquire an asset. The time scale of a finance lease is set such that at the end of the initial leasing period, the lessor has more than recovered the cost of the asset. At such a time, the lessee is given the option to continue leasing the asset at a nominal rental, or sell the item on behalf of the lessor, and retain the bulk of the proceeds.

The cash flow pattern of a finance lease is such that cash flow is evenly spaced throughout the leasing period, and the company acquiring an asset is not therefore required to pay out a large sum of cash in one go in order to obtain the use of that asset. The interest rate charged for the finance is usually fixed for the duration of the lease, and the predictability of the outgoing cash flow in such circumstances can be very useful in helping smaller companies to plan their finances. One possible area of uncertainty in relation to fact that under such an agreement the lessee is responsible for maintenance costs of the equipment/machinery. Such costs may not be readily predictable, and be related to level of usage.

A cash flow advantage may arise because of the tax treatment of finance leases. Some businesses may be earning insufficient profits to allow them to take advantage of all the capital allowances that may be available to them if they choose to purchase machinery and equipment outright. Where a finance lease is used, no capital allowances may be claimed, but instead the company may claim tax relief against the full leasing cost. The lower annual cost may mean that the company is able to maximise its use of tax relief, and so reduce the effective cost of the leased equipment.

An alternative source of medium-term finance is a bank loan. In terms of cash flow, the loan agreement will define the level of regular repayments, which will be a mix of capital repayment plus an interest component. The loan may be subject to either a fixed or a variable rate of interest. In the latter case, the repayments may change over the life of the loan, if interest rates alter. Under such circumstances the cash flow pattern is clearly less certain than under a finance lease based on a fixed finance charge.

The company can claim capital allowances on the purchase, and so obtain tax relief to reduce its mainstream corporation tax liability. As indicated above, such tax relief is only of value if the company has profits against which the relief can be offset. This means that the tax paying position of a company plays a critical role in determining the comparative advantage of leasing versus borrowing to pay for a business asset.

A third source of finance to pay for acquisition of a business asset is the use of existing cash holdings/funds on deposit. Where funds are withdrawn from deposit, there will be a cash-flow impact in terms of the loss of regular interest receivable. Furthermore, the conversion of the current asset of cash into a fixed asset (piece of equipment) alters the structure of the company's balance sheet. The outflow of a single large cash payment will reduce the liquidity of the business (at least temporarily). If cash-flows from operations are adequate to meet regular cash outgoings, this will not matter. If, however, there is a potential cash shortfall, this is not a sensible source of funding for asset purchases. As with loan finance, the purchase of the asset for cash means that capital allowances can be claimed, and the same considerations on the usefulness of those allowances need to be taken into account.

(b)   **Workings**

(i)   *Capital Allowances*

		Allowances £
Year 1	25% × 120,000	30,000
Year 2	75% × 30,000	22,500
Year 3	75% × 22,500	16,875
Year 4	75% × 16,875	12,656
		82,031
Year 5	Balancing allowance (120,000 – 82,031)	£37,969

(ii)   *Taxable profits and tax liability*

Year	Cash savings	Capital allowance £'000	Taxable profits	Tax at 30%
1	50	30	20	06
2	50	22.5	27.5	08.25
3	50	16.875	33.125	09.94
4	50	12.656	37.34	11.20
5	50	37.969	12.03	03.61

(iii)   *Tax savings on capital allowances*

Year	Capital allowance £	Tax relief at 30% £
1	30,000	
2	22,500	9,000
3	16,875	6,750
4	12,656	5,063
5	37,969	3,797
6		11,390

◈ FOULKS*lynch*

Acquisition decision

Year	Equipment £'000	Cash savings £'000	Tax £'000	Net cash flow £'000	Discount factor at 15%	Present value £'000
0	(120)			(120)	1.000	(120)
1		50		50	0.870	43.50
2		50	(6)	44	0.756	33.26
3		50	(8.25)	41.75	0.658	27.47
4		50	(9.94)	40.06	0.572	22.91
5		50	(11.2)	38.80	0.497	19.28
6			(3.61)	(3.61)	0.432	(1.56)
					NPV	24.86

The NPV is positive and so the company should acquire the machine.

Present value of purchase

Discounting cash-flows at the after tax cost of borrowing i.e. $13\% \times 0{\cdot}7 = 9{\cdot}1\%$ (say 9%).

Note: This is approximate, as tax relief is lagged by one year.

Year	Item	Cash flow £	Discount factor at 9%	Present value £
0	Purchase cost	(120,000)	1.000	(120,000)
2	Tax savings from allowances	9,000	0.842	17,578
3		6,750	0.772	15,211
4		5,063	0.708	13,585
5		3,797	0.650	12,468
6		11,390	0.596	16,788
			NPV of cost	(94,370)

Present value of leasing

Year	Lease payment £	Tax savings £	Discount at 9%	Present value £
0 – 4	(28,000)		4·239	(118,692)
1 – 5		8,400	3·890	32,676
			Net PV leasing	(86,016)

This means that it is cheaper to lease the machine than to purchase it via the bank loan.

21   Benland plc

Key answer tips

This will be quickly recognised as a DCF question, so use your initial read through of the information in the question efficiently. Note the types of cash flow that arise and any unusual points that may be missed later – such as the fact that the raw material (tyres) will actually represent an income rather than a cost, the existence of the non-tax-deductible penalty clause, and the fact that seals are rising by 10% wholly due to volume rises (so other volume dependent cash flows will increase by 10% as well). A horizontal layout for the DCF computation is probably best, with workings shown separately, either before or after the main computation. Make and state any necessary assumptions.

In part (b), the requirement to "discuss" probably excludes detailed sensitivity computations – it is fairly clear which cash flows are most significant. The main marks will be awarded for the discussion on risk management.

(a)   *Workings*

Starting from year one, and taking into account the sales increases of 10% per year:

Year	Receipts from garages (£'000)	Savings on particles (£'000)	Tyre processing costs (£'000)
1	3,200	280	3,003
2	3,520	308	3,299
3	3,872	339	3,625
4	4,259	373	3,983
5	4,685	410	4,377

Tax Cash Flow (excluding capital allowances)

£'000

Year	1	2	3	4	5
Receipts	3,200	3,520	3,872	4,259	4,685
Savings	280	308	339	373	410
Costs	(3,003)	(3,299)	(3,625)	(3,983)	(4,377)
Taxable Cash Flow	477	529	586	649	718
Tax at 33%	(157)	(175)	(193)	(214)	(237)

Capital Allowances and Associated Tax savings
Assume purchase of the machine in year 0, and claim of the first capital allowance in the same year. This gives rise to the first cash flow from tax savings on allowances in year one.

£'000

Year	Allowance (from preceding year)	Tax saving
1	265	87
2	199	66
3	149	49
4	112	37
5	84	28
6	136	45

	£'000
Investment cost	1,060
Receipts from disposal	115
Total	945

Balancing allowance   = (945–809)
                       = £136,000

Cash Flows
£'000

Year	0	1	2	3	4	5	6
Machine purchase/sale	(1,060)					115	
Tax savings							
On Machine Purchase		87	66	49	37	28	45
Processing costs		(3,003)	(3,299)	(3,625)	(3,983)	(4,377)	
Savings on particles		280	308	339	373	410	
Receipts from garages		3,200	3,520	3,872	4,259	4,685	
Penalty charge	(100)						
Tax on cash flows (excluding capital allowances)		(157)	(175)	(193)	(214)	(237)	

Net cash flow	(1,160)	564	438	460	493	647	(192)
Disc factor	1.0	0.893	0.797	0.712	0.636	0.567	0.507
PV of cash flow	(1,160)	504	349	328	343	367	(97)

Net present value = £634,000

The net present value of the investment is positive, and so it is advisable that Benland purchase the machine.

(b) The most important costs are those of the equipment itself and the tyre processing. The final sales volumes and estimated receipts from garages per tonne of tyres recycled are also critical in determining the viability of the investment. A significant change in any of these figures could alter the attractiveness of the investment.

The purchase price of the equipment is of critical importance, but this is a one-off cost, and so the time scale of its variability is strictly limited. Once Benland has signed a purchase contract, the cost is fixed. In order to avoid any risk of a price change in the immediate short term, Benland should ask the supplier to provide a fixed price quotation, which remains valid for a prescribed period. As long as the purchase is made within the defined period, the company can be certain of the price to be paid. The second-hand value of the equipment at the end of the investment period is not of great significance, as its estimated present value is just £65,000, or 10% of the net present value.

In order to avoid the risk of large scale changes in processing costs, it may be possible for Benland to use engineering calculations to assess the expected processing time, maintenance requirements, and yields per tonne of used tyres. (There is insufficient detail on the question to assess which of these aspects is most important in determining the overall cost.) It may also be possible to obtain general cost information from other users of similar equipment, in order to verify the accuracy of Benland's current estimates. Once production has commenced, statistical process controls can be used to help the company to accurately record the processing time and yields, and the amount of machine downtime can be recorded via job-sheets. In this way changes in costs can quickly be identified. If any costs change by a significant amount Benland may need to revise its NPV forecast, and if necessary look at the feasibility of disinvesting. The cash flow forecast suggests that the investment is feasible partly because processing costs are less than the receipts from garages for used tyre disposal. If this situation were to be reversed, then the viability of the investment may be altered.

Management of the cash flows from receipts from garages and other possible suppliers of the used tyres should be more straightforward. If there is a cost advantage to such parties relative to the cost of land-fill, then Benland can be assured of raw material supplies at a predictable cost. The only circumstances under which the revenue may become less certain is if sales of the playground equipment, and hence the company's demand for rubber particles, rose to a level beyond that which could be supplied from existing sources of used tyres. In such a case, the price paid for the tyres may increase, or the company may have to revert to the use of outside suppliers to meet the shortfall in supply. This seems unlikely, but Benland should formally assess the likelihood of sales reaching such high levels, and monitor the company's demand for particles relative to supply, in order to avoid any risk of a sudden large cost increase.

An aspect of the cash flow which is outside the control of Benland, but may nevertheless have a potentially significant effect on the investment's viability is the tax position. The appraisal is based on the assumption of tax allowances granted on the basis of 25% of the reducing balance, and a corporation tax rate of 33%. If either the allowances or the tax rate were to change, the NPV of the investment would be affected. For example, if tax allowances were altered to give a 100% first year allowance, then the cash flow impact of additional tax savings would be considerable. Conversely, if the tax rate is reduced to, say, 25%, then the tax savings created via the capital allowances would be reduced, but so also would the corporation tax payable on profits, and so the NPV would change. Assessing the likelihood of changes in the tax regime is difficult, as tax rates tend to reflect political opinion, but it is highly unlikely that tax rates would be dramatically changed. The tax aspects of the cash flow are important, but they must be viewed as of less significance than the equipment cost, processing costs and revenues already discussed.

Overall, the NPV of the project is sufficiently high to allow for some changes in all of the key variables without the risk of making the project non viable.

Costing systems and techniques (including decision making)

22   A polytechnic

Key answer tips

The flow diagram for part (a) is not difficult, but the time allowance for 3 marks does present problems. However, time spent on ensuring that a correct picture of the cost apportionments is depicted will not only gain these marks but help a great deal in answering part (b).

Part (b) is basically an arithmetic exercise. Good use of the flow diagram will help in breaking this down into a series of apportionments. The model answer uses a 'step' approach. Students should adopt this approach; any attempt to apportion all the costs in a single table is likely to fail.

There is no one answer for part (c). Use your common sense and make brief general statements.

(a)   **Flow diagram**

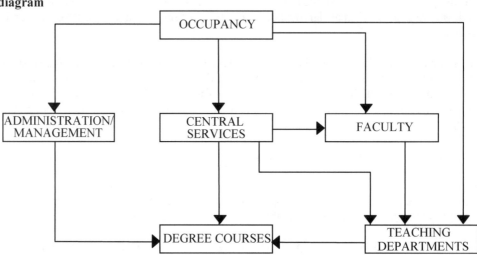

(b)   **Average cost per graduate**

Step 1

Apportion occupancy costs: $\left(\dfrac{£1,500,000}{37,500 \text{ sq ft}} = £40 \text{ per sq ft} \right)$

	£'000
Administration/Management	280
Central Services	120
Faculty	300
Teaching Departments	800
	1,500

Step 2

Apportion central services costs:

$\left(\dfrac{£1,000,000 + £120,000}{\text{External Costs } £1,600,000} \right) = 70\text{p per } £ \text{ of external cost}$

	£'000
Faculty	168
Teaching Departments	560
Degree Courses	392
	1,120

Step 3

Apportion teaching department costs (includes 100% of Faculty costs) and Administration/Management costs, to degree courses.

Teaching department: £800,000 + £560,000 + (£300,000 + £168,000 + £700,000) + £5,525,000 = £8,053,000

Administration/management: £280,000 + £1,775,000 = £2,055,000

Total degree courses costs: £8,053,000 + £2,055,000 + £392,000 = £10,500,000

Average polytechnic cost per student $= \dfrac{£10,500,000}{2,500 \text{ students}} = £4,200$

Step 4

Analyse £10,500,000 by degree course (in round £'000s).

	Business Studies	Mechanical Engineering	Catering Studies
	£'000	£'000	£'000
Teaching department	242	201	564
Administration/management	51	103	82
Central services (based on external costs)	22	34	22
	315	338	668
Average cost per graduate	£3,938	£6,760	£5,567

(c) **Discussion**

The average cost per graduate will differ from one degree course to another for several reasons, the most obvious of which is the very different nature of the courses.

The engineering and catering courses will require much greater use of expensive machinery and equipment, which in turn will need more room. In addition these courses will probably require much greater lecturer input than on the business studies courses. The much lower staff/student ratio will push up the teaching costs per student.

Another factor to be considered is the variability in the student numbers. This variable is unlikely to have an impact on many of the polytechnic costs, which are mainly fixed in nature. For example, if in the following year intake is up to sixty on the mechanical engineering degree, with a similar level of costs, the average cost per student would fall to nearly that being reported for a catering studies student.

These average cost figures must be interpreted with great care by the management. They give a 'rough' guide to the relative cost of degree courses but the arbitrary apportionments render them very nearly useless for decision-making. For decision-making, incremental costs are required.

23 Amazon plc

Key answer tips

This is a question that combines process costing with joint product pricing. However, it is a straightforward application of each of these topics, with losses but no work in progress and offers some easy marks for the reasonably well-prepared candidate. These can, however, also be easily lost by poor presentation or unclear workings!

(a) Cost per kg $= \dfrac{\text{Total cost} - \text{Scrap value of normal loss}}{\text{Expected output}} = \dfrac{3,500 + 4,340 - (700 \times 0.40)}{7,000 - (10\% \times 7,000)} = £1.20/\text{kg}$

Transfer to process 2 $= 6,430 \text{ kg} \times 1.20 = £7,716$

Expected output	$= 7,000 - (10\% \times 7,000) =$	6,300 kg
Actual output		6,430 kg
Abnormal gain		130 kg

Net gain = 130 kg × (1.20 − 0.40) = £104

(b)   *Costs of process 2*

		£
Transfer from process 1	6,430 × 1.20	7,716
Labour and overhead		12,129
		19,845
Less net income of by-product (1.80 − 0.30) × 430		645
		19,200

(i)   *Weight of output*   *Share of joint costs*

	kg		£
E	2,000	$\dfrac{2,000}{6,000} \times 19,200$	6,400
F	4,000	$\dfrac{4,000}{6,000} \times 19,200$	12,800
	6,000 kg		19,200

Cost/kg

Type E	£6,400/2,000kg = £3.20/kg
Type F	£12,800/4,000kg = £3.20/kg

Profits/(losses)

Type E	1,100kg × (7 − 3.20) = £4,180
Type F	3,200kg × (2.50 − 3.20) = (£2,240)

Stock values

Type E	(2,000kg − 1,100kg) × 3.20 = £2,880
Type F	(4,000kg − 3,200kg) × 3.20 = £2,560

(ii)   *Market value of output*   *Share of joint costs*

		£		£
Type E	2,000kg × £7 =	14,000	14/24 × 19,200	11,200
Type F	4,000kg × £2.50 =	10,000	10/24 × 19,200	8,000
		24,000		19,200

Cost/kg	Type E	£11,200/2,000kg	=	£5.60/kg
	Type F	£8,000/4,000kg	=	£2/kg

Profits	Type E	(7 − 5.60) × 1,100kg	=	£1,540
	Type F	(2.50 − 2) × 3,200kg	=	£1,600

Stock values	Type E	(2,000kg − 1,100kg) × 5.60	=	£5,040
	Type F	(4,000kg − 3,200kg) × 2	=	£1,600

(c)   The main purpose of apportioning joint costs is for financial reporting. We apportion the joint costs in order to calculate the stock value and the cost of sales. The main problem is that the choice of apportionment method is subjective and can have a profound effect on stock values and profits. For instance in part (b) above:

(1)   Type E was valued at £3.20/kg or £5.60/kg and gave a profit of £4,180 or £1,540.

(2)   Type F was valued at £3.20/kg or £2/kg and gave a loss of £2,240 or a profit of £1,600.

24   Miozip Co

Key answer tips

This is an average standard question but, having no 'units' with which to work, it does present problems.

Part (a) is the standard question about absorption costing with changing stock levels resulting in different profits. Don't lose easy marks by failing to present your answer in report format.

Part (b) is not difficult, but with no variable costs per unit with which to work, it is necessary to use total amounts after deducting the fixed factory overhead.

Part (c) is reasonably straightforward. Remember the problem of using pre-determined absorption rates in periods of changing activity levels.

In part (d), concentrate on the usefulness of marginal costs in decision-making (but full cost systems ensure that no costs are ignored).

(a)   **REPORT**

To: The Board of Directors, Miozip Co
From:
Subject: **Profitability**

From the summarised profit and loss accounts (estimated 20X2, budgeted 20X3), it is apparent that two periods with equal sales revenue are reporting profits/losses which differ by £210,000. The difference can be entirely attributed to the valuation of opening/closing stock.

The factory cost of goods sold for 20X2 is £60,000 lower than that expected for the level of sales achieved because of the lower overhead absorption rate used in 20X1. Some of the goods produced in this period, being attributed with a lower cost, were sold in 20X2. All units budgeted to be sold in 20X3 carry the full £3.60 overhead.

In addition, the level of activity budgeted in 20X3 (100,000 direct labour hours) is only two-thirds of that achieved in 20X2. This will result in an increased under-absorption of overhead charge of £150,000. This, together with the £60,000 above, accounts for the £210,000 differential.

(b)   **Marginal costing statement**

Workings

	£	%
20X1:		
Factory cost of production	1,000,000	100.00
Fixed factory overhead absorbed		
(£600,000 − £300,000)	300,000	30.00
∴ Other variable factory costs	700,000	70.00
20X2 (similar percentage for 20X3):		
Factory cost of production	975,000	100.00
Fixed factory overhead absorbed		
(£600,000 − £150,000)	450,000	46.15
∴ Other variable factory costs	525,000	53.85

◈ **FOULKS**_lynch_

Based on marginal costs:

	Actual 20X1		Estimated 20X2		Budgeted 20X3	
	£	£	£	£	£	£
Sales		1,350,000		1,316,250		1,316,250
Opening stock	70,000		140,000		192,500	
Variable factory cost of production	700,000		525,000		350,000	
	770,000		665,000		542,500	
Closing stock	(140,000)		(192,500)		(70,000)	
Variable cost of goods sold		630,000		472,500		472,500
Contribution		720,000		843,750		843,750
Fixed costs:						
Factory overheads		(600,000)		(600,000)		(600,000)
Administrative and financial costs		(220,000)		(220,000)		(220,000)
Net profit/(loss)		(100,000)		23,750		23,750

(c)   **Potential problems**

The decision to increase the selling price by using the cost-plus formula without considering the effect upon demand from customers, could result in an increase in the under-absorbed overhead. The higher price might result in a fall in demand and a fall in the number of direct labour hours worked. Thus, the absorption of overheads would fall with the reduction in direct labour hours and a larger proportion of the overheads incurred would not be absorbed.

(d)   **Use of absorption and marginal costing**

Management accounting theorists favour marginal costing because it will tend to give the most relevant costs to assist a decision-maker. Marginal costs are usually differential, incremental costs and are important in most decisions, including pricing special orders, production scheduling with limiting factors, and make or buy decisions. By contrast, full costing systems, by including fixed costs in product costs, can often lead to sub-optimal decisions being taken if the effect of 'fixed costs per unit' is not fully understood.

However, full costing systems appear to be used extensively in practice. This could be for the following reasons:

(i)   automatically ensures compliance with SSAP 9

(ii)   provides more realistic matching of total costs with revenues

(iii) a large part of the costs of most companies are now fixed; using marginal costing may result in these substantial costs being overlooked e.g. under-pricing using a marginal cost-plus formula resulting in losses

(iv)   analysis of under/over-absorbed overhead is useful to identify inefficient utilisation of production resources.

25   Your company

Key answer tips

The examiner has stated that he intends to set at least one entirely discursive question in each exam. The key to gaining good marks on these is good structure – so take some time to plan your answer before ploughing in. Although this question starts with a small scenario, it has little detail, and your answer can be quite general about the problems of processing costing. The examiner gives you a guide as to some important areas to include, but note that there will be marks for additional aspects considered. Note that report format generally requires an introduction, and some sort of conclusion.

REPORT

To: The Board of Directors   **Date:**
From: Management Accountant

Report on the problems associated with process costing

I have now completed my review of the problems associated with using process costing and describe my findings below.

My findings have been divided between five principal areas which are:

–   The treatment of overheads

–   Valuation at the point of separation of by-products and joint products

–   Normal and abnormal gains and losses

–   The valuation of work-in-progress and finished goods (equivalent units) including the valuation of materials used

–   Others (sub-contractors etc)

The treatment of overheads

Overheads, the indirect expenditure such as non-manufacturing labour and maintenance materials, light and heat etc. has to be included in process costs using marginal costing or absorption costing.

Marginal costing only includes the variable overheads in the process costs i.e. those overheads which vary directly with production.

Absorption costing includes all the manufacturing overheads in the process costs. Those overheads which cannot be identified and traced to a specific process are apportioned between the processes according to some arbitrary basis such as floor area, number of employees, etc.

The overheads are then charged to production via a direct labour or machine hour rate. For example, for every direct labour hour worked an amount will be added to the cost of the process to recover the overheads. Costs can only be described as accurate up to the point of their marginal cost. Costs attributed to products via absorption costing can in no way be described as accurate and should not therefore be used for decision-making purposes.

The main problem here is whether to use marginal costing or absorption costing. It must be stressed that if absorption costing is used, the data which it provides should not be used for decision-making purposes.

The valuation at the point of separation

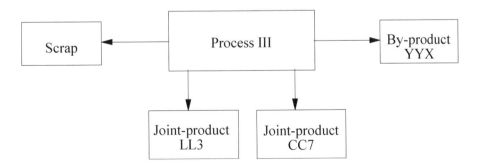

Figure 1: A valuation problem

The above diagram illustrates the problem which has to be faced. How much of process III should be charged, if any, to scrap, the by-product and the two joint products respectively? All three products and the scrap were produced in the same process. A number of treatments can be used. Some examples are:

–   scrap – of low saleable value, value at nil

–   the by-product – value it at its selling price. This reduces the process cost

–   the joint products – share the remaining process cost out in proportion to their weighted selling prices or weighted market values. Sharing the process cost between them using weight alone e.g. the process cost per kilo, fails to recognise the fact that the two products are different.

The problem here is that a selection has to be made of the method for valuing the products at the point of separation. It must also be emphasised that the methods used simply share the process costs between the products, and cannot be regarded as accurate.

Normal and abnormal gains and losses

The principle of not charging abnormal losses or including abnormal gains in the process cost is well-established. The key problem to be solved is arriving at what is abnormal. This would involve consultation with the appropriate production personnel and would to a large extent depend upon past experience and future expectations.

The valuation of work-in-progress and finished goods

The valuation depends upon:

–   The estimation of the degree of completion. This should be done by those production personnel who are competent to make such an assessment. The estimation will need to take account of opening stocks, inputs from an earlier process, materials, labour and overheads.

–   The recording of labour for each process and the treatment of idle time, bonus payments and overtime.

–   A selection will also have to be made of the method of valuation of materials which are issued to each process e.g. FIFO (first in, first out), LIFO (last in, first out), AVE CO (average cost), STD CO (standard cost) etc. The method adopted could have a significant impact on the process costs e.g. FIFO in times of rising prices could in effect be understating the process costs in terms of the material content. The above-mentioned valuation methods also have an impact where stocks are brought forward in cases where there have also been movements in labour rates and overhead rates.

Others

Sub-contractors:

The work undertaken by sub-contractors can be included as a direct cost of the next process or the finished product in cases where there is no further processing. The concern here is the maintenance of quality and the keeping of delivery pledges.

Activity-based costing (ABC):

An alternative to the marginal costing and absorption costing approaches is ABC. This method shares out the overheads via 'cost drivers' i.e. the reason why the cost has been incurred e.g. the number of purchase orders. However, this would need careful consideration and could be the focus of a future report.

Please do not hesitate to consult me should you want more information about the contents of this report.

26   Brunti plc

Key answer tips

In part (a) you have already been given the traditional absorption rates, so the main work in (i) is simply converting unit revenues and costs to totals for each product. For (ii) new activity based absorption rates for the individual categories of overheads need to be computed from the cost driver information supplied. These are then applied to products according to their relative use of the cost drivers.

In part (b) the best answers to this part will be those that draw on information given/derived in (a) to illustrate the points being made. The tendency otherwise may be to talk in vague terms about "more representative cost allocation" without specifically explaining why that is the case.

(a)   (i)   **Absorption costing profit statement**

			Products			
		XYI '000		YZT '000		ABW '000
Sales/production (units)		50		40		30
	£'000	£'000	£'000	£'000	£'000	£'000
Sales		2,250.00		3,800.00		2,190.00
Less: Prime cost	1,600.00		3,360.00		1,950.00	
Overheads						
Machine dept	120.00		240.00		144.00	
Assembly dept	288.75	2,008.75	99.00	3,699.00	49.50	2,143.50
Profit (loss)		241.25		101.00		46.50

Total: £388.75

(ii)

	Machining services	Assembly services	Set-ups	Order processing	Purchasing
			Cost pools		
(£'000)	357	318	26	156	84
Cost drivers	420,000 machine hours	530,000 direct labour hours	520 set-ups	32,000 customer orders	11,200 suppliers' orders
	£0.85 per machine hour	£0.60 per direct labour hour	£50 per set-up	£4.875 per customer order	£7.50 per suppliers' order

Activity-based costing profit statement

		XYI '000		YZT '000		ABW '000
Sales/production (units)		50		40		30
	£'000	£'000	£'000	£'000	£'000	£'000
Sales		2,250.0		3,800.0		2,190.0
Less: Prime cost	1,600.0		3,360.0		1,950.0	
Cost pools						
Machine dept at 0.85	85.0		170.0		102.0	
Assembly dept at 0.60	210.0		72.0		36.0	
Set-up costs at £50	6.0		10.0		10.0	
Order processing at £4.875	39.0		39.0		78.0	
Purchasing at £7.50	22.5		30.0		31.0	
		1,962.5		3,681.0		2,207.5
Profit/(loss)		287.5		119.0		(17.5)

Total: £389

(b)   Activity-based costing (ABC) is considered to present a fairer valuation of the product cost per unit for the following reasons:

   –   It overcomes some of the problems which are associated with conventional absorption costing. In part (a) (i) all of the production overheads and some other overheads had to be allocated or apportioned to the two cost centres, machine department, assembly department and to service cost centres. Those overheads which could not be identified with a particular cost centre would have had to be shared between cost centres using some arbitrary basis such as floor area or the number of employees. In addition, the service department costs would have been apportioned to production cost centres using some arbitrary basis or technical estimates. The total overheads for each production cost centre would then be divided by the estimated number of machine hours or direct labour hours, as appropriate. This meant that costs which could have been more accurately related to the product were not e.g. set up costs vary more with the number of set-ups than with the number of machine hours or direct labour hours.

   –   In (a) (ii) it can be observed that by having a number of 'cost pools' and dividing them by their 'cost driver' i.e. the activity which causes the cost, a more accurate and realistic assessment can be produced. The information so produced using ABC, can be significantly different to that which is generated by traditional absorption costing. The differing levels of activity incurred on behalf of each product in terms of the 'cost drivers' e.g. the number of set-ups, customer orders etc, can, and do, have quite a significant impact on the product cost per unit.

27   ABC plc

Key answer tips

For Part (a), (i) the computations will only account for 1-2 marks, so don't waste time by repeating detail from the question - start with the operating profit figures given, and deduct the allocated overhead costs as a total figure for each store. Explanation of the term 'cost driver' should be reasonably straightforward from a rudimentary knowledge of ABC; for what is required for 'volume' and 'complexity' in both explanation and comment, you must focus on the area of cost allocation and think how these issues can affect it.

Part (a), (ii) the apportionment of individual overhead costs between cost centres on different bases is a procedure that should be familiar to you. The relevant bases are fairly obvious from the cost driver information given in the question, with the exception of warehouse costs (depreciation and part of HO costs). Don't waste time worrying about the 'right' basis to use, make a rational decision, jot it down, and carry on. Again, the computations account for a minority of the allocated marks - ensure you allow enough time to consider what the figures show. Try not to be too categorical – 'this method now produces the correct allocation of costs and shows that store C is unprofitable and must be closed' - as any method of allocating true central shared costs between units will have some arbitrary element and needs to be used with care in decision making. Remember fixed costs are fixed whatever fancy methods are used to split them.

In the computations, time could be saved by working in £'000s and using a total column.

In part (b), do not waste any of the few marks allocated to this part by explaining the mechanics of the techniques themselves; think how they can be applied in this particular context. Discuss both regression and correlation

(a)   (i)   **From:**

              To: Group management

              Subject: Reporting store's profits

              Date:

       This report presents the budgeted profits for 20X8 of stores A, B and C based on the method of sharing central costs that was originally employed by the group - sales value. As a result of discussions with management at various levels alternative 'drivers' of these costs have been revealed. This is explained and then applied to the results budgeted for 20X8, finally drawing some conclusions.

	A £	B £	C £
Central costs	416,667	333,333	250,000
Operating profit	840,000	370,000	290,000
Net profit	423,333	36,667	40,000

Cost drivers are events or activities which result in the incurrence of a cost. They are commonly used to allocate costs to cost objectives or reported and 'managed' in order to 'manage' the costs they influence. It is argued that in many traditional costing systems the cost drivers or allocation bases which were used had 'volume' implications. For example number of units produced or sold, machine hours worked or in our case, sales value. It is clear that there are many other factors which give rise to costs being incurred or resources consumed. It is not only the volume of business but the way that business is done which causes costs. Dealing with a small volume of business in a complex product or for a difficult customer is sometimes more costly than a large volume in a familiar situation. It is important that cost reports reveal this issue of complexity so that management can take steps to deal with any business issues which arise. In the original allocation it is implied that store A which makes the most sales consumes the greatest proportion of the central resources. This need not be the case, it depends on what and how it sells and how it is served by the central resource.

Our company has used sales value to allocate all central costs. It is unlikely that this accurately reflects the way central resources have been consumed by the three stores. The basis seems to be one which is conveniently available and one which is related more to what each store can 'bear' of the central costs rather than any cost causality. It has a tendency to penalise a store if its sales are high e.g. store A. It is therefore a discouragement to a better performing store. Additionally, it may influence the accuracy of the budgets in that stores may deliberately understate their budgets in order to attract a lower overhead charge.

(ii)   A revised profit for each store is shown below which uses the information obtained from recent discussions with staff at all locations.

Head office	Total £	W'hse Opns. £	A £	B £	C £
Salary	200,000	20,000	60,000	60,000	60,000
Advertising	80,000	-	33,333	26,667	20,000
Establishment	120,000	12,000	36,000	36,000	36,000
		32,000			
Warehouse					
Depreciation	100,000	-	40,000	30,000	30,000
Storage	80,000		32,000	24,000	24,000
Opns/Desp	120,000+32,000		55,000	45,000	52,000
Delivery	300,000		100,000	71,429	128,571
Store costs			356,333	293,096	350,571
Operating profit			840,000	370,000	290,000
Net profit/(loss)			483,667	76,904	(60,571)

The revised calculations show that the costs identified with store C exceed the current level of operating profit and an overall loss is disclosed. A and B show improved results based on these allocations. The bases selected are believed to bear a closer relationship to how the resources are consumed in providing service to the three stores. The allocation reflects the benefit they receive rather than their 'ability to bear' the cost. There are however still some costs which will always prove difficult to identify and these inevitably result in an arbitrary allocation (if management requires them to be allocated) e.g. advertising. It is useful for management to be aware of this analysis, though they should use it with care, it does not directly make decisions for them. It does not give any information about the efficiency with which store C is managed nor does it indicate that the company would make more profit by closing store C.

It would be useful to see a trend of this information over a period of years, likewise it would be important to know the extent of competition in the area and the market being served.

In the current situation it may be uneconomic to service C at its present volume. Having made this point C has the smallest gross margin percentage (37%), compared with A (44%). It has a different sales mix or different pricing structure. From the further statistics it is also a difficult store to support. It requires proportionately more despatches and greater delivery distances to be travelled. This information suggests there is scope to rationalise delivery to reduce costs, consider direct delivery from some suppliers, examine vehicle routing schedules etc.

Further investigation and discussion is required before taking any firm decisions but the information presented above has highlighted issues which would not have been disclosed by the allocation method previously adopted.

(b)   Regression analysis and the use of r^2 would demonstrate the association between some of the central costs and allocation bases proposed. In the case of delivery miles it would be necessary to accumulate cost of delivery for a number of periods, say quarterly for three years and set these against the miles travelled. The value would require adjusting for accruals and inflation over the three year periods. A regression equation would identify the variable and fixed elements of the cost. The coefficient of determination (r^2) would express the degree of association between the variable cost and the delivery miles. A close association between these would produce a value for r^2 of close to 1.

28   EXE and WYE

Key answer tips

Part (a) is a standard apportionment and re-apportionment exercise, using the step-wise method - take care to choose the correct order in which to clear service departments. This part only attracts 6 marks (11 minutes' worth) so don't spend hours on presentation, explanations etc.

In part(b), when advising on the acceptability of accepting additional orders, the main question to ask is - can it be completed using solely spare capacity, or will it necessitate the curtailment of existing business? If the former, then the basic principle is that the order is acceptable provided the price covers the variable cost of manufacture. If the latter, then the opportunity cost of lost contribution from existing business needs to be brought into the equation. In either case, it is variable unit cost that is relevant here, and any apportioned fixed costs should be ignored. So your first task is to compute the variable cost per unit of WYE, including its share of the service departments' variable costs.

Now use this information to determine the decision in (a) on financial grounds, then comment on other less quantifiable aspects that may need to be brought into the decision.

For (ii) you need to recognise that some of the new business would be met from spare capacity, and some by giving up existing business, and an overall gain/loss must be computed (again in contribution terms). Then, stand back from the numbers to make some practical comments on other impacts of accepting this order.

The main consequence here is the inevitable under-absorption of overheads resulting in adverse volume variances. Try to think of some positive aspects too, and bring in numbers (from the previous parts) if you have time and they add to your argument.

(a)

	EXE	WYE	Stores	Maintenance	Admin
Material	1.800	0.700	0.100	0.100	
Other variable	0.800	0.500	0.100	0.200	0.200
Gen factory	1.440	1.080	0.540	0.180	0.360
					0.560
Admin	0.224	0.168	0.112	0.056	(0.560)
				0.536	
Maintenance	0.268	0.134	0.134	(0.536)	
			0.986		
Stores	0.592	0.394	(0.986)		
	5.124	2.976			
Volume	150,000	70,000			
	£	£			
Full cost	34.16	42.51			
Price	42.70	53.14			

The prices of EXE and WYE based on the target mark up are £42.70 and £53.14 respectively.

(b)　(i)　The full cost and the cost plus price both include an allocation of fixed overheads. As the company has some spare capacity they should be aware also of the product variable cost to help with this sort of decision. It can be shown that by focusing on the variable cost only, an extra unit of WYE costs £20.97.

	EXE	WYE	Stores	Maintenance	Admin
Material	1.800	0.700	0.100	0.100	
Other variable	0.800	0.500	0.100	0.200	0.200
					0.200
Admin	0.080	0.060	0.040	0.020	(0.200)
				0.320	
Maintenance	0.160	0.080	0.080	(0.320)	
			0.320		
Stores	0.192	0.128	(0.320)		
	3.032	1.468			
Volume	150,000	70,000			
	£	£			
Variable cost	20.21	20.97			

The price offered makes some contribution to the fixed costs and profit of the company though not as much as the normal business.

For 3,000 units, the reported profit will increase by 3,000 × (£35 – £20.97)= £42,090. The company should not replace normal business but if this is additional it appears worth while. They should ascertain that it will not affect their relationship with existing customers or the prices they can command in the market, i.e. the markets are segregated. As a loss leader in this market it may create further business opportunities, though sales should not all be at this sort of price level. Even allowing for the approximation involved in some of the budgeted costs and the arbitrariness of some allocations of costs it appears that the extra revenue exceeds the extra cost and for this volume there is a minimal risk.

(ii)　Enquiry price £42.51 + 10% = £46.76

Normal price (from a)　　= £53.14

Unlike the scenario in (i) above the volume of this potential order is significant. The price being indicated is above the full cost but below the normal selling price. Some extra volume is attractive but to meet this order the company would have to operate at capacity and turn away existing business. A financial evaluation can be made by comparing the contribution from the volume which is the subject of the enquiry at the offer price with that from the business which must be sacrificed at normal price levels.

			£
Gain from new business 50,000 × (£46.76 – £20.97)		=	1,289,500
Existing trade lost　　20,000 × (£53.14 – £20.97)		=	643,400
Net gain		=	646,100

There is a danger of major goodwill implications for the company in their move to refuse some of their existing business for this product, if that is the option they adopt. This may also extend to products other than the one in question here for which we have no detail. The price being suggested of cost plus 10% is a steep change from the normal price of this product and if it applies to a significant volume, it may well alter the market position of the product. We are not however in a position to bring this into any calculation. If they take the order they are also reliant on the business of one customer and will need to consider the chance of repeat orders from this source.

The analysis assumes that the company is comfortable operating at the 100,000 capacity indicated and that the current cost levels apply, that is, the same variable costs and no change in the total fixed costs. Although the increase in contribution/profit for the order looks attractive the company would be advised to look beyond the current year to longer term negotiation on both price and volume. To turn away existing business which may have a future for the one-off enquiry applied to only one year may be inappropriate. If a longer term contract with price terms which may be attractive to both parties could be established, this may encourage the company to invest in order to expand capacity and not lose any business.

(c) Generally, using a volume base of maximum capacity, rather than budget volume, will result in lower overhead recovery rates per unit. This is caused by the fixed overheads being spread over a greater volume which will inevitably lead to a lower product cost being compiled.

The cost would not be representative of the average actual product cost being achieved in the current year, unless current volumes are the same as the maximum capacity level. The company must expect an adverse volume variance to be reported if such a costing approach is incorporated into a management information system.

This approach will reveal a target product cost which can be achieved if high levels of business volume are achieved. In this way it can be a motivation to management to go out, be more competitive and attract new business. It will show just how low overhead rates and product costs can get.

The revised product cost can be computed by adjusting the fixed overhead component of the product cost for WYE.

	£ per unit
Original full cost	42.51
Variable cost	20.97
Original fixed cost	21.54
Revised fixed cost	15.08*
Add back variable cost	20.97
	36.05

*This is achieved by adjusting the original fixed cost by the proportion 70:100. An alternative would be to re-examine the overhead apportionment, though it would come to the same conclusion.

Management should be aware that full product costs, including as they do arbitrary overhead allocation and volume levels, are approximations. Pricing and other decisions are usefully informed by a range of values which include variable costs and full costs based on alternative approaches. The accountant must ensure however that management are fully aware of the assumptions contained in the cost calculations which he/she presents.

29   Rayman Company

Key answer tips

In part (a), it is probably a good idea to do a *quick* sketch of the flow diagram to get the logic sorted, then produce the finished version with quantities etc on it.

In part (b) these are two common methods of splitting fixed costs between joint products, and you should have a good idea of the best way to lay out your workings. Don't forget to comment.

In part (c), when decision-making comes into a joint products question, you must remember the golden rule - consider incremental costs versus incremental revenue, disregarding any unit costs you may already have calculated involving apportioned fixed costs. In this case, producing more of one product will inevitably mean the production of more of the other, with associated common costs. The decision will ultimately depend upon the possible uses of the excess 'other' product.

(a)

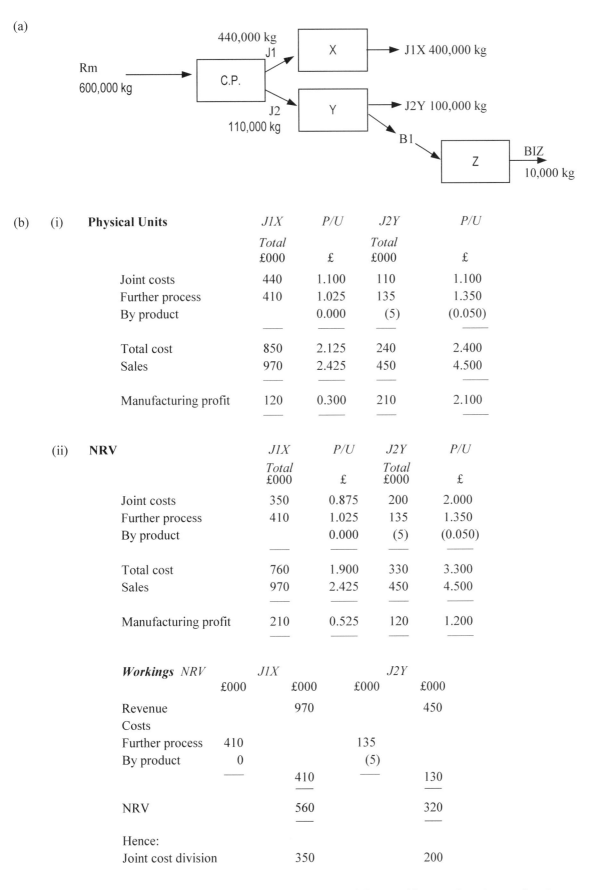

(b) (i) **Physical Units**

	JIX	P/U	J2Y	P/U
	Total £000	£	*Total* £000	£
Joint costs	440	1.100	110	1.100
Further process	410	1.025	135	1.350
By product		0.000	(5)	(0.050)
Total cost	850	2.125	240	2.400
Sales	970	2.425	450	4.500
Manufacturing profit	120	0.300	210	2.100

(ii) **NRV**

	JIX	P/U	J2Y	P/U
	Total £000	£	*Total* £000	£
Joint costs	350	0.875	200	2.000
Further process	410	1.025	135	1.350
By product		0.000	(5)	(0.050)
Total cost	760	1.900	330	3.300
Sales	970	2.425	450	4.500
Manufacturing profit	210	0.525	120	1.200

Workings *NRV*

	JIX		J2Y	
	£000	£000	£000	£000
Revenue		970		450
Costs				
Further process	410		135	
By product	0		(5)	
		410		130
NRV		560		320
Hence:				
Joint cost division		350		200

Note: The above tables enable the cost per unit and the monthly manufacturing profit to be extracted and are presented for the sake of clarity. A candidate would be able to produce the answers required in this question without reproducing all the detail in the tables.

There is no single correct way to divide the joint costs between the two products involved. The above are two possibilities. The physical units method is the most simple and results in the same unit joint cost of the two products. If management want to undertake this product costing for the purposes of stock valuation and stocks are not material in the context of overall volume then the physical unit method may be convenient and appropriate but it has little else to commend it.

The NRV method takes account of the respective market values in addition to the quantities produced. If management want to make some judgements about profitability of the products this method is to be preferred. However, they should be warned about drawing any conclusions about individual products. In joint product situations this is not possible. The emphasis must be on the whole process rather than individual products. With this method the individual products will be shown to be profitable if the whole process is profitable. It is preferable to produce cost and profit reports which show joint products with a similar level of profitability than for these to be distorted when products have very different market values and this is not taken into account.

(c)   (i)   Extra costs incurred for 10,000 kg of J2Y
(i.e. 10% of current volume of J2Y)

	£	£
Emphasis on variable costs only:		
10% of Common Facility costs		50,000
10% of finishing process (Y)		13,000
Subtotal of costs		63,000
Sales revenue of J2Y		
10,000 × £4.00	40,000	
Contribution from sale of B1Z		
10% of current volume (1,500 – 700)	800	
		40,800
Shortfall in revenue		22,200

The price of £4.00 per kg is not sufficient to cover all of the costs of manufacturing the 10,000 of J2Y. On the face of it a price in excess of £6.22 would be more appropriate. It should be noted however that in undertaking this production of J2Y the company will also manufacture 40,000 kg of intermediate product J1 which can be developed into J1X. A decision rests on what can be done with this output. If J1X can be sold at a price which exceeds the shortfall in revenue and the variable further processing costs then this should be undertaken. The minimum revenue for the sales of the excess J1X to make the whole deal profitable is £22,200 plus £38,500 (10% of process X £385,000 variable further processing costs). This represents a minimum price of approximately £1.52 per kg.

(ii)   There are a number of assumptions and further questions applicable to the above approach. It is stated that this business is extra to the present level of business, it needs to be confirmed that all present output is committed and cannot be used to meet this order. Following on from this it is uncertain that the company has the capacity to cope with this extra business, though it is only 10% of volume, not all businesses have the flexibility to cope with this sort of volume change, it depends on their existing capacity.

Given that some increase in production is likely if the approach is to be entertained then in the calculations above it is assumed that the extra costs will be variable costs only. This assumes that the unit variable costs have been identified with some accuracy and there are no incremental fixed costs incurred for this order. If there are any additional costs they need to be incorporated.

The attractiveness of the order may well depend on what can be done with the extra J1X that is produced, therefore its market potential and the price it can command may be a decisive factor in responding to this approach. This is presently unknown.

The prevailing market price of J2Y is £4.50, if this order is taken at £4.00, or close to it, the effect on the existing customers and the prices currently being achieved needs to be considered. If further discussion with this new customer takes place it may have to be made clear that business at this special price may not be possible in the future. Indeed, there is no indication of the chances that this approach may lead to further business, but this could be a factor which the company may wish to consider.

30   Zorro Company

Key answer tips

In part (a) use the information given to split out the costs between fixed and variable elements. Variable costs only should be attributed to individual products - you can either initially ignore the fixed costs completely, or put them in as a lump sum (which is quite useful to check your figures). Now explain the implications of your figures, including reference to the avoidable fixed costs relating to product Y. The requirement to 'qualify' your answer is basically asking you to talk about the assumptions upon which it is based, and further information that may help to improve its validity.

In part (b) think carefully about what is being asked - you have already discussed the advisability of withdrawing Y on short-term financial grounds in (a), so what further is required here? The key here is that we are now looking at the long term position, and not necessarily purely on quantifiable financial grounds. So consider what might change in the future (e.g. capacity) and what other knock-on effects withdrawal of a product might have, to give you some ideas.

In part (c) the requirement gives you the structure of your answer in identifying three options to consider. Remember, the approach is to consider incremental costs and revenues, so start with the status quo, continuing Y, then consider the impact on the revenue and cost figures of each of the other options.

(a)   **Workings**

	W £000	X £000	Y £000	Z £000	Total £000
Sales	2,000	2,500	1,000	500	6,000
Variable costs:					
materials	300	400	200	40	940
labour	500	600	400	100	1,600
factory overhead	240	320	200	40	800
selling overhead	100	125	50	25	300
Total variable costs	1,140	1,445	850	205	3,640
Contribution	860	1,055	150	295	2,360
CS ratio	43%	42%	15%	59%	39%
Less fixed costs:					
manufacturing					1,200
selling					600
Net profit					560

The table given in the question includes an arbitrary allocation of fixed costs to product Y. This form of presentation is not always the most helpful in reaching product discontinuation decisions. From the workings above it can be seen that Y makes a contribution of £150,000 and this exceeds the £100,000 fixed costs which would be saved if Y were to be withdrawn. In the short-term if Y is discontinued all of the remaining fixed costs will still be incurred. Profit would fall by £50,000 to £510,000 if Zorro were to discontinue Y at this time. It is apparent however that Y, in financial terms, is the poorest performing product in the line and it should therefore receive some detailed consideration.

The above explanation assumes that variable costs can be accurately identified by the percentages given in the question. Labour costs are assumed to be variable, in other words there is some casual labour which can be reduced with immediate effect and there are no other costs, for example redundancy costs, related to the withdrawal of Y. The discussion regarding Y also assumes that the current situation will continue, that is, there is no scope for price rises in the future or for costs to be significantly reduced through efficiency or cost changes.

(b) (i) The decision related to product Y turns on the incremental expenditure and incremental costs involved in producing and selling the product over the relevant time period. In the present position of spare capacity and the fact that Y is making a contribution, in the short-term, it should remain in the product line.

If the amount of the fixed costs which may be saved by withdrawing Y are low and there are no other lump sum savings of expenditures by withdrawing Y then it could be retained over the longer term on the basis that it is contributing to profit. Additionally, if its abandonment would cause the reduction in the sales of other products in the line, then these implications should also be taken into account. However, to proceed too far with this argument could be dangerous and the company could find it is using this reasoning to retain a wide range of low volume/low contribution products. These would add to the complexity and hence the costs of manufacture, but very little to the overall profit. It would be wise therefore for the company to regularly examine the low volume/low contribution products in its range. This may be what the chief executive has in mind. The ability of a product to cover its costs, including its somewhat arbitrarily allocated costs may be a useful general indicator to its viability.

(ii) If the company were able to develop another product, offering a better contribution, with similar characteristics which would utilise the same plant as Y, then Y should naturally be re-evaluated. If sales of the existing products expand sufficiently to require the capacity currently devoted to Y, then Y would be a candidate for withdrawal. Alternatively, if the company was faced with significant capital expenditure to maintain its production capacity then consideration could be given to withdrawing Y rather than incurring that expenditure. This would depend on the capacity involved, amount of the investment and the extent to which withdrawal of Y would affect sales of other products in the line.

(c) If Y were to be continued the financial result would be the same as that shown in (a) above. This could be summarised in terms of the respective contributions of the products and the total fixed costs as:

Product	£000
W	860
X	1,055
Y	150
Z	295
Total contribution	2,360
Fixed costs	1,800
Net profit	560

If Y were to be withdrawn completely the implications would be £300,000 extra sales of Z and a reduction in the sales of W by 10%. Additionally, £100,000 fixed costs would be saved, thus:

Product		£000
W	Less 10% of the contribution	774
X	Unchanged	1,055
Y	Withdrawn	
Z	Additional £300,000 × 59%	472
Total contribution		2,301
Fixed costs	Less £100,000	1,700
Net profit		601

If Y were to be retained to service only the customers for product W, this would imply 20% of the present sales of Y would be achieved (i.e. 80% reduction). The extra £300,000 sales of Z would still apply and there would be no reduction in the sales of W because these customers would be satisfied. The fixed costs saved would be only £50,000 in this case as some manufacturing capacity of Y is retained, hence:

Product		£000
W	As original	860
X	Unchanged	1,055
Y	Only 20% sold	30
Z	Additional £300,000 × 59%	472
Total contribution		2,417
Fixed costs	Less £50,000	1,750
Net profit		667

On financial grounds it would appear that the best option for Zorro is to retain manufacture and sale of product Y for the customers of product W only. There is the implication that Y has a trend of poor profit performance in the recent past and no indication that this will change. The opportunity cost of dropping Y completely, given the consequent loss of sales of W, is high and this is the main reason for keeping it in the portfolio. It is still reasonable for the company to look to develop a product with a better level of profit than Y and one which has the characteristics suitable for product W customers. This would improve their profit position even further.

31   Holiday Company

Key answer tips

For part (a)) look at the analysis given and jot down any points that immediately spring to mind (mainly the need for cost analysis between fixed and variable). Then read the text below to pick up more ideas – actual capacity levels, fixed/variable elements, sunk costs. Now look at the requirement – the need for figures per customer and break-even figures. You now have a summary of the revisions you need to make to the original statement.

Part (b) has three requirements – first, identification of the shortcomings of the original analysis, the material for which you have from your initial review in (a). Just write out what you thought was poor, and why. Now turn to the revisions you made, explaining why they overcome the problems you have just discussed. Finally, step back from the detail and tell the story of your revised statement in words. Breaking down the requirement like this will help to structure your answer and ensure you have properly addressed all aspects required.

(a)   The analysis calls for recognition of cost behaviour and cost relevance to each holiday. It will start with an analysis by customer and then by the number of customers per holiday.

		Sports Holidays £ /Customer		Culture Holidays £ /Customer		Special Interest Holidays £ /Customer
Revenue		420		480		300
Commission		63		48		60
		357		432		240
Variable Costs						
Hotels etc.	168		198		72	
*Office etc.	45		45		45	
		213		243		117
Contribution per customer		144		189		123

	£ /Package	£ /Package	£ /Package
Total Contribution (x 70/80/60 respectively)	10,080	15,120	7,380
Courier costs	1,500	1,500	1,750
	8,580	13,620	5,630
Air travel costs	8,100	8,400	7,800
Surplus/(Deficit)	480	5,220	(2,170)

*Office overhead etc. by High/Low method: $\dfrac{£225,000}{5,000} = £45$ per person

Break-even number of customers:

One possible break-even point is the number of customers required to cover the specific fixed costs of each holiday type.

	Sport	Culture	Special Interest
BEP = $\dfrac{FC}{CPU}$	$\dfrac{9,600}{144}$	$\dfrac{9,900}{189}$	$\dfrac{9,550}{123}$
No of passengers	67	53	78

Another possible break-even point calculation could be based on the above fixed costs plus the allocated fixed customer costs and office overheads which can be determined from the table given in the question after deduction of the variable element.

	Sport	Culture	Special Interest
BEP = $\dfrac{FC}{CPU}$	$\dfrac{£9,600+6,060}{£144}$	$\dfrac{£9,900+7,380}{£189}$	$\dfrac{£9,550+1,680}{£123}$
No of passengers	109	92	92

A further possibility is to focus only on incremental fixed costs of the local courier, all other fixed overhead for this season being ignored because they are sunk costs.

	Sport	Culture	Special Interest
BEP = $\dfrac{FC}{CPU}$	$\dfrac{£1,500}{£144}$	$\dfrac{£1,500}{£189}$	$\dfrac{£1,750}{£123}$
No of passengers	11	8	15

Note: Any one of the above answers is acceptable for this part of the question. No specific comment is required in this part but the outcome of the calculations may form a basis for part of the discussion which follows in part (b).

(b)   The original analysis is related to 100 passengers when experience has shown that on average fewer customers are attracted. It is not appropriate to analyse the situation at full capacity only; the implications for the expected capacity should also be reviewed.

There is also an attempt to associate all costs with the holidays, including those costs common to all holidays which will exist whether or not these holidays are undertaken. Whilst for long-term pricing it is considered desirable to cover all costs, it is also appropriate for the short-term to focus on 'contribution business'. That is, to identify only variable and relevant costs and revenues.

The costs of air travel and the local courier are fixed costs but specific to each holiday so they need to be set against each one. In this analysis the costs of air travel is shown separately from courier costs because the courier support can still be negotiated or cancelled. It would appear that contracts for the flights have been signed and therefore the costs cannot be avoided, i.e. they are sunk costs. It is considered appropriate that these costs are separately set against the holidays to which they relate. For the purposes of supporting the assessment, separate subtotals of the surplus, after each cost, are provided.

At the current level of occupancy it is the special interest holidays which are the least viable. Based on the current prediction, they fail to cover the variable and fixed costs of the holiday. In immediate financial terms the company would be better off still undertaking the holiday because it cannot avoid the flight costs which have already been booked. It should be noted that in the present analysis the holiday is not covering any general company costs which have been removed from the analysis. The company should attempt to increase occupancy at least in the short-term to above the break-even level of 78 customers, or increase the holiday price, or both. Sporting holidays also show limited profitability, they cover all of the specific fixed costs of the holiday but make only a limited surplus to contribute to corporate fixed costs.

It should be noted that any conclusions drawn from the figures relies on the predictions contained in the information about cost behaviour and number of customers etc. No allowance has been made for exchange rate fluctuations applicable to the holidays in question, this could add to the riskiness of each venture. Likewise inflationary factors concerned with the extrapolation of the variable costs elements have been ignored as instructed. One could ask if there is variability about the average number of customers provided in the question. It may be that the package holidays are very popular in the peak of the season and it is only in off-peak times that questions about viability should be asked. It may be possible also for the company to price the holidays for any seasonality observed. Dealing with these points will however require a separate analysis, and we can draw no definite conclusions from the figures currently available.

32 Plastic tools

Key answer tips

Part (a) is a textbook discussion of cost-plus pricing. Start with an explanation of the various possible cost bases that may be used (full/marginal/opportunity/target), and where each may be appropriate. Then briefly discuss the drawbacks of cost-plus, in that prices cannot be set in isolation from demand.

For part (b), you first need to establish a unit cost (full and marginal) to which a mark-up can be applied. Such a cost will be based upon specific material and layout costs (given) and overhead charges based upon an analysis of the budgeted data given for the company. This means first following the instructions given to reallocate general factory overhead to the productive departments. The total costs of each department need to be absorbed by the cost units via machine hour rates, as more than one product will be using these departments. Budgeted machine hours are used, rather than practical capacities, as the latter would lead to significant under-absorption.

Once a full cost per unit has been established, show a range of full-cost-plus prices between 25% and 35% mark ups.

The marginal cost information should include both the variable cost per unit and a share of *incremental* fixed costs, which represent a true marginal cost of undertaking the new product project.

Part (c) requires you to look at the numbers you have produced and come up with a sensible pricing strategy. Use all the information you are given in the question, and some general knowledge about pricing new products, to present a reasoned argument.

(a) Cost-based approaches to pricing involve use of either full cost or marginal cost, or a combination of the two. To the cost, a desired profit margin may be added, hence cost-plus basis of pricing. It may seem that a full-cost plus basis is safe because it ensures that a profit will be earned. This is only true however if the volume that was used to estimate the product cost is actually achieved. If the sales demand falls below the volume used to predict the product cost the total sales revenue may be insufficient to cover all costs including the total fixed costs. One situation where the cost-plus approach may be the only feasible method is in the production of one-off special products. Where management have to quote for the production of a unique item it is logical to seek to recover all applicable costs in the price.

If a firm is faced with spare capacity, in the short run, then any price above the marginal cost will increase profit, provided normal business is not affected. Marginal costs may also be employed in situations where a firm is seeking to identify a minimum short-run price to obtain business which has some long-run profit potential. The existence of fixed costs, which must be covered in the long-run, must not be lost sight of. There is a case therefore for being aware of the full-cost in addition to the marginal cost of a product or service.

A major objection to cost-plus pricing is that, in its basic form, it tends to ignore what the customer is prepared to pay or what the level of demand is likely to be at various prices. There is, therefore, a strong theoretical argument to support the economic model. This model suggests a price/demand schedule should be established and this should be compared with costs, both fixed and variable, at different volume levels to locate the maximum profit point. The practical problem with this approach is the complexity of obtaining this demand / price / cost information for the many products or services which a typical firm offers.

(b)   *Calculation of overhead rates*
Variable overhead

	Moulding £000	Finishing £000	General Factory £000
Sub Total	1,600	500	1,050
Re-allocation	600	450	(1,050)
	2,200	950	
Machine hours	800	600	
Rate per hour	£2.750	£1.583	

Fixed overhead

	Moulding £000	Finishing £000	General Factory £000
Sub Total	2,500	850	1,750
Re-allocation	1,050	700	(1,750)
	3,550	1,550	
Machine hours	800	600	
Rate per hour	£4.4375	£2.583	

Product Costing

			£
Direct material			9.00
Direct labour	2 × £5	10.00	
	3 × £5.50	16.50	
			26.50
Variable overhead	4 ×£2.750	11.00	
	3 × £1.583	4.75	
			15.75
Variable manufacturing cost			51.25
Fixed overheads	4 × £4.4375	17.75	
	3 × £2.583	7.75	
			25.50
Full manufacturing cost			76.75

Price based on full manufacturing cost:

Mark up %	25%	30%	35%
	£	£	£
Mark up	19.19	23.03	26.86
Proposed price	95.94	99.78	103.61

Price based on variable cost and incremental fixed costs:

	£
Variable manufacturing cost (as above)	51.25
Incremental fixed costs £167,000/20,000 units	8.35
	59.60

(c)   The full cost approach using the existing allocation methods and mark-up practices suggests prices in the range of £96 to £104. At the top of this range it is a little above the current market price but the product is suggested to offer some improvements over competitors. The management may find, additionally, that as they go into full production, that they are able to increase their efficiency and lower their costs. The fact that the full cost price is broadly similar to the prevailing market price is an indicator that the company is not too far out of line with the cost of manufacture of this product.

The product variable cost is £51.25. In the very short term this could be taken to be a minimum price but which offers no contribution to overheads or profit. Management may see it as appropriate to cover at least the incremental fixed costs specific to this product. Working on an assumption of 20,000 unit sales per annum raises the minimum price to £60, though this value is dependent on the accuracy of the volume base used to apply the specific fixed overheads.

In the present situation the management should be guided more by the prevailing market price and full cost recovery than a marginal approach. The price should not be pitched too low because they may want to reinforce the impression that the product offers improvement.

Standard costing and variance analysis

33   Material variances

Key answer tips

Part (a) is a very basic mix/yield question although it is designed to 'unnerve' students by including variances of zero in January.

In part (b) the zero variances should be mentioned.

(a)   **Standard cost**

Material X	60% @ £30		18
Material Y	40% @ £45		18
	100%		36
Standard loss	10%		
Standard yield	90%	$=$ $\dfrac{£36}{90\%}$ $=$ £40 per tonne	

Price variance

	January £	February £	March £
Material Y	Nil	Nil	Nil
Material X:			
Total material cost	32,400	31,560	38,600
Less: Cost of Y 360 × £45	16,200	16,200	16,200
Actual cost of material X	16,200	15,360	22,400
Standard price @ Actual quantity:			
540 × £30	16,200		
480 × £30		14,400	
700 × £30			21,000
Price variance	Nil	960 A	1,400 A

Material variance summaries

	January			February			March		
	Product X	Product Y	Total	Product X	Product Y	Total	Product X	Product Y	Total
Mix variance									
Actual quantity									
@ Actual mix	540	360	900	480	360	840	700	360	1,060
Actual quantity									
@ Standard mix	540	360	900	504	336	800	636	424	1,060
Mix variance				24 @ £30	24 @ £45		64 @ £30	64 @ £45	
			Nil	= £720 F	= £1,080 A	360 A	= £1,920 A	= £2,880 F	£960 F
Yield variance									
Actual quantity									
@ Standard mix	540	360	900	504	336	800	636	424	1,060
Standard quantity for									
actual production		$810 \times \frac{100}{90}$			$765 \times \frac{100}{90}$			$900 \times \frac{100}{90}$	
@ Standard mix	540	360	= 900	510	340	= 850	600	400	= 1,000
Yield variance				6 @ £30	4 @ £45		36 @ £30	24 @ £45	
			Nil	= £180 F	= £180 F	£360 F	= £1,080 A	= £1,080 A	£2,160 A
Usage variance									
Actual quantity									
@ Actual mix	540	360		480	360		700	360	
Standard quantity for									
actual production									
@ Standard mix	540	360		510	340		600	400	
Usage variance				30 @ £30	20 @ £45		100 @ £30	40 @ £45	
			£Nil	= £900 F	= £900 A	Nil	= £3,000 A	= £1,800 F	£1,200 A

(b)   Production in January is exactly according to standard. The price of Y has remained at standard for the whole period. The price of X is £2 $\left(\frac{960}{480} \text{ and } \frac{1,400}{700} \right)$ in excess of standard in February and March. If this continues the standard price of X will need to be increased. The proportion of X in the mix changed to $\frac{4,400}{840} = 57\%$ and $\frac{700}{1,060} = 66\%$ in February and March respectively. The cost increase in February, shown as an adverse mix variance of £360, is caused by dearer Y being used instead of cheaper X. There is an improvement in yield in February. The increased yield could be viewed as an abnormal gain of 9 tons (840 × 90% = (756 − 765) × £40 = £360). There is also a reduction in volume produced in February.

In March the significant increase in the proportion of X (which is cheaper) used has caused a favourable mix variance and may have contributed to the large adverse yield variance. Production in March is considerably higher than for January and February - this may be a reason for the adverse yield variance.

Overall there appears to be a link between mix and yield. If the proportion of Y is increased, causing adverse mix variance as Y is more expensive, the yield is improved - as occurred in February; the opposite took place in March.

There could also be a link between yield and the volume of production - in February production is low and yield is high, whereas in March production is high and yield is low.

(c)   This information helps to explain the increased proportion of Y used in February - if not used Y would be wasted, which could involve disposal costs. It could therefore be argued that the adverse mix variance on Y of £1,080 in February is a sunk cost i.e. using a greater proportion of Y has not increased the purchase quantity. Using more of Y has improved yield.

In March the restriction on Y has resulted in adverse yield arising from the increased proportion of X needed to increase production volume - this has resulted in an overall adverse usage variance of £1,200. This excess cost should be included in the evaluation of decisions to try to obtain more of Y by, for example, paying a premium price.

It would be necessary to ascertain whether and how the quality of the final product is affected by changes in mix and whether the quality is then acceptable to customers.

34   Perseus Co Ltd

Key answer tips

This is a straightforward variances question, and provided you are well-prepared on this topic is quite manageable in the time allowed. Note in the answer to (a), the two statements have been combined in columnar form, which saves time. Whilst the answer interprets "standard costing profit statement" as a flexed budget, it would be equally acceptable to base this statement on the budgeted activity level.

Whether you include a sales volume variance in part (b) depends upon the approach taken in (a); note that mix and yield variances are not generally required unless specifically requested or the working of the question indicates they would be useful/relevant.

(a)   **Profit statements**

(15,400 units) *	Standard £	Standard £	Actual £	Actual £
Sales (at £140)		2,156,000	(at £138.25) 2,129,050	
Less: Costs				
Materials				
Mat. 007				
(6 kilos × 15,400)				
= 92,400 × £12.25	1,131,900		1,256,640	
			(given)	
Mat. XL90				
(3 kilos × 15,400)				
= 46,200 × £3.20	147,840		132,979	
			(given)	
Labour				
(4.5 hours × 15,400)				
= 69,300 × £8.40	582,120		612,766	
			(given)	
Fixed overheads	86,400		96,840	
	(given)		(given)	
		1,948,260		2,099,225
Profit		207,740		29,825

* A standard based on the original budget of 16,000 units could have been used in part (a) and then adjusted by means of a sales volume variance in part (b).

(b)   **Reconciliation**

		£
Standard profit on 15,400 units (as above)		207,740

Variance	£	*(+)* *Favourable* £	*(−)* *Adverse* £

Sales price
    Standard – Actual
    (£2,156,000 – £2,129,050)
			26,950

Materials			

Mat. 007 usage
    (Standard – Actual) × Standard price
    (92,400 – 98,560) × £12.25
			75,460

Mat. XL90 usage
    (Standard – Actual) × Standard price
    (46,200 – 42,350) × £3.20
		12,320	

Mat. 007 Price
    (Actual quantity × Actual price)
    (Actual quantity × Standard price)
	1,256,640
	1,207,360
			49,280

Mat. XL90 Price
    (Actual quantity × Actual price)
    (Actual quantity × Standard price)
	132,979
	135,520
		2,541	

Labour			

Efficiency
    Standard hours – Actual hours*
    (69,300 – 70,840) = 1,540 × Standard rate £8.40
			12,936

Rate
    Standard – Actual
    (£8.40 – 8.65) = £0.25 × Actual hours 70,840
			17,710

Overheads			

Fixed overheads
    Standard – Actual
    (£86,400 – £96,840)
			10,440

		14,861	192,776

(177,915) (A)

		£
Actual profit		29,825

$$* \quad \frac{£612,766}{£8.65} = 70,840 \text{ hours}$$

(c)   Variances may be inter-related e.g. the reason why one variance is favourable could also help explain why another variance is adverse.

Using poor quality materials could result in a favourable price variance because of paying a lower price. The poor quality material could be the cause of an adverse material usage variance and an adverse labour efficiency variance e.g. materials more difficult to work with, more rejects/spoilt work, more waste.

If a higher grade of labour was used, compared with that which was planned, there would most certainly be an adverse labour rate variance. The higher skill level employed could well be the reason for a favourable labour efficiency variance and a favourable material usage variance e.g. a lower number of rejects and less waste of materials.

35   Acca-chem Co plc

Key answer tips

In parts (a) and (b), before leaping into the first calculation, think a little about how you can most efficiently process and present the data required to produce all the material variances requested - for example, in a 'line-by-line' approach for all of (a). Or you could incorporate (b) as well, by preparing a table that analyses the variances by product right from the start - using total figures for (a), and the individual figures for (b). But ensure you clearly identify your answers.

In part (c) note that you are asked for the variances for each of the departments - and no mix/yield analysis is required. A tabular approach can again be used to process the information clearly and efficiently. Note that the activity level is measured in terms of batches

In part (d) there is just one product, so the basic sales variances are total, price and volume. Here, in particular, there are different approaches that are equally acceptable to the examiner

In part (e) it is easy to overlook short written parts at the end of a longish computation question, but some of the easiest marks can be gained here. It entails an interpretation of your computations, particularly in (b), to identify possible reasons for the adverse yield variance. As this part comes at the end of the whole question, it may indicate that other aspects may also be relevant - e.g. the possible link between efficiency of labour and materials usage.

(a)   **Material variances**

(i)	Actual quantity at actual price (given)		£17,328

(ii)	Actual quantity at standard price:		£
	F 1,680 × £4		6,720
	G 1,650 × £3		4,950
	H 870 × £6		5,220
			16,890

(iii)	Standard yield × Standard cost		
	(32 × 120) × £4.50 (W1)		£17,280

(iv)	Actual yield × Standard cost		
	3,648 × £4.50		£16,416

Variances		£
Price	(i) – (ii)	438 A
Usage	(ii) – (iv)	474 A
Cost	(i) – (iv)	912 A
Mix	(ii) – (iii)	390 F
Yield	(iii) – (iv)	864 A
Usage (as above)		474 A

Workings

(W1) Standard cost per kilo $= \dfrac{£144}{32 \text{ kilos}} = £4.50$

Variances

A = Adverse   F = Favourable

(b)   **Further analysis of material variances**

Mix	Total	F	G	H
Standard (kilos)		1,800	1,440	960
Actual (kilos)		1,680	1,650	870
		120 F	210 A	90 F
× Standard price (£)		4	3	6
	£390 F	£480 F	£630 A	£540 F

Price	Total	F	G	H
			£	£ £
Standard		4.00	3.00	6.00
Actual		4.25	2.80	6.40
		0.25 A	0.20 F	0.40 A
× Actual kilos used		1,680	1,650	870
	£438 A	£420 A	£330 F	£348 A

(c)   **Labour variances**

	Total	Dept P	Dept Q
Cost variances	£	£	£
Standard cost	6,240	4,800	1,440
Actual cost	7,872	6,360	1,512
(i)	1,632 A	1,560 A	72 A

	Total	Dept P	Dept Q
Efficiency variances	£	£	£
Standard hours		480	240
Actual hours		600	270
		120 A	30 A
× Standard rate per hour (£)		£10	£6
(ii)	£1,380 A	£1,200 A	£180 A

	£	£	£
Rate variances			
Standard rate		10.00	6.00
Actual rate		10.60	5.60
		0.60 A	0.40 F
× Actual hours worked		600	270
(iii)	£252A	£360A	£108 F

Proof: (i) = (ii) + (iii)

(d)   **Sales variances**

	£
Budgeted sales for actual level of activity (120 × 32 × £16)	61,440
Actual sales (3,648 × £16.75)	61,104
	336 A

Made up of:

	£
Volume variance(3,840 – 3,648 kilos) × £16	3,072 A
Price variance (£0.75 × 3,648)	2,736 F
	336 A

(e)   The actual mix used had the same weight as the standard mix i.e. 4,200 kilos but used a different combination to the standard mix [as indicated in (b)]. It used less than planned of materials F and H, and more than planned of material G, a lower cost material. In addition to substituting the lower cost material for F and H which could affect the yield, the adverse yield variance could have also been caused by using materials of a lower quality than that which was planned e.g. the lower price per kilo of G gives a favourable price variance, but this could be due to buying a lower quality material.

The labour efficiency variance could have been caused by poor quality materials taking longer to process. It could also be caused by a lack of motivation on the part of employees e.g. the employees in department Q getting a pay rise lower than expected, could have caused them to work more slowly and to waste more material because of not taking as much care as they should. This could also help to explain the actual yield, 30.4 kilos per batch being lower than the standard yield of 32 kilos per batch.

36   Component RYX

Key answer tips

In part (a), depending upon the way you compute variances, you may compute all four in one working (e.g. using the "line by line" method) or separately (using formulae etc). Whichever method, make sure you clearly identify the variances required - making sure you get the efficiency and capacity variances the right way round (these being a split of the volume variance). The summary statement required should show how the three subsidiary variances add up to the overall cost variance. Note that (b) tells you that these should all be adverse.

Part (b) is testing your understanding of the relevance of the figures you have just computed, and carries half the marks of the question - do not underestimate it! The best approach is, for each variance, start by defining the variance itself - i.e. how it is calculated. Then you have to look for possible causes of an *adverse* result. Give specific examples of events that may have contributed - don't just talk vaguely of 'over-spending' or 'inefficiency' .

In part (c) the inter-relationships again need specific examples for illustration. Since overhead efficiency variances are computed on the same basis as labour efficiency, once you have linked the material and labour variances, the overhead variance should follow.

(a)   Budgeted fixed overhead rate

$$\frac{£22,260}{8,400 \text{ hours}} = £2.65 \text{ per hour}$$

Standard labour hours per unit of production

$$\frac{8,400}{1,200} = 7 \text{ hours per unit}$$

Production fixed overhead cost variance:

Standard labour hours for actual production 1,100 × 7 = 7,700 standard hours

	£
Actual cost	25,536
Less Standard cost (7,700 × £2.65)	20,405
	5,131 (A)*

Fixed production overhead expenditure variance:

	£
Actual cost	25,536
Less Standard cost as per budget	22,260
	3,276 (A)

Fixed production overhead efficiency variance:

Actual hours	7,980
Less Standard hours	7,700
	280 × £2.65 = £742 (A)

Fixed production overhead capacity variance:

Actual hours	7,980
Less Budgeted standard hours	8,400
	420 × £2.65=£1,113 (A)

* (A) = Adverse
  (F) = Favourable

Proof Production fixed overhead variances:

	£
Expenditure variance	3,276 (A)
Efficiency variance	742 (A)
Capacity variance	1,113 (A)
Cost variance	5,131 (A)

(b)   *The production fixed overhead expenditure variance.* This is the difference between the budgeted and actual overhead for the period and provides an indication of the efficiency in keeping to the spending targets which are set.

An adverse variance is an indication of over-spending in one or more of the component parts which make up the overhead cost e.g. rent of premises, light and heat, insurance of buildings etc. The causes of such variances could have been a higher than planned inflation rate, an unexpected outcome to a rent review, colder weather, the area in which the firm is situated becoming a higher risk area for insurance purposes, etc.

However, it should be noted that under-spending is not always an indication of efficiency and should be investigated.

The production fixed overhead efficiency variance compares standard and actual efficiency in terms of hours, multiplied by the standard rate applicable to the actual production. An adverse variance means that more hours than planned were taken because of, for example: using different skill levels of labour, poor quality materials which take longer to work on or result in more spoilt work, poor training, poor motivation/morale, poor working conditions, poor supervision, etc.

The production fixed overhead capacity variance compares the actual and planned capacity and is the difference between the budgeted and actual levels of activity, valued at the standard overhead rate. Adverse variances could be caused by a failure to attract orders e.g. because of a poor assessment of demand and/or not monitoring competitors. It could have also been caused by machines breaking down e.g. as a result of poor servicing and maintenance, or using defective or poor quality materials, power failures, or labour disputes, etc.

(c)   Two examples of the inter-relationships between the overhead efficiency variances and the labour and material variances are as follows:

Using an unskilled or semi-skilled worker to do the work usually performed by a skilled worker will tend to lead to a favourable labour rate variance, an adverse labour efficiency variance and an adverse material usage variance and an adverse overhead efficiency variance.

Using defective or poor quality materials could lead to an adverse material usage variance, an adverse labour efficiency variance and an adverse overhead efficiency variance, and in some cases a favourable material price variance.

37   Alpha

Key answer tips

In part (a) the analysis of costs between fixed and variable elements is basically done for you - it is mainly a question of combining the manufacturing and selling costs for each element, in order to obtain a standard marginal cost of sales per unit and the total period budgeted fixed costs. These are then used in the computation of break-even, and predicted loss for the *actual* sales level.

In part (b) (i) the proof of the volume variance given is fairly straightforward, but 3 out of the 5 marks are for the explanation of its significance - don't miss this out. Just a quick explanation as to how it arises will get some marks, even if you're not sure of how it may be useful information.

In part (b)(ii) the variable selling overhead variance is purely an expenditure (or rate) variance - based upon *actual sales* volume. When considering the fixed overhead variances, this could in fact be restricted to just the expenditure variance (*budget* total cost versus actual) as the profit statement could imply that it is not absorbed into units sold but treated as a period cost. It is, however, possible to compute a volume variance if this is not assumed - and the marks indicate that this is required.

Part (c) of the question is the explanation of why a budgeted loss, using marginal costing principles (calculated in (a)) turns to a profit when actual values and absorption costing is used. A moment of thought before launching into the mechanics should identify two basic reasons for this - one is the differences between budgeted and actual revenues/costs (as highlighted by variances) and the other is stock valuation (the overriding factor in this case).

You have already got some variances from the question and (b); the only additional variance required is sales price (sales margin volume is not required as you are starting with budgeted loss for *actual* sales), and you also don't need fixed cost volume variances . The remaining reconciling item is the difference in stock valuation under marginal and absorption costing. Finally, don't lose the last 3 marks by failing to explain what you have shown (or attempted to show) with your figures.

(a)   Break-even point

$$= \quad \frac{£140,000}{£17-£7.50} = \frac{£140,000}{£9.50}$$

$$= \quad 14,737$$

		£
Sales	12,400kg × £17	210,800
Marginal costs	12,400kg × £7.50	93,000
		117,800
Fixed costs		140,000
Loss		22,200

(b)   (i)   Manufacturing volume variance:

	£
Budgeted volume	20,000kg
Actual volume	18,400kg
	1,600kg
Manufacturing fixed overhead rate	£5.00
Volume variance	£8,000

The volume variance is caused by the month's actual production level falling below the volume that was used to compute the fixed overhead recovery rate. It is an under-recovery of fixed overhead, which the company has charged against the profits for period 1. It does not specifically represent an extra cost or a loss to the company as these fixed costs would be incurred anyway. It acts as a convenient reconciliation (a book-keeping bridge) between the budgeted and actual volume of the period. It occurs because an absorption costing system identifies fixed overhead costs with products based on a unit rate.

(ii)   Variable selling overhead:

	£
12,400 × £1.5	18,600
Incurred	17,500
Expenditure variance	1,100 Fad.
Fixed selling overhead:	
Recovered:	
12,400 × £2	24,800
Budget	40,000
Volume variance	15,200 Adv.
Budget	40,000
Incurred	38,300
Expenditure variance	1,700 Fav.

NB: Different approaches are acceptable and note that not all of these values are used in part (c).

(c)
	£	£
Predicted loss		22,200
Expenditure variances		
Manufacturing	5,500 A	
Variable sales	1,100 F	
Fixed sales	1,700 F	
Selling price variance	2,000 A	
Fixed overhead carried forward in stock value	30,000 F	
		25,300
Actual profit		3,100

The reconciliation is achieved when all the differences between the two statements are accounted for. This involves expenditure variances which were not in the budgeted statement (a) but were adjusted in the profit statement given. It is not appropriate to adjust for volume variances as both statements ultimately reflect the actual fixed costs and these are the only costs to which volume variances apply.

The actual profit statement reports the sales value of £208,800 but 12,400 units at a standard price of £17 should return £210,800 so a price variance of £2,000 is deduced.

Finally, and most significantly, a variable costing statement applies variable manufacturing costs only to stock values. An absorption costing statement, which the company uses for reporting purposes, values stock at full manufacturing cost. The production and sales levels for P1 imply 6,000kg were added to stock, therefore a difference between the two stock values accounts for a difference in profit. The absorption costing statement is adjusted (relieved of cost) by the fixed overhead carried forward in the increased stock value. That is 6,000kg at £5 per kg fixed overhead rate, £30,000. By allowing for the direction of these adjustments a reconciliation is achieved.

38   Hairdressing

Key answer tips

In part (a) in order to be able to reconcile them you need to first determine what the budgeted and actual profit figures are. Now move onto the variance analysis, treating clients like product units and commissions like variable labour costs. Using a marginal costing approach, as required, results in sales mix and quantity variances being valued at standard contribution (revenue - commission) and there being no fixed overhead volume variance.

In part (b) you've computed the numbers in (a) - now use them to tell a story. State what the figures are showing (not 'adverse cost variance' but 'costs higher than expected'), then try to suggest a cause. Since the examiner specifically asked for the mix variance, it is important that you comment on it here. Look for links between variances wherever possible.

In part (c) some of the comments that may be made relate to all variances, not just sales - inappropriateness of standards, outdated standards etc. But you must quickly focus on the sales aspects, and the relevance of the mix/quantity analysis for possibly unrelated products is an important point to raise. As usual, try to gear your answer to the particular business concerned whenever possible.

(a)

	Budget £	Actual £
Sales – Male	30,000	16,000
Sales – Female	18,000	40,000
Commission – Male	12,000	7,000
Commission – Female	10,000	22,000
Fixed costs	20,000	24,000
Profit	6,000	3,000

Profit variance £3,000A

		£
Price variances –	Male 2,000 (8.0 – 7.5)	1,000F
	Female 2,000 (20.0 – 18.0)	4,000F
Mixture variance		4,200F
Quantity variance		5,200A
Fixed overhead expenditure (20,000 – 24,000)		4,000A
Labour rate variance –	Male 2,000 × (3.0 – 3.5)	1,000A
	Female 2,000 × (10.0 – 11.0)	2,000A
		3,000A

Workings – mixture and quantity variances

AC AM SC	AV BM SC	BV BM SC
9,000	14,400	18,000
16,000	6,400	8,000
25,000	20,800	26,000

mixture £4,200F   quantity £5,200A

AV AM SC is actual volume × actual mix × standard contribution.
$$4,000 \times 0.5 \times £4.5 = £9,000$$
$$4,000 \times 0.5 \times £8.0 = £16,000$$

AV BM SC is actual volume × budget mix × standard contribution
$$4,000 \times 0.8 \times £4.5 = £14,400$$
$$4,000 \times 0.2 \times £8.0 = £6,400$$

BV BM SC is budget volume × budget mix × standard contribution
$$4,000 \times 4.5 = £18,000$$
$$1,000 \times 8.0 = £8,000$$

(b)

MEMORANDUM

To: Manager   **Franchise Ref:**

The overall result is below the budget expectations, the variance analysis will help to explore the reasons for this. It appears that it has been possible to put prices up beyond the level that was envisaged, or clients have been requiring different treatments which has lifted the overall price. This applies to both male and female clients, as the price variances are both in the same direction.

The level of business was significantly less than planned, only 80% of the planned number of clients were attracted to the business. There was a significantly favourable move concerning the mix of clients. Far more female clients attended and they had a higher level of contribution than male clients, resulting in a favourable mix variance. In overall terms the effect of the sales side on the profitability of the business was favourable compared to the original budget.

The adverse profit implications came from higher than planned commission rates paid to staff, perhaps this was likely given the higher than average selling prices achieved. The other negative impact reported was the variance on fixed overhead expenditure and further detail is required here before any corrective action can be anticipated. It may be difficult to change fixed overheads and, depending on further analysis, it may be necessary to amend the budget figure.

(c)   When interpreting the disaggregation of the profit variance with particular reference to sales variances various limitations can be suggested. In the particular business environment envisaged it may be difficult to set 'standard' selling prices, so any variances need to be interpreted with care. It may not be possible, for example, to apply the same rigour as in manufacturing situations, however these approximate targets may prove useful.

It should be noted that the actual sales performance is being compared to a budget which may have been set some time ago. In this regard the extent to which it may have become out of date must be considered. A more recently revised forecast could be used as an alternative.

The splitting of price and volume implications in these variances, whilst common in both theory and practice, needs care in interpretation. There is little doubt that in many market situations the prices and quantities are interrelated, one cannot be read without the other. In the example in part (a) it is possible to suggest that the situation represents a move along the demand curve.

Finally, the attempt to report mix and quantity variances may be dubious. A mix variance seems to imply some relationship between the respective products and that this is incorporated in the planning process. To provide management with a mix variance where no relationship exists is spurious, they should perhaps tackle the quantity differences separately. In the simple example produced in part (a) there may be no connection between the change in male/female attendance.

39   Information source

Key answer tips

In parts(a) and (b) take care to clearly distinguish four purposes (and no more) and three performance levels (and no more). Whilst the latter is standard textbook material, the former needs more thought to avoid launching into a standard reply on the role of budgets.

In part (c) there are two distinct parts so ensure you address both. However, with only four marks overall, don't spend too long. State your view, then support it with a brief explanation and one or two examples.

Part (d) of the question is designed to test your 'higher skills'. You may be able to compute variances in your sleep, but can you stand back from the mechanics and critically evaluate the assumptions and principles upon which they are based? Even if you can't think of much to say, you must be seen to address each of the specified types of variances in your answer.

(a)   A standard costing system can support a wide range of management requirements. For example:

- It can help in the development of budgets; standards are in effect the building blocks of periodic budgets.

- If handled correctly by management the existence of an appropriately set standard can act as a target and hence become a source of employee motivation.

- To the extent that standards are measures of expected performance by departments or individuals, standard costs are the basis for measuring performance.

Following on from the above, the variances that are derived from standard costs act as a control device by highlighting those activities which are different from plans. This signals to decision makers the need for action to take advantage of any circumstances which have produced favourable variances or minimise the repercussions of any adverse variances.

Standard costs are predicted future costs which can be used to support decision making, for example in making pricing decisions.

In manufacturing companies a key requirement of costing is the valuation of stock. Standard costs simplify the process of tracing costs to products for stock valuation.

NB: The question asks for four of the above.

(b)   Three different levels of performance are as follows:

Basic standards – such standards are left unchanged for a long period, perhaps from the inception of the product or service concerned. They may be useful in demonstrating a progression of improved performance over a period of time, but do not represent current targets. Therefore, they do not motivate, they do not result in representative unit costs and are inappropriate as predicted costs for decisions.

Ideal standards – these represent perfect performance and the most efficient operating conditions reflecting the lowest possible costs. They are a useful objective to which the firm can aspire over the long term but firms will rarely achieve this level of performance consistently. As a result adverse variances will almost always be reported, this will inevitably have an adverse effect on employee attitude and motivation. They represent budget figures which are too tight and inappropriate from which to set prices or to use directly as performance measures in most circumstances.

Currently attainable standards – these standards represent costs which should be attained under current efficient operating conditions. They are a reasonable target and represent a likely level of future costs if operations are managed efficiently. They are a level of performance which does not demotivate staff. They are therefore the figures which can be used to manage the current operations of a business unit. They are figures which can support planning and decision-making and as current cost levels they are appropriate for stock valuation. It should be expected that most companies will run their systems based on these standards. The first two levels mentioned above may, on the other hand, be useful for strategic purposes, demonstrating on an adhoc basis, how far the company has come or how far it has to go.

(c)   Standard costing is most suited to organisations whose activities consist of a series of common or repetitive operations. Typically, mass production manufacturing operations are indicative of its area of application. It is

◆ FOULKS*lynch*

also possible to envisage operations within the service sector to which standard cost may apply, though this may not be costed with the same degree of accuracy of standards which apply in manufacturing. For example, hotels and restaurants often use standard recipes for food preparation, dealing with conference attendance can be like a mass production environment. Similarly, banks will have common processes for dealing with customer transactions, processing cheques etc. It is possible therefore that the principles of standard costing may be extended to service industries.

In modern manufacturing and service businesses, continuous improvement and cost reduction are topical. In order to remain competitive it is essential that businesses address the cost levels of their various operations. To do this they have to deal with the costing of operations. But the drive to 'cost down' may mean in some cases that standards do not apply for long before a redesign or improvement renders them out of date. In such a setting an alternative to the use of standard costs is to compare actual costs with those of the previous operating period. We have seen in (a) above that a standard costing system has a variety of purposes. It is for management to judge their various reasons for employing standard costing, and consequently whether their aims of continuous improvement and cost reduction renders the system redundant.

(d)   Standard costing variances are a convenient way of summarising the results of an operating period by focusing on the financial impact of deviations from a budgeted result. The variances, which can be identified as to cause and responsibility, are in total the absolute difference that actual results bear to an original plan. The exercise of variance analysis is not without difficulty however, and the following is a critique of the technique, bringing out some of the practical problems.

For direct costs the traditionally adopted formula creates an analysis of price and usage variances. However, this division is only by the convention of the variance formula and the existence of joint variances influenced by a combination of price and usage could also be compiled in certain circumstances, say when remuneration is based on the results of the reported variance. The complexity of the variance calculation can at times however, be taken too far, for example the extraction of mix, yield and price variances say in relation to materials costs can be questionable. Most of these variances can be inter-related. It is dangerous to interpret individual variances in isolation, interdependency should be recognised.

Concerning variable and fixed overheads, the level of costs are controllable against a budget and this is often a fixed budget. When activity levels change it is important to remember that the variable costs need to be flexed to allow for this. This raises the problem of which costs to flex and what measure of activity (i.e. number of units, hours of work etc.) to use as the basis of flexing. There is unlikely to be exact correlation between the measure of activity chosen (say labour hours) and the cost change, therefore care should be exercised in the interpretation of these variances. A comparison of the actual and standard activity levels facilitates the extraction of an efficiency variance in relation to variable overheads. Whether the results of such analysis reflect a more or less efficient use of variable overhead resources has been questioned.

Perhaps the variance which attracts most criticism is the fixed overhead volume variance. This variance represents the fixed overhead cost or benefit of working at a volume level below or above that which was budgeted. Though it is important to reconcile budget and actual volumes, the value applied to the volume variance does not report a meaningful cost in all circumstances. For example, as costs are fixed, by definition, extra volume, if available, is 'free' up to a certain limit. In other circumstances if time is scarce then the cost of any time wasted, for example, may be far higher than the fixed overhead rate. It has been pointed out that the calculation of an overhead recovery rate per unit or per hour applied to fixed overheads may be unhelpful because it is in effect treating fixed overheads as if they were variable costs.

N.B. In the latter stages of this question, especially parts (c) and (d), there is scope for slightly different content or views to be expressed than those in the outline answer. Credit will be given for points other than those stated above.

40   Performance meeting

Key answer tips

The main difficulty you may encounter in part (a) is the summation of formulae – but there are only two marks overall, so spend a minimal amount of time on it.

The main approach in part (b) is to write down the relevant formula (in whatever form you like), plug in the known values and rearrange to find the required unknown. If your computation of one part relies on an answer to a previous part, which you haven't been able to compute, then make something up! The examiner wants to see that you can use the formulae, even with the wrong numbers.

Part (c) builds on (b), and the same comment applies to figures you haven't got. Set out a proforma computation (type of cost, std qty × std price – std cost) then start to fill in the blanks. Look back at the original data in the question to pick up those figures that can be slotted in straightaway, then use your answers to (b) to deduce the rest.

Part (d) – there is only one overall cost variance for variable overheads, but you can still talk about its interpretation in terms of the possible underlying efficiency and rate variances. The fixed overhead variance is analysed out, and you can be more specific about the causes. You should at least state that the volume variance is due to lower production levels than budgeted; using the data to calculate the extent of this will be the icing on the cake.

(a)   Rate variance $AH(SR – AR)$
                                     or $(AH \times SR) – (AH \times AR)$

Efficiency variance $(SH – AH)SR$ or $(SH \times SR) – (AH \times SR)$
Adding the second expressions in each case:
$$(AH \times SR) – (AH \times AR) + (SH \times SR) – (AH \times SR)$$

Clear brackets and cancel common terms leaves:
$$(SH \times SR) – (AH \times AR)$$

(b)   (i) $\dfrac{\text{Actual wages cost}}{\text{Actual rate per hour}}$

$\dfrac{£97,350}{£8.85}$

$= 11,000$ hours

(ii)   LRV $= AH(SR – AR)$

£1,650 $= 11,000(SR – £8.85)$

£0.15 $= SR – £8.85$

SR $= £9.00$

(iii)   LEV $= SR(SH – AH)$

£9,000 $= £9.00(SH – 11,000)$

£1,000 $= SH – 11,000$

SH $= 12,000$ hours

(iv)   Number of units $= \dfrac{12,000}{3} = 4,000$ units

(v)   DMPV $= (SP – AP)AU$

$– £5,700 = (– £0.30) AU$

AU $= 19,000$ kg

(vi) $\dfrac{\text{Actual cost}}{\text{Actual usage}}$

$\dfrac{£62,700}{19,000 \text{ kg}}$

Actual price $= £3.30$ per kg.

(vii)   Standard price of material = £3.30 – £0.30 = £3.00 per kg.

DMV   = SC – AC

£2,700   = SC – £62,700

SC   = £60,000

$$\text{Standard usage} = \frac{\text{Standard Cost}}{\text{Standard Price}}$$

$$= \frac{£60,000}{£3}$$

= 20,000 kg

Note: Alternative calculations are acceptable, e.g.
Standard usage   = Actual units × SQ per unit
= 4,000 × 5 kg
= 20,000 kg.

(c)   The solution to this part is contained in the right-hand column.

	Actual cost	Variance	Total standard cost recovered	Standard cost per unit	
	£	£	£	£	£
			(4,000 units) (12,000 std.hrs.)		
Dir. Matl.	62,700	(2,700)	60,000	5 kg at £3	15.00
Dir. Labour	97,350	10,650	108,000	3 hrs at £9	27.00
Var. o/hd.	19,500	(1,500)	18,000	3 hrs at £1.50	4.50
Fixed o/hd.	106,500	(16,500)	90,000	3 hrs at £7.50	22.50
			276,000		69.00

(d)   **Fixed overhead variances**

The fixed overhead expenditure variance of £1,500 indicates that spending was higher than the level set by the fixed budget. As these costs have been categorised as fixed the target spending level will not have been changed from that which was originally budgeted in spite of any changes in business volume. The volume variance of £15,000 adverse shows that the volume of business actually achieved (4,000 units or 12,000 standard hours) was below that which was budgeted for the period. The volume variance is in effect identifying the under recovery of fixed overheads. It is possible to determine the shortfall in production that occurred by dividing the variance by the fixed overhead recovery rate, that is, £15,000/£7.5 = 2,000 standard hours of work or 667 units. The original budgeted production was 14,000 hours and the original budget of fixed overheads £105,000.

Variable overhead variance

Variable overheads are applied to the product using standard hours. As there was a favourable labour efficiency variance reported it follows that the favourable effect of this efficiency on costs could apply, not only to direct labour, but also to variable overheads, i.e. all costs that vary with hours worked. The implication is that greater efficiency enabled time to be saved and hence a lower expenditure on variable costs was to be expected. However, management appear to have elected not to report this variance separately and hence there is only one variance related to variable overheads, £1,500 Adv. This is therefore reflecting the combined effect of both spending and efficiency. For the month in question any efficiency saving that may have occurred was outweighed by the fact that the actual expenditure, i.e. bills paid, was greater than the flexible budget set by the number of hours.

41   Food manufacturer

Key answer tips

Your are given an original budget, followed by some post-budget planning changes, and then actual figures. This should lead you into thinking along the lines of planning and operational variances. However, four things point towards these being required as part of the discussion in (c) rather than as an explicit part of the variance analysis in (b):

- the question states that the original budget is to be used as a reference point
- there is no detail about the changes to the methods of working
- there is no mention of planning and operational variances in requirement (b)
- the budget prepared in (a) is based upon the original figures.

So parts (a) and (b) are standard budget/variance analysis computations. Whilst the examiner has incorporated some of his workings in the discussion in (c), you are best advised to set these out clearly following your answer to (b).

It is in part (c) that you should make use of the information regarding post-budget planning changes. Start with an overall summary of the picture painted by the analysis in (b), then look at individual variances, tying them in to the changes where possible. You must also address the specific areas required by the question, interrelationships and overheads.

(a)

	Flexed Budget		Actual		Variance	
Units	240,000		240,000			
	£000	£000	£000	£000	£000	£000
Sales		1,200		1,080		120A
Ingredients	480		520			40A
Labour and energy	120		110			10F
	———	600	———	630		
Contribution		600		450		
Fixed O'heads		300		340		40A
		———		———		———
		300		110		190A

NB: The answer only specifically required the flexible budget.

(b)   An overall reconciliation of profit is as follows:

	£000	£000
Budget profit		200.0
Sales volume contribution variance	100.0F	100.0
		———
Budget profit for actual sales		300.0
Sales price variance	120.0A	
Ingredient usage variance	74.7A	
Ingredient price variance	34.7F	
Labour and energy variance	10.0F	
Overhead expenditure variance	40.0A	
	———	(190.0)A
Actual profit		110.0

An alternative layout of the above table is acceptable.

For the material variances, the standard quantity for actual output is 1,200,000 kg, the actual quantity used is 1,386,667 kg. (£520,000/£0.375). Hence, the usage variance is 186,667 kg at the standard price of 40p = £74,667A. The material price variance is the price reduction of 2.5p per kg on all of the ingredients used, i.e. 1,386,667 kg = £34,667F. The table above is shown in £'000 and the variances have been rounded to one decimal place. Explanation of some of the other variance calculations occurs within the commentary which follows.

(c)   Commentary

The budgeted sales volume was 200,000 packs whereas 240,000 packs were actually sold, a volume increase of 20%. The material, labour and energy costs are dealt with as totally variable costs. This results in the contribution margin (using the original budget) being £2.50 per pack (£1,000,000–£400,000–£100,000)/200,000. It can be seen that the increased volume earned £100,000 extra standard contribution (40,000 × £2.50) compared to the original budget. The price reduction of 50p per pack, however, caused sales revenue and hence profits to fall by £120,000. It would be useful to examine the sales price and volume variances together because of the interrelationship between them. The price reduction will have had an impact on the volume sold and this, which was probably anticipated, should be noted by the management. This marketing tactic, of trading off price and volume (moving along the demand curve), does not appear to have been entirely successful, but we have no information about the experiences of other manufacturers of similar products. There could have been an unexpected downturn of the whole market. For example, the position could have been worse if the company had not decided to reduce the price. To investigate further they should perhaps, look outside the organisation for more market intelligence.

The actual total cost of material exceeded that which was planned by £40,000. It is possible to analyse this difference further from the information supplied. The price reduction obtained was worth £34,667, a favourable variance. A substantial adverse usage variance of £74,667 occurred. The purchasing department would appear to have succeeded in making purchases of ingredients at favourable prices. If, however, after further investigation the ingredient usage variance is found to be due to waste caused by poorer quality purchases, this has been a false economy. This is a further example of possible interrelationships among variances and should be noted to inform future decisions on ingredient sourcing. It is not appropriate from current information to jump to conclusions about poor quality ingredients; theft or an error in the figures collected could be the cause. If, however, the ingredients are of a poorer quality then there may also be long-term repercussions in subsequent sales of these or other products, another example of interrelationships between the variances which should be borne in mind.

The labour and energy costs show a small favourable variance so the changed method of working has made a difference, providing these are completely variable costs. The actual costs incurred were more than the original budget but less than the budget when it is flexed for the increased volume. From the information given it is not possible to isolate labour and energy variances separately. Nor is it possible to identify rate and efficiency variances for these variable costs.

The actual fixed overheads were greater than the budget by £40,000. The detailed expenses should be consulted to identify any reasons for cost differences, to judge whether the costs are controllable and what action is needed, or whether the budget should be revised. Reduction of fixed overheads in the short-term may be particularly problematic. Scope to 'manage' the fixed costs (see expenditure variance) may occur when there is some potential to renegotiate prices or use resources more efficiently perhaps resulting in some resources being disposed of, including staffing economies. However, some of the fixed costs may be uncontrollable in the short-term, for example, the rates applied to premises cannot change unless some premises are vacated. Such changes cannot be made immediately, there may therefore be, at best, a lag in any economies in this area. The company is attempting to increase market share through increased sales, this should result in a greater total contribution to overall costs, but this in itself does not reduce costs.

Budgeting, budgetary control and decision-making

42   Cepheus Transport Co Ltd

Key answer tips

This question focuses on budgetary control information in a service business scenario. Part (a) is quite an open requirement, and you need to think carefully about the type and format of the performance measures you use. As well as doing some sort of overall profit computation, you should think about costs per unit. Although cost units are typically more difficult to define for service industries, transport companies will often use miles or some variant (passenger-miles), and the data in the question lends itself to this.

Direct your answer to part (b) towards the particular business concerned, using as much of the information given as possible, including any numerical data, to illustrate the points made.

REPORT

To: Mrs Cepheus
Chief Executive
Cepheus Transport Co Ltd

Date:

(a) **An evaluation of current performance**

I have now completed my evaluation of the data which you supplied. From the limited amount of data which you provided, it can be observed that currently, your company is making an overall profit of £21,870 which is computed as follows:

	£
Revenue received	165,702
Less: Operating costs (including depreciation)	85,612
Gross profit	80,090
Less: Administration costs and other fixed overheads (including rent)	58,220
Net profit	21,870

The revenue generated *per mile* is:

Type of vehicle	*Type F*	*Type P*	*Type U*
From holding company	£1.825	£1.675	£1.225
From other companies	£3.200	£2.645	£1.900
Operating cost (per mile) (including depreciation)	£1.055	£1.082	£1.062

The revenue per mile for each type of vehicle is in excess of the operating cost per mile. However, the revenue per mile from the holding company is well below that which is generated from dealing with other companies. This will have the effect of increasing the holding company's own profits, because they are apparently paying below market rates for the service which you provide, and reducing your own profits. If you are to be judged on your performance, it is important that you take up this matter with the holding company. If the holding company can pay rates which are nearer to the market rates this will raise your profits and provide you with funds for the expansion of your business and for the replacement of motor vehicles and other fixed assets.

Depreciation policy

In my opinion, in view of the high cost of motor vehicles, it would be fairer to compute your depreciation using the 'time apportionment' basis i.e. you charge depreciation on say a month-by-month basis, from the date of purchase to the date of disposal.

Information needed

Should you wish me to do a more in depth appraisal of your performance I would need copies of your published accounts and access to your financial accounting recording system.

Pricing policy

There was also insufficient data relating to your pricing policy. However, I must stress the need for you to monitor:

– your costs
– your competitors e.g. their prices and services
– the economic environment e.g. social factors, legislation etc. which may have a direct impact on your business.

(b) **Improvements to the management accounting information system**

I suggest that you consider giving a higher priority to management accounting, so that you may receive information which is up-to-date, and relevant, information which will help you with planning, control and decision-making. I propose that you consider making the following improvements.

More detailed records for each individual motor vehicle of:

- the revenue, analysed between the holding company and others
- their operating costs in terms of fuel, wages, insurance, etc
- the amount spent on repairs and maintenance
- the depreciation charged to date, using the time apportionment basis
- the mileage
- an analysis of waiting time
- the revenue per mile, cost per mile, fuel consumption per mile etc.

At the moment, the fuel consumption can only be calculated for each group of vehicles, as follows:

Vehicle	Type F	Type P	Type U
Diesel (gallons) (Fuel cost ÷ 2)	2,184	702	876
Miles	40,600	15,520	24,480
Miles per gallon	18.59	22.11	27.95

The information above provides the average miles per gallon for each class of motor vehicle. Hidden in the average, could be one or more vehicles which for various reasons are performing badly. The information needed to produce this analysis can be extracted from the log sheets/records which are kept by the drivers.

Using budgetary control

Budgets will provide the company with targets for revenues and costs and provide a means of control via the frequent comparison of budgeted and actual figures. This should help the company to take appropriate corrective action to put right that which is not going according to plan. All the aspects of the business would be taken into account in producing the 'master budget' i.e. a budgeted trading and profit and loss account, balance sheet and cash budget.

To illustrate the need for budgeting, consider its application to the repairs and maintenance of vehicles expenditure. The budgeting process will require planning of what maintenance is to be done and when it is to be done for each vehicle. Spending targets will be compared with actuals on say, a monthly basis, and significant adverse variances highlighted on reports and investigated so that management can decide upon what action needs to be taken.

Devoting more time/resources to the management accounting activities

You need information for planning, control and decision-making purposes. You need information which can help you:

- make vehicle-by-vehicle internal comparisons
- to decide whether or not to use a sub-contractor
- to compare buying vehicles with leasing vehicles
- to review the possibility of using other forms of transport e.g. rail, air, sea
- to evaluate the cost of carrying out your own maintenance of vehicles with the cost of using a garage
- to formulate your pricing policy
- to assess the performance of vehicles loaned to you for testing purposes.

Improving efficiency

Other areas which you will need to look at are:

- route planning, to avoid hold-ups that could cost you time and money
- scheduling, to make the best possible use of vehicles in terms of capacity, loading etc
- monitoring the efficiency of keeping to delivery times
- making use of idle capacity, especially on return journeys.

Fixed costs

One final observation which needs to be drawn to your attention is the high level of fixed costs which you have to recover. The fixed costs make up around 63% of the operating costs, excluding the overtime premium and the fixed element, if any, included in the operating and maintenance costs. The company's current break-even point, based on the above assumptions, may be computed as follows:

	£'000
Revenue	166
Less: Variable costs	31
Contribution	135 (81% of the revenue)

$$\text{Fixed costs } £54,000 \times \frac{100}{81} = £67,000 \text{ break-even point (40\% of revenue)}$$

To break even, the company needs to operate at around 40% of current capacity. In the event of a downturn in the economy causing the company's operations to fall below its break-even point, a loss-making situation would arise.

Conclusions and recommendations

One of the principal findings to the lower earnings made was in connection with the work performed for the holding company. If you are to stand on your own feet and be responsible for your own performance, you need to be able to charge the holding company a fair price. This should enable you to generate more funds for re-investment and make you better able to assess your profitability.

More resources need to be devoted to the provision/ supply of management accounting information which will assist you to plan and control the company more effectively and help you with your decision-making. This includes introducing a system of budgetary control which provides targets for both costs and revenues, and by continuous comparison with actuals, provides an 'early warning' of where things are going wrong.

In view of the limited amount of data which was provided, and the wide scope of this report, I will be pleased to discuss any of the above matters with you personally in greater detail.

43   Flexible budgeting

Key answer tips

In part (a) having decided that the budget needs flexing, you then have to be careful not to over-complicate matters by flexing fixed costs, which will result in the total variance incorporating a volume variance. The format of the statement in the question is along marginal costing lines (cost of sales are all variable) so stick with this. The re-drafting of the statement should be kept as simple as possible, to allow enough time for comments on possible causes. Note that the examiner has awarded one mark for a general conclusion, in which the major differences are highlighted.

Note that in part (a) all *variable* budget costs / revenues have been flexed by multiplying by a factor of 720/640 = 1.125. Fixed costs are unflexed. The variances calculated are thus those expected in an MC operating statement, though the layout is more consistent with absorption costing.

In part (b) you are asked to explain the rationale of the adjustments you have made in (a).

In part (c) many of the general problems in forecasting future costs and revenues are relevant here, but do try to include particular considerations of flexible budgeting, that depends upon a reasonable understanding of the cost behaviours involved.

(a)   **Revised operating statement based on sales of 720,000 units**

	Budget £'000	Actual £'000	Variance £'000	*Possible reasons for the variance*
Sales	1,152	1,071	(81)	Sales made to certain segments at lower prices. Bulk discounts given to customers.
Cost of sales				
Materials	189	144	45	Buying in bulk and attracting discount. Buying lower quality materials.
Labour (variable)	270	288	(18)	More time taken to work, lower quality material. More overtime worked to cope with increased volume.
Labour (fixed)	100	94	6	Fixed lower than budget could be caused by employees leaving and not being replaced.
Overheads	36	36	Nil	
	595	562	33	
Gross profit	557	509	(48)	(As above)
Other overheads				
Selling and distribution				
Fixed	72	83	(11)	Additional fixed advertising cost.
Variable	162	153	9	Better vehicle utilisation.
Administration				
Fixed	184	176	8	Staff leave but not replaced
Variable	54	54	Nil	immediately
	472	466	6	
Net profit	85	43	(42)	(As above)

The principal reasons for the variation between budgeted and actual net profits are the sales revenue being lower than planned and the £45,000 less than planned expenditure on materials plus the increased variable labour costs.

Note: The above statement could have used a marginal costing format, and other reasons for variances are possible.

(b)   When budget and actual figures are compared, and variances extracted, it is most important that 'like is compared with like' i.e. that the budgeted 'level of activity' is the same as the actual 'level of activity'. The statement provided is not a fair and valid comparison, as it is comparing sales and costs for 640,000 units with an actual of 720,000.

(c)   The problems associated with forecasting figures which are to be used in flexible budgeting are:

–   Using past information to forecast the future does not always provide reliable forecasts. What happened in the past does not always hold true for the future e.g. records showing how much material was used are just a starting point in the assessment of what quantities should be used.

–   Flexible budgeting relies on being able to separate costs into their fixed and variable elements. This is not always an easy task e.g. direct labour can be fixed or variable or a combination of the two such as a fixed salary plus a bonus based on output.

–   The computation of step-fixed costs also needs to be considered. Fixed costs can go up or down as output increases/decreases e.g. shedding labour, hiring/renting more machinery and equipment.

–   Another problem is concerned with sorting out the underlying assumptions upon which the budget is to be based e.g. the rate of inflation, the level of sales, constraints imposed by limiting factors, judgements re probability, etc.

44   Sychwedd plc

Key answer tips

In part (a) a machine hour rate needs total budgeted overheads for the period (given in the question) and total machine hours budgeted to be worked. The latter is determined from budgeted product activity levels (here, production = sales) and machine hours by products (here given in terms of hours per 1,000 kg).

In part (b) the computations required are not complex, but there are a lot of numbers to work through. You need to make sure you set out your answer in such a way that the examiner can award marks for method even if you make the odd slip here and there. Set up a proforma statement first, ensuring you can identify the contribution line as well as profit, then use separate workings where necessary to compute the figures. These should be referenced in to your statement.

In part (c) it is a temptation to think that by the time you have worked your way through the data for the first two parts, you're virtually there, and it needs only a quick note or two for this part. When there are this many marks involved, this is a dangerous strategy. At the very least, as the question specifically refers to the sales trend, you can assess what is happening to each product in this respect. Consider both the sales volumes and the resulting contributions, as you have this information for both periods. On the whole, you should be ignoring fixed costs in your analysis as they are absorbed on a relatively arbitrary basis. Then look for any other points worthy of mention – e.g. high proportion of material costs.

(a)

	Machine group	
Period 2	*1*	*2*
Product		
R (10 × machine hours per 1,000)	750	800
S (25 × machine hours per 1,000)	750	2,750
T (50 × machine hours per 1,000)	2,500	2,500
Budgeted machine hours	4,000	6,050
Overheads (given)	£40,800	£68,365
Machine hour rate	£10.20	£11.30

(b)

		Product Profitability Analysis		
Period 2		*Product R*	*Product S*	*Product T*
	Kilos	10,000	25,000	50,000
		£	£	£
Sales	(A)	110,000	250,000	450,000
Direct materials		45,080	127,400	306,250
Variable labour and overheads		5,650	12,500	16,000
	(see W1)			
Sales commission at 4%		4,400	10,000	18,000
Variable cost	(B)	55,130	149,900	340,250
Contribution	(A)–(B)	54,870	100,100	109,750
Fixed overheads	(W2)	16,690	38,725	53,750
Budgeted net profit		38,180	61,375	56,000

◈ FOULKS*lynch*

Workings

(W1) **Variable labour and overheads**

Machine group Direct labour hours:			Labour and overhead rate per hour	Products R £	S £	T £
	R	S	T			
1	30 :	10 :	20	£7.50	225	75	150
2	40 :	50 :	20	£8.50	340	425	170
					565	500	320
Number of batches					10	25	50
Variable labour and overheads					£5,650	£12,500	£16,000

(W2) **Fixed overheads**

Machine group Machine hours			Machine hour rate	Products R £	S £	T £
	R	S	T			
1	75 :	30 :	50	£10.20	765	306	510
2	80 :	110 :	50	£11.30	904	1,243	565
					1,669	1,549	1,075
Number of batches					10	25	50
Fixed overheads					£16,690	£38,725	£53,750

The net profit figures have been calculated using absorption costing i.e. absorbing fixed overheads into the product costs via arbitrary bases such as floor area, number of employees etc, in addition to the variable costs.

The fixed overhead recovery rate uses machine hours i.e. an output based measure, when in fact a lot of the fixed overheads will tend to vary more with time than output. Absorption costing is an attempt to ensure that costs are recovered. It does not attempt to provide accurate and realistic product costs. The marginal costing contribution approach, only includes those costs which vary with output i.e. the variable costs, and by indicating the amount which each product contributes towards the recovery of the fixed overheads and profit, is considered to be the more appropriate method for decision-making purposes.

(c)   At the outset it should be noted that the budgets are only estimates and that the assumptions on which they were based could change. They provide targets against which the actual performance can be compared as and when the information becomes available.

For decision-making purposes management need to use a contribution approach and also assess where the product is in its life cycle.

The sales of product R are expected to fall. If this continues in the future, the product will be in the decline stage of its *life cycle* and a time could come when its contribution would not cover the fixed overheads assigned to it, meaning that they would have to be recovered out of the contributions generated by the other products.

Product S, if it continues to remain static in terms of the sales demand would appear to have reached its peak. However, there should be a significant increase in period two in its contribution, possibly resulting from increased efficiency, improved productivity and cost reductions.

Product T could well be into its growth stage with an anticipated 25% increase in volume planned for period two. Here also the selling price is expected to remain unchanged and increases in efficiency etc should help to increase the contribution per kilo from £1.89 to around £2.20.

The management need to consider what action they can take to reverse the trends in products S and T and search for new products.

Management also needs to be made aware of the very high proportion of material costs e.g. material cost for all products as a percentage of the total cost is over 73%. This high level of investment in materials should make inventory management a very high priority. In order to reduce material costs and expensive holding costs, management will need to monitor and review the situation at frequent intervals. They could consider actions which would reduce waste e.g. better design/production methods, or reduce the cost e.g. by using substitutes.

45   Rolling budgets

Key answer tips

In part (a), even if you can't remember exactly what a rolling budget is, the question itself makes this fairly clear. Give a concise explanation of how such a budget is prepared, and then think about its advantages - again, even if you haven't specifically learnt these, you should be able to come up with some common sense ideas.

In part (b) in the introduction to the data in the question, it refers to 'the cost behaviour' of each cost item. This should alert you to the possibility that some will be fixed costs (which should be obvious), some will be purely variable (change proportionately with volume) and some will be semi-variable (change with volume, though not proportionately). You thus need to determine the fixed and variable elements of the costs from the Q1 to Q3 data, and apply these to Q4.

In part (c) this budget is prepared for three different production levels, using the Q4 unit and fixed costs computed in (b). Note that as the stock adjustment is at a standard cost, not necessarily matching that used in valuing Q4 production, you cannot simply use the sales volume to get cost of sales directly.

In part (d), given both the requirement to produce your answer in summary form only and the number of marks you have for this and comment, you need to think before launching into long repetitive revised budgets. Basically, if you produce the extra 8,000 units instead of using stock, the profit will be charged with the extra actual variable cost instead of the standard full factory cost for these units. The difference between these costs gives you most of the profit difference. You then need to recognise the impact of the bonus - which helps with the discussion part that follows.

(a)   Accounting budgets are typically prepared for the year ahead, each year being divided into months or quarters. A company can then monitor its progress as the year passes. A variation and extension of the annual budget is to regularly add a further quarter to a budget as the immediate quarter passes so that a full budget year is always in view. This approach is called a rolling or continuous budget. As Q1 progresses, Q2 is reviewed and revised in some detail, at the same time the budget for the other quarters are reviewed and updated.

Benefits of this approach are that management can always have in front of them plans for a full year. This will emphasise the longer term focus of the organisation. It also ensures that managers are constantly thinking about planning for the future and the validity of these plans. It keeps planning at the front of the manager's mind all of the year, not just at the annual budget round. As a result of this it is likely that the actual performance is being compared with a more realistic target than if the budget was prepared only once a year.

(b)   The costs are variable, semi-variable or fixed. It is necessary to determine the cost behaviour from Q1–Q3, then adjust this for Q4.

| | Q1 – Q3 | | Q4 | |
	Variable Costs £	Fixed Costs £	Variable Costs £	Fixed Costs £
Material	2.5	–	2.75	–
Labour	5.0	80,000	5.0	80,000
Factory overhead	1.5	140,000	1.5	147,000
Admin overhead	–	30,000	–	30,000
Selling overhead	0.5	20,000	0.5	21,000

Note: sample calculations:

$$Material\ Q1\quad \frac{£50,000}{20,000} = £2.5$$

$$Labour\ Q3 - Q1\quad \frac{£230,000 - £180,000}{30,000 - 20,000} = £5$$

Fixed element £230,000 – (30,000 × £5) = £80,000

Factory overhead

$$Q2 - Q1 \quad \frac{£200,000 - £170,000}{40,000 - 20,000} = £1.5$$

Fixed element £200,000 – (40,000 × £1.5) = £140,000

Selling overhead (based on sales)

$$Q2 - Q1 \quad \frac{£37,000 - £29,000}{34,000 - 18,000} = £0.5$$

Fixed element £37,000 – (34,000 × £0.5) = £20,000

Note: further calculations made with data from other quarters would confirm the rates and costs computed above.

(c)   Flexible Budget Profit Statements

	Low	Most Likely	High
	000s	000s	000s
Sales	38	44	50
Production	30	36	42
	£000	£000	£000
Material	82.5	99.0	115.5
Labour	230.0	260.0	295.0
Factory Overhead	192.0	201.0	210.0
Admin. Overhead	30.0	30.0	30.0
Selling Overhead	40.0	43.0	46.0
Cost of Production	574.5	633.0	696.5
Add stock adjustment	104.0	104.0	104.0
Prodn. Cost of sales	678.5	737.0	800.5
Sales	684.0	792.0	900.0
Profit	5.50	55.0	99.5

(d)   The change in profit will be caused by the change in costs as a result of greater production, rendering the stock adjustment undertaken for the quarter (based on absorption costing principles) unnecessary. Change in costs = 8,000 units × variable production cost £9.25.

Production (000's) units	38	44	50
	£000	£000	£000
Variable production costs	74	74	74
Additional bonus	–	10	20
Stock adjustment	104	104	104
Increase in profit	30	20	10

Under the assumption of a simple linear relationship of variable costs to volume the only extra costs for 8,000 units are the variable production costs which are £9.25 per unit. For any volume above 40,000 units there is also the bonus payment to incorporate (in the case of the high volume the incremental bonus payment). If the budgeted production volume is made equal to sales then the stock level at the start of quarter four will remain at the end. There is no need for a stock adjustment, or put another way, the adjustment made in part (c) can be added back. The above table shows the profit increase which will occur for the three volume levels.

Under the original volume prediction (and absorption costing principles) quarter four was being charged with fixed overhead contained in the opening stock value in addition to the fixed overhead of the period. Such overhead being transferred to that quarter from earlier accounting periods where production exceeded sales. With the revised stocking policy, the production for quarter four is equal to the sales of the quarter, and this fixed overhead is, in effect, being passed into the following year.

Regarding managerial motivation and production levels, it is apparent that the reported profit levels, under absorption costing, respond to changes in the levels of production. We have seen that during a quarter, an increase in the production results in an increase in the reported profit. This presents the possibility of opportunistic behaviour by managers wishing to enhance the level of profit being reported in any one period. They may deliberately over-produce, compared to prevailing sales demand, this production would be held in stock to be sold later, and reported profits would increase. This action would occur if they were placed in a position of needing to achieve a target profit for their bonus or performance appraisal purposes. It may be storing up trouble for the future however, because future production may have to be cut back in order to allow stock levels to be reduced. It would really only be justified if, for example, future sales were expected to be so high that they could not be met by the existing production capacity.

46   Budget compilation

Key answer tips

In part (a) the key is to remember the flow of the budgets - starting with the sales units given, *add* closing stock (finished goods) and *subtract* opening stock to get to production. This will determine materials usage, which then needs to be adjusted for opening and closing stock of raw materials in the same way to arrive at materials purchases.

In part (b) we are looking at one month only, and the main working required is that of closing stock value, incorporating the overhead absorption rate appropriate to that month's production.

In part (c), having used the company's 'monthly' system of overhead absorption in (b), you are now asked to assess its implications. You should start by stating the obvious - that stock value will fluctuate with production levels, even though budgeted overhead for the month is constant - then think how this might affect the information conveyed by the management accounts.

Part (d) is a straightforward textbook explanation of a time series and its components, and should give easy marks.

(a)   *Production Budget (units)*

	Dec	Jan	Feb	Mar	Apr
Sales	14,000	16,000	22,000	17,000	20,000
Closing stock	4,000	5,500	4,250	5,000	6,000
	18,000	21,500	26,250	22,000	26,000
Opening stock	3,500	4,000	5,500	4,250	5,000
Production	14,500	17,500	20,750	17,750	21,000

Purchases Budget (units)

	Dec	Jan	Feb	Mar
Production	14,500	17,500	20,750	17,750
Closing stock	1,750	2,075	1,775	2,100
	16,250	19,575	22,525	19,850
Opening stock	1,450	1,750	2,075	1,775
Purchases	14,800	17,825	20,450	18,075

Note: columns for January to March only are required in an answer to (a) though candidates will find that they will need some data from December for the cash budget, as well as the production for April for the purchases budget.

(b)   *Working: Product unit manufacturing cost for January*

	£
Material	10
Variable overhead and labour	16
Fixed overhead	12
	38

Note: The fixed overhead rate for January is calculated using the budgeted monthly overhead and production thus: £210,000/17,500.

Budgeted profit and loss account January 20X9

		£000	£000
Sales	16,000 × £58		928
Raw material usage	17,500 × £10	175	
Variable overhead and lab.	17,500 × £16	280	
Fixed overhead	17,500 × £12	210	
Manufacturing cost	17,500 × £38	665	
Closing stock	(5,500 × £38)	(209)	
	12,000 × £38	456	
Opening stock	4,000 × £40	160	
			616
Gross Profit			312
Selling costs			
variable	16,000 × £7	112	
fixed		164	
			276
Net Profit			36

Cash receipts and payments January 20X9

		£000	£000
Receipts			
sales	7,000 × £58		406
	8,000 × £58		464
			870
Payments:			
Material		148	
Variable overhead & labour		280	
Fixed overhead (210,000 – 54,000)		156	
Variable selling		112	
Fixed selling		164	
			860
Cash surplus			10

(c) Under a system of absorption costing an overhead rate is used to apply overheads to each unit produced. At present the company applies each month's overhead to products based upon the budgeted production levels and the budgeted expenditure in each month which are used to establish a separate predetermined rate for each month. As a result unit overhead costs fluctuate if production levels fluctuate because the fixed overheads are spread over fluctuating volumes.

It can be disconcerting and misleading for production and sales staff to be dealing with product costs which fluctuate on a monthly basis. This is especially so when the fluctuation has not been caused by changes in production efficiency and it bears no relation to changes in the general market price.

One way to overcome this is to compute an overhead rate which is based on a longer time period, for example quarterly, or a predetermined annual rate as mentioned in the question. This enables large fluctuations in, and extreme values of, product costs to be avoided. This would mean that management would be able to monitor the business volume and overhead costs on which the calculations were based to ensure that over the longer-term the average product costs which were predicted were in fact achieved.

(d) A time series is the name given to a set of observations taken at equal intervals of time in order to obtain an overall picture of what is taking place. For example, monthly sales covering a period of, say, five years. A time series consists of various components, such as trend, cyclical, seasonal and residual components.

To develop this explanation a little further, the trend component is the way in which the series appears to be moving over a long interval, after other fluctuations have been smoothed out. The cyclical component is the wave-like appearance which occurs in the series when taken over a fairly long period, a number of years. Generally it is caused by the booms and slumps in an industry or trade cycle.

A seasonal component is the regular rise and fall of values over specified intervals of time, within say one year. Though the term seasonal is used it does not have to align with seasons, but any regular variations over short time periods. Residual components are any other variations which cannot be ascribed to any of those mentioned above, essentially random factors and due to unpredictable causes.

47 Budget behaviour

Key answer tips

Part (a) should not present much difficulty, requiring a discussion of four purposes of budgeting, a list of at least six of which should be imprinted on your mind! However, you should not just reproduce the 'heading' in your list - expand it out with a couple of sentences.

Part (b) needs a bit of careful thought and planning to first of all decide exactly what it is you are being asked, and then how to answer it. The key word here is *behavioural* - do not discuss other problems of budgetary control, even if you do know a lot more about them! The best approach to a structured answer might be to think (1) what are the behavioural factors to take account of (target setting, motivation, participation etc) (2) how would they ideally be incorporated into the system and (3) what are the practical problems that may arise?

(a) An answer should cover four purposes from the six provided below.

Planning

The budget is a major short-term planning device placing the overall direction of the company into a quarterly, monthly and, perhaps, weekly focus. It ensures that managers have thought ahead about how they will utilise resources to achieve company policy in their area.

Control

Once a budget is formulated a regular reporting system can be established so that the extent to which plans are, or are not, being met can be established. Some form of management by exception can be established so that deviations from plans are identified and reactions to the deviation developed if desirable.

Co-ordination

As organisations grow the various departments benefit from the co-ordination effect of the budget. In this role budgets ensure that no one department is out of line with the action of others. They may also hold in check anyone who is inclined to pursue his or her own desires rather than corporate objectives.

Communication

The construction of the budget can be a powerful aid to defining or clarifying the lines of horizontal or vertical communication within the enterprise. Managers should have a clearer idea of what their responsibilities are, what is expected of them, and are likely to work better with others to achieve it.

Performance Evaluation

When budgets are 'tailored' to a department or manager they become useful tools for evaluating how the manager or department is performing. If sales targets are met or satisfactory service provided within reasonable spending limits then bonus or promotion prospects are enhanced.

Motivation

The value of a budget is enhanced still further if it not only states expectations but motivates managers to strive towards those expectations. This is more likely achieved if a manager has had some involvement in the budget construction, understands its implications and agrees it is fair and controllable by him/her.

(b)   If budgetary control is to be successful, attention must be paid to behavioural aspects, i.e. the effect of the system on people in the organisation and vice versa. The following are some of the points which should be borne in mind:

Budget Difficulty

It is generally agreed that the existence of some form of target or expected outcome is a greater motivation than no target at all. The establishment of a target, however, raises the question of the degree of difficulty or challenge of the target. If the performance standard is set too high or too low then sub-optimal performance could be the result. The degree of budget difficulty is not easy to establish. It is influenced by the nature of the task, the organisational culture and personality factors. Some people respond positively to a difficult target others, if challenged, tend to withdraw their commitment.

Budgets and Performance Evaluation

The emphasis on achievement of budget targets can be increased, but also the potential for dysfunctional behaviour, if the budget is subsequently used to evaluate performance. This evaluation is frequently associated with specific rewards such as remuneration increases or improved promotion prospects. In such cases it is likely that individuals will concentrate on those items which are measured and rewarded neglecting aspects on which no measurement exists. This may result in some aspects of the job receiving inadequate attention because they are not covered by goals or targets due to the complexity of the situation or the difficulty of measurement.

Managerial Style

The use of budgets in evaluation and control is also influenced by the way they are used by the superior. Different management styles of budget use have been observed, for example:

budget constrained	–	placing considerable emphasis on meeting budget targets
profit conscious	–	where a balanced view is taken between budget targets, long-term goals and general effectiveness
non-accounting	–	where accounting data is seen as relatively unimportant in the evaluation of subordinates.

The style is suggested to influence, in some cases, the superior/subordinate relationship, the degree of stress and tension involved and the likelihood of budget attainment. The style adopted and its implications are affected by the environment in which management is taking place. For example, the degree of interdependency between areas of responsibility, the uncertainty of the environment and the extent to which individuals feel they influence results are all factors to consider in relation to the management style adopted and its outcomes.

Participation

It is often suggested that participation in the budget process and discussion over how results are to be measured has benefits in terms of budget attitude and performance. Views on this point are varied however, and the personality of the individuals participating, the nature of the task (narrowly defined or flexible) and the organisation structure influence the success of participation. But a budget when carefully and appropriately established can extract a better performance from the budgetee than one in which these considerations are ignored.

Bias

Budgetees who are involved in the process from which the budget standards are set are more likely to accept them as legitimate. However, they may also be tempted to seize the opportunity to manipulate the desired performance standard in their favour. That is, they may make the performance easier to achieve and hence be able to satisfy personal goals rather than organisational goals. This is referred to as incorporating 'slack' into the budget. In this context there may be a relationship between the degree of emphasis placed on the budget and the tendency of the budgetee to bias the budget content or circumvent its control.

Any organisational planning and control system has multiple objectives but primary amongst these is encouraging staff to take organisationally desirable actions. It is never possible to predict with certainty the outcomes of all behavioural interaction however it is better to be aware of the various possible behavioural implications than to be ignorant of them.

48   Planning and control

Key answer tips

Although you may not feel you know much about the terms in (b), parts (a) and (c) offer some fairly straightforward marks for those with a good basic knowledge of budgeting. When thinking about the potential difficulties of responsibility accounting, run through in your mind how you would go about allocating responsibility for, say, the variances in a standard operating statement. The adverse labour rate variance would appear to be the responsibility of the production manager, but what if overtime was incurred in completing a rush order accepted by the sales manager? Suppose wage rates were re-negotiated during the year by general management? Suppose there was quite a lot of training time involved in the period, which will benefit future periods? These questions identify the problems of dual responsibility, uncontrollable costs and short-termism.

Note that the diagrams given in (b) are the standard, textbook, diagrams of the control systems; the examiner did not necessarily expect you to put the diagrams into the context of budgetary control. Your written explanations, however, must do so.
Note the requirement in (c) to give examples of the purposes of budgets from a non-profit organisation. Use those with which you are familiar – a college, library, hospital etc.

(a)   Responsibility accounting is a system of reporting that compares budget performance with actual performance for responsibility centres, often departments of an organisation. It is based on the recognition of individual areas of responsibility as specified in a firm's organisational structure and job descriptions. It seeks to trace the costs, revenue and investment to responsibility centres so that deviations from budget can be attributed to the person(s) in charge.

Three potential difficulties in operating a system of responsibility accounting are as follows:

- Clear and unambiguous identification of areas of responsibility. For example where events or desired courses of action may be dictated, or influenced, by more than one person or department. The problem is often referred to as dual responsibility.

- Identification of controllable costs and revenues from those which are uncontrollable by a particular person or department. This is influenced by the organisational level or hierarchical level of authority the manager occupies and the time span involved. A top manager can, in effect, control all costs by closing a department, middle management can only influence some departmental costs. Additionally, a cost which is uncontrollable over a month may be controllable over five years.

- It may encourage focus on the short-term performance, that is, achievement of the current budget, which may neglect the long-term performance of the organisation as a whole.

(b)   Control through feedback is where actual results (outputs) are compared with those which were planned for the budget period. Likewise, the actual inputs (costs) are compared with the budget, taking account of the actual level of outputs. This comparison of actual with plan takes place after the event. The intention is to learn for the future so that future deviations of actuals and plans are avoided or minimised. It is a reactive process.

Control through feed-forward is where prediction is made of what outputs and inputs are expected for some future budget period. If these predictions are different from what was desired/planned, then control actions are taken which attempt to minimise the differences. The aim is for control to occur before the deviation is reported, in this way it is more proactive. Budget generation is a form of feed-forward in that various outcomes are considered before one is selected.

A feedback control system

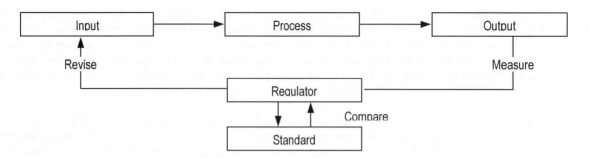

A feed forward control system

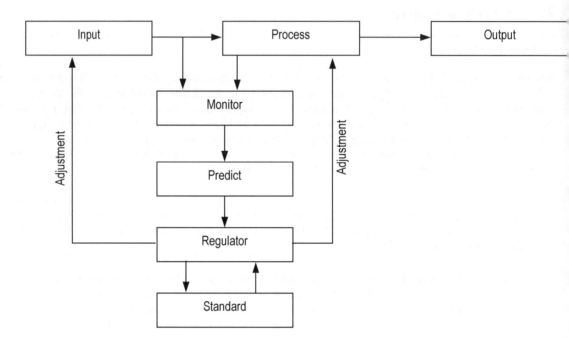

(c)   (i)   *Resource Allocation:* Budgets enable the business to estimate the amount of physical and financial resources required/available over a future period. Information can also be collected on the environment in which the business operates in order to identify any strengths, opportunities etc. which may exist. It is then possible for members of the organisation to discuss how these resources can be allocated to different parts of the business in order to create an optimal plan.

In the context of a non profit organisation this can be illustrated by making a choice, for example, between spending on education, care of the elderly, or leisure provision. The budget planning process helps to prioritise, to decide where the financial resources should be spent in the current planning period.

(ii)   *Authorisation:* In some budget systems, expenditure which has passed through the budget review procedure automatically becomes approved for commitment without additional formality. In other words, the identification of an expense for a particular budget centre is the formal approval that the head of the centre may go ahead and incur such an expense. No further detailed control in relation to this would occur until the actual expenditure was reported as part of the budgetary control system. This has particular relevance in some non profit sectors because any spending is based on an allocation of revenue which is fixed.

For example, a school may have a certain sum allocated for part-time teaching staff. It would be left to the head of the school to decide when and on whom this budget was spent. No further reference need be made for permission to spend.

(iii)   *Control:* Budgets are not used to best effect if, once prepared, they are buried away in files. They should be consulted regularly to ensure that the business is on track, that planned outcomes are being achieved. That is, they should be used to control the enterprise. Control is the comparison of actual performance with plans so that deviations from plans can be identified and action taken in the light of this comparison. The purpose of budget variance reports is to direct the attention of management to problem areas of the business, which are in need of control. It may result in action to ensure that the original plans are met or revision of those plans.

The management accounting department of a hospital will circulate summaries of the actual expenditure incurred, often analysed by different departments, to the managers of these departments. This can be compared with the planned expenditure and will highlight where spending was at variance from the plans.

Control is achieved because future actions and/or future plans may be modified in the light of this information. The extent to which this is produced after the event means that the benefit of control is only limited and in its simplest form it does not show what has been achieved with the expenditure.

Scenario-based questions

49   Manray plc

Key answer tips

Part (a) is a straightforward NPV computation, once you've sorted out the cash flows and their timings! The benefits (cash inflows) of the investment are in the form of incremental revenues and net cost savings; don't forget to take account of the tax effects of these. These are matched against the cost of the investment itself, again net of tax effects (CAs). You will have to make assumptions where the text is not absolutely precise.

Part (b) requires a "before" and "after" computation of the EPS. Note that there is some question as to whether the extra £400,000 fixed costs include the depreciation on the new equipment or not (tutorial note). The best thing, as always, is to state your assumption and work consistently within it.

In part (c) , you should be aware that there are various definitions of operating gearing, although they all basically show the same thing. Note the requirement is to explain, not define, so you should start by summarising what operating gearing is in words, rather than just stating a formula.

Part (d) is textbook stuff, and part (e) examines your knowledge (or otherwise) of macro-economics. Whilst it is tempting to rush this last part of a long question, note that it accounts for 25% of the marks, so you should be devoting at least 18 minutes to it.

(a)   **NPV of project**

In order to determine whether or not the project is worthwhile it is necessary to compare the present value of the inflows and outflows of the project after tax adjustments. In this scenario the discount rate (cost of capital) is set at 15%. The actual interest rate of the borrowing being used is therefore irrelevant as this is deemed to be inherent in the discount rate.

The project outflow is £2m (£3m borrowed less £1m used to repay the overdraft).

The project will be eligible for capital allowances of 25% per annum over 4 years. This amounts to £500,000 per annum, assumed to be available from year 1 (when the equipment is brought into use) until year 4 inclusive. After tax this allowance amounts to £500,000 × 33% = £165,000 per annum. The present value of this tax saving is found using the 4-year annuity factor for years 2-5 inclusive (because tax is paid one year in arrears).

15% annuity factor years 1 – 5	=	3.352
15% annuity factor year 1	=	(0.870)
15% annuity factor years 2 – 5	=	2.482

The present value of the capital allowance is thus: £165,000 × 2.482 = £409,530

The change in costs and revenues arising from the project is as follows:

		£
Revenue: Additional 10,000 units @ £35 =		350,000
Variable costs: New cost = 90,000 × £10 (W1)		
Old cost = 80,000 × £20 (W1)		
Saving = (80,000 × £20) – (90,000 × £10) =		700,000
		1,050,000
Fixed costs: Increase by		(400,000)
Net pre-tax operating inflow		650,000

Since the loan is to be repaid 'in three equal instalments, every two years over the anticipated lifetime of the equipment' the project has a life of 6 years.

The present value of the net pre tax operating inflow is thus found using the 15% annuity factor for years 1–6:

£650,000 × 3.784 = £2,459,600

The tax charge resulting from the increase in pre-tax operating inflow is £650,000 × 33% = £214,500 which will arise in years 2–7 inclusive (because tax is paid 1 year in arrears). The 15% annuity factor for years 2–7 inclusive is:

15% annuity factor years 1–7	=	4.160
15% annuity factor year 1	=	(0.870)
15% annuity factor years 2–7		3.290

The present value of the tax charge is thus: £214,500 × 3.290 = £705,705

Present value summary:

	£
Investment outflow	(2,000,000)
Capital allowance inflow	409,530
Operating inflow	2,459,600
Operating tax outflow	(705,705)
Net present value	163,425

Since the project has a positive net present value it is clearly worthwhile.

(b)   **Earnings per share (EPS)**

$$\text{Earnings per share} = \frac{\text{Profit available for ordinary shareholders}}{\text{Number of ordinary shares}}$$

$$= \frac{£456,000}{4\text{m}} = 11.4 \text{ pence per share}$$

If the new project is introduced the revised profit and loss account is:

	£'000	£'000
Sales	3,150	
Less: Variable expenses	900	
Fixed costs	650	
		(1,550)
Operating profit		1,600
Less: Interest payable (£3m × 10%) (W2)		(300)

Profit before tax	1,300
Taxation (33% × £800,000 (W3))	(264)
	1,036
Less: Preference dividend	(80)
Profit available for ordinary shareholders	956

The new earnings for share is thus: $\dfrac{£956,000}{4m}$ = 23.9 pence per share

This represents an increase of 12.5 pence per share or 110%.

(Tutorial note: Although this is the answer that was published by the ACCA as part of the old Paper 8 Pilot Paper, there is clearly an inconsistency over the treatment of fixed costs. In (a) the additional £400,000 has been taken as extra **cash** fixed costs. However, on purchasing a new asset, additional **depreciation** of £2m ÷ 6 = £ $\frac{1}{3}$ m will be charged in the profit and loss and **should** appear in (b).*)*

(c)   **Operating gearing**

Operating gearing is the relationship between the level of fixed and variable costs incurred by a business. In relative terms the higher the level of fixed costs the greater is the proportion of revenue required to cover those costs. As a consequence the greater the level of relative fixed costs, the greater the risk of making losses (due to the impact of sales volume changes). In contrast, once the fixed costs have been covered the greater the proportionate fixed costs, the greater is the growth in profits.

Operating gearing can be measured by:

$$\frac{\text{Fixed costs}}{\text{Total costs}} \quad \text{or} \quad \frac{\text{Fixed costs}}{\text{Sales}}$$

In the case of Manray these calculations before and after the introduction of the project are:

Before: $\dfrac{£250,000}{£1,850,000} = 13.5\%$ $\dfrac{£250,000}{£2,800,000} = 8.9\%$

After: $\dfrac{£650,000}{£1,550,000} = 41.9\%$ $\dfrac{£650,000}{£3,150,000} = 20.6\%$

(Tutorial note: The most common definition is percentage change in profit ÷ percentage change in sales or contribution ÷ profit. Using this formula, operating gearing has increased from 126% to 178%.*)*

(d)   **Break-even analysis**

The breakeven point equals:

$$\frac{\text{Fixed costs}}{\text{Contribution / unit}}$$

In the case of Manray this can be calculated before and after the project is introduced:

Before: $\dfrac{£250,000}{(£35-£20)} = 16,667$ units

After: $\dfrac{£650,000}{(£35-£10)} = 26,000$ units

Both of these calculations ignore interest, which if included has the following effect:

Before: $\dfrac{(£250,000+£150,000)}{(£35-£20)} = 26,667$ units

$$\text{After:} \quad \frac{(£650,000+£300,000)}{(£35-£10)} = 38,000 \text{ units}$$

Note: the preference dividend is ignored because although it is fixed rate capital it is an appropriation of profit and not a cost.

(e)   **Cause of interest rate rises and problems**

There are a number of economic reasons why interest rates change. Possible reasons for an increase in interest rates include:

(i)   increased borrowing by the government; interest rates rise so as to increase the funds available for gilt purchase by taking funds away from other investments

(ii)   an increase in the funds demanded by the private sector; again interest rates rise to encourage such investors

(iii)   a rise in actual price inflation; causing notional interest rates to rise so that real interest rates remain constant

(iv)   a rise in the expected rate of inflation; so that investors, especially in respect of fixed rate investments, raise their interest rate demands so as to maintain a constant level of real income

(v)   government legislation to reduce the funds available for lending (e.g. by banks); so that interest rates rise to reduce the demand for funds

(vi)   government action to strengthen the value of currency on the world currency markets.

When measuring difficulties in this way it is necessary to identify how such a difficulty would be measured. In the following it is assumed that the director is concerned about the company's ability to earn profits and make appropriate dividend payments to shareholders. Manray's level of interest cover after the introduction of the new project is:

$$\frac{\text{Operating profit}}{\text{Interest payable}} = \frac{£1,600,000}{£300,000} = 5.33 \text{ times}$$

This means that the interest payable can increase more than five-fold before the operating profit is eliminated, however this would then result in no dividends to either preference or ordinary shareholders. The ordinary shareholders, as the risk-takers, would expect their return to increase in line with interest rate changes in the longer term. Thus it can be stated that any significant increase of the interest cost in isolation has an important implication if it becomes the norm in the longer-term. However, when considering the added effects of reductions in operating income together with increases in interest rates the problem becomes more acute.

Workings

(W1)   Present variable costs are £1,600,000/80,000 = £20/unit.
        The saving of £10/unit reduces the variable cost to £10/unit.

(W2)   The interest charge assumes that the present overdraft is refinanced - this would appear worthwhile as the present interest rate on the overdraft is 15% (£150,000/£1m) and the new loan rate is only 10%.

(W3)   Taxable profit = £1,300 – £500 (capital allowances).

50   Netherby plc

Key answer tips

At first sight, this question looks to be an investment appraisal question, but in fact the NPV computation in part (a) is straightforward, and accounts for less than 20% of the marks. The remaining parts consider the effects of this project, its method of finance and its risks on the company undertaking it. Although some of the requirements of the question are quite technically demanding, there are six basically independent parts, so it is quite easy to miss out parts if necessary. Just answering parts (a), (c) and (f), perhaps the most straightforward requirements, could earn more than half marks. Note, in part (f), the question asks for *operating* risks, so don't waste time talking about finance, or gearing, risk.

(a) Assuming that the restructuring cost is a revenue item, and that all costs are incurred in year 0, the estimated cash flow profile is:

Cash flow profile (£m)

Item	0	1	2	3	4	5	6
				Year			
Closure costs	(5)						
Tax saving		1.65					
Cash flow increase		2.00	2.00	2.00	2.00	2.00	
Tax payment			(0.66)	(0.66)	(0.66)	(0.66)	(0.66)
	(5)	3.65	1.34	1.34	1.34	1.34	(0.66)

NPV (£m) $= -5 + 1.65(\text{PVIF}_{15,1}) + 2(\text{PVIFA}_{15,5}) - 0.66(\text{PVIFA}_{15,6} - \text{PVIFA}_{15,1})$

$= -5 + 1.65(0.870) + 2(3.352) - 0.66(3.784 - 0.870)$

$= -5 + 1.44 + 6.70 - 1.92 = +1.22$ (i.e. $+$ £1.22m)

Hence, the restructuring appears worthwhile.

(b) A semi-strong efficient capital market is one where security prices reflect all publicly-available information, including both the record of the past pattern of share price movements and all information released to the market about company earnings prospects. In such a market, security prices will rapidly adjust to the advent of new information relevant to the future income-earning capacity of the enterprise concerned, such as a change in its chief executive, or the signing of a new export order. As a result of the speed of the market's reaction to this type of news, it is not possible to make excess gains by trading in the wake of its release. Only market participants lucky enough already to be holding the share in question will achieve super-normal returns.

In the case of Netherby, when it releases information about its change in market-servicing policy, the value of the company should rise by the value of the project, assuming that the market as a whole agrees with the assessment of its net benefits, and is unconcerned by financing implications.

Net present value of the project = £1.22m

Number of 50p ordinary shares in issue = £5m × 2 = 10m shares

Increase in market price = £1.22m/10m = 12.2p per share.

(Alternatively, the answer could be expressed in terms of Netherby's price-earnings ratio. This would necessitate an assumption about Netherby's sustainable future earnings per share after tax.)

(c) Arguments for and against making a rights issue include the following:

For

(i) A rights issue enables the company to at least maintain its dividends, thus avoiding both upsetting the clientele of shareholders, and also giving negative signals to the market.

(ii) It may be easy to accomplish on a bull market.

(iii) A rights issue automatically lowers the company's gearing ratio.

(iv) The finance is guaranteed if the issue is fully underwritten.

(v) It has a neutral impact on voting control, unless the underwriters are obliged to purchase significant blocks of shares, and unless existing shareholders sell their rights to other investors.

(vi) It might give the impression that the company is expanding vigorously, although this appears not to be the case with Netherby.

Against

(i)   Rights issues normally are made at a discount, which usually involves diluting the historic earnings per share of existing shareholders. However, when the possible uses of the proceeds of the issue are considered, the *prospective* EPS could rise by virtue of investment in a worthwhile project, or in the case of a company earning low or no profits, the interest earnings on un-invested capital alone might serve to raise the EPS.

(ii)   Underwriters' fees and other administrative expenses of the issue may be costly, although the latter may be avoided by applying a sufficiently deep discount.

(iii)   The market is often sceptical about the reason for a rights issue, tending to assume that the company is desperate for cash. The deeper the discount involved, the greater the degree of scepticism.

(iv)   It is difficult to make a rights issue on a bear market, without leaving some of the shares with the underwriters. A rights issue which 'fails' in this respect is both bad for the company's image and may also result in higher underwriters' fees for any subsequent rights issue.

(v)   A rights issue usually forces shareholders to act, either by subscribing direct or by selling the rights, although the company may undertake to reimburse shareholders not subscribing to the issue for the loss in value of their shares. (This is done by selling the rights on behalf of shareholders and paying over the sum realised, net of dealing costs.)

(d)   *Note:* candidates are not expected to display a knowledge of FRS 14.

A rights issue normally has to be issued at a discount in order, firstly, to make the shares appear attractive, but more importantly, to safeguard against a fall in the market price below the issue price prior to closure of the offer. If this should happen, the issue would fail as investors wishing to increase their stakes in the company could do so more cheaply by buying on the open market. Because of the discount, a rights issue has the effect of diluting the existing earnings per share across a larger number of shares, although the depressing effect on share price is partly countered by the increased cash holdings of the company.

The two possible issue prices are now evaluated.

(i)   *A price of £1*

It is assumed that to raise £5m, the company must issue £5m/£1 = 5m new shares at the issue price of £1.

In practice, it is possible that the number of new shares required might be lower than this, as the post-tax cost of the project is less than £5m due to the (delayed) tax savings generated. The company might elect to use short-term borrowing to bridge the delay in receiving these tax savings, thus obviating the need for the full £5m.

Ignoring this argument, the terms of the issue would be '1-for-2' i.e. for every two shares currently held, owners are offered the right to purchase one new share at the deeply-discounted price of £1.

The ex-rights price will be:

[Market value of 2 shares before the issue + cash consideration]/3

$$= [(2 \times £3) + £1]/3 = £7/3 = £2.33$$

(ii)   *Similarly, if the issue price is £2*, the required number of new shares = £5m/£2 = 2.5m, and the terms will have to be '1-for-4'

The ex-rights price will be [(4 × £3) + £2]/5 = £14/5 = £2.80.

Clearly, the smaller the discount to the market price, the higher the ex-rights price.

(e) Ignoring the impact of the benefits of the new project:

The rights issue at £2 involves 2.5m new shares.

The EPS was £15m/10m = £1.50p per share.

Hence, EPS becomes $\dfrac{£15m}{10m + 2.5m} = £1.20$

With the debt financing, the interest charge net of tax = [12% × £5m] [1 – 33%] = £0.40m

Hence, EPS becomes $\dfrac{£15m - £0.40m}{10m} = £1.46$

Allowing for the benefits of the new project

The annual profit yielded by the proposal, after tax at 33% = (£2m × 0.67) = £1.34m, although the cash flow benefit in the first year is £2m due to the tax delay.

After the rights issue, the prospective EPS will become:

[£15m + £1.34m]/12.5m = £1.31 per share

With debt finance, the financing cost, net of tax relief, of £0.40m pa reduces the net return from the project to (£1.34m – £0.40m) = £0.94m pa.

(In the first year, the cash flow cost will be the full pre-tax interest payment. Thereafter, Netherby will receive annual cash flow benefits from the series of tax savings.)

The EPS will be: £15.94m/10m = £1.59 per share.

Therefore, in terms of the effect on EPS, the debt-financing alternative is preferable, although it may increase financial risk.

(f) A range of factors could be listed here. Among the major sources of risk are the following:

(i) *Reliability of supply.* This can be secured by inclusion of penalty clauses in the contract, although these will have to be enforceable. The intermediation of the European Bank for Reconstruction and Development may enhance this.

(ii) *The quality of the product.* Again, a penalty clause may assist, although a more constructive approach might be to assign a UK-trained total quality management (TQM) expert to the Hungarian operation to oversee quality control.

(iii) *Market resistance to an imported product.* This seems less of a risk, if retailers are genuinely impressed with the product, and especially as there are doubts over the quality of the existing product.

(iv) *Exchange rate variations.* Netherby is exposed to the risk of sterling depreciating against the Hungarian currency, thus increasing the sterling cost of the product. There are various ways of hedging against foreign exchange risk, of which use of the forward market is probably the simplest. Alternatively, Netherby could try to match the risk by finding a Hungarian customer for its other goods.

(v) *Renewal of the contract.* What is likely to happen after five years? To obtain a two-way protection, Netherby might write into the contract an option to renew after five years. If the product requires re-design, Netherby could offer to finance part of the costs in exchange for this option.

51 Bardsey plc

Key answer tips

In part (a) you are required to compute cash flow for the coming year. As the main cash flow will be from operations, the starting point is last year's operating profit. The key to earning full marks here was the careful reading of information given in the question and requirement - this served to considerably simplify the computations. The only adjustment to last year's operating profit to get it to this year's operating cash flow was thus depreciation. This then needs adjustment for *cash payments* to be made next year in respect of this year's tax and dividend creditors, and next year's interest and investment.

In part (b), although the requirement for the report seems quite general, both the information supplied and the requirement itself drop heavy hints as to what is expected. The requirement mentions ratio analysis - so this should clearly be part of your answer. Which ratios? You are given a list relating to the stores sector, so these are the main ones to consider (although you may feel others are also relevant). The question also specifically requires comparison of Bardsey's ratios with those of the sector (this means both in numbers *and* comment) and discussion of the limitations of such an analysis. Once you have identified these elements, think about how you are going to structure your answer. Although you are likely to do the computations first, these could be put in an appendix at the end of your report. Once you have the numbers, look for clues from the question as to possible reasons for differences between Bardsey and the sector. Once all specific requirements of the question have been met, you should draw a short conclusion as to the overall picture drawn from your analysis.

In part (c), it is essential that you focus on the business and market defined in the question in order to avoid making irrelevant, impractical or inappropriate comments. Look at the type and size of business it is, the market in which it is operating, the picture given by its financial statements and the information you have derived in earlier parts (including, in particular, the amount of external finance that will be required). This should restrict your discussion of sources of finance to those that are actually of practical application to Bardsey (note the marking guide implied at least four were to be suggested). You can be more general when discussing interest rates.

In part (d), the first thing to check is that you have understood the requirement. In contrast to (c), where the aim was to *raise* additional finance, here we are looking at ways to *invest* surplus cash. The same contextual focus is required, as in (c), a sufficient variety (again, at least four distinct uses).

(a)   Bardsey appears to be a strong generator of cash. Ongoing investment needs are partly met out of depreciation provisions, a deduction before calculating operating profit. Assuming no changes in operating activity or in the net working capital position, cash generation for 20X7 is likely to be:

	£m
Operating profit plus	60
Depreciation	8
Working capital	-
	—
Operating cash flow	68
Less	
Replacement investment	(10)
Interest due for 20X7	(15)
Taxation due from 20X6	(12)
Dividends due from 20X6	(20)
	—
Net cash flow	11
	—

(b)   *Report on Bardsey plc's financial health and performance*

This report focuses mainly on the financial ratios which can be calculated from the accounts and the industrial comparators given, but it is important to acknowledge the drawbacks with this form of performance appraisal:

-       it is usually desirable to examine ratios over a series of years, long enough to iron out any random influences but short enough not to be distorted by structural changes such as divestment.

-       it is important to recognise that the end-of-year accounts may not be representative either of the trading year concerned, given the tendency to 'window dress' accounts at year end (e.g. speeding up debtors collection), or of current trading circumstances, given the delay in preparation of accounts.

- other companies may prepare accounts on different bases, using different policies and over different financial years.

- in practice, it is difficult to define the boundaries of an industry given the differences in product offerings and product mixes produced and sold by companies.

- it is often not sufficient to examine financial ratios alone. A more balanced approach to performance appraisal might focus on aspects such as customer satisfaction and rate of innovation.

1   The company is achieving a pre-tax return on long-term capital of £60m/[£283m + £100m] = 15.7%, which compares well enough with the industry as a whole. In fact, given the recent asset revaluation, this may indicate better than average performance if other companies have not conducted similar revaluations.

2   The return on equity at £33m/£283m = 11.7% is well below that of the industry, probably reflecting a higher equity base following the recent revaluation. Alternatively, other companies may operate at higher gearing ratios, thus increasing their ROEs if the interest cost of debt is lower than the ROE. This is borne out by examination of the industry gearing figures.

3   Bardsey trades with an operating profit margin of £60m/£150m = 40%, well in excess of the sector. This could suggest a number of things. Perhaps Bardsey is more efficient than its competitors, perhaps it applies higher prices, competing on quality of service, or maybe it sells higher quality products which appeal to a more affluent clientele.

4   The fixed asset turnover ratio is often taken as an indicator of efficiency. At just £150m/£300m = 0.5 for Bardsey, this compares unfavourably with the sector average of 1.2, but this is probably partly explained by the asset revaluation.

5   Lengthy stock periods are common in the furniture trade, which often holds high value-added goods for display purposes. Bardsey's stock period (stocks/cost of sales as the figure for purchases is not given) is £60m/£90m × 365 = 243 days, well in excess of the industry figure of 180 days, although if it is serving a higher quality market segment, this might be expected. Against this, if the industry figure is based on purchases, the two figures are not directly comparable.

6   As suggested above, Bardsey's capital gearing (£100m/£283m = 35% at book values) is lower than that of the sector, although the sector figure cited includes short-term debt which Bardsey does not presently use.

7   Interest cover at £60m/£15m = 4 appears safe, implying that profits could drop substantially without endangering Bardsey's ability to pay interest. However, the issue is really much more complex than this, depending on the balance of fixed and variable costs i.e. operating gearing, which is probably quite high in this sector.

8   Dividend cover at £33m/£20m = 1.65 is low, perhaps reflecting pressure by the dominant shareholders to pay high dividends. Alternatively, this ratio could be inflated by temporarily low profits as Bardsey emerges from recession. Besides, there is no problem in financing a high payout given Bardsey's substantial cash holdings and strong cash flow.

9   In addition, the liquidity ratios appear satisfactory at £200m/£117m = 1.71 for the current ratio and £140m/£117m = 1.20 for the acid test. However, debtors are very high at £100m, with debtor days of £100m/£150 × 365 = 243 days probably reflecting the impact of special offers such as lengthy interest-free credit periods. However, no industry comparators are given.

Overall, Bardsey presents a picture of sluggish performance in the mature market of retailing quality products, continued demand for which ensures adequate profitability and strong cash flow. The relatively low P:E ratio suggests the market is not expecting substantial growth from Bardsey, nor, given the concentration of shareholders, is it likely to be subject to a take-over.

Without attempting to diversify into new markets and products, there is probably a case for paying even higher dividends to prevent even greater over-capitalisation.

(c)   Bardsey requires finance of (£50m plus £20m) for its new developments. £11m of this can be internally financed, leaving a substantial net external financing requirement of (£70m less £11m) = £59m. Some possible financing alternatives are:

Run down cash holdings

Bardsey is currently holding substantial cash balances, which would largely cover the additional financing needs. However, some degree of liquidity may be thought desirable as protection from adverse contingencies. There are no 'rules' in this respect, but a buffer stock of highly liquid assets held in cash and/or money market investments would be prudent.

Rights issue

Bardsey appears currently to be over-capitalised. There is little point in issuing more equity in this situation, especially as the current ROE is relatively weak, and the relatively low P/E ratio already applied by the market hints at a possibly unfavourable reaction.

Short-term borrowing

On the 'matching' principle, it looks sensible to undertake short-term financing for at least part of the working capital requirements. Short-term overdraft financing is usually cheaper than equity financing, especially allowing for tax relief on debt interest (the 'tax shield'). Given Bardsey's strong asset backing, a modest increase in gearing does not seem risky. Even without the benefits from the new projects, borrowing perhaps £10m at say, 3% above base rate i.e. 11%, thus imposing extra interest charges of (11% × £10m) = £1.1m, would lower interest cover only to £60m/[£15m + £1.1m] = 3.7 times.

Long-term borrowing

There is considerable scope for increasing gearing, as noted, but whether it is wise to increase long-term borrowing is doubtful unless this can be achieved on a variable rate basis, given that interest rates are expected to fall. If not, it seems better to use short-term debt pending the fall in interest rates, and then to re-finance with long-term debt as and when rates fall. If anything, there seems a case for repaying some of the existing long-term debt (if permitted) given that it costs 15% (before tax relief) to finance.

Sale-and-leaseback (SAL)

SAL involves selling 'quality' assets (usually property in 'good' sites, which command high rents and are likely to increase in value) to a financial institution in exchange for the right of continued occupation. It seems likely that many of Bardsey's assets would qualify, but if 'out-of-town' developments are taking sales from city centres, this could already be undermining property values in some locations.

Interest rates

A critical element in the financing decision is expectations about the future course of interest rates and the economic determinants of interest rate changes. In this case, people are expecting falling rates. Among the possible reasons for a fall in interest rates are the following:

(i)   lower government borrowing, thus reducing downward pressure on the price of 'gilts' (government stock)

(ii)   lower demand for investment funds by the private sector

(iii)   an unexpected fall in the actual rate of price inflation

(iv)   a fall in the expected rate of inflation, caused perhaps by upward adjustment of the exchange rate, or a fall in the national level of wage settlements

(v)   looser regulation of the monetary system, for example, a decrease in prudential ratios, enhancing the ability of banks to lend using the bank multiplier effect

(vi)   less need for the monetary authorities to intervene to dampen speculative pressure on the exchange rate.

Clearly, Bardsey will have to take a view on the reasons why, in the current context, people expect a cut in interest rates, and the likelihood of these events occurring. Indeed, if the money market is efficient, it might be argued that expected lower rates are *already* factored into the existing term structure of interest rates.

Lower future rates may provide an opportunity to borrow long-term on a fixed rate basis thus locking into a historically low interest rate. Conversely, short-term financing at a variable interest rate may be a good hedge against further falls in rates. Lower interest rates also tend to favour running down cash holdings and short-term financing, and will increase asset values, which favours a SAL. Against this, if the inflation rate is falling, the borrower does not enjoy the benefit of the falling real value of debts.

(d)   **Possible uses of 'spare' cash include:**

Pay out higher dividends

Dividend cover at £33m/£20m = 1.65 times is below the sector average of 2.1 times, reducing scope for higher distribution. However, this would be preferable to investing in projects with dubious prospects of generating adequate returns and would presumably impress those institutional shareholders seeking income rather than capital appreciation.

Paying higher dividends also promotes expectations of at least the same level of dividends in the future, expectations which Bardsey may have difficulty in meeting, given its present sluggish performance. For these reasons, temporarily cash-rich companies often pay a 'Special Dividend', emphasising their 'one-off' nature.

However, the ownership structure of Bardsey is important here. Arguably, a family-dominated company might want to avoid yet higher dividends which may not be tax-efficient for some members paying higher rate tax. These could prefer capital gains on which tax can be deferred. In addition, there is a higher tax threshold on capital gains compared to that on income, and gains can also be indexed.

Take-overs

Spare cash could be used to acquire other companies. This is a short-cut to growth but requires specialised skills in valuing the target(s) and integrating newly-acquired companies. There is a danger of over-paying for the target company, especially in the excitement of a contested bid. Much will depend on the track record of Bardsey in this respect. If it has not previously acquired other companies, attempting to do so at this juncture could well provoke adverse market reaction.

Share repurchase

Under certain conditions, UK companies are allowed to buy back a certain proportion of their shares on the market. This tends to raise EPS, and exerts upward pressure on share price. It could be interpreted adversely as a signal that the company has exhausted ideas for profitable expansion, as seems likely in the case of Bardsey.

Repay debt

Bardsey has £100m of debentures outstanding, with a coupon rate of 15%. Allowing for tax, this requires a cash outflow of £15m (1–33%) = £10.05m per annum i.e. an effective cost of about 10% (although lower than this when expressed at market values). The ROE is currently only just above this, so unless Bardsey expects to improve its ROE, it may be desirable to lower long-term indebtedness. This may depend also on the attitudes to risk of the predominant shareholders.

Social responsibility

Bardsey could take the opportunity to improve its public image by increased 'social expenditure'. For example, it might upgrade the health, welfare and sporting facilities provided for its employees. It could also adopt policies designed to promote the welfare of the community at large e.g. sports sponsorship, provision of educational endowments and environmental programmes. Such policies generally have a beneficial effect on a company's standing in the community which may translate into improved sales and profitability, although this is difficult to quantify in practice.

52   Marton Ltd

Key answer tips

In part (a) these types of evaluations arise quite frequently in this exam, and tend to involve the same basic computations - interest saving from reduced debtors, discount costs, service charges etc. The first of these is often overlooked, although it can be one of the most significant savings arising. The approach is to first ascertain the amount by which (average) debtor days have been reduced, then multiply this by average daily sales to find debtor reduction. The interest saving can then be calculated. When commenting upon your results, state the conclusion based initially on the figures alone, then consider the validity of the assumptions used.

Part (b) is really just another method of management of debtors, and a very similar approach to that used in (a) should be taken - cost versus benefits. Go through each line of text in the relevant paragraph of the question, noting the general impact on costs or revenues of each piece of information given. Then evaluate them on an expected value basis where necessary, using the interest rates and probabilities provided. In the comments, when computations involve expected values, it is always worth considering the possible impact of the best and/or worst actual outcomes arising.

You have to stop and think carefully before answering part (c) to avoid wasting time on irrelevancies. The main point to note is that you are looking at this from the supplier's viewpoint, rather than the customer's, for which you may have a standard list of benefits.

In part (d) there are two aspects - 'factor' and 'overseas'. The first requires a brief description of the general services a factor offers, and the second requires specific additional benefits that an overseas factor will bring.

In part (e)(i) which way will the exchange rate need to move to make a loss? A loss means getting less £ for the $ receipt than currently offered; this means a lower £/$ rate, or a higher $/£ rate. So look at the effects of the highest rate given.

In part (e) (ii) an opportunity cost will arise if the actual future spot rate is such that it yields a greater £ value for a $ receipt than the forward rate. This will be if the £/$ rate is higher, or the $/£ rate is lower. So here we compare the £ value at 1.55 with that at the lowest rate given.

A good answer to (iii) will consider the specific circumstances of the hedge in the question as well as the general pros and cons of hedging.

(a)   The relative costs and benefits of each option are calculated as follows:

Option 1 – Factoring

Reduction in debtor days	=	15 days
Reduction in debtors	=	$\dfrac{15}{365} \times £20m$
	=	£821,916

Effect on profit before tax:

Interest saving	=	$(13\% \times £821,916)$ =	£106,849
Administrative savings		=	£200,000
Service charge	=	$(1\% \times £20m)$	= £(200,000)
Insurance premium		=	£(80,000)
			————
Net profit benefit		=	£26,849

Option 2 – The discount
With year-end debtors at £4.5m, the debtor collection period was:

£4.5m/£20m × 365 = 82 days

The scheme of discounts would change this as follows:

10 days for 20% of customers
20 days for 30% of customers
82 days for 50% of customers

Average debtor days becomes:
(20% × 10) + (30% × 20) + (50% × 82) = 49 days

Hence, average debtors would reduce from the present £4.5m to:
49 × £20m/365 = £2,684,932

The interest saving would be:

13% × £4.5m – £2.685m)   = £235,950

The cost of the discount would be:

(3% × 20% × £20m) + (1.5% × 30% × £20m)   = (£210,000)

The net benefit to profit before tax would be:

(£235,950 – £210,000)   = £25,950

The figures imply that factoring is marginally the more attractive but this result relies on the predicted proportions of customers actually taking up the discount and paying on time. It also neglects the possibility that some customers will insist on taking the discount without bringing forward their payments. Marton would have to consider a suitable response to this problem.

Conversely, the assessment of the value of using the factor depends on the factor lowering Marton's debtor days. If the factor retains these benefits for itself, rather than passing them on to Marton, this will raise the cost of the factoring option. The two parties should clearly specify their mutual requirements from the factoring arrangement on a contractual basis.

(b)   *The JIT arrangement*

Existing sales to customer	=	20% × £20m	=	£4m
Enhanced sales with premium	=	£4m (1 + 5%)	=	£4.2m
Reduction in debtors	=	30/365 × £4m	=	£328,767
Interest saving	=	£328,767 × 13%	=	£42,740 (a)
Sales increase			=	£200,000 (b)
Expected value of penalty cost:	=	5% × 10% × £4.2m	=	(£21,000) (c)
Bank interest	=	13% × £0.5m	=	(£65,000) (d)
Increased depreciation	=	£0.5m/5	=	(£100,000) (e)
Net change in profit (items a – e)			=	£56,740

Thus, participation in the JIT arrangement appears to be worthwhile. However, it should be noted that although the chance of having to pay the penalty is low, if it *is* triggered, the resulting penalty of (10% × £4.2m) = £420,000 represents a sizeable proportion (over 5%) of total profit. It may thus be prudent to insure against this risk, the premium payable lowering the net benefits of JIT.

(c)   In addition to a higher price and quicker settlement by its main customer, such a JIT agreement offers several benefits to the supplier of goods. Among these are:

–   A guaranteed order from a major customer will facilitate output planning and the ordering of materials as inputs into its own production. Marton may be able to negotiate JIT arrangements with its own suppliers using the experience gained.

–   The close cooperation inherent in a JIT agreement may encourage Marton and its customer to engage in joint research and development into planning future products.

–   The experience gained in supplying a major customer may give Marton the confidence and reputation to negotiate JIT agreements with other customers.

(d)   Many overseas factors are subsidiaries of UK banks or their agents, which offer facilities to companies with export credit sales usually of above £0.25m. Overseas factors perform largely the same range of functions as factors in UK markets, namely debt collection and administration of accounts payable and provision of finance.

An additional and highly valuable service particularly for smaller firms without large overseas forces is the provision of advice on the creditworthiness of overseas customers, using their own experience, or tapping the expertise of agents who act on their behalf in the pursuit of debts.

If factoring is provided on a non-recourse basis, the factor will bear the risk of bad debts, thus enabling the exporter to sell on open account without risk of default. Even allowing for the additional charge made by the factor, this may well be a much cheaper means of arranging overseas transactions than more formal methods such as letters of credit.

(e)   (i)   From Marton's viewpoint, an adverse outcome is depreciation of the dollar against sterling as this lowers its income when converted into sterling. The worst outcome is thus an exchange rate of US$1.60:£1.

At present, its dollar income is £5m × 1.45 = $7.25m. At US$1.60:£1, its sterling income would fall to $7.25m/1.60 = £4.53m. Hence, the worst outcome is a loss (compared to the current rate) of (£0.47m).

(ii)   If Marton hedges all its expected dollar income over the next year at US1$1.55: £1, this will generate guaranteed (ignoring other sources of risk) sterling income of $7.25m/1.55 = £4.68m. If the actual rate of exchange moved to US$1.3: £1, it would have made sterling earnings of £5.58m. This indicates an opportunity cost of hedging of £0.90m.

(iii) In theory, foreign exchange earnings should not be hedged, as the chances of an adverse movement are equivalent to those of a favourable one, so that in the long-term, exporters like Marton should break even. This can be inferred from the figures above – the chances of the dollar appreciating are equal to the chances of it depreciating against sterling (30%).

Indeed, when allowance is made for the wider spread between the rates at which banks will buy and sell currency as between spot and forward transactions, use of the forward market is more costly. However, failure to hedge can leave firms exposed to the risk of erratically large adverse currency movements, perhaps large enough to bankrupt the smaller firm. So, although the risks in the long-term are roughly symmetrical, many companies deem it prudent to hedge at least some part of their overseas earnings, especially those relating to major contracts.

53   Stadium Eats

Key answer tips

In part (a) there are 10 marks, so you need to spend a little time thinking of various issues that may be discussed. You have very little detail in the profit and loss account (indeed, this is one point to raise), so you are expected to look at the broad figures - level of turnover, margins etc - and then comment on the feasibility of achieving these for a brand new enterprise, and possible impact on the existing business. Some of your criticisms cannot be taken into account when redrafting the profit and loss, but some sensible assumptions are needed as regards turnover and margins to produce revised (lower) figures.

Part (b) gives you a chance to display your general knowledge of gearing before having to relate it to the scenario. Don't stint on your explanation of the meaning of capital gearing - the marks allow you to give a little detail about different definitions and which types of debt may be included etc. You then need to consider the impact of high gearing levels on both lenders and equity investors.

In part (c) you need to apply what you have discussed in general terms in (b) to the data and circumstances of the question. Make it clear which definition of gearing you are using in your calculations. You cannot come to any firm conclusions without any benchmarks for comparison, but you can discuss particular aspects of the restaurant business that may affect the impact of the gearing level.

In part (d) you can initially recall your sources of finance "checklist", but before writing about any of them, you must think whether they will apply in this particular context. And don't forget the all important source - equity - that appears to be perhaps most appropriate in this case.

In part (e) there are two parts to this requirement - a general discussion on the AIM, followed by the specific factors to be considered in obtaining a listing. The latter actually carries more marks, and should not be skimped on.

(a)   The forecast covers only the first trading year. This is unlikely to be representative of the longer term trading position of the business and hence a forecast over a three to five year period would be more appropriate.

The question indicates that the forecast is loosely based on the current Stadium Eats figures. There would in fact appear to have been some questionable assumptions made in constructing the forecast.

Firstly, sales of £600,000 (in excess of the current sales of £425,000) may be viewed as rather ambitious for the first year. It is unrealistic to assume sales will be even close to equivalent to those of the original restaurant within such a short time. Furthermore, it may be that some customers simply switch from eating at Stadium Eats to eating at the new location. The forecast makes no mention of the sales for the overall operation, and the possible interdependence of sales between the two outlets.

The figures given in the forecast are lacking in any detail. There is insufficient information and no comparative data to show sales trends over time. It is impossible to learn anything about the costs of the restaurant from the information given. A detailed breakdown of costs by type, and over time, would be very helpful. The operating profit margin is difficult to appraise without further information on the average rate for similar restaurant businesses, but seems excessive when compared with the margin currently achieved. A forecast cash flow would also be useful.

The forecast may also be criticised for failing to take account of the likely need to employ new managerial staff to take responsibility for the existing outlet, in order to free up the partners to concentrate on the new site.

Working on sales in Stadium Eats at present, annual turnover is equal to £2,833 per cover. The estimate for the new restaurant is equal to £3,333 per cover per annum. Being pessimistic sales of perhaps £1,500 per cover pa may be assumed, and this would give a turnover of £270,000 instead of the forecast £600,000.

The current operating profit margin is 11%, which against the forecast sales of £600,000 would yield £66,000 before interest, as opposed to the £135,000 suggested figure for operating profit. This figure assumes management drawings are maintained at just £22,000 each.

Re-working the forecast to use an adjusted sales figure, and maintaining the 11% net margin gives:

	£
Sales	270,000
Operating Profit	29,700
Less Interest	(18,000)
Profit before tax	11,700

In practice, it is likely that the lower turnover (compared with the existing outlet) will lead to a reduction in net margin, leading to an even lower operating profit and lower profit before tax. If the margin is reduced to 10%, then on sales of £270,000, the operating profit of £27,000 is reduced to just £9,000 profit before tax.

This is a great deal lower than the forecast, and significantly alters the potential viability of the business, hence the need for a longer term forecast set of figures.

(b) The term capital gearing refers to the extent to which a company is funded by fixed return finance as opposed to equity. Two different formulae may be used when measuring capital gearing.

The first is:
Capital gearing = Debt plus preference share capital/Equity
This measures the ratio of fixed return capital to equity finance within a business.

An alternative formula, commonly used, measures the proportion of fixed return capital in relation to the total capital of a business. The formula is as follows:

Capital gearing = Debt + preference share capital/Total long-term capital

In both cases, debt may be measured as either long-term debt, or all interest bearing debt. Clearly the gearing level will vary depending on the formula selected, and the type of debt included, but in all cases the level of gearing rises as the proportion of fixed return finance increases. It is not possible to specify a precise dividing line between high gearing and low gearing. Gearing is a relative measure, and should be assessed in terms of the gearing levels of comparable companies in the same business sector. Companies in different industrial sectors may exhibit very different levels of capital gearing.

The level of gearing is of interest to a bank, which is lending to a business, because it reflects the extent to which the owners of the business are risking their own capital relative to that of the bank. At the same time, the bank will recognise that increased loan finance, which is not matched by an increase in equity investment, will lead to an increase in capital gearing. As the level of debt increases, if sales figures decline or are static, businesses may find it increasingly difficult to meet the interest payments due on the debt. The bank will therefore look for an increase in cash flows from operations to help to pay any incremental interest due on new borrowing. One problem, however, is that gearing does not measure cash flows.

The equity investor should be cautious of highly geared companies, because the return on equity in such a business will be very sensitive to changes in profit before interest. When gearing is high, and interest payments are also high, a dramatic fall in the profit before interest figure may result in a collapse in the profit attributable to equity. Equally, a large rise in pre interest profit may lead to a surge in the profit attributable to equity, if earnings were already more than sufficient to meet interest payments. In summary, high gearing is of concern to the equity investor because it increases the volatility of the return on equity.

(c)   Using the first formula for capital gearing:

Long-term Debt/ Equity = 195/176   = 1.108 or 110.8%
or
Interest Bearing Debt/ Equity = 195/176   = 1.10 or 110.8%

In this case, the absence of short-term interest bearing debt means that the gearing calculation gives the same result for both calculations.

Alternatively, using the second formula:

Long-term Debt/Total Long-term Capital = 195/371   = 0.526 or 52.6%
or
Interest Bearing Debt/Total Long-term Capital = 195/371 = 0.526 or 52.6%

As before, the fact that long-term debt is the only form of interest bearing debt, results in a common value for the scale of gearing.

The gearing level appears quite high, inasmuch as debt is a significant source of funding for the business, although the bulk of the debt is of a long-term nature and is secured against property. The restaurant business is a volatile one, subject to changing tastes, and sales volatility needs to be taken into account when analysing financial gearing. For most businesses in a volatile market, the risk of falling sales means that high levels of debt can leave a business facing difficulties in meeting its interest payments. The restaurant business, however, is cash generating, when compared with other types of businesses dependent upon credit sales. In view of this, the new restaurant should have fewer problems in servicing interest payments. Nonetheless, if the owners wish to limit their risk it may be advisable to reduce the level of gearing to below one (depending on the formula used), so that a sharp drop in sales would not threaten the long-term survival of the business. It is often the case that banks will only be prepared to lend to small businesses on the basis of 'matching funds' i.e. £100 loan per £100 equity. As the gearing is in this case already over one, the owners would be unable to increase their borrowing if the matched funds approach was used.

The adjusted profit and loss account given in answer to (a) shows interest cover is poor. This would serve to confirm that gearing is uncomfortably high.

Furthermore, the figures do not reveal the true level of indebtedness and risk for the proprietors, who are in fact borrowing £75,000 in order to purchase their equity stake. For them the company is a very risky venture.

(d)   The accounts clearly indicate that the business would be best suited to seeking out new equity investors, rather than further borrowing, but the access to such investors will depend on the forecast profitability and medium term growth potential. In order to attract investors, Stadium Eats would need to prepare a Business Plan which included detailed Profit and Loss, Balance Sheet and Cash Flow forecasts, together with information on company strategy and marketing plans. Such a plan could then be studied by potential investors, allowing them to make their own estimates of the business' potential, and the risk that they would be taking in buying an equity stake.

Possible sources of such finance might include Business Angels, Venture Capital Trusts or wealthy relatives/individuals looking to obtain tax relief via the Enterprise Investment Scheme. The latter scheme offers tax relief to individuals investing in a qualifying company, up to a maximum of £100,000; the Stadium Eats project would therefore be well suited to this source of funding. It is possible that it could encourage customers to sign up as investors, in return for discount vouchers on meals. Business Angels may also use the Enterprise Investment Scheme, but they will also be individuals who are used to dealing with small businesses, and may have some expertise to offer. Some Business Angels will request a seat on the Board of Directors in order to monitor the progress of their investment. Venture Capital Funds vary widely in size, from small regional funds (often part financed by local authorities) through to large scale funds which operate as investment trusts, raising money through the issue of shares to the general public.

Equity is not the sole source of funding which might be available. If the restaurant is located in an economic development area, such as an inner city or rural community, then there may be job creation grants/soft loan funds provided by local or central government. In certain areas, a limited amount of grant finance is also available via the European Union.

(e)   AIM is the Alternative Investment Market, which was set up in London to replace the Unlisted Securities Market. AIM serves as the market place in which it is possible for smaller companies to raise equity capital. The issue costs and annual registration fees are much lower than for the main stock exchange, and the investors are more likely to be looking for higher risk investments. As relatively new and fast growing businesses, many AIM companies choose to retain a large proportion of their profits, and so they offer low dividend yields to potential investors. The attraction of such investments lies in the potential for substantial capital gains if the business is successful.

Amongst the factors to be considered when seeking a stock market quotation are:

- Does the company need a large-scale injection of equity?

- Public quotation involves greater reporting requirements and openness.

- A listing increases take-over risks.

- The owners are likely to see a reduction in the scale of their shareholding, and perhaps lose overall control.

- Are growth rates sufficient to give potential investors their required rate of return?

53   Buntam plc

Key answer tips

In part (a) start by jotting down all the factors you can think of that will be relevant. Start your answer with a general introduction to traded investments, mentioning the main factors from your list that need to be considered. Then try to illustrate each factor by reference to various types of investment, particularly those for which you have been given data.

In part (b) again, start with an introduction to the general role of intermediaries, giving examples of institutions that act as such. Then go through their particular uses to *private* investors – whilst their advisory role is important here, it is not the only aspect to consider.

In part (c) when discussing these equity measures, don't be too technical - it is probably better to describe them in words rather than simply quoting formulae, although you may find it useful to jot these down for your own use in the computations. Once you have completed a calculation, make sure your figures appear sensible.

In part (d) the valuation of shares, in practice, is an inexact science, with various market, economic and investor perception factors playing a part. However, you are asked to come up with an estimate using the data given and you should therefore use this as a guide to the approach required. Your first thought should be for the theoretical dividend valuation model, so check whether you have the perception factors playing a part. However, you are asked to come up with an estimate using the data given and you should therefore use this as a guide to the approach required. Your first thought should be for the theoretical dividend valuation model, so check whether you have the relevant information for this. If you can't remember the growth version, assuming a fixed dividend will be better than nothing. Otherwise, you need to start with an estimate of the average annual growth rate.

In part (e) your answer should start with a yield curve plotted from the gilt data given. Remember to label the axes clearly. Once plotted, give a brief explanation of its shape. (f) requires you to explain the relevance of such curves to the private investor - link this to your explanation of its shape in (e).

REPORT

To: Private Clients
Subject: Traded Investments
Author:
Date:

(a)   The term 'traded investment' refers to the purchase of an investment asset, which is traded in the financial markets. Examples include government and company bonds, ordinary shares, preference shares, warrants, and options or futures contracts. The range of such investments is therefore wide, and it is important to recognise that each type of investment has unique characteristics in terms of its cost, rate of return and risk. All of these factors must be taken into account when selecting an investment.

The price of bonds and shares will vary, depending upon economic conditions and the financial performance of the individual companies. Interest rates directly affect the price of gilt-edged stock and corporate bonds, such that as interest rates rise, the price of bonds falls. This represents a capital risk to the investor, who cannot be certain of the price at which the bond can be sold. This uncertainty is counter-balanced by the fact that such investments offer a fixed rate of return. If an investor buys, for example, 10% Treasury Stock 20Y1, at a price of £105, he/she can be certain that the interest payable is £10 per bond, equal to a return of 10/105, or 9.5% gross. This interest is payable annually (usually in two instalments) until the date of maturity of the bond, when the bond is redeemed for the nominal value of £100. The return earned on bonds will generally, though not always, be higher than that available through interest bearing deposit accounts. Ordinary shares present a much riskier form of investment, particularly for private individuals, who may incur high charges for the purchase and sale of shares. The price of ordinary shares varies daily, depending on factors within the market in general, and also specific to the company. An investor may earn a return via dividends and/or capital gains. The amount of dividends receivable is dependent, amongst other things, upon the profits of the company, and hence is not predictable with certainty. Individual share prices are definitely not predictable with any level of certainty. Consequently, investment in ordinary shares is relatively risky, but may offer good returns, which historically have been shown on average to be higher than the returns on bonds.

The purchase of derivatives, such as futures or options, as a way of investing in traded securities, may be highly risky unless they are covered trades. The potentially very high returns from such investments reflects the associated high risk.

In conclusion, when comparing the different traded investments, it is essential that the composition of the investment portfolio matches both the liquidity and risk needs of each individual investor.

(b)   Financial intermediaries are important to the efficient functioning of the financial markets, as they act to bring the borrowers/companies and lenders/equity providers together. Financial intermediaries include pension funds, insurance companies, retail and merchant banks, and unit trust companies. In relation to private investors, their functions include the following.

(i)   *The provision of investment advice and information.*

Financial intermediaries provide investors with advice and information on the range of investment opportunities available, and the associated risks and returns. Access to such expert information and advice saves the private investor a great deal of time in searching for the investment most suited to his/her needs. Stockbrokers can act on client instructions to buy/sell stocks, but may also offer an advisory service which offers suggestions on investments to add to a portfolio. Many brokers also offer private investors hands-free investment management, whereby the investor leaves all the decisions on investment selection in the hands of the broker, in return for a management fee. The investor is protected from the risk of loss through negligence or mismanagement on the part of the intermediary, by the regulatory systems which govern the financial markets.

(ii)   *Reduction of risk via aggregation of funds*

Intermediaries serve to reduce investment risks for individuals by creating an investment portfolio. Unit trusts are a good example of how the process works. An individual investor will usually lack the funds to own an equity portfolio, but by investing money in a unit trust the trust can aggregate all the small individual investments and invest in a wide spread in stocks across the whole market. In this way, the returns to the individual investor are less volatile than if they invested in the equities directly on a small scale.

(iii)   *Maturity transformation*

It will often be the case that there is not a perfect match between the time period for which a company needs funds and the time period over which a private individual is willing to invest.

Financial intermediaries play a role here in performing the function of maturity transformation. For example, a building society will lend out money for periods of 20 or 30 years, but their investors will still wish to be able to withdraw cash that they have in deposit accounts at random intervals. By taking advantage of the constant turnover of cash between borrowers and lenders, the building society can lend long-term whilst holding short-term deposits. It is this process which is referred to as maturity transformation.

Financial intermediaries can therefore be seen to be extremely useful to the private investor, as they may provide useful advice and make it easier for the individual to take advantage of the returns that can be earned in the financial markets (via, for example, personal pension funds), whilst at the same time leaving investors with a wide range of opportunities because of maturity transformation, aggregation and reduced risk.

(c)   (i)   *Gross dividend*

At the end of the financial year, companies will announce the profits or losses that they have earned, and a figure for net profit after tax. A company can choose either to pay any profit out in dividends or to re-invest it in the business. Dividends are paid out per share, and so the more shares that you own in a business, the more dividend income that you will receive. Using the example of Buntam plc, the figures indicate a gross dividend yield of 5%. This means that the dividend paid equals 5% of the share price, or eight pence, in this case. The term gross means that this is the dividend paid before tax. The equivalent calculation for Zellus plc means that the dividend yield of 3.33% is equivalent to a gross dividend payment of nine pence. (***Note:*** dividends are now paid by companies net of 10% tax (as at May 2001). Therefore the net dividend receivable is 8 pence per share. Ultimately many investors pay more tax than this on dividend income.)

The gross dividend figure is of relevance to an investor as it facilitates direct comparison of the dividend figure and dividend yield paid out by different companies, as well as comparison with interest yields on fixed return investments. (***Note:*** since the abolition of ACT most newspapers publish net dividend figures.)

The tax liability is determined by the individual circumstances of each investor, and so its inclusion would serve only to confuse any comparative analysis. The dividend figure is also relevant to an investment decision because it is a way of earning income from investments, as opposed to capital gains, which can only be realised when the investment is sold.

(ii)   *Earnings per share*

Earnings per share (EPS) is calculated as profit attributable to ordinary shareholders divided by the weighted average number of ordinary shares outstanding during the period (FRS 14). EPS thus represents what is available to be paid out as dividends.

Clearly, therefore, if the number of shares in issue remains fixed, the EPS will rise as the net profit attributable to equity increase.

The value of EPS can be calculated by dividing the share price by the P/E ratio. For Buntam this means EPS equals eight pence. In other words, the earnings per share is equal to the gross dividend payable. For Zellus, the EPS is equal to 18 pence (270/15), which compares with a gross dividend of nine pence. On first sight, therefore, it is tempting to view Zellus as a better investment because its EPS is higher. On the other hand, an investor has to pay 270 pence per share to get earning of 18 pence, compared with 160 pence to get earning of eight pence. The EPS figure is of limited value on its own; it needs to be judged in conjunction with the share price, and hence the P/E ratio.

(iii)   *Dividend cover*

Dividend cover measures the relationship between earnings per share and net dividends per share. The higher the level of dividends (for any given level of EPS) the lower will be the level of profit retained and re-invested within the business. This can have an effect on the balance of returns available to an equity investor.

The returns from investing in shares may take the form of either income i.e. dividends, which are paid twice yearly or capital gain/loss which is earned when the shares are sold. Some investors may prefer one type of return to the other, often for tax reasons.

Dividend cover is measured as follows: Earnings per share (net)/dividend per share (net).

Using the example of Zellus plc, the net EPS is 18 pence. The gross dividend is nine pence, and so if tax is payable at 20%, then the net dividend equals 7.2 pence. Using the formula, dividend cover equals 18/7.2, which gives a dividend cover of 2.5.

In other words, Zellus' earnings are sufficient for the company to be able to pay out dividends at a rate 2.5 times their current level. By comparison, Buntam has an EPS of eight pence and a net dividend per share of 6.4 pence, giving a dividend cover of just 1.25.

Investors need to understand the relationship between dividend cover and investment returns. As a general rule, the greater the level of retention (and dividend cover), the greater the likelihood that a share will yield capital gain rather than income. From the examples given above, it would thus appear for Buntam plc (paying out almost all their earnings as dividends), there is limited scope for capital growth in the share price. By contrast, Zellus has a relatively high dividend cover, and so the reinvestment of profits should generate capital gains.

As with all investor ratios, dividend cover has to be interpreted with caution, and alongside a number of other measures.

(d)   The dividend growth model suggests a method whereby share values can be estimated from information on the required return on equity and the expected dividend payable. The theory suggests that the value of a share is equivalent to the discounted value of the future dividend stream, where the discount rate is determined by the return required by the investor.

For example, if I decide that an investment is very risky, the result may be that I require a return of 20%, and the dividend flows will be discounted at this rate. In this way, the price that an investor places on a share is a reflection of his perceived risk re that investment together with his dividend expectations.

Using Crazy Games plc as an example, the formula for share valuation under the dividend growth model is as follows:

$$\text{Market value of share} = \frac{D_1}{R-G}$$

Where D_1 = Next year's dividend
R = Investor's required return on the equity
G = Growth rate of the dividends

From the figures given relating to Crazy Games plc,

G = 16.36%
i.e. $\sqrt[4]{5.5/3} - 1$
R = 20%
D_1 = 5·5 (1·1636) = 6.40 pence

$$\text{Market value} = \frac{6.40}{0.2 - 0.1636}$$

Market value = 175.8 pence

This means that to buy 1,000 shares in Crazy Games would cost £1,758.

It is important to note that the model bases share prices on dividend growth rates even though, as in this case, there is often a significant difference between the rate of growth of dividends and that of earnings.

(e)   Based on the data given in the question, the yield curve has the following shape.

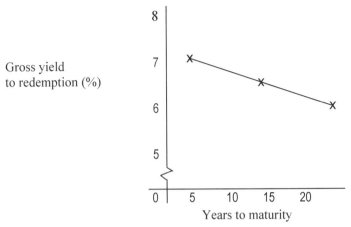

The yield curve clearly shows that as the years to maturity increase, the yield earned on the gilt investment falls.

The shape of the curve drawn above is contrary to that which would be expected from liquidity preference theory. Theory suggests that investors require increasing levels of compensation as the time to maturity lengthens – the curve drawn above shows the exact opposite. The reason for the difference between the theoretical and the observed shape of the curve is market expectations. The market believes that over the long term interest rates will fall, and the effect of market expectations is currently greater than the effects of liquidity preference.

The slope of the yield curve shows not only how much an investor can expect as investment returns, but also the cost of debt finance to the government.

(f)   The term gilts refers to government issued bonds, which are 'gilt' edged because of the associated risk of default is negligible.

For the private investor, gilts are an attractive form of investment because they offer fixed rates of return, they may be index-linked, and the investment risks are low. Gilts have a nominal value of £100 but they may trade at prices above or below that value depending on the current level of interest rates. If the current interest rate exceeds the coupon rate payable on the gilt, then it will sell for a price below its nominal value, and vice versa.

Yield curves are relevant to the private investor because they give an indication of interest rate expectations and trends. A downward sloping yield curve, such as that shown above, indicates a long-term downward trend in interest rates. For a gilt investor, this means that he can expect gilt prices to rise over the same time period.

55   The Independent Film Co

Key answer tips

Part (a) is a standard DCF computation, and a well organised and laid out answer should gain high marks. The best layout is probably a horizontal one, with columns for each year. Start by annotating the list of costs for those that have to be multiplied up by 3, and those that are increasing. Set up a proforma computation table, and put in all the operating cash flows first (including effects of increases etc). Sales will be based on an expected value. The tax is very simple here, as there are no capital allowances, so you just need to multiply the net cash flow by 33% and delay it by one year.

Be very careful in part (b) - you are being asked to discuss the use of *expected values* in investment appraisal, not DCF. A simple example, such as that shown in the examiner's answers, is not essential, but helps to illustrate the limitations.

The success or otherwise of your answer in part (c) (i) hangs upon whether you know what a profitability index (PI) is! Using it to decide between projects in a capital rationing situation is a form of key factor analysis - equivalent to using contribution per unit of scarce resource in product mix problems. Whilst a quick example of the calculation of the index is useful, with a brief explanation of its use, you probably wouldn't have time to go into the detail the examiner has in his answer.

Parts (c)(ii) and (iii) - don't worry if you are not confident about your answer to (a), you should still use your answer here to get the project's PI. The examiner will be looking for understanding of its application, not necessarily the right answer! Note that here, a bit of trial and error is needed to decide the optimal investment plan, as the projects are non-divisible (so you can't go for all of Y and ¾ of the filmmaking company project, as the PI ranking would indicate). This difficulty gives you your first point for (iii); then you need to think of 2 or 3 more.

Part (d) is a fairly straightforward discussion.

(a)   *Cash flows £'000*

		0	1	2	Year 3	4	5	6
Purchase of Company		(400)						
Legal/Professional			(20)	(20)	(20)	(20)	(20)	
Lease rentals			(12)	(12)	(12)	(12)	(12)	
Studio hire			(540)	(540)	(702)	(702)	(702)	
Camera hire			(120)	(120)	(120)	(120)	(120)	
Technical staff			(1,560)	(1,716)	(1,888)	(2,077)	(2,285)	
Screenplay			(150)	(173)	(199)	(229)	(263)	
Actors' salaries			(2,100)	(2,310)	(2,541)	(2,795)	(3,074)	
Costumes/Wardrobe			(180)	(180)	(180)	(180)	(180)	
Non Production Staff Wages			(60)	(66)	(73)	(80)	(88)	
Set design			(450)	(450)	(450)	(450)	(450)	
'Lost income' from office accommodation			(20)	(20)	(20)	(20)	(20)	
Sales			5,900	6,195	6,505	6,830	7,172	
Cash flow before Tax		(400)	688	588	300	145	(42)	
Tax				(227)	(194)	(99)	(48)	14
Net Cash Flow		(400)	688	361	106	46	(90)	14
Disc. Factor		1	0.877	0.769	0.675	0.592	0.519	0.456
P.V. Cash Flow £'000		(400)	603	278	72	27	(47)	6

NPV = £539,000

(b)   An expected value is calculated by using forecast probabilities to weight the values of alternative outcomes and thus compute an arithmetic mean for the overall expected result. There are three main problems with the use of expected values for making investment decisions:

(i)   The investment may only occur once: it is certainly very unlikely that there will be the opportunity to repeat the investment many times. The average of the anticipated returns will thus not be observed.

(ii)   Attaching probabilities to events is a highly subjective process. In investment decisions, probability may often be used in relation to sales forecasts derived from market research. The subjectivity involved in setting probabilities means that the judgements may be incorrect, even though the Net Present Value for the investment may be highly sensitive to changes in the probability distribution.

(iii)   The expected value does not evaluate the range of possible NPV outcomes.

The limitations of expected values can be demonstrated by means of a simple example. Suppose that an individual places a £10 bet with a colleague that it will rain within the next 24 hours. The weather forecast predicts the likelihood of rain with the 24 hour period at 60%. The expected value of the bet can thus be calculated as: $(0.6 \times £10) - [0.4 \times (£10)] = £2$. In reality, the expected value can never be observed, because the person will never be just £2 better off, only £10 richer or poorer depending on the success of the bet.

(c)   (i)   A profitability index for an investment project may be defined as the ratio of the net present value of the cash flows relative to the capital invested. The formula is thus:

$$\frac{\text{NPV Cash flows}}{\text{Capital investment}} = \text{Profitability Index}$$

For example, an investment which yields an NPV of £250,000 as a result of an investment of £100,000 would yield a profitability index of 2.5.

In cases where companies do not have unlimited funds available for investment, the profitability index can be used as the criteria for rationing of the scarce available capital where investments can be assumed to be divisible (i.e. any amount can be invested up to the desired level). Projects with the highest profitability index will be selected first, and selection will continue until all available funds have been used up.

For example, suppose that the NPV of two projects is calculated, based on a common discount rate, and Project A yields an NPV of £150,000 whilst Project B yields an NPV of £50,000. The yield per £ invested can be calculated if project costs are known. If Project A cost £20,000 then the yield per £ invested is £7.5. In contrast, if Project B costs £5,000, then the yield per £ is higher at £10. This means that B is the preferred investment and capital should be allocated accordingly.

Suppose then that a company had £15,000 available for investment, then the optimal investment strategy is to put £5,000 into Project B and the balancing £10,000 into Project A. The net yield will then be as follows:

£5,000 x £10 per £	= £50,000
£10,000 x £7.5 per £	= £75,000
Total Yield	= £125,000
Profitability index	$= \dfrac{125}{15}$
	= 8.33

In this way the company has maximised the Net Present Value per £ invested. A key assumption, however, is that investments can be split.

(ii)   Purchase of the film production company yields an NPV of £539,000 on an investment of £400,000. This gives a profitability index of 539/400 = 1.35.

Investment X

NPV = (200 × 0.877) + (200 × 0.769) + (150 × 0.675) + (100 × 0.592) + (100 × 0.519) + (100 × 0.456) − 200 = 387

Profitability Index   = 387/200
                       = 1.94

Investment Y

NPV = (80 × 0.877) + (80 × 0.769) + (40 × 0.675) + (40 × 0.592) + (40 × 0.519)+ (40 × 0.456) − 100 = 121

Profitability Index   = 121/100
                       = 1.21

Note: profitability indices may also be calculated as Present Value/Initial Outlay instead of Net Present Value/Initial Outlay. The ranking will remain the same regardless of the formula used. The profitability index cannot be applied in this case because of non-divisibility.

The choices available are:

− X plus Y at a cost of £300,000 and yielding an NPV of £508,000.

− Purchase of the company costing £400,000 and yielding an NPV of £539,000.

If the objective is to maximise the sum of the Net Present Values, which can be achieved subject to the budget constraint, then the optimal investment strategy is to purchase the film production company.

(iii)   There are several problems with using the profitability index as the basis for profit selection under capital rationing.

First, as has been shown above in the answer to (ii), the method is of limited use when projects are indivisible, because it ignores the opportunity to maximise the sum of the net present values from all projects.

Secondly, the criterion for selection is relatively simplistic in nature, and takes no account of the potential strategic value of individual projects. In the case of the Independent Film Company, for example, we have no information about the nature of investments X and Y. It is however clear that the investment in a filmmaking business involves some vertical integration of the company's activities and this may be important to its future survival in the industry. The discounted cash flow for the purchase shows that it yields a positive return, and is thus a viable investment, even if it offers a lower rate of return than project X. The use of a Profitability Index effectively takes no account of strategic considerations.

A third problem of the approach relates to the fact that it is of limited use when projects have differing cash flow patterns. The index selects purely on the basis of NPV per £ invested, but the pattern of cash flows from projects will vary. This means that in multi-period rationing it is possible for the project with the highest index to be the slowest in generating returns. The cash flow pattern of returns may, however, be important to a company as it will affect the timing and availability of funds for future investment.

Finally, the profitability index ignores the absolute size of individual projects. An investment may yield an index of 10, but the sum invested is just £5,000. By contrast, an investment with an index of 3, and hence less attractive on this criterion, may involve the investment of £500,000. An absolute return of £50,000 is clearly less attractive then one of £1.5 million, but comparison of the alternatives is not straightforward in practice. The company should look at all the alternatives open to it, within the bounds of the capital available, and maximise the total NPV which can be achieved. The most useful tool for this type of analysis is linear programming, which allows maximisation of an objective subject to specified constraints, but this assumes divisibility.

(d)   The tax treatment of capital purchases can affect an investment decision because where tax relief is available, the tax benefits serve to reduce the effective cost of an investment. For example, suppose that a company estimates the net present value of a two year project to be £10,000, but that this is in the absence of any capital allowances being available on capital purchase. If the government then introduces 100% first year allowances, the company can use the allowances claimed on purchases to offset its corporation tax liability. If capital purchases totalled £15,000 and tax was payable at a rate of 33%, the cash impact of the capital allowances would be (£15,000 x 0.33) or £5,000 in reduced tax liabilities. This amounts to a 50% increase in the NPV. The impact on NPV will be less marked where the capital allowances take the form of writing down allowances instead of a large first year allowance, but the general effect is the same.

Clearly the example given above is an extreme case, but it illustrates the fact that on potentially marginal projects, it is possible that tax benefits could serve to convert a negative NPV into one which is positive. For this reason, capital allowances on investments can be viewed as a tool of government economic policy. If the economy is suffering from low levels of industrial investment, then an increase in the level of allowances can be used to encourage such investment.

Obviously the tax treatment of capital purchases will only affect investment decisions in cases where the investing company is able to take advantage of the reliefs available. For loss making companies or those with tax liabilities below the threshold of the tax relief created by allowances, the situation is more complex, and investment decisions may be made irrespective of the tax position. Similarly, there may be some investments which are being made for strategic reasons, and which would be made regardless of the tax treatment of capital purchases. It is oversimplifying the situation to argue that higher tax allowances will definitely lead to an increase in industrial investment.

56   Sprinter plc

Key answer tips

Don't be put off by the amount of data given in the question. These long scenario-based quotations will inevitably have to give quite a lot of information up front, but the requirements are usually broken down into manageable parts, as here. Although this is set in a foreign exchange context, the number of marks awarded for detailed technical knowledge of forex techniques is very low, most of it can be tackled by a logical, common sense approach. In (a) you have to reconstruct *total* sales figures from an historic *UK* sales figure, its growth rates and the proportions these represent of total (be careful – these change from year to year).

Part (b) builds upon the answers to (a), but, as always, the examiner is looking for correct method, so you can still get full marks even if your answers to (a) were not wholly correct. It is a good idea to summarise your answers once you have worked through them for each year, to assist both you (in seeing trends for part (c)) and the examiner (in seeing what you final answers are).

In order to give a sensible answer to (c), you must sort out in your own mind what is meant by, and the implications of, sterling strengthening. This means the £ costs more in other currencies, so more Yen/£ or less £/Yen. This may, indeed, lead to sales to Japan falling; you should first recognise this (using the data), and then go on to consider other possible factors that may come into play. Here, show that you have read the initial information in the question by considering the nature of the product being sold.

Part (d)only has 2 marks, so don't get too technical. You would not have time do an example as in the answer.

Parts (e) and (g) move onto perhaps more familiar ground, the general management of working capital, although still in a foreign trade context. All of the principles of domestic management of debtors etc apply here, with additional points to be made regarding the particular delays and risks involved with overseas trading. Note that in (g) you are expected to first *calculate* the profit impact of the longer overseas working capital cycle. This is basically the cost of funding the cost of goods sold for the extra time before recouping the cost from sales revenue(note that the answer acknowledges that cost of funding debtors is usually done on the basis of sales value, and you would have got equal credit for using this basis instead). The remaining 4 marks or so will be given for sensible comment; as there is not much more to say about the actual impact figures, it makes sense to talk about how it may be reduced.

(a)   20X7 UK sales = £6.5 million, which is 70% of total sales of £9.29 million
       20X8 estimate = £6.5m × 1.12 = £7.28 million
       20X9 forecast = £7.28 × 1.12 = £8.15 million

       20X8 UK sales = 65% of total
       20X8 total sales = £7.28/0.65 = £11.20 million

       20X9 UK sales = 60% of total
       20X9 total sales = £8.15/0.60 = £13.58 million

(b)   Working from 20X7 as the first known value.
       Sterling Values
       20X7.10% of total = £0.93 million
       20X8.14% of total = £1.57 million
       20X9.12% of total = £1.63 million

       20X5 and 20X6 sales need to be calculated from the UK sales figures.
       20X6 UK sales = £6.5/1·08 = £6.02 million. This equals 50% of total sales of £12.04 million. Japanese sales are 19% of total i.e. £2.29 million

       20X5 UK sales = £6.02/1·08 = £5.57 million. This equals 40% of total sales of £13.93 million. Japanese sales are 25% of total i.e. £3.48 million

       Summary of sterling value of sales to Japan (£ million)

20X5	3.48
20X6	2.29
20X7	0.93
20X8	1.57
20X9	1.63

◈ FOULKS*lynch*

Converting these at the exchange rates given, the yen (million) value of sales is as follows:

20X5 Y 185.65 × 3·48 = Y 646.06
20X6 Y 190.50 × 2·29 = Y 436.25
20X7 Y 209.75 × 0·93 = Y 195.07
20X8 Y 196.83 × 1·57 = Y 309.02
20X9 Y 188.30 × 1·63 = Y 306.93

(c)   The Finance Director's view is that sales have fallen as a result of the strength of sterling. The effect of exchange rate movements on sales depends, to some extent, on company pricing policy. For many companies adopting fixed sterling prices is the simplest approach, and this is the policy used by Sprinter. One effect of the policy is to make the UK exports appear comparatively expensive to Japanese customers, as their weaker currency will buy fewer pounds sterling. The result is that sales to Japan may fall when sterling strengthens, and vice versa.

Over the period 20X5–20X8 the exchange rate figures indicate that sterling is strengthening against the yen, and so the Finance Director is suggesting that it is for this reason that the value of sales to Japan has declined over this same period. As the statistics show, the sterling value of sales in 20X7 was only a little over one quarter of the value of sales two years earlier. Moreover the forecast is for the Yen to recover in 20X8 and the forecasts show a simultaneous recovery in sales. In fact the forecast recovery may simply reflect the Finance Director's belief.

If the direction of the movement in the exchange rate is compared with the direction of change in sales we can see the following trends:

20X5–20X6 yen depreciates and sales (yen value) fall
20X6–20X7 yen depreciates and sales (yen value) fall
20X7–20X8 (Estimate) yen appreciates and sales (yen value) rise
20X8–20X9 (Forecast) yen appreciates and sales (yen value) fall

The fact that the figures suggest that Japanese sales fall as sterling strengthens (and vice versa) certainly implies that the market is sensitive to exchange rate movements. Nevertheless, it cannot be expected that the exchange rate is the only influence on Japanese sales figures. Demand for a product is dependent upon a wide variety of both macro and micro economic influences. The state of the economy, the competitive environment, the savings ratio, trends in personal income levels, demographic trends and fashion will all play their part in determining sales levels. In the case of Sprinter's 'designer' watches, they are fashion products aimed at younger customers. The demand for them is thus likely to be very sensitive to trends in youth culture and fashion, and the size of the population in the relevant age group. It is by no means clear that currency movements are the primary explanation for the recent dramatic decline in sales, and it would therefore be dangerous to assume that if the yen appreciates again (as forecast) that sales to Japan will recover. The Finance Director is therefore over-simplifying the issue.

(d)   *Note:* this answer contains substantially more detail than would be required from candidates under examination conditions.

A forward contract is an agreement to buy/sell a foreign currency at a fixed rate of exchange at an agreed date in the future. Such contracts are useful for protecting against transaction risks which arise when there is a time lag between the date that a company issues an invoice in a foreign currency, and the date that it receives payment.

For example, if 90 days credit is granted, it is possible for the exchange rate to move by several percentage points during that time, and so the value of the payment received when converted back into the domestic currency is different from the sum anticipated when the invoice was issued.

Example
Invoice date 1 July 20X9: invoice value US$5,000
Payment date 1 October 20X9
Exchange rates (spot): 1 July $1.62/£
                        1 October $1.70/£

The sterling value of the invoice on the date of issue   = 5,000/1.62 = £3,086.42
The sterling value on the date of payment   = 5,000/1.70 = £2,941.18

The difference represents a potential loss to the UK exporter of £142.24 equal to 4.6% of the original invoice value. For a company selling on tight margins, this could make the difference between a profit and a loss. The company can protect its position by purchasing a forward contract. Suppose that it can buy a contract to sell the dollars receivable on 1 October at a rate of $1.65/£, it will then be 'guaranteed' to receive £3,030.30. This is still less than the exchange rate at the date of issue of the invoice, but the value is now fixed. If the company takes the risk of not purchasing the contract, and decides to risk selling them in the spot market, the risk is potentially open-ended. Purchase of a forward contract therefore hedges (limits) the level of foreign exchange risk.

(e)

Days in working capital cycle:

		Total Sales	UK Sales
Raw Materials Days	$= \dfrac{\text{Raw Materials} \times 365}{\text{Purchases}}$	76	76
Work in Progress	$= \dfrac{\text{WIP} \times 365}{\text{Cost of goods sold}}$	44	38
Finished Goods	$= \dfrac{\text{F.G.} \times 365}{\text{Cost of goods sold}}$	50	43
Debtors	$= \dfrac{\text{Debtors} \times 365}{\text{Sales}}$	127	73
Trade Creditors	$= \dfrac{\text{Creditors} \times 365}{\text{Purchases}}$	42	42
Total		255	188

(f) The key reason for the difference in the length of the working capital cycle is the additional time taken to receive payment from overseas debtors. It takes 251 days to obtain payment from an overseas customer: this is more than three times as long as the period outstanding for UK debtors. It is also noticeable that both WIP and finished goods stocks are considerably higher on overseas sales. Work in progress stocks for overseas amount to 58 days compared with 38 days for the UK. Similarly, finished goods stocks are 66 days compared with a UK figure of 43 days. The higher stock levels perhaps suggest that there is a longer lead time needed to organise export packing and delivery. The longer credit period granted to foreign customers arises because of the combined effect of an increased delivery time, the period required for processing the associated paperwork, and the conversion of foreign currency receipts. It is also likely that the resolution of any problems arising with deliveries in respect of foreign sales will take longer, and such delays simply add to the value of the debtors outstanding.

(g) The difference in the length of the total versus the UK cycle is 67 days. In other words, the company has as a consequence of choosing to sell world-wide, increased its working capital requirements. Extra is needed to fund additional stocks and debtors and the increases will only be partially offset by greater trade credit. The effect is thus an increase in the borrowing requirement equal to a maximum of 67 days worth of cost of sales, or £1,492,000. At a cost of capital of 12% this represents additional costs of £179,040. This sum could theoretically be added to profit if the company's borrowing could be reduced by £1.492 million. Given that the current gross profit (Total Sales less COGS) is equal to £1.16 million, the impact of such extra earnings would be very significant.

In practice it is unlikely that Sprinter could bring the cycle time for overseas sales down to a level which matches that of UK sales, except perhaps, by the use of an overseas factor to take responsibility for collection of the foreign debts. As indicated in (i), there are practical issues involved in managing foreign sales, the logistics of which may result in additional stock (per £ sales) being carried or debts taking longer to collect. These factors will combine to make it almost inevitable that the working capital cycle will lengthen when a company begins to sell overseas. In the light of this, it becomes even more important to manage working capital very tightly. It is also important to try and measure any change in the length of the working capital cycle and calculate the additional borrowing costs, as this is an incremental cost arising from the decision to sell abroad. As such, that cost must be set against any contribution from the sales, in order to assess the viability of selling overseas. The world-wide sales strategy adds £185,000 to gross profits, but if this is eroded by additional borrowing cost of £179,040, then the net increase in profit amounts to just over £5,000. Sprinter should therefore monitor foreign sales very closely, as it would appear to be a marginal area of business in terms of its profitability.

Alternatively, the additional borrowing cost may be based on the sales figure, rather than cost of sales. This approach may be justified by arguing that the bulk of the increase in cycle length is caused by an additional longer debt collection period. Borrowing a sum equal to 67 days of sales increases the cost still further to £204,600. The ideal method is to calculate the additional borrowing needs by a pro rata calculation which takes into account the funding needed for stock as opposed to debtors. Borrowing for stock needs is calculated on the basis of cost of goods sold, whilst debtors are calculated against sales.

Section 8

OLD SYLLABUS EXAMINATIONS

June 2000 Questions

Section A - THIS question is compulsory and MUST be attempted

1 Spender Construction plc

Spender Construction plc is an expanding UK based building company wishing to raise funds to invest in building a new headquarters and IT centre with upgraded facilities for its logistics and project management business. The total investment required is estimated to be £7 million. The financial justification for the investment is based upon estimates that the new centre will cut fixed administration costs by approximately £500,000 per annum, and reduce the cost of sales by 2%. Sales for the year to 31 December 20X1 are forecast to rise 15% above 20X0 levels (regardless of the investment decision), and so the company anticipates a need for higher working capital funding, in addition to finance for the capital expenditure.

Spender's finance director has commented that in raising funds the Board need to be conscious of the fact that the company operates in a sector which is notorious for its volatility of demand, and also that the company has relatively high levels of fixed operating costs. The industry average is for fixed operating costs to equal 7% of sales revenue. Summarised financial statement for Spender Construction plc are shown below:

Profit and Loss Account Year Ending 31 December 20X0

	£'000
Turnover	55,258
Cost of sales	41,827
Gross profit	13,431
Selling & distribution costs	348
Administration costs	8,250
Operating profit	4,833
Interest charges	327
Profit before tax	4,506
Corporation tax payable	1,352
Profit after tax	3,154
Dividend payable	1,520
Retained profit	1,634

Balance Sheet as at 31 December 20X0

	£'000
Fixed Assets	5,800
Current Assets	27,928
Current Liabilities	20,076
Net Current Assets	7,852
Total Assets less Current Liabilities	13,652
10% Debentures 20X6	1,200

Net Assets	12,452

Capital and Reserves

Ordinary share capital	4,000
Share premium account	800
Profit and loss account	7,652
Equity shareholders' funds	12,452

Additional information

(1)   The nominal value of ordinary share capital is 50 pence per share.

(2)   Costs are classified as fixed or variable as follows:

Cost of sales: 100% variable
Selling and distribution: £100,000 per annum fixed, balance variable
Administration costs: £7 million per annum fixed, balance variable

(3)   The current rate of corporation tax is 30%

(4)   Current liabilities as at 31 December 20X0 includes a £2 million overdraft, and a £450,000 VAT bill

(5)   The current market price of ordinary shares in Spender plc is £6.50.

(6)   Working capital needs are expected to rise in line with sales.

(7)   The dividend forecast for year ending 31 December 20X1 is 25 pence per share

(8)   Bank interest charges for the year to 31 December 20X1 are forecast to be £280,000. Interest is charged at 12.5% per annum.

(9)   Depreciation charges on fixed assets for the year to 31 December 20X0 are £435,000

(10)   Assume that payments totalling £2.5 million were made during 20X0 in respect of creditors outstanding at the end of the previous year.

(11)   Working capital requirements for 20X0 were the same as those for the previous year.

Required:

(a)   Explain and illustrate, using the above data, each of the following terms and comment upon the implications of these two forms of gearing for the equity investors in Spender Construction plc:

(i)   operational gearing
(ii)   financial gearing.   **(14 marks)**

(b)   Calculate how much external finance Spender must raise in order to finance the planned sales growth and the investment in the new HQ and IT centre. Assume that both additional working capital and the capital funds are required in full immediately i.e. on 1.1.20X1.   **(8 marks)**

(c)   Given that it currently has an overdraft of £2 million, under what circumstances would it be prudent for Spender plc to replace this short-term funding with long-term debt finance?   **(5 marks)**

(d)   Evaluate (by comparison of shareholder risks and returns, including EPS) the relative merits of raising the £7 million required for the capital investment via a 1 for 6 rights issue priced at £5.25, or a 10% debenture issue redeemable in 20 years time. Ignore issue costs.   **(10 marks)**

(e)   Explain the meaning of the term dividend cover and, using the forecast figures for the year ending 31 December 20X1, calculate the dividend cover for Spender plc assuming the debenture issue is made.

(3 marks)
(Total: 40 marks)

Section B - ONE question ONLY to be attempted

2   Investment appraisal

(a)   Explain and illustrate (using simple numerical examples) the Accounting Rate of Return and Payback approaches to investment appraisal, paying particular attention to the limitations of each approach.   **(6 marks)**

(b)   (i)   Explain the differences between NPV and IRR as methods of Discounted Cash Flow analysis.   **(6 marks)**

(ii)   A company with a cost of capital of 14% is trying to determine the optimal replacement cycle for the laptop computers used by its sales team. The following information is relevant to the decision:

The cost of each laptop is £2,400. Maintenance costs are payable at the end of *each full year* of ownership, but not in the year of replacement, e.g. if the laptop is owned for two years, then the maintenance cost is payable at the end of year 1.

Interval between replacement (years)	Trade-in value (£)	Maintenance cost
1	1,200	Zero
2	800	£75 (payable at end of Year 1)
3	300	£150 (payable at end of Year 2)

Required:

Ignoring taxation, calculate the equivalent annual cost of the three different replacement cycles, and recommend which should be adopted. What other factors should the company take into account when determining the optimal cycle?   **(8 marks)**
(Total: 20 marks)

3   Delcars plc

(a)   Explain, with the use of a numerical example, the meaning of the term 'cash operating cycle' and its significance in relation to working capital management.   **(6 marks)**

(b)   Delcars plc own a total of ten franchises, in a variety of United Kingdom locations, for the sale and servicing of new and used cars. Six of the franchises sell just second hand vehicles, with the remaining four operating a car service centre in addition to retailing both new and used vehicles. Delcars operate different systems for banking of sales receipts, depending on the type of sale. All monies from new car sales must be banked by the garage on the day of the sale; receipts from second hand car sales are banked once a week on Mondays, and receipts from car servicing work are banked twice a week on Wednesdays and Fridays. No banking facilities are available at the weekend i.e. Saturdays and Sundays. The sales mix of the three elements (as a percentage of Delcars' total revenue) is as follows: 60% new vehicles; 25% second hand vehicles; 15% servicing. Total sales for all three business areas amounted to £25 million in 1999. Delcars pays interest at a rate of 8.5% per annum on an average overdraft of £65,000, and the company's finance director has suggested that the company could significantly reduce the interest charge if all sales receipts were banked on the day of sale. All the garages are open every day except Sunday. Assume that the daily sales value (for all three areas of business) is spread evenly across the week.

Required:

Calculate the value of the annual interest which could be saved if all ten franchises adopted the finance director's suggestion of daily banking.   **(8 marks)**

(c)   Using the example of a car dealership such as Delcars, as given in (b) above, outline the advantages and disadvantages of centralisation of the treasury function.   **(6 marks)**
(Total: 20 marks)

Section C -TWO Questions ONLY to be attempted

4   Public sector organisation

A Public sector organisation is extending its budgetary control and responsibility accounting system to all departments. One such department concerned with public health and welfare is called 'Homecare'. The department consists of staff who visit elderly 'clients' in their homes to support them with their basic medical and welfare needs.

A monthly cost control report is to be sent to the department manager, a copy of which is also passed to a Director who controls a number of departments. In the system, which is still being refined, the budget was set by the Director and the manager had not been consulted over the budget or the use of the monthly control report.

Shown below is the first month's cost control report for the Homecare department

Cost Control Report - Homecare Department
Month ending May 20X0

	Budget	Actual	(Overspend)/ Underspend
Visits	10,000	12,000	(2,000)
	£	£	£
Department expenses:			
Supervisory salary	2,000	2,125	(125)
Wages (Permanent staff)	2,700	2,400	300
Wages (Casual staff)	1,500	2,500	(1,000)
Office equipment depreciation	500	750	(250)
Repairs to equipment	200	20	180
Travel expenses	1,500	1,800	(300)
Consumables	4,000	6,000	(2,000)
Administration and telephone	1,000	1,200	(200)
Allocated administrative costs	2,000	3,000	(1,000)
	15,400	19,795	(4,395)

In addition to the manager and permanent members of staff, appropriately qualified casual staff are appointed on a week to week basis to cope with fluctuations in demand. Staff use their own transport, and travel expenses are reimbursed. There is a central administration overhead charge over all departments. Consumables consist of materials which are used by staff to care for clients. Administration and telephone are costs of keeping in touch with the staff who often operate from their own homes.

As a result of the report, the Director sent a memo to the manager of the Homecare department pointing out that the department must spend within its funding allocation and that any spending more than 5% above budget on any item would not be tolerated. The Director requested an immediate explanation for the serious overspend.

You work as the assistant to the Directorate Management Accountant. On seeing the way the budget system was developing, he made a note of points he would wish to discuss and develop further, but was called away before these could be completed.

Required:

(a)   Develop and explain the issues concerning the budgetary control and responsibility accounting system which are likely to be raised by the management accountant. You should refer to the way the budget was prepared, the implications of a 20% increase in the number of visits, the extent of controllability of costs, the implications of the funding allocation, social aspects and any other points you think appropriate. You may include numerical illustrations and comment on specific costs, but you are not required to reproduce the cost control report.

(14 marks)

(b)   Briefly explain Zero-Based Budgeting (ZBB), describe how (in a situation such as that above) it might be implemented, and how as a result it could improve the budget setting procedure.   **(6 marks)**

(Total: 20 marks)

5   Fish processing

A fish processing company has a contract to purchase all the fish caught by a fishing vessel. The processor removes the head and skeleton which are waste (Process 1) and is then able to sell the fish fillets which remain. The waste is estimated to be 40% by weight of the fish bought and is sold at 30p per kilo for animal food.

The fish fillets are inspected for quality and three categories are identified (standard, special and superior). Half the catch is expected to be of standard quality. Of the remainder there is twice as much special as superior.

For one contract period, the vessel contains a total of 36,000 kilos of whole fish and the contract price is £1.50 per kilo irrespective of quality. The labour cost for Process 1 is £28,000 for this quantity.

As an alternative to sale as fresh produce, the fillets of fish may be cooked and coated in bread crumbs (Process 2). The process of cooking the fillets and coating them in bread crumbs costs 10p per kilo for material and 60p per kilo for labour. Current market prices of fresh fillets and the bread crumbed alternatives are as follows:

	£ per kilo	
Category	*Fresh*	*Bread crumbed*
Superior	7.50	8.70
Special	6.80	7.50
Standard	4.00	5.20

In Process 1 the overhead costs are recovered based on 120% of labour costs; one third of these overheads are variable. In process 2 the overhead rate set is 180% of labour costs, one quarter being variable.

Required:

(a)   An often quoted phrase used in management accounting is 'different costs for different purposes'. To demonstrate the appropriateness of this phrase, list and briefly describe three purposes of preparing product costs in a manufacturing organisation.   **(5 marks)**

(b)   Prepare statements of total net profit or loss per period for each category of fish if all sales are in the fresh state (i.e. after Process 1) and on the assumption that the total net cost is shared between the three categories based on:

    (i)   weight

    (ii)   market value.   **(6 marks)**

(c)   If a loss were revealed for a category under either (b) (i) or (ii) above, explain how the management should react.
                                                                                            (4 marks)

(d)   Determine for each category whether it is profitable for the company to further process the fillets, and make brief comments.   **(5 marks)**
                                                                            (Total: 20 marks)

6   BML

BML has three product lines: P1, P2 and P3. Since its creation the company has been using a single direct labour cost percentage to assign overhead costs to products.

Despite P3, a relatively new line, attracting additional business, increasing overhead costs and a loss of market share, particularly for P2, a major product, have convinced the management that the costing system is in need of some development. A team, led by the management accountant was established to develop an improved system of costing based on activities. The team spent several weeks collecting data (see tables below) for the different activities and products. For the accounting period in question, given in the tables below is data on BML's three product lines and overhead costs:

	P1	P2	P3
Production volume	7,500 units	12,500 units	4,000 units
Direct labour cost per unit	£4	£8	£6.40
Material cost per unit	£18	£25	£16
Selling price per unit	£47	£80	£68
Materials movements (in total)	4	25	50
Machine hours per unit	0.5	0.5	0.2
Set-ups (in total)	1	5	10
Proportion of engineering work	30%	20%	50%
Orders packed (in total)	1	7	22

Activities	Overhead cost £
Material receiving and handling	150,000
Machine maintenance and depreciation	390,000
Set-up labour	18,688
Engineering	100,000
Packing	60,000
Total	718,688

Required:

(a)   Calculate the overhead rate and the product unit costs under the existing costing system.   **(4 marks)**

(b)   Identify for each overhead activity, an appropriate cost driver from the information supplied, and then calculate the product unit costs using a system that assigns overheads on the basis of the use of activities.   **(9 marks)**

(c)   Comment on the results of the two costing systems in (a) and (b) above.   **(7 marks)**

(Total: 20 marks)

June 2000 Answers

1   Spender Construction plc

(a)   (i)   *Operational gearing* may be defined as a measure of the impact of a change in sales upon Earnings Before Interest and Taxation (EBIT). The following formula can be used to calculate the level of operational gearing for a unit output level of Q:

$$\text{Level of operational gearing at point } Q = \frac{Q(P-VC)}{Q(P-VC)-FC}$$

Q   = Units of output
P   = Selling price per unit
VC = Variable cost per unit
FC = Total fixed costs

The numerator in the formula can be seen to be the same as total contribution, and the denominator is equal to EBIT. Hence for any given level of output the level of operational gearing is:

Contribution/EBIT

A company's level of operational gearing is dependent upon the ratio of fixed to variable costs and the current level of profit. If a company has a high level of fixed costs, then beyond break-even a change in sales levels will lead to especially magnified percentage increases in profit, but the percentage change declines as profit continues to grow. Applying the formula shown above to the 20X0 financial statements for Spender plc, we can compute the current level of operational gearing within the company:

$$\text{Operational gearing} = \frac{\text{Contribution}}{\text{EBIT}}$$

For 20X0:
Contribution = Sales – variable costs
            = £55.258m – (41.827m + 0.248m + 1.250m)
            = £11.933m

EBIT   = £4,833m

Operational gearing   = 11,933/4,833
                      = 2.47

(ii)   *Financial gearing* is measured by comparing a company's use of long-term debt finance relative to equity. The higher the proportion of debt finance, the higher the level of gearing. Financial gearing affects the sensitivity of the profit attributable to equity to changes in EBIT. Using debt as a source of finance commits a company to the payment of debt interest which, for any given level of operating profit, erodes the amount of profit attributable to equity investors. However, once operating profits are sufficient to cover the interest payments due, then (ceteris paribus) no further such erosion can take place, and so all additions to operating profit will be fully allocated to equity investors.

The textbooks contain a number of different formulae for financial gearing which include the following alternatives:

(1) $$\frac{\text{Long - term interest bearing debt} + \text{preference share capital}}{\text{Equity plus reserves}}$$

(2) $$\frac{\text{Long - term interest bearing debt} + \text{preference share capital}}{\text{Total long - term capital}}$$

(3) $$\frac{\text{Profit before interest}}{\text{Profit after interest}}$$

◈ FOULKS*lynch*

Some writers also suggest that a further variation on the formula should be applied which includes short-term interest bearing debt in the numerator. In this way financial gearing is then measuring the proportion of total borrowing relative to total capital, rather than just the proportion of long-term loans in the total capital base.

It is useful to note the differences between the formulae. The first two differ only in relation to the denominator, but this has the effect of altering the resulting figure for financial gearing. This can be illustrated by reference to Spender plc, using formula (i) in respect of the 20X0 financial statements.

$$\text{Financial gearing} = \frac{1,200}{12,452}$$
$$= 0.0964 \text{ or } 9.64\%$$

Using formula (ii):

$$\text{Financial gearing} = \frac{1,200}{13,652}$$
$$= 0.0879 \text{ or } 8.799\%$$

The second figure is lower because the denominator is larger. This means that care must be taken in interpreting figures for financial gearing to ensure that there is consistency in the formula chosen for the calculation. Finally, applying formula (iii), which uses figures from the profit and loss account (as opposed to the balance sheet), and so is more consistent with the operational gearing calculation done earlier, we get:

$$\text{Financial gearing} = \frac{\text{Profit before interest}}{\text{Profit after interest}}$$

$$= \frac{4,833}{4,506}$$

$$= 1.07$$

Clearly the use of this formula yields a very different result to the other two, and so serves to underline further the need for caution in interpretation of gearing figures.

Financial gearing is sometimes referred to as 'second tier' gearing because it affects the profit going to equity but not until the impact of operational gearing has already affected the level of EBIT. This means that if a company trades with a high level of operational gearing then EBIT is already highly sensitive to changes in sales revenue. If this is then combined with the potential for further erosion of the returns to equity via large debt interest payments caused by high financial gearing then the overall risk to equity investors is high. This overall effect is most important to investors, and means that attention needs to be given to a company's level of operational and financial gearing in combination.

Spender's fixed costs (excluding interest payments) equal over 12.5 % of sales, compared with the industry average of just 7%. The potential risk of this gearing lies in the sales volatility that is often associated with construction firms. The industry is very sensitive to the state of the economy, and an economic downturn can hit sales quite dramatically. Under such circumstances, and with an operational gearing level of 2.47, Spender plc could find that a 10% fall in sales from current levels would cause a drop of almost 25% in operating profit. It is worth noting, however, that this gearing level will come down next year as a result of increased sales and reduced fixed costs. It is probably in recognition of this sensitivity of profits to changes in sales that the company has chosen to keep its level of financial gearing relatively low at 1.07.

Spender's financial gearing cannot be compared with that of the industry because the relevant information is not available. The lower level helps to limit the potential impact of sales changes upon the profit available to equity and so limit the overall risk to equity investors. Nonetheless, Spender plc must be regarded as a somewhat risky choice for equity investors and the example clearly demonstrates how a company needs to think about how it mixes its levels of financial and operating gearing in such a way as to limit the risk to equity shareholders.

(b)   The additional working capital required is expected to rise in line with sales i.e. growth of 15%.

Working capital 20X1 = 1.15 (Net Current assets in 20X0)
                     = 1.15 (£13.174 million)
                     = £15.15 million

(*Note:* the net current asset figure in the balance sheet has been adjusted to exclude the overdraft and VAT bill, plus tax and dividends payable as detailed in the additional information.)

This represents an increase of £1.98 million (i.e. £13.174 × 0.15).

In addition to the capital expenditure investment of £7 million this gives a funding requirement of £8.976 million, which may be raised either from external or internal sources. Internal funding will come from operations and the cash flow can be deduced from the profit and loss account and additional information.

The profit and loss account for 20X0 shows cash inflows from operations equal to £4.956 million (i.e. £4.506 million plus £450,000 VAT), and after adjusting for depreciation this gives an operating cash flow of £5.391 million. The net cash available for investment within the business can thus be calculated as follows:

	£'000	£'000
Cash from operations		5,391
Cash outflows		
Tax	(1,802)	
Interest payments	(327)	
Dividends	(1,520)	
Other payments	(2,500)	
		(6,149)
Net addition to cash		(758)

The total funding requirement equals £8.976 million, of which none can be met from internal resources. (Note that this excludes any allowance for additional working capital required to pay either debenture interest of dividends in the year 20X1, although these may be funded out of future profits, and includes corporation tax plus VAT payable.)

(c)   In considering whether to replace short-term with long-term borrowing, Spender plc needs to look at the current structure of its balance sheet and its forecast capital requirements. From (a) we saw that the current level of financial gearing in the company is relatively low, partly to compensate for relatively high operating gearing. Converting short- into long-term borrowing will slightly affect the level of financial gearing as calculated in (a)(i), and (a)(ii), but the impact on (a)(iii) will depend upon relative short-term and long-term interest rates. The main factors that Spender plc need to consider are the need for flexibility in access to short-term funding and the relative cost and risk of alternative funding sources.

The overdraft facility offers the advantage of flexibility, but the cost is relatively high if the funds are borrowed on a semi-permanent basis. In other words, if Spender plc does not expect to utilise its overdraft except for brief periods throughout the year, it may be prudent and cheaper to retain it. On the other hand, if the overdraft is being used to finance 'permanent' working capital within the business, and Spender plc is regularly borrowing at close to the overdraft limit, then it may be prudent to convert the borrowing into a long-term loan. As a general rule, long-term finance is slightly cheaper, and given that the company is already having to raise funds for other purposes, the marginal cost of raising an additional £2 million would be small. As a general principle, it is a good idea for companies to divide working capital requirements into temporary and permanent, with the funding for these being short-term or long-term respectively. The forecasts suggest that Spender plc will be experiencing rising sales, and an associated high level of cash generation, although this will be linked to a related increase in its need for working capital. By converting the overdraft into a long-term loan, the company can leave itself renewed access to short-term borrowing whilst reducing the average cost of its working capital funding by an increased use of long-term money. The only time when it may not be sensible to convert the overdraft is if economic forecasts suggested that interest rates were due to fall dramatically in the near future. In such a case, it would make sense to wait until interest rates had bottomed out before converting the overdraft.

(d)   Number of shares in issue 8 million (i.e. £4m/£0.50)

EPS 20X0 39.4 pence (i.e. £3.154m/8m)

Dividend per share 20X0 19 pence (i.e. £1.520 million/8 million)

In comparing the alternative funding sources of a rights issue versus a debenture issue, it is important to take account of the effect of each alternative on the returns to ordinary shareholders, and the level of risk to those shareholders. It is reasonable to assume that if we are asking shareholders to accept a higher level of risk (operational or financial) then they will expect to receive an increase on their returns in compensation. The two alternative methods of funding affect only the level of financial risk in the company. As a form of loan finance, the debenture issue will increase the level of financial gearing whilst the rights issue will reduce the level of financial gearing. As at December 20X0 the financial gearing of Spender Construction was 1.07. In selecting the most appropriate source of funding, therefore, consideration must be given as to whether such changes would be acceptable to the equity shareholders. A comparison of the forecast EPS under both types of funding is useful in assessing the likely shareholder response. Care must be taken, however, in interpreting the forecast, because only one year's data is available.

Forecast Profit and Loss Account, Spender Construction Year ending 31 December 20X1

	Assuming debenture issue £'000		*Assuming rights issue* £'000
Turnover	63,547		63,547
Cost of Sales	47,139	i.e. 0.98(41,827 × 1.15)	47,139
Gross Profit	16,408		16,408
Selling and Distribution	385	i.e. {(248 × 1.15) + 100}	385
Administration Costs	7,938	i.e. (1,250 × 1.15) + 6,500	7,938
Operating Profit	8,085		8,085
Interest Charges	1,100	(120 + 700 + 280)	400
Profit before Tax	6,985		7,685
Corporation Tax	2,096		2,306
Profit for Year	4,889		5,379
Dividend Payable	2,000		2,333
Retained Profit	2,889		3,046

Assuming debenture is issued:
Forecast EPS Year ending 31 December 20X1
EPS = 4,889/8,000 = 61.1 pence
Change in EPS = 55.1% growth

Assuming rights issue
Forecast EPS Year ending 31 December 20X1
EPS = 5,379/9,333 = 57.6 pence
Change in EPS = 46.2% growth

The figures show that if the sales targets are achieved, the EPS will grow faster if the debenture funds are selected, but in both instances the growth is substantial. This is largely because profits are already sufficiently high to meet the interest payments required and so, helped substantially by other changes, such as the fixed cost savings, all increases in profit (net of tax) can accrue to equity investors. The rights issue generates a smaller EPS because the number of shares in issue has been increased by 1.33 million, and so the equity earnings are shared more widely. In either case the investors benefit from a growth of EPS which exceeds the rate of growth of sales. However, if sales were to fall, then EPS would fall at a rate greater than the drop in sales, again because of the leverage effect. This risk from additional borrowing must be acknowledged and explained to shareholders.

If investors are looking for rapid growth of earnings, it is marginally preferable to fund the investment by the debenture issue, however the effect of this choice on shareholder risk needs to be taken into account, because Spender's financial gearing will be increased by the debenture issue. Whether investors will accept the higher risk or not depends to some extent on industry and economic forecasts. If the outlook for the construction industry is good, then investors are likely to accept such a proposal; conversely if the future prospects look poor then the rights issue is the safer choice. The attractiveness of the higher returns from using debenture funds needs to compensate for the marginal additional risk created by the issue, and given that the use of debentures yields an EPS 6% greater than if the rights issue is made then it is likely that this is the case.

In addition to financial considerations which may affect the choice of funding source, Spender plc should also take into account the organisational aspects of the two alternatives, including the speed of issue, issue costs, and prevailing stock market conditions. Rights issues will tend to be slower to arrange and complete than a debenture issue, but rights do offer the advantage that the issue costs may be kept low as it is not a requirement (though it is usual practice) for them to be underwritten. At the same time, debentures may be easier to sell if the stock market is volatile or on a bear run.

In conclusion, the debenture issue should be the chosen source of funding provided that market forecasts indicate rising future sales and earnings. The rights issue should be the chosen source of finance provided that the directors believe that shareholders are highly risk averse, and would prefer to avoid any additional financial gearing, and that stock market conditions are favourable to such an issue.

(e) Dividend cover is calculated by dividing the profit available to equity by the total dividend payable, and it measures the extent to which equity investors can view their dividend as being 'secure'. As the level of cover rises, so does the security of the dividend, inasmuch as equity investors can still expect there to be sufficient profit available to pay the dividend. A high dividend cover offers a reasonable certainty that dividend levels can be maintained, but it should also lead investors to question how the retained profits are being utilised. By definition, a high dividend cover implies that a large proportion of profits are being retained within the business, and unless these funds are being invested wisely, the equity investor may be better off if the cash is paid out to shareholders, who can then re-invest it elsewhere to earn a better rate of return.

For Spender plc, the forecast profit available to equity (from (d)) if the debentures are issued equals £4.889m and the dividend forecast for the year is £2m. This gives a dividend cover of:

4.889/2 = 2.44

This means that over half of the profit is being retained for re-investment. If the re-investment can be expected to maintain the profit growth achieved between 20X0 and 20X1, then investors have little to be worried about. If, however, Spender plc gives little indication of how it intends to use this money, then those investors should be concerned that dividend cover is perhaps a little high.

2   Investment appraisal

(a) *Accounting rate of return (ARR)* is a measure of the return on an investment where the annual profit before interest and tax is expressed as a percentage of the capital sum invested. There are a number of alternative formulae which can be used to calculate ARR, which differ in the way in which they define capital cost. The more common alternative measures available are average annual profit to initial capital invested, and average annual profit to average capital invested. The method selected will affect the resulting ARR figure, and for this reason it is important to recognise that the measure may be subject to manipulation by managers seeking approval for their investment proposals. The value for average annual profit is calculated after allowances for depreciation, as shown in the example below:

$$\text{If ARR is defined as: } \frac{\text{Average profit (after depreciation)}}{\text{Initial capital invested}} \times 100$$

then a project which costs £5 million, and yields average profits of £1,250,000 per year after depreciation charges of £500,000 per year, will give an ARR of:

1,250,000/5,000,000 × 100 = 25%

If the depreciation charged is increased to £750,000 per year as a result, for example, of technological changes which reduce the expected life of an asset, the ARR becomes:

1,000,000/5,000,000 × 100 = 20%

The attraction of using ARR as a method of investment appraisal lies in its simplicity and the ease with which it can be used to specify the impact of a project on a company's profit and loss account. The measure is easily understood and can be directly linked to the use of ROCE as a performance measure. Nonetheless, ARR has been criticised for a number of major drawbacks, perhaps the most important of which is that it uses accounting profits after depreciation rather than cash flows in order to measure return. This means that the capital cost is over-stated in the calculation, via both the numerator and the denominator. In the numerator the capital cost is taken into account via the depreciation charges used to derive accounting profit, but capital cost is also the denominator. The practical effect of this is to reduce the ARR and thus make projects appear less profitable. This might in turn result in some worthwhile projects being rejected. Note, however, that this problem does not arise where ARR is calculated as average annual profit as a percentage of average capital invested.

The most important criticism of ARR is that it takes no account of the time value of money. A second limitation of ARR, already suggested, is that its value is dependent upon accounting policies and this can make comparison of ARR figures across different investments somewhat difficult. This may be important in an international company where accounting policies vary between nations. A further difficulty with the use of ARR is that it does not give a clear decision rule. The ARR on any particular investment needs to be compared with the current returns being earned within a business, and so unlike NPV for example, it is impossible to say 'all investments with an ARR of X or below will always be rejected.

The *payback* method of investment appraisal is very widely used by industry - generally in addition to other measures - perhaps because, like ARR, it is easily calculated and understood. The payback approach simply measures the time required for cumulative cash flows from an investment to sum to the original capital invested.

Example
Original investment £100,000

Cash flow profile: Years 1–3 £25,000 pa: Years 4–5 £50,000 pa.; Year 6 £5,000

The cumulative cash flows are thus:

End Year 1	£25,000
End Year 2	£50,000
End Year 3	£75,000
End Year 4	£125,000
End Year 5	£175,000
End Year 6	£180,000

The original sum invested is thus returned via cash flows some time during the course of Year 4. If cash flows are assumed to be even throughout the year, then the cumulative cash flow of £100,000 will have been earned halfway through year 4. The payback period for the investment is thus 3 years and 6 months.

This approach is useful for companies which are seeking to claw back cash from investments as quickly as possible. At the same time the concept is intuitively appealing as many businessmen will be concerned about how long they may have to wait to get their money back, because they believe that rapid repayment reduces risks. This means that the payback approach is commonly used for initial screening of investment alternatives.

The disadvantages of the payback approach are as follows:

(i)   Payback ignores the overall profitability of a project by ignoring post payback cash flows. In the example above, the cash flows between 3–5 years and the end of the project sum to £80,000. To ignore such substantial cash flows is somewhat naive, and as a consequence the method is biased in favour of fast return investments. This can result in investments which generate cash flows more slowly in the early years, but which are overall more profitable, being rejected if the payback system is used for investment decisions.

(ii)   As with ARR the method ignores the time value of money.

(iii) The payback method, in the same way as ARR, offers no objective measure of what is the desirable return, as measured by the length of the payback period.

(b)   (i)   Discounted cash flow analysis is the term used to describe the technique whereby the value of future cash flows is discounted back to a present value, so that the monetary values of all cash flows are equivalent, regardless of their timing. The logic for discounting is that the value of money declines over time because of individual time preferences and the impact of inflation in eroding spending power. People value money received sooner rather than later because as soon as cash is received they can increase consumption, or re-invest the capital.

NPV uses discounting to calculate the present value of all cash flows associated with a project. The present value of cash outflows is then compared with the present value of cash inflows, to obtain a net present value (NPV). If cash out exceeds cash in then the NPV will be negative, and vice versa. The size of the NPV is dependent upon the cash flow pattern and the rate of discount which is applied. The general rule is that a company will discount the forecast cash flows at a rate equal to its cost of capital. The reason for this is that if a company has an overall cost of capital of, for example, 12%, it is essential that the rate of return exceeds 12% or the funding costs will not be covered. Hence if the cash flows are discounted at the cost of capital and the project yields a positive NPV this implies that the return exceeds the cost of capital. When using NPV for investment appraisal then a simple rule is applied: invest if NPV is positive, and do not invest if it is negative.

IRR uses discounting in a slightly different way to determine the profitability of an investment. The Internal Rate of Return is defined as the discount rate at which the net present value equals zero. For example, an investment may yield a forecast NPV of £15,000 when the cash flows are discounted at 10%. If the rate of discount is increased, the net present value will fall, and the IRR represents the effective, break-even discount rate for the investment. Suppose, for example, that the IRR is 15%, this figure can then be used to establish a decision rule for investments. An IRR of 15% means that if the cost of capital exceeds 15% then the investment would generate a negative NPV. If the company is currently having to pay 12% on its investment funds, then it knows that it can afford to see its cost of capital rise by 3% before the investment will become financially non-viable. As long as the IRR exceeds the cost of capital, then the company should invest and so, as a general rule, the higher the IRR the better.

NPV and IRR measures may sometimes contradict one another when used in relation to either mutually exclusive investments or projects which have multiple yields. An example of the ambiguity which can occur when choosing between mutually exclusive decisions is when one of the investments has a higher NPV than the other, and so is preferable on that basis, but at the same time it has a lower IRR. When IRR and NPV give conflicting results, the preferred alternative is the project with the highest NPV. In the case of projects with multiple yields, caused by cash flows which change from positive to negative and vice versa on several occasions, there may be more than one IRR. In this situation it is once again preferable to use NPV as the decision criteria.

In conclusion then, although both NPV and IRR use discounted cash flows as a method of arriving at an investment decision, the results that they generate need to be interpreted with care, and they do not always yield the same investment decisions. NPV is the preferred criteria where the two approaches give ambiguous results.

(ii)   If the laptops are replaced every year:

NPV of one replacement cycle	$= £(2,400) + 1,200/1.14$
	$= £(1,347.47)$
Equivalent Annual Cost	$= £1,347.47/0.877$
	$= £1,536.64$

If replacement occurs every two years:

NPV of one replacement cycle	$= £(2,400) + 800/1.14^2 + (75)/1.14$
	$= (£1,850.21)$
Equivalent Annual Cost	$= £1,850.21/1.647$
	$= £1,123.38$

If replacement occurs every three years:

$$\overset{202.49\qquad 115.42\qquad 65.79}{}$$

NPV of one replacement cycle	$= £(2,400) + 300/1.14^3 + (150)/1.14^2 + (75)/1.14$
	$= (£2,378.72)$
Equivalent Annual Cost	$= £2,378.72/2.322$
	$= £1,024.43$

Conclude:

The optimal cycle for replacement is every three years. Other factors which need to be taken into account are the non-financial aspects of the alternative cycle choices. For example, computer technology and the associated software is changing very rapidly and this could mean that failure to replace annually would leave the salesmen unable to utilise the most up to date systems for recording, monitoring and implementing their sales. This could have an impact on the company's competitive position. The company needs to consider also the compatibility of the software used by the laptops with that used by the in-house computers and mainframe. If system upgrades are made within the main business which render the two computers incompatible, then rapid replacement of the laptops to regain compatibility is essential.

3 Delcars plc

(a) The working capital (or operating) cycle is the length of time between when a business makes payments to its suppliers for raw materials and goods entering into stock, and when the business receives payment for those resources from its customers. The number of days in the cycle is equal to:

Debtor days + Stock days (Finished goods + WIP + raw materials) – Creditor days

For example, if analysis of company financial statements revealed the following statistics:

	DAYS
Debtors	45
Raw material stocks	20
Work in progress	25
Finished goods	15
Creditor days	50

The working capital cycle = 45 + 20 + 25 + 15 – 50 = 55 days

The number of days in the cycle represents the length of time for which the business requires funding for working capital if it is to continue trading. As the length of the cycle increases, therefore, the amount of working capital required by the business also increases. Working capital may be funded from either long-term or short-term sources of finance, but as a general rule it is argued that 'permanent' working capital should be paid for by long-term sources and 'temporary' working capital by short-term sources. Debentures are an example of a long-term source of funds, and an overdraft facility is an example of a short-term source.

The significance of the cycle for working capital management lies in the fact that if a company can reduce the length of the cycle, it can lower its funding needs, and this can in turn increase the potential ROCE. The length of the operating cycle can be reduced in a number of ways, which vary from the very simple to the sophisticated. The use of tight credit controls, Just in Time stock management and debt factoring are various examples of ways in which the cycle can be reduced.

(b) Annual sales £25 million, split as follows:

New vehicles (60%) £15 million
Secondhand vehicles (25%) £6.25 million
Servicing (15%) £3.75 million

Secondhand vehicle sales -
Weekly value £6.25m/52 = £120,090
Daily value £ 120,090/6 = £20,032
Daily overdraft cost = 8.5%/365

The cost of not banking receipts can be calculated daily with the maximum delay equalling 4 days for sales made on Tuesday but not banked until the following Monday. The total days delay in any one week is thus equal to:

Sales	Delay
Monday	Nil
Tuesday	6 days
Wednesday	5 days
Thursday	4 days
Friday	3 days
Saturday	Nil
Total:	18 days

Weekly cost of delay = 18 × £20,032 × 8.5%/365 = £83.97

Annual cost of the delay = £83.97 × 52 = £4,366

Using the same approach to calculate the cost of delayed banking of receipts from vehicle servicing

Weekly sales value £3.75m/52 = £72.115
Daily sales value £72,115/6 = £12,019

Total days banking delay

Sales	Delay
Monday	2
Tuesday	1
Wednesday	Nil
Thursday	1
Friday	Nil
Saturday	2
Total:	6 days

Weekly cost of delay = 6 × £12,019 × 8.5%/365 = £16.80

Annual cost of delay = 52 × £16.80 = £874
Total cost of delays in banking both sets of receipts = £4,366 + £874 = £5,240

Note: the calculation assumes that Delcars plc are operating on an overdraft on every working day of the year and hence the sooner that money is banked, the greater will be the associated interest saving. In practice, it is likely that the level of overdraft will vary throughout the year and when the account is in credit, the company will gain no interest saving benefit from the faster banking of receipts.

(c)   Management of the banking side of a business' operations is just one of the functions of the treasury department. The treasury is also responsible for the raising of short- and long-term finance for a business, the control of cash and investment of cash surpluses, foreign currency risk management, management of capital investment procedures and organisation of insurance for company assets. When treasury activities are centralised, these activities become the sole responsibility of the central unit, and local divisions of a business simply hold cash for day to day transactions, and do not get involved in raising finance, hedging foreign exchange risk etc. The primary advantage to be gained from centralisation of the treasury is the increased control that it offers. For a company such as Delcars, the need is to maximise overall corporate profit. This means, for example, that if one dealership is currently running a cash surplus, and all surpluses come back to the central treasury, the treasury can then use that money to fund any of the dealerships which may be running a cash deficit. In this way the need to look for external funding is reduced or eliminated. Consequently, it is argued, centralised treasurership can save a company money via reduced borrowing requirements and lower bank charges. Lower banking costs may also be available via the use of the central department to negotiate finance when required. If, for example, a dealer wished to acquire and develop a new retail site then if the organisation was decentralised, the funding terms would be negotiated between the individual dealership and the local bank. If all funding requirements are dealt with via the central treasury it is likely that the terms available will be preferable because the overall account will be larger, and the company regarded as a more 'important' bank customer.

A secondary benefit of centralisation is the elimination of the need for each element within a group company to employ staff with treasury skills. This reduces duplication, and should work to raise the overall standard of treasury provision as the skills and experience of the centre's staff are likely to be greater than those of staff working n the smaller individual divisions.

For some businesses which buy/sell in foreign markets, the role of central treasury in managing the process of hedging foreign exchange risk can be very important. Delcars are unlikely to require such hedging but if they did then a central department can offer the advantage of expertise that is often scarce at a local level.

The main disadvantage of centralisation of treasury activities is that it can lead to slower decision making and the potential loss of local market advantage as a result. If a local manager wishes to obtain funds to buy assets e.g., secondhand car stock, he may have to put a business case to head office to obtain the funds. In the time taken to process the application, the buying opportunity may disappear and with it the opportunity to increase profit. At the same time, many writers would argue that the independence of local management is important to good performance, because responsibility serves to motivate staff. Giving responsibility to the centre can simply demotivate, whilst at the same time eradicating the detailed understanding of local conditions.

There is no clear cut answer as to whether centralised or decentralised treasury functions are preferable. The choice is ultimately dependent upon the specific needs of the individual company.

4   Public sector organisation

(a)   Budget Preparation

It would be in line with the principles of modern management if the department manager was encouraged to participate more in setting the budget. In this way his commitment to the organisational goals in general and the budget in particular would be more likely to occur. He is closer to the activity and hence the relevance and accuracy of the budget should be improved. This involvement should extend also to discussion of the form and frequency of the reporting which is to take place for his/her department.

Activity Volume

The volume of visits undertaken is 20% greater than that budgeted. It is inappropriate to compare the actual costs of visiting 12,000 clients with a budget for 10,000 clients. Costs such as wages, travel expenses and consumables would be expected to be higher than the fixed budget in these circumstances.

One way to deal with this is to adjust or flex the budget to acknowledge the cost implications of the higher number of visits, or to be aware of it when making any comparison. If a factor of 1.2 is applied to the overall wages budget (i.e. on the assumption that it is a variable cost) the flexed budget £5,040 (£4,200 × 1.2) is greater than the actual cost of £4,900. On a similar basis actual travel expenses are exactly in line with the flexed budget, but the consumables seem to be highly overspent, though the nature of this cost item may make expenditure on it difficult to predict.

To circulate a report as originally constructed seems to highlight and publicise some invalid comparisons on which inappropriate conclusions may be drawn. It is recommended that for cost control purposes a report is prepared which compares actual spending with a flexible budget based on the actual activity. This would require an estimate of the variable, fixed and semi-variable nature of the cost items.

Controllability

It is possible to question whether all the costs shown need to feature on the report. For example, the allocated administrative costs and equipment depreciation are book entries which do not directly affect the department and are not likely to be controllable by members of the department. There are, therefore, adverse variances on the report contributing to the overall overspend which are not the responsibility of the departmental manager. The difference between actual and budgeted cost of administration serves no useful purpose on this report, as the manager can take no action to directly influence this. The only justification to include this is if the manager can bring about some pressure to reduce this spending by someone else.

It may be unwise to adopt the guide of a 5% deviation to judge variances. The key is whether a cost is out of control and can be corrected by managerial action. Also, 5% of some values can be significant whilst on others are of little consequence.

Funding Allocation

The Director is correct in pointing out that 'the department must live within its funding allocation'. It is not like a commercial organisation where more output can result in more revenue and hence more money to spend. Increased funding will only be achieved if this organisation and the department is allocated more funds as a result of National or Local Government decisions to support an increase in services.

It would be appropriate for the funding allocation to be compared with the flexible budget (based on actual activity) to encourage the managers to be aware of and live within the budget allocation. Ways can always be found to spend more money and so authority structures must be in place to ensure that requests to spend have been budgeted and appropriately funded. Hence the organisational arrangements which authorised the increased visits would be examined.

The nature of the activity for which the budget is being developed should not be lost sight of. It is more complex to deal with budget decisions related to the welfare needs of society than those for a typical manufacturing firm. There are no clear input-output relationships in the former and hence it is difficult to judge what is justifiable spending for the department compared with other departments and Public Sector organisations.

Other Aspects

One possible outcome from discussion over the appropriate form of report would be the use of non-financial measures. The total staff hours worked, client satisfaction and size of the potential client population are all examples of extensions to the reporting procedure which would help to place the results in context.

The style of the approach adopted by the Director may show some lack of behavioural insight. The despatch of a memo to deal with a prototype report may result in lower staff morale and increased tension in the Homecare department. This may lead to inappropriate future decisions on spending and budget 'game playing' within the department. It may, of course, be a conscious decision of the Director to place the manager in the position of having to reduce spending to the allocated level.

Although this is the first month's report, in the future it may be helpful to use an additional column of the report to show the year to date figures. This would help to identify trends and assist discussion of whether costs are being controlled over the longer term. To show future results for only one month may be insufficient; for example, the repairs to equipment may not follow a regular pattern and this would be revealed if cumulative data existed.

(b)   Traditional budgeting, sometimes called incremental budgeting, takes a current level of spending as a starting point. Discussion then takes place on any extra expenditure or what, of the current expenditure, to cut. Zero Based Budgeting (ZBB) is an approach which takes nothing for granted, it requires justification of all expenditure. This technique would not suit expenditure planning in line departments of a manufacturing company because clear relationships of input and output will exist and be defined by standard values. In less clearly defined areas such as service departments or non-profit orientated businesses ZBB might have some value if selectively applied.

ZBB would involve describing all of the organisation's activities in a series of decision packages, for example, visit frequency, level of eligibility for visit, type of support (medical care, food preparation, wash and clean, shopping needs etc). The packages can then be evaluated and ranked: what is essential, highly desirable, desirable and so on. The resources would be allocated according to the packages selected, discussion could also take place between other departments so that a wider allocation of funding is brought into the discussion. Once the budget is set the packages are adopted up to the spending level indicated, this is the cut-off point.

It is possible that economies and increased efficiency could result if departments were to justify all, not just incremental, expenditure. It is argued that if expenditure were examined on a cost/benefit basis, a more rational allocation of resources would take place. Such an approach would force managers to make plans and prioritise their activities before committing themselves to the budget. It should achieve a more structured involvement of departmental management and should improve the quality of decisions and management information, enabling such questions as: Should this be done?, At what quality/quantity?, Should it be done this way?, What should it cost?

ZBB may not be simple and easy to install, could be expensive in time and effort to analyse all expenditure and difficult to establish priorities for the activities or decision packages. Managers are often reluctant to commit themselves to ZBB because they believe they already do it. Critics of ZBB have asserted that no real change in funding allocation takes place as a result of the exercise. However, any system which encourages managers to examine, and communicate about, their spending and performance levels must be useful providing it does not prevent individuals fulfilling their other duties and responsibilities.

5   Fish processing

(a)   In a manufacturing organisation the purposes of preparing product costs include:

- *Stock valuation:* so that the closing stock of finished products and work-in-progress can be correctly valued on the balance sheet. This also has implications for the calculation of profit and loss in that it assists in the identification of the cost of goods sold to be matched against the sales revenues generated in an accounting period. The cost used in this situation is usually the cost of manufacture only.

- *Pricing:* it is common for many companies to consult the cost of a product in order to help set a selling price, this is by adding a desired mark-up percentage. The form of cost used in this case may be manufacturing cost, total or full product cost including administrative and selling costs. It is sometimes referred to as a long-run average cost which prices must exceed to ensure the continued viability of the business.

- *Tactical decisions:* on occasions management in some organisations may wish to make short-run decisions on, for example, special pricing offers, make or buy/sell or further process opportunities, or the utilisation of spare capacity. In this situation it may be desirable to refer only to those costs which are likely to change in the circumstances, the marginal costs. This notion of relevant cost is at times simplified to be a product's variable costs only.

(b)   **Process 1**

Costs	£
Material 36,000 kilos × £1.50	54,000
Labour	28,000
Overhead 120%	33,600
	115,600
Waste (40%) 14,400 kilos × 30p	(4,320)
Total net cost of output	111,280

(i)   The cost assigned to the superior quality is £111,280 × 3,600/21,600 = £18.547. A similar approach is taken for calculations related to the special and standard quality.

	Superior	Special	Standard	Total
Weight (kilos)	3,600	7,200	10,800	21,600
	£	£	£	£
Sales	27,000	48,960	43,200	119,160
Cost	18,547	37,093	55,640	111,280
Profit/(Loss)	8,453	11,867	(12,440)	7,880

(ii)   The cost assigned to the superior quality is £111,280 × £27,000/£119,160 = £25,215. A similar approach is taken for calculations related to the special and standard quality.

	Superior	Special	Standard	Total
	£	£	£	£
Sales	27,000	48,960	43,200	119,160
Cost	25,215	45,722	40,343	111,280
Profit	1,785	3,238	2,857	7,880

(c)   If a loss was revealed for one category under (b) (i) the management should not be unduly concerned, providing an overall profit was reported for all categories together. Method (i) allocates the cost equally to each kilo produced, ignoring the potential market price of these joint products. Inevitably if the products command different market prices then some products will look more profitable than others and, in this case, the 'standard' quality reveals a loss because the market price is lower than the average cost.

Method (ii), by allocating costs using market value (quantity and selling price), ensures that each category makes the same proportion of profits/losses to sales. In this case if the whole operation is profitable then each product must look profitable, in the same proportion of profit to sales. If a loss is revealed it will thus be for all categories and management should react to the fact that the whole operation is unprofitable.

In fact there is no 'correct' method of sharing these joint costs and no judgement should be made about the separate profitability of any one of these three categories. It is only the overall profit revealed by the contract which management should take account of. If the overall profit is unacceptable then management could ask questions about the current market price levels, the costs they incur or the proportions of each category.

(d)   For this decision it is necessary to compare the incremental revenue and incremental costs of each category. Thus:

| | £ per kilo | | |
	Superior	Special	Standard
Incremental revenue	1.20	0.70	1.20
Incremental costs			
Material	0.10	0.10	0.10
Labour	0.60	0.60	0.60
Variable overhead	0.27	0.27	0.27
	0.97	0.97	0.97
Contribution/incremental profit/(loss)	0.23	(0.27)	0.23

The extra costs of processing the special category is greater than the extra revenue from the sale of breadcrumbed fillets so this is not worthwhile. The incremental revenue from further processing the superior and standard categories exceeds the incremental costs in the short-term, therefore it appears that it is more profitable to further process them.

The above analysis ignores any fixed costs of further processing which are recovered at a rate of 135% (180% × 0.75) of labour costs. From further processing superior and standard categories a total contribution of £3,312 ((3,600 × £0.23) + (10,800 × £0.23)) emerges. The total labour cost for this is £8,640 ((3,600 × £0.60) + (10,800 × £0.60)) which is already accounted for; however the fixed overhead which would be assigned, based on the labour cost, is £11,664 (£8,640 × 135%). When set against the incremental contribution of £3,312 this suggests an overall loss of £8,352. So process 2 does not appear profitable and there may be a case not to operate it at all. A decision on this turns on the extent to which the assigned fixed costs may be saved in the medium to long-term, or whether they represent allocated corporate costs and sunk costs which would not change with any decision about this process.

6   BML

(a)

Existing Costing System:	P1	P2	P3
	£	£	£
Direct materials	18.00	25.00	16.00
Direct labour cost	4.00	8.00	6.40
Overhead cost at 462% of DL	18.48	36.96	29.57
Unit cost	40.48	69.96	51.97

Calculation of overhead rate:

Labour cost = (£4 × 7,500) + (£8 × 12,500) + (£6.40 × 4,000)
        = £155,600

$$\text{Overhead rate} = \frac{\text{Overhead cost}}{\text{Labour cost}} \times 100\%$$

$$= \frac{£718,688}{£155,600} \times 100\%$$

$$= 462\%$$

(b)

Activity-Based Costing	P1	P2	P3
	£	£	£
Direct materials	18.00	25.00	16.00
Direct labour	4.00	8.00	6.40
Overhead costs:			
Receiving/materials handling	1.01	3.80	23.73
Maintenance and depreciation	18.06	18.06	7.22
Set-up labour	0.16	0.47	2.92
Engineering	4.00	1.60	12.50
Packing	0.27	1.12	11.00
Sub total overhead costs	23.50	25.05	57.37
Total unit cost	45.50	58.05	79.77

See below for an indication of the cost drivers used for the ABC product cost calculations.

ABC workings:
Receiving and handling materials cost = £150,000
Cost Driver: Number of materials movements = 4 + 25 + 50 = 79 movements
Cost per material movement = £150,000/79 = £1,898.73
Cost per unit of P1 = (£1,898.73 × 4)/7,500 = £1.01 per product unit

Maintenance and depreciation cost = £390,000
Cost Driver: No of machine hours = (0.5 × 7,500) + (0.5 × 12,500) + (0.2 × 4.000) = 10,800
Cost per machine hour = £390,000/10,800 = £36.11 per machine hour
Cost per unit of P1 = £36.11 × 0.5 = £18.06 per product unit

Set-up labour cost = £18,688
Cost Driver: Number of set-ups 1 + 5 + 10 = 16;
Cost per set-up = 18,688/16= £1,168 per set-up
Cost per unit of P1 = £1,168/7,500 = £0.16 per product unit

Engineering cost = £100,000
Cost Driver: Based on proportion of engineering work
Cost per unit of P1 = (£100,000 × 30%)/7,500 = £4.00 per product unit

Packing cost = £60,000
Cost Driver: No of orders packed 1 + 7 + 22 = 30
Cost per order = £60,000/30 = £2,000
Cost per unit of P1 = £2,000/7,500 = £0.27 per product unit

An alternative approach to the ABC calculations would be to allocate the total overhead costs to each product line using the cost drivers identified above, finally dividing by the number of units to arrive at the unit cost, thus:

	Total £	P1 £	P2 £	P3 £
Receiving and handling	150,000	7,595	47,468	94,937
Maintenance/depreciation	390,000	135,417	225,694	28,889
Set-up labour	18,688	1,168	5,840	11,680
Engineering	100,000	30,000	20,000	50,000
Packing	60,000	2,000	14,000	44,000
Sub-total overhead costs	718,688	176,180	313,002	229,506
Number of units		7,500	12,500	4,000
Unit overhead cost (£)		£23.49	£25.04	£57.38

Any difference between the figures for unit overhead costs derived by the two methods is due to rounding.

(c)   P1 is shown to have lower unit costs under the original system than on the ABC basis. This is caused by its relatively higher machine hour usage and smaller proportion of labour cost, compared to the other products, and the effect this has on the overhead cost allocation. Using ABC the product is shown to have a very small margin indeed. This must therefore raise questions about its viability at this price.

It is a relatively simple product to make. For example, it seems to consist of just one production run and one packing order for the whole output which means it does not use much of these supporting resources. But it does use a considerable proportion of machine hours which is what gives rise to much of its allocated overhead cost.

In comparison to P1, P3 seems to be a complex product to administer, made in small batches with small orders. In the original system P3 was being undercosted, being subsidised by P2. It appears to offer a good margin based on its original cost, but the ABC analysis shows that it does not manage to cover all of the direct and overhead costs assigned to it.

There is, therefore, little surprise that this new line is attracting additional business as it is priced below the cost to make it if all of the activities the company undertakes are needed. The company cannot afford to continue business at this price and needs to find some way of managing up the price of this product to make it viable in the future. An alternative may be to re-examine the way it is manufactured and the ABC system may offer some help in this by assisting with an analysis of what is involved in its manufacture. Presently it is the high proportion of overhead costs for material movement, engineering and packing which make it expensive. If it is seen to have a future, BML may need to re-engineer their manufacturing methods in relation to this product which makes quite modest use of machining resources.

P2 has the highest volume of the three products, though we are told it is suffering a loss of market share. It is the most labour intensive product and this resulted in serious overcosting under the original system, because overhead was apportioned on a labour cost basis. To put it another way the ABC cost is lower because the product makes less use of engineering machine hours etc, than the other products. It would seem competitors discovered that they could manufacture this and sell it for a lower price and still make a profit. BML should realise that its major cost is in the use of machinery and for the volume produced it makes little use of other support costs. It is therefore quite economical to make, though the original system does not reveal this. BML still make a good volume of this product and although we do not know much about the market for it a lower price might stimulate demand, and offer higher sales volumes recovering some of the market share.

Note: the above comments are based on the information as presented in the question. We know nothing about any other overhead costs relating, for example, to administration and selling. No information about the market for the three products is supplied, e.g. market shares or competitors' prices. Such information as this would place the company in a better position to judge the adequacy of the results of its costing system.

December 2000 Questions

Section A – This ONE question is compulsory and MUST be attempted

1   Amber plc

Amber plc operates a daily return high-speed train service between the UK and mainland Europe, via the channel tunnel. In an attempt to reduce overheads, the company is considering using an outside supplier to take over responsibility for all on-train catering services. Amber invited tenders for a five-year contract, and at the same time the senior management accountant drafted a schedule of costs for in-house provision of an equivalent service. This cost schedule, together with the details of the lowest price tender which was received, are given below. (See Table 1 and additional information).

Table 1: In-House Provision of Train Catering Services
Schedule of Costs, Amber plc

Variable Costs	*Pence Per £ Sales*
Direct material	55
Variable overhead	12
Fixed Costs (allocated to products)	
Labour (Year 1)	10
Purchase/storage management	3
Depreciation (catering equipment)	4
Insurance	2
Total cost	86

The train service operates 360 days per year and a single restaurant carriage is adequate to service the catering needs of a train carrying up to 600 passengers. The tendered contract (and the in-house schedule of costs) is for the provision of one catering carriage per train. Past sales data indicates that 45% of passengers will use the catering service, spending an average of £4.50 each per single journey or £9.00 per return journey. This is expected to remain unchanged over the next five years, unless Amber invests in quality improvements.

Statistical forecasts of the level of demand for the train service, under differing average weather conditions and average exchange rates over the next five years, are shown in Table 2.

Table 2: Forecast Passenger Figures (per single journey)

	UK Weather conditions		
Exchange rate Euro/£	Poor	Reasonable	Good
1.52	500	460	420
1.54	550	520	450
1.65	600	580	500

The differing weather conditions are all assumed to be equally likely.

Based upon historical trends, the probability of each different exchange rate occurring is estimated as follows:

Exchange Rate Euro/£	Probability
1.52	0.2
1.54	0.5
1.65	0.3

Additional information:

(1)   Labour costs are expected to rise at a rate of 5% per year over the next five years.

(2)   Variable costs per £ sales are expected to remain unchanged over the next five years.

(3)   Some catering equipment will need to be replaced at the end of Year 2 at a cost of £500,000. This would increase the depreciation charge on catering equipment to 5 pence per £ sales. The equipment value at the end of Year 5 is estimated to be £280,000.

(4)   The outside supplier (lowest price tender) has agreed to purchase immediately (for cash) the existing catering equipment owned by Amber plc at a price equal to the current book value i.e. £650,000. The supplier would charge Amber a flat fee of £250 per day for the provision of this catering service, and Amber would receive 5% of gross catering receipts where these exceeded an average of £2,200 per day in each 360 day period. The quality of the catering service is expected to be unaffected by the contracting out.

(5)   In the event of Amber deciding to contract out the catering, the following fixed costs will be saved:

Depreciation	£35,000 per year
Purchasing/storage costs	£18,000 per year
Insurance	£3,000 per year
Labour costs	£74,844 (Year I)

(6)   The cost of capital for Amber plc is 12%.

Assume that all cash flows occur at the end of each year. Taxation may be ignored in answering this question.

Required:

(a)   Calculate the expected number of passengers per single journey for the train service.   **(5 marks)**

(b)   Draft a table of annual cash flows and, using discounted cash flow analysis, determine which of the two alternatives (in-house provision or contracting out) is preferred.   **(16 marks)**

(c)   Calculate and comment upon the financial effect on the decision of a forecast ten per cent increase in the number of passengers purchasing food and beverages on each train if the in-house catering service were to be improved. Any such improvement would require Amber investing £10,000 per year over five years on staff training.   **(7 marks)**

(d)   Comment on the limitations of using demand forecasts, such as that given in Table 2, for the purposes of the decision in question.   **(5 marks)**

(e)   Identify and critically comment upon three non-financial factors which need to be taken into account when a business is considering this type of decision.   **(7 marks)**
          (Total: 40 marks)

Section B – ONE question ONLY to be attempted

2   News For You

News For You operate a chain of newsagents and confectioner's shops in the south of England, and are considering the possibility of expanding their business across a wider geographical area. The business was started in 20X2 and annual turnover grew to £10 million by the end of 20X6. Between 20X6 and 20X9 turnover grew at an average rate of 2% per year.

The business still remains under family control, but the high cost of expansion via the purchase or building of new outlets would mean that the family would need to raise at least £2 million in equity or debt finance. One of the possible risks of expansion lies in the fact that both tobacco and newspaper sales are falling. New income is being generated by expanding the product range stocked by the stores, to include basic foodstuffs such as bread and milk. News For You purchases all of its products from a large wholesale distributor which is convenient, but the wholesale prices leave News For You with a relatively small gross margin. The key to profit growth for News For You lies in the ability to generate sales growth, but the company recognises that it faces stiff competition from large food retailers in respect of the prices that it charges for several of its products.

◆ FOULKS*lynch*

In planning its future, News For You was advised to look carefully at a number of external factors which may affect the business, including government economic policy and, in recent months, the following information has been published in respect of key economic data:

(i)   Bank base rate has been reduced from 5% to 4.5%, and the forecast is for a further 0.5% reduction within six months.

(ii)   The annual rate of inflation is now 1.2%, down from 1.3% in the previous quarter, and 1.7% 12 months ago. The rate is now at its lowest for 25 years, and no further falls in the rate are expected over the medium/long term.

(iii)   Personal and corporation tax rates are expected to remain unchanged for at least 12 months.

(iv)   Taxes on tobacco have been increased by 10% over the last 12 months, although no further increases are anticipated.

(v)   The government has initiated an investigation into the food retail sector focusing on the problems of 'excessive' profits on certain foodstuffs created by the high prices being charged for these goods by the large retail food stores.

Required:

(a)   Explain the relevance of each of the items of economic data listed above to News For You.   **(10 marks)**

(b)   Explain whether News For You should continue with their expansion plans. Clearly justify your arguments for or against the expansion.   **(10 marks)**
    (Total: 20 marks)

3   Ply, Spin and Axis

Food Retailers: Ordinary Shares, Key Stock Market Statistics

Company	Share price (pence)			Dividend Yield (%)	P/E Ratio
	Current	52 week high	52 week low		
Ply	63	112	54	1.8	14.2
Axis	291	317	187	2.1	13.0
Spin	187	201	151	2.3	21.1

Required:

(a)   Illustrating your answer by use of data in the table above, define and explain the term P/E ratio, and comment on the way it may be used by an investor to appraise a possible share purchase.   **(6 marks)**

(b)   Using data in the above table, calculate the dividend cover for Spin and Axis, and explain the meaning and significance of the measure from the point of view of equity investors.   **(8 marks)**

(c)   Under what circumstances might a company be tempted to pay dividends which are in excess of earnings, and what are the dangers associated with such an approach?

    You should ignore tax in answering this question.   **(6 marks)**
    (Total: 20 marks)

Section C – TWO questions ONLY to be attempted

4   Contribution approach to decisions

(a)   In a marginal costing system only variable costs would be assigned to products or services, in which case management may rely on a *contribution approach to decisions*.

Required:

Explain and discuss the contribution approach to decisions giving brief examples and drawing attention to any limitations.   **(6 marks)**

A full absorption costing system would involve the assignment of both variable and fixed overhead costs to products. A traditional full absorption costing system typically uses a *single volume related allocation base (or cost driver)* to assign overheads to products. An activity based costing (ABC) system would use *multiple allocation bases (or cost drivers),* taking account of *different categories of activities and related overhead costs* such as unit, batch, product sustaining and facility sustaining.

Required:

(b)   Describe the likely stages involved in the design and operation of an ABC system.   **(4 marks)**

(c)   Explain and discuss volume related allocation bases (or cost drivers), giving an example of one within a traditional costing system. Contrast this with the multiple allocation bases (or cost drivers) of an ABC system.
                                                                                                  (6 marks)

(d)   Briefly elaborate on the different categories of activities and related overhead costs, such as unit, batch, product sustaining and facility sustaining, which may be used in an ABC system.   **(4 marks)**
                                                                                                  (Total: 20 marks)

5   Bud plc

A division of Bud plc is engaged in the manual assembly of finished products F1 and F2 from bought-in components. These products are sold to external customers. The budgeted sales volumes and prices for Month 9 are as follows:

Product	Units	Price
F1	34,000	£50.00
F2	58,000	£30.00

Finished goods stockholding budgeted for the end of Month 9, is 1,000 units of F1 and 2,000 units of F2, with no stock at the beginning of that month. The purchased components C3 and C4 are used in the finished products in the quantities shown below. The unit price is for just-in-time delivery of the components; the company holds no component stocks.

	Component	
Product	*C3*	*C4*
F1 (per unit)	8 units	4 units
F2 (per unit)	4 units	3 units
Price (each)	£1.25	£1.80

The standard direct labour times and labour rates and the budgeted monthly manufacturing overhead costs for the assembly and finishing departments for Month 9 are given below:

Product	*Assembly*	*Finishing*
F1 (per unit)	30 minutes	12 minutes
F2 (per unit)	15 minutes	10 minutes
Labour rate (per hour)	£5.00	£6.00
Manufacturing overhead cost for the month	£617,500	£204,000

Every month a predetermined direct labour hour recovery rate is computed in each department for manufacturing overhead and applied to items produced in that month.

The selling overhead of £344,000 per month is applied to products based on a predetermined percentage of the budgeted sales value in each month.

Required:

(a)   Prepare summaries of the following budgets for Month 9:

    (i)   component purchase and usage (units and value)

    (ii)   direct labour (hours and value)

    (iii)   departmental manufacturing overhead recovery rates

    (iv)   selling overhead recovery rate

    (v)   stock value at the month-end.   **(8 marks)**

(b)   Tabulate the standard unit cost and profit of each of F1 and F2 in Month 9.   **(3 marks)**

(c)   Prepare a budgeted profit and loss account for Month 9 which clearly incorporates the budget values obtained in (a) above.   **(3 marks)**

(d)   Explain clearly the implications of the company's treatment of manufacturing overheads, i.e. computing a monthly overhead rate, compared to a predetermined overhead rate prepared annually.   **(6 marks)**
    (Total: 20 marks)

6   Consultant engineers

A firm of consultant engineers makes hourly charges to clients in order to recover labour and overhead costs incurred by the firm. The current combined labour and overhead rate is £55 per hour. This rate is based on annual budgets which are then analysed into four equal quarterly periods for the purposes of reporting and control.

The annual budgets and predetermined hourly rates are shown below. It should be assumed that budgeted labour hours and budgeted fixed costs are the same per quarter.

All of the chargeable hours have been incorporated into the budget, as all of the hours worked by these engineers should be chargeable to clients.

	Budget	
Total hours	24,000	
	£	*£ per hour*
Labour and variable overhead costs	720,000	30
Fixed overhead costs	600,000	25
Total labour and overhead costs	1,320,000	55

In the first quarter of the year the hours of work chargeable, invoiced to and recovered from clients were 5,550 hours. The total time actually worked in the period (and theoretically chargeable) by the engineers for which they were paid, was 5,700 hours.

The accountant wishes to reconcile the total cost recovered from clients with the actual costs incurred and explain the difference using variance analysis in as much detail as possible. For this quarter the actual costs incurred were:

	£
Labour and variable overhead costs	174,000
Fixed overhead costs	157,000
Total	331,000

Required:

(a)   Reconcile the actual costs incurred with those recovered from the clients using variance analysis in as much detail as possible. Interpret and explain your results.   **(15 marks)**

(b)   In relation to cost analysis explain least squares regression (you should not quote a formula). Specify three practical requirements related to gathering data for carrying out least squares regression.   **(5 marks)**
    (Total: 20 marks)

December 2000 Answers

1   Amber plc

(a)   The expected number of passengers using the service is dependent upon the demand at each particular exchange rate.

At 1.52 Euro/£ expected demand $= (500 + 460 + 420)/3$
$= 460$

At 1.54 Euro/£ expected demand $= (550 + 520 + 450)/3$
$= 506.67$ (rounded)

At 1.65 Euro/£ expected demand $= (600 + 580 + 500)/3$
$= 560$

The expected demand is thus:

$= (0.2) (460) + (0.5) (506.67) + (0.3) (560)$
$= 92 + 253.33 + 168$
$= 513.33$ per train
$= 1,026.7$ per day

(b)   *Workings*

45% of passengers use the catering service, spending £4.50 per head on average. Two trains are run daily, for 360 days per year. This gives:

Annual Revenue $= 0.45 \times 513.3 \times £4.50 \times 2 \times 360$
$= £748,440$
$= £748,440/360 = £2,079$ per day

Costs

Direct material $= (0.55) (£748,440)$
$= £411,642$

Labour
Year 1 $= (0.1) (£748,440)$
$= £74,844$

Rising by 5% per year; this gives:
Year 2 £78,586
Year 3 £82,516
Year 4 £86,641
Year 5 £90,973

Variable overhead $= (0.12) (£748,440)$
$= £89,813$

Purchase and insurance $= 0.05 (£748,440)$
$= £37,422$
Less savings   (£21,000)
_____
£16,422
_____

Contract cost per year $= (250)(360) = £90,000$
Gross catering receipts are less than an average of £2,200 per day, therefore the 5% commission does not apply.
Contribution from the current service:
Contribution £246,985 per year

Cash flows: in house option

Year	1	2	3	4	5
Sales	748,440	748,440	748,440	748,440	748,440
Variable costs	(501,455)	(501,455)	(501,455)	(501,455)	(501,455)
Contribution	246,985	246,985	246,985	246,985	246,985
Labour costs	(74,844)	(78,586)	(82,516)	(86,641)	(90,973)
Purchase & insurance	(37,422)	(37,422)	(37,422)	(37,422)	(37,422)
Asset sale/purchase		(500,000)			280,000
Net cash flow	134,719	(369,023)	127,047	122,922	398,590
Discount Factor at 12%	0.893	0.797	0.712	0.636	0.567
PRESENT VALUE	120,304	(294,111)	90,457	78,178	226,000

Net present value = £220,828

Cash flows: contract out option

Year	0	1	2	3	4	5
Contract Fee		(90,000)	(90,000)	(90,000)	(90,000)	(90,000)
Asset purchase/Sale	650,000					
Fixed Costs		(16,422)	(16,422)	(16,422)	(16,422)	(16,422)
Net Cash flow	650,000	(106,422)	(106,422)	(106,422)	(106,422)	(106,422)
Discount Factor	1.0	0.893	0.797	0.712	0.636	0.567
Present Value	650,000	(95,035)	(84,818)	(75,772)	(67,684)	(60,341)

Net present value £266,350

This option thus offers an NPV which is £45,522 greater than the in-house option, which means that profits could be increased by contracting out the catering service.

Alternative solution

Differential cash flows: contracting out versus in-house provision

Year	0	1	2	3	4	5
Asset purchase/Sale	650,000		500,000			(280,000)
Lost contribution		(246,985)	(246,985)	(246,985)	(246,985)	(246,985)
Fixed costs savings		95,844	99,586	103,516	107,641	111,973
Contract fee		(90,000)	(90,000)	(90,000)	(90,000)	(90,000)
Net cash flow	650,000	(241,141)	262,601	(233,469)	(229,344)	(505,012)
Discount Factor	1.0	0.893	0.797	0.712	0.636	0.567
Present Value	650,000	(215,339)	209,293	(166,230)	(145,863)	(286,342)

Net present value = £45,519

The positive NPV means that the cash flows from contracting out exceed those from keeping the service in-house.

[Note the £3 difference between the NPV of the two alternative approaches is merely a result of rounding.]

Contracting out the catering service is thus the preferred alternative and it is recommended that Amber plc accept the tender from the outside supplier.

(c)   The financial effect can be assessed by comparison of the present value of the additional costs incurred with the present value of the incremental contribution.

Workings

Present value of the additional expense	= 3.605 × £10,000
	= £36,050

The additional contribution amounts to 10% per year i.e.

Years 1-5 Additional contribution	= £24,699 per year
Present value at 12% per year	= 3.605 × £24,699
	= £89,040

The net present value of the additional investment in staff training is thus £89,040 less £36,050. This means that the net present value can be increased by £52,990 by retaining the service in-house, but increasing demand via improved services.

This additional net present value is greater than the £45,522 which can be created by switching to an outside provider for the catering service. The decision to contract out is therefore changed, although Amber plc must be wary of the fact that the difference between the in-house and the contracted out service is only £7,468 i.e. (£52,990–£45,522). The advantage is therefore relatively insignificant. Perhaps more importantly, the forecast that demand can be increased by as much as ten per cent for the relatively small investment of £10,000 per year (less than 2% of current variable costs) suggests that Amber plc should perhaps look more closely at the possible opportunities for increasing their contribution from the in-house catering service, before they choose to contract out. If demand is very sensitive to both price and quality it may require little investment to make the catering service very profitable.

The gains from investing internally, however, must be weighed against the potential gains to be earned from higher demand for a contracted out service. The additional information shows that the company will receive 5% of gross sales receipts once daily sales exceed £2,200. At present sales are at £2,079 and so, if the external contractor was able to raise demand by 10%, Amber plc would receive 5% of the new annual revenue i.e. £41,164 without incurring any additional expense. The choice, therefore, of whether to use the outside supplier or keep the service in-house is very dependent on the anticipated levels of future demand.

(d)   The primary limitation of making demand forecasts lies in the fact that they are forecasts and hence their reliability is unknown. Most forecasts are based upon a mix of historic information and expectations in relation to relevant influential variables. For example, the exchange rate forecasts, where the highest probability is attached to a rate of 1.54 Euro/£, is likely to be based on the statistical pattern of historic exchange rates (including the standard deviation) such that 1.54 Euro/£ constitutes the most frequently observed rate. This does not, however, necessarily mean that the rate will be similar in the future – history does not always repeat itself.

Another limitation relates to the nature of the data being forecast. Weather forecasts are notoriously unreliable because nature is such an uncontrollable force. Even if the UK weather has been hot, on average, for the past five years, this does not imply that this will be the case in the future. The factors which dictate the weather are uncontrollable and consequently to a large degree unpredictable.

The forecast also runs into problems because it seeks to link two unrelated variables. The state of the weather is totally independent of the exchange rate, and vice versa, and they can only be linked in the way suggested by the table if the range of alternative observations is restricted. This is ultimately a distortion of a reality which is far more complex.

(e)   There are numerous non-financial factors which may be relevant to a decision to contract out, and the type of factors are likely to be dependent upon the process/service which is the subject of the decision. Amongst the most important of the non-financial considerations will be the impact of any decision on the company's competitive position. For example, in the case of Amber plc, if the on train catering facility is sufficiently high class, it may attract new clientele to use their trains, thereby giving Amber plc a competitive advantage. The opposite may also be the case. In other words, the strategic impact of a decision needs to be taken into account, in addition to the directly measurable financial effects.

Another factor which needs to be taken into account is the question of management control of service quality. Once a service moves 'out of house' the only control mechanism which rests with the purchasing company may be a variety of penalties, the extreme one being termination of the contract. If the service remains inside the company it may be easier to change things in response to changing customer needs. In other words, contracting out may be linked to a reduction in the level of management control.

Staff morale may be affected by contracting out, and any such effects need to be carefully considered. Staff in departments which remain in-house may begin to feel threatened and view their service as the next on the 'hit list' for external contracting. It is important for managers to help allay such fears, and make clear the criteria on which any future outsourcing decisions will be based.

Other non-financial factors which may be useful to consider include:

- environmental effects, such as changes in food packaging policies

- the terms of any contract for outside supply, and the willingness of the supplier to respond to changes in market demand as and when necessary

- the capabilities of the business to manage the external supply process. If a large number of contracts are in place, this can possibly become a logistical headache.

2   News For You

(a)   Economic opinion on the effect of an interest rate change upon News For You may vary. Keynesian economists believe that if base rate (and other interest rates) fall then the demand for money will rise, and this will in turn lead to an increase in consumer demand. Unfortunately, however, even if News For You accept the argument that the recent drop in the base rate will increase demand, it is unlikely to have any significant impact on their particular business. Sales are likely to remain unchanged because newspapers and small confectionery items are low cost purchases, often bought on impulse. Interest rate movements will not make such items suddenly affordable where before they were not.

Monetarists believe that the level of demand in the economy is unaffected by interest rates. As already suggested, in the case of this particular business, this is likely to be true. News For You need to think about other ways in which the interest rate change might affect their business, and particularly its impact on business costs. If the company has an overdraft facility then the cost of borrowing will have been reduced. At the same time the expansion plans require the business to raise £2 million, and changes in interest rates affect the cost of all types of capital-loans and equity. Corporate borrowing rates are generally linked to the prevailing base rate, with companies paying a premium above base for the loan. The drop in rates will therefore affect the return that may be earned on the proposed expansion. If News For You appraise their investment by the use of Discounted Cash Flow analysis, then the fall in the cost of capital which has resulted from the drop in the base rate will mean that a lower discount rate can be applied to the forecast cash flows. A lower rate of discount, *ceteris paribus*, will result in a higher Net Present Value for any given proposal.

Keynesian economists do not, however, agree that changes in interest rates affect corporate investment decisions. They argue that investments are dependent more upon the level of business confidence. It may be possible to suggest that News For You see the fall in the base rate as stimulating general economic confidence, and hence they are more confident about the future of their particular business, and so regardless of any changes in the cost of capital, they are more willing to undertake the expansionary investment.

The figures on the rate of inflation are useful to News For You because they can directly affect profit and cash flow forecasts. A rise in the rate of inflation can indirectly lead to a rise in interest rates in order to curb demand, resulting in the business being affected on two fronts. The cash and profit impact of inflation will be to a large degree dependent on the relative rates of increase in wages, the cost of wholesale supplies for the shop, and the prices that News For You can charge its customers. The quoted rate of inflation is very low at just over 1% per year and, although the rate is not expected to fall any further, its current level is unlikely to have a dramatic effect on the ability of the business to trade profitably. The greater risk for the business may come from the problem that, because inflation is so low, customers are not prepared to tolerate any price rises at all, and News For You may become more vulnerable to loss of business to the large food stores which can draw away customers via price cutting campaigns.

Personal and corporation tax rates are relevant to the owners of News For You because they will affect the net gain to the business that may be generated by expansion. As with interest rates, tax rates can affect personal spending patterns, and therefore affect the turnover of a particular business. News For You, however, is unlikely to have a business which is sensitive to tax rates, because its products are basic essentials and low cost items. Nonetheless, the information that tax rates will remain unchanged is useful because it allows the business to be certain of the amount of tax relief that may be available on loan finance, and the relief that equity investors may claim for investing in a small unquoted company. This information may be useful in deciding whether or not to go ahead with the expansion, because it may affect the relative cost and availability of capital.

The changes in taxes on tobacco may be expected to have had a significant effect on News For You because it is one of the relatively high value products sold by the stores. The question indicates that tobacco sales have been falling, but it is unclear whether this drop is linked to the 10% rise in tax over the last twelve months, or simply a result of the population becoming more health conscious and so buying fewer cigarettes. If customers are price sensitive in their purchasing of tobacco, News For You may once again find itself vulnerable to competition from the food retailers which can exercise greater buying power and sell similar products at lower prices. The high cost of these items also means that stocking costs are high, and if stock turnover is reduced because of tax increase, then the amount of working capital required by News For You will rise.

The investigation into the food sector may prove to be detrimental to News For You if it serves to initiate a price war amongst the retailers, all of whom will be anxious to prove that they look after their customers. The business grew very quickly between 20X2 and 20X6, but since then turnover has increased by just 2% per year, and the owners must be concerned that further growth potential is limited, at least within the existing outlets. Moving into the sale of basic foodstuffs has been used as a strategy to compensate for loss of sales in other products such as tobacco, but these days in many countries a large proportion of people do their food shopping in large retail outlets. By expanding their product range, News For You has also created for itself another set of competitors in the form of food retailers. The only way in which the business may gain from this investigation is if it also covers food wholesaling, and the result is a drop in the prices that News For You have to pay for their stock.

(b)   Arguments in favour of the expansion include the following:

–   The figures on turnover suggest that there is only limited opportunity for the business to continue to grow organically. The business is seeking to replace sales of tobacco and newspapers with sales of foods, but as suggested in answer to (a),the potential of this side of the business may be limited. News For You may be advised to grow their sales via the acquisition of new outlets instead.

–   If News For You are being forced into paying relatively high prices for supplies from a local wholesaler, then expansion may allow them to gain more bargaining power, and purchase at reduced rates from a national wholesale chain. Increased size will offer the opportunity to take advantage of possible economies of scale via bulk ordering. In this way, margins could be widened and the overall business made more profitable.

–   With a larger number of stores covering a wider geographic area, News For You will be able to broaden the nature of their business base, so that they are less vulnerable to regional economic trends.

Arguments against any expansion include the following:

–   The potential to increase sales substantially via food sales is very limited. The majority of people purchase most of their food from larger stores, and will only use a local shop for small low cost items where it is not worthwhile making a special car journey to the supermarket for just one or two products. It is unlikely that it is possible to run a profitable business based on this type of sale.

–   The widespread ownership of televisions and access to differing forms of mass media communications is likely to mean that fewer people will purchase newspapers on a daily basis. This is particularly true of those papers which are also published in electronic form. Many newsagents are dependent for the bulk of their sales upon customers who come into the shop to buy a newspaper and then purchase additional items at the same time. If customers do not come in for the paper, then the associated sales income will also be lost. Expanding a business where there is such a risk of demand falling away may be regarded as very risky.

–   The information in the question suggests that the competitive environment for News For You is becoming much tougher on a number of different fronts simultaneously with rising excise duties, powerful food retailers and a reduction in tobacco and newspaper purchases. Expansion usually occurs because a business is very confident of the future, but in this case it is questionable whether News For You has much about which to be confident.

It would therefore seem to be advisable for News For You to postpone their expansion plans, and perhaps look at ways of using their existing outlets to sell very different products, thereby 're-inventing' their business, perhaps by moving completely away from confectionery and into, for example, video rental.

3   Ply, Spin and Axis

(*Note:* this answer contains a level of detail beyond that which would be expected of an examination candidate.)

(a)   The P/E, or Price Earnings Ratio is calculated as:

Current share price/Earnings per share

The P/E ratio is generally regarded as an important ratio for equity investors. The P/E for a company may be used as a basis for comparison with other companies, especially in the same business sector. A P/E ratio can be described as an indicator of potential earnings. The higher the P/E ratio, the greater the future expectations in terms of earnings growth. Earnings potential is determined very much by the sector of business, and so the P/E ratio of any single company should simply be used for intra-sector comparisons and not cross-sector comparison. The P/E ratio also reflects the level of financial risk in the company because the share price will be adjusted to compensate for such risk.

Using the information in the table the P/E ratio for Ply is 14.2, which means that if an investor were to purchase shares in the business, then based on current earnings it would take over 14.2 years before the cumulative earnings per share equalled the price paid for the share (if there was no earnings growth). By way of contrast, the P/E for Spin is 21.1.

The P/E ratio is used, as already suggested, to indicate growth potential, and so the higher figure of 21.1 for Spin indicates that the market believes that the company has a greater chance of increasing its profits and earnings per share than does Ply. The reason for the different potential may lie in better quality management, a different investment strategy or better investment opportunities. The P/E ratio simply indicates the market's explicit recognition of that potential.

The P/E ratio therefore changes in response to announcements which affect a company's share price. Suppose, for example, Ply were to announce that its quarterly sales figures had grown much quicker than expected, then the price of the share might rise in response. The P/E ratio relates the earnings for the last financial year to the *current* share price and since the P/E is based on last year's earnings (which are unchanged), the higher share price results in a higher P/E ratio. In other words, the market is now more confident about the company's future.

This can be illustrated as follows:

Share price 1 December 20X0 is 63 pence; EPS 4.44 pence; P/E ratio 14.2
5 December 20X0 the company announces a 15% sales increase over the last quarter; and the share price rises to 70 pence in response.
New P/E ratio = 70/4.44 = 15.77

Such price changes mean that a P/E ratio can vary quite substantially over the course of the year. For Ply, if the P/E ratio is 14.2 at a price of 63 pence, then at the year's highest price of 112 the P/E would be 25.2, and at the 52 week low price of 54 it would be 12.2. The range for the ratio is thus quite wide over the course of the year. Similar ranges could be calculated for the other two companies for the purposes of comparison.

From the brief information in the table, the market would appear to be most confident about the future earnings potential of Spin, and least confident about Axis. Spin has the highest current P/E ratio, and the least volatile share price, whilst Axis is the reverse. The investor can therefore use information on P/E ratios to identify high growth companies in which they may wish to invest because of their long-term capital growth potential.

(b)   Dividend cover is a measure of the relationship between dividends and earnings, and may be calculated for the whole company or on a per share basis, but both methods will yield the same results. In order to calculate the dividend cover from the information given, it is first necessary to calculate the earnings per share.

A value for earnings per share can be obtained from the P/E ratio and current share price since the share price is the EPS multiplied by the P/E ratio. Applying some simple algebra,

P/E = Share price/EPS
And so EPS = Share price/P/E ratio
For Spin, this means EPS = 187/21.1 = 8.86 pence.
For Axis, this means EPS = 291/13 = 22.38 pence

The EPS figure gives us a measure of total profit per share (after tax and preference share dividends) before it has been divided into dividends and retained earnings. Companies are free to choose the proportion of earnings which are paid out in dividends, and this is clearly indicated by the dividend cover which is measured as:

$$\frac{\text{Earnings per share}}{\text{Dividend per share}}$$

The table shows dividend yield but not the dividend value required to compute the cover. The value can be calculated by multiplying the share price by the percentage dividend yield:

i.e. Dividend value = Dividend yield (%) × Share price

For Spin this gives a dividend per share of $0.023 \times 187 = 43$ pence. For Axis the dividend per share is $0.021 \times 291 = 6.11$ pence.

This means that, combining the information on EPS and dividend per share, the dividend cover for Spin and Axis can be calculated as:

Spin	= 8.86/4.3
	= 2.06 times
Axis	= 22.38/6.11
	= 3.66 times

An alternative method of calculation is:

Dividend cover	= (100/P/E ratio)/dividend yield
For Spin	= (100/21.1)/2.3 = 2.06 times
For Axis	= (100/13.0)/2.1 = 3.66 times

The lower cover for Spin indicates that they have chosen to pay out more of their earnings in dividends. The figure of close to 2 for cover means that almost half of earnings have been paid out in dividends. For Axis, the figure of over 3 for cover means that less than one third of their earnings have gone in dividend payments.

The extent to which a company retains profit is indicative of its desire to re-invest to maintain or increase future profits. This means that, as a general rule, the higher the dividend cover for a business, the greater the potential for future capital growth. The level of dividend cover varies widely between industries, because the scale of investment required to maintain/improve production varies across industries. Consequently, investors should take care to ensure that they only compare the dividend cover of companies that are in the same sector.

(c)   If dividends per share are in excess of earnings per share, then a company must be making the dividend payment out of reserves. In other words, the net asset value of the business will be reduced by the extent of the difference in value between the dividend payout and the earnings.

Erosion of the net asset value will be a matter of concern to the investor if either:

–   the fall in value is substantial, or
–   the company adopts this strategy over a number of successive years.

One reason why a company may adopt such a policy can be explained by the common perception that the share price will fall if dividends are reduced. Hence market forces encourage company directors to feel that it is preferable to pay the necessary dividend out of reserves if such a strategy will help to maintain the share price. An alternative reason is that if a company has a very high level of reserves, and is unable to find suitable uses for the funds, then it may feel that paying those funds back to investors is a sensible and more appropriate policy. In this case, the dividend which is higher than earnings is merely a repayment of earnings from earlier years back into the hands of the equity investors. In such instances, directors are often criticised for their inability to identify suitable investment opportunities, and the strategy may well only be adopted as a last resort measure.

The dangers of making payments out of reserves are three-fold. First, the action might trigger a stock market reaction which sends the share price on a downward spiral, and this means that in the medium to longer term the shareholders are worse off. In the short term, they have been compensated by the high dividend, but in the longer term this may be insufficient to cover the fall in the value of the shares. Secondly, the fall in the net asset value of the business may make it more vulnerable to a take-over. The market is also likely to react to the implementation of such a policy and this may mean a downward adjustment in the share price. Finally if a company makes payments out of reserves over an extended period of time, this may bring into question its future trading viability. In practice, however; it is unlikely that such a situation would arise.

4   Contribution approach to decisions

(a)   In some decision-making situations, contribution is often pointed out as the 'key' to reaching a financial recommendation, because in certain circumstances the only values which change are the sales and variable costs. This applies in particular to short-term tactical decisions when fixed costs are assumed to remain unchanged and perhaps the only changes are those caused by changes in volume.

If a firm has spare capacity then any further business it can attract is worthwhile providing the additional sales revenue exceeds any additional variable costs incurred, i.e. any contribution is better than no contribution at all. This idea is often linked to the pricing of off-peak business or special orders.

Contribution is also used as a basis to rank products given the existence of a limiting or constraining factor. The most financially advantageous product to sell in this case is the one which maximises the contribution relating to the limiting factor.

It is dangerous to proceed too enthusiastically with the contribution concept, however, as there are a number of simplifying and limiting assumptions contained in it. It assumes that an organisation can separate the variable and fixed costs that it incurs and, if a range of volume is considered, that unit selling prices and variable costs will be constant over the range or that we can know when and by how much they change.

In its simple form it ignores the incurrence of fixed costs because 'they will be incurred anyway'. Such a step is argued because this is only dealing with the short-term. It can be dangerous, however, to ignore fixed costs over the longer term and to think of basing all decisions on contribution alone, because in the long run all costs must be covered. There may also be some incremental fixed costs and any decision-maker using contribution should be clear on the financial consequences of these in addition to the contribution.

(b)   The first step in the design of an ABC system is the identification of the activities in the organisation. In manufacturing, some of these will be traditional such as machining, others may not have been previously separated e.g., material handling or ordering. It is then necessary to identify the factors which influence the cost of each particular activity; such as machine hours, number of times material moved, orders created, telephone calls etc. These are the 'cost drivers' and are indicative of the amount of work throughput in the activity. It is important to use the cost driver which is the most appropriate indicator of work undertaken and cost incurrence for the activity.

The next step is for cost centres or cost pools to be created for each activity or group of activities. This process is similar to the departmental or cost centre costs which apply in traditional systems, but there are likely to be many more activities and activity cost pools in an ABC system than departments in a traditional system. This depends, however, on the degree of detail applied to the ABC system. Following this, the incidence of each cost driver for each product or service must be established. The final step is to trace the costs of each activity cost pool to products or services based on the products/services' demand for these activities, using the cost drivers as a measure of that demand.

(c)   A cost driver is an event or force which is a significant determinant of the cost of an activity. In traditional product costing a volume-related cost driver is used as an 'allocation base' to assign overheads to products in the second stage of allocation. This driver changes approximately in proportion to the number of units produced or services delivered (hence volume-related, strictly product-volume related). Examples of volume-related cost drivers are labour hours or machine hours. The greater the volume of units produced, the greater the number of labour hours or machine hours worked. This results in an allocation of the total overhead cost in question which reflects the volume of units produced. That is, a high proportion of total overhead is assigned to the products/services with a high volume of throughput.

Advocates of an ABC system argue that some overhead costs do not respond to the volume of units produced or services delivered. Rather, for example, they respond to the complexity of the service and support processes involved. They point out that the use of volume-related cost drivers distort the product cost, often resulting in high volume products being over-costed and low volume products being under-costed. This is because, they argue, the cost of some service and support activities does not increase in proportion to the number of units produced. Within manufacturing the cost to set up a machine is the same irrespective of the number of units being manufactured. Likewise the cost to generate and manage an order or expedite delivery by the purchasing function, is not dependent on the quantity being ordered and delivered.

Unlike the traditional approach which used 'volume' related drivers such as hours of work, a system based on activities uses multiple measures, some product-volume related, some not. It relies on the premise that activities cause costs, and products or services consume activities. It is argued therefore that the approach delivers a more 'accurate' cost and one which more appropriately facilitates overhead cost management

The ABC system must take into account how the company currently manufactures its products or delivers its services. It must address the nature and extent of the business activities performed. This will move away from departmental analysis and place greater emphasis on processes and activities undertaken to produce, distribute or support products and services.

(d)   A further development of an ABC system is the subdivision of the activities and overheads into different categories. These categories have different characteristics when being related to products or services. Unit related activities and costs are those which can be closely related to each item produced, such as direct labour and energy costs. Batch related activities are not identifiable with individual items but with groups or batches of product, for example, machine set up or material ordering.

Product-sustaining activities relate to different products but are independent of units or batches; engineering resources for individual products or specific product enhancements are examples. Finally facility-sustaining activities, such as plant management and administration and factory heating, support the general manufacturing capability but not individual products. Such analysis is important when decisions are being made about profitability, volume of production or retiring individual products. For example, deleting an individual product or service would result in saving of direct costs naturally, plus unit and batch related overhead. Only if a product were deleted would product sustaining costs be removed, and facility sustaining costs would still be incurred unless the whole facility were closed down. From a decision-making point of view facility sustaining costs would not be assigned to individual products, instead they are regarded as common to all products.

5   Bud plc

(a)   *Preliminary workings:*

Budgeted Sales (units and value)

Product	Units	Price	Value (£)
F1	34,000	£50.00	1,700,000
F2	58,000	£30.00	1,740,000
			3,440,000

Budgeted Production (units)

Product	Sales	Stock increment	Production
F1	34,000	1,000	35,000
F2	58,000	2,000	60,000

(i)   *Component purchase and usage budget (units and value)*

Product	Component C3	Component C4	Total
F1	280,000 u	140,000 u	
F2	240,000 u	180,000 u	
	520,000 u	320,000 u	
Value	£650,000	£576,000	£1,226,000

(ii)   *Direct labour budget (hours and value)*

Product	Assembly	Finishing	Total
F1	17,500 hours	7,000 hours	
F2	15,000 hours	10,000 hours	
	32,500	17,000	
Value	£162,500	£102,000	£264,500

(iii)   *Departmental manufacturing overhead recovery rates:*

	Assembly	Finishing
Total overhead cost per month	£617,500	£204,000
Total direct labour hours	32,500	17,000
Overhead rate (per direct labour hour)	£19.00	£12.00

(iv)   *Selling overhead recovery rate*

Total overhead cost per month	£344,000
Total sales value (Month 9)	£3,440,000
Selling overhead rate	10%

(v)   *Closing stock budget*

Product	Units	Cost £	Value £
F1	1,000	32.80	32,800
F2	2,000	19.40	38,800
			71,600

(b)   *Standard unit cost (Month 9)*

		Product			
		F1		*F2*	
			£/unit		£/unit
Material	C3	8 × £1.25	10.00	4 × £1.25	5.00
	C4	4 × £1.80	7.20	3 × £1.80	5.40
Labour	Assembly	30/60 × £5	2.50	15/60 × £5	1.25
	Finishing	12/60 × £6	1.20	10/60 × £6	1.00
M'fg. overhead	Assembly	30/60 × £19	9.50	15/60 × £19	4.75
	Finishing	12/60 × £12	2.40	10/60 × £12	2.00
Manufacturing cost			32.80		19.40
Selling overhead			5.00		3.00
Total cost			37.80		22.40
Selling price			50.00		30.00
Profit			12.20		7.60

(c)   *Budgeted profit and loss account (Month 9)*

Cost element	£
Components	1,226,000
Direct labour	264,500
Manufacturing overhead	821,500
Subtotal	2,312,000
Less closing stock	71,600
Manufacturing cost of sales	2,240,400
Selling overhead	344,000
Total cost	2,584,400
Sales	3,440,000
Net profit	855,600

(d)   Under a system of absorption costing an overhead rate is used to apply overheads to each unit produced. At present the company applies manufacturing overhead to products based upon the budgeted labour hours and the budgeted expenditure in each month. Such figures are used to establish a separate predetermined rate for each month. As a result unit overhead costs fluctuate if production levels fluctuate because any fixed element of overheads is spread over fluctuating volumes.

It can be disconcerting and misleading for production and sales staff to be dealing with product costs which fluctuate on a monthly basis. This is especially so when the fluctuation has not been caused by changes in production efficiency and it bears no relation to changes in the general market price.

One way to overcome this is to compute an overhead rate which is based on a longer time period, for example quarterly or a predetermined annual rate as mentioned in the question. This enables large fluctuations in, and extreme values of, product costs to be avoided. This would mean that management would be able to monitor the business volume and overhead costs on which the calculations were based to ensure that, over the longer term, the average product costs which were predicted were in fact achieved.

6   Consultant engineers

(a)   *Labour and overhead variance calculations*

			Variance £
Total variance	5,550 × £55 = 305,250	−331,000	25,750 A
Labour and variable overhead total	5,550 × £30 = 166,500	−174,000	7,500 A
Expenditure	5,700 × £30 = 171,000	−174,000	3,000A
Efficiency	(5,550 − 5,700)	× £30	4,500 A
Fixed overhead total	5,550 × £25 = 138,750	−157,000	18,250 A
Expenditure	6,000 × £25 = 150,000	−157,000	7,000 A
Volume	(5,550 − 6,000)	× £25	11,250 A
Volume efficiency	(5,550 − 5,700)	× £25	3,750 A
Volume capacity	(5,700 − 6,000)	× £25	7,500 A

Variance summary	£	£
Labour and variable overhead:		
expenditure	3,000 A	
efficiency	4,500 A	
		7,500 A
Fixed overhead:		
expenditure	7,000 A	
efficiency	3,750 A	
capacity	7,500 A	
		18,250 A
Total variance		25,750 A

(*Note:* The layout shown above is a traditional form, but other presentations are acceptable. Likewise, in the context of the question, credit will be given if slightly different terminology is used, for example, for the capacity variance – budgeted hours not worked and for the efficiency variance – hours paid not charged. Candidates may combine the 'efficiency' implications for variable and fixed overheads in one calculation.)

The costs incurred on labour and overheads exceeded those recovered from clients by £25,750. This will result in a profit lower than that which was budgeted and is attributable to differences related to both variable and fixed elements.

Although only 5,550 hours were chargeable (i.e. recovered), 5,700 hours were worked and paid for – that is, overhead invoices received and payments made from the payroll. This needs to be investigated. If there is some reason why hours worked were not recoverable from clients (e.g., mis-recording of engineers' travelling or due to carrying out administrative duties) some adjustment may need to be made to the way these are accounted for or results will be continually distorted. In part (a) this is labelled as an adverse efficiency variance. In this situation 'efficiency' should be interpreted somewhat less rigorously than as typical manufacturing setting in which variance analysis originated.

Based on the number of hours worked (5,700) and assuming the labour and variable overhead costs vary with hours worked, then the costs (invoices and payroll) exceeded those allowed for in the budget rates by £3,000. Possible reasons are: differences in the rates of pay; the mix of staff paid on different rates; a difference in the cost of variable overhead items, travel costs for example.

The fixed overheads were under-recovered by £18,250. This was due in part to invoices for fixed overhead items being £7,000 higher than the original fixed budget. The volume of work undertaken for clients was below the budget by 450 hours which also contributed to the under-recovery of overheads. This can be traced to both the absolute number of hours worked being 300 below budget and the fact that ISO hours worked were not chargeable to clients. They thus failed to achieve the capacity which was planned (perhaps there was no more work available) and the time that was worked was, on the face of it, inefficient.

(*Note:* Credit will also be given if candidates' answers (in place of some of the above) addressed appropriate practical aspects such as the need to incorporate an allowance for non-chargeable hours or the interpretation of 'efficiency' in this context.)

(b) Determining how cost will change with output or other measurable factor is important for decisions, planning and control. When seeking to estimate cost behaviour or predict a level of cost for a certain measure of activity a series of observed part cost and activity measures may be collected, being the dependent and independent variables, respectively. Least squares regression determines mathematically the 'line of best fit' for all of the observations. It is based on the principle of minimising the squared (hence removing negative signs) vertical deviations from the line, of all the observations made.

Practical requirements in gathering data are as follows:

– Care in selecting the activity base which is best likely to describe the cost. This would be assisted by undertaking mathematical tests on the relationship between the dependent and independent variables.

– The cost and activity should be related to the same time periods. If there is a lag in the incurrence of a cost this must be allowed for.

–   A reasonable number of observations should be made, from the most recent periods rather than from the distant past. A balance between these must be established between getting a sufficient number of observations yet not having recourse to old and possibly non-representative time periods.

–   For the whole time period covered it is important that there was no change in the accounting techniques or policies adopted. If this has taken place adjustment would be required.

–   Similarly; if data is drawn from periods some years previous it may be that technological changes may have to be allowed for; or, for example, the existence of an inflationary element in some of the cost values.

(Three points only required.)

June 2001 Questions

Section A – THIS ONE question is compulsory and MUST be attempted

1   Kolb plc

Kolb plc produces high quality fountain pens, ballpoints and writing sets which it has traditionally sold by mail order. Sales and profit growth were strong and consistent over the period 1990-1998. Since 1998 the company has seen sales growth slow dramatically as a result of growing competition from retailers on the World Wide Web (Internet).

Management consultants brought in by Kolb estimate that rapid sales growth can be re-established if the company invests in setting up its own Web site. The designs sold via the Internet will have a different brand name from those sold via mail order, in order to allow Kolb to set different, and possibly more competitive prices for its Web sales.

Allowing for the current slow down in the growth of mail order sales, and the introduction of the new Web site, total sales are expected to increase in value by 30% per year for each of the next two years. The Web site is expected to reduce total operating costs (excluding depreciation) to 82% of sales.

Kolb's balance sheet at the close of the last financial year is summarised below. Fixed assets, including freehold land and buildings, are shown at historic cost, net of depreciation. The debenture is redeemable in two years time, although early redemption without penalty is permissible.

Balance sheet as at 30 November 2000

	£m	£m	£m
Fixed assets:			
Freehold land & buildings	15.0		
Machinery	30.0		45.0
Current assets:			
Stocks	20.0		
Debtors	5.0		
Cash	5.0	30.0	
Current liabilities:			
Trade creditors		(24.0)	
Net current assets			6.0
Total assets less current liabilities			51.0
10% Debenture			(8.0)
Bank loan (12%)			(4.0)
Net assets:			39.0
Financed by:			
Issued share capital (par value 50p):			8.0
Profit and loss account			31.0
Shareholders' funds			39.0

Additional Information for Kolb

(i)   Operating profit for the year ended 30 November 2000 was 12.5% of sales of £120 million, after deduction of depreciation of £5 million. The depreciation charge for the next two years is expected to remain unchanged, and all depreciation provisions qualify for tax relief.

(ii)   Dividends are increased by 10% per year, and in the financial year ended 30 November 2000 dividends of £3.75 million were paid.

(iii)   Corporation tax is levied at 30%.

(iv)   The Web site became fully operational on 1 December 2000.

(v)   Interest charges are expected to remain unchanged over the next two years.

(vi)   The value of stock, debtors and trade creditors are expected to increase at the same rate as sales over the next two years.

The following information is also available regarding key financial indicators for Kolb's major competitor:

Return on (long-term capital employed	15%
Return on equity	12.8%
Operating profit margin	10%
Current ratio	1.25:1
Acid-test	1:1:1
Gearing (total debt/equity)	33%
Interest cover	6%
Dividend cover	3%

Required:

(a)   Draft a profit and loss account for the year ended 30 November 2000, and a forecast profit and loss account and balance sheet for the year ending 30 November 2001. (Values should be calculated to the nearest £10,000.)   **(6 marks)**

(b)   Discuss the performance and financial health of Kolb in relation to that of its major competitor, as at 30 November 2000.   **(8 marks)**

(c)   At present Kolb's main market is Western Europe, and the company wishes to expand into the North American market where there is strong demand for 'collector pens' and high priced specialist designs. Kolb has been advised that the best way of establishing a strong US sales base is to seek a joint venture or merger with a North American company. In order to fund such a venture, the company is planning a 1 for 8 rights issue in March 2002. The rights shares will be priced at a 25% discount on the share price current at the time of the issue

Required:

(i)   Calculate the market capitalisation of Kolb and the price per share *immediately prior* to the rights issue, assuming that the shares trade on a PE. of 8 based on the previous year's earnings.
(3 marks)

(ii)   Calculate the issue price of the rights shares, and the theoretical ex-rights price.   **(2 marks)**

(iii)   What assumptions are implied in the calculation of the theoretical ex-rights price?   **(3 marks)**

(iv)   Under what circumstances might Kolb's share price after the rights issue be higher than the theoretical ex-rights price?   **(3 marks)**

(v)   Critically comment upon the effect that the rights issue will have on the gearing of Kolb. (Detailed calculations are not required.) Your answer should pay particular attention to the impact upon the return on equity.   **(6 marks)**

(d)   The following model shows that the growth rate of dividends can be calculated by using the formula:
$g = rB$
Where r = the post tax return on equity
    B = the proportion of profits re-invested.

Required:

(i)   Using this formula, calculate the potential growth rate in dividends for Kolb, based on the forecast accounts for the year ending 30 November 2001.   **(4 marks)**

(ii)   Critically comment on your findings, taking into account the proposed US expansion of the business   **(5 marks)**
(Total: 40 marks)

Section B – One questions ONLY to be attempted

2   Sludgewater plc

(a)   Sludgewater plc, a furniture manufacturer, has been reported to the anti-pollution authorities on several occasions in recent years, and fined substantial amounts for making excessive toxic discharges into the air. Both the environmental lobby and Sludgewater's shareholders have demanded that it clean up its operations.

If no clean up takes place, Sludgewater estimates that the total fines it would incur over the next three years can be summarised by the following probability distribution (all figures are expressed in present values.)

Level of fine	Probability
£1.0m	0.3
£1.8m	0.5
£2.6m	0.2

A firm of environmental consultants has advised that spray painting equipment can be installed at a cost of £4m to virtually eliminate discharges. Unlike fines, expenditure on pollution control equipment is tax-allowable via a 25% writing-down allowance (reducing balance, based on gross expenditure). The rate of corporation tax is 30%, paid with a one-year delay. The equipment will have no scrap or resale value after its expected three year working life. The equipment can be in place ready for Sludgewater's next financial year.

A European Union grant of 25% of gross expenditure is available, but with payment delayed by a year. The consultant's charge is £200,000 and the new equipment will raise annual production costs by 2% of sales revenue. Current sales are £15 million per annum, and are expected to grow by 5% per annum compound. No change in working capital is envisaged.

Sludgewater applies a discount rate of 10% after tax on investment projects of this nature. All cash inflows and outflows occur at year ends.

Required:

(a)   Calculate the expected net present value of the investment.
      Briefly comment on your results.   **(12 marks)**

(b)   Write a memorandum to Sludgewater's management in respect of the potential investment taking into account both financial and non-financial criteria.   **(8 marks)**
                                                                                       (Total: 20 marks)

3   Capital

Answer any FOUR of the six parts of this question.
Each part carries five marks.

(a)   Briefly explain the main features of:

            -   Sales and leaseback;
            -   Finance leasing.   **(5 marks)**

(b)   Explain the difference between hard and soft capital rationing, and give reasons why a company may deliberately choose to restrict its capital expenditure.   **(5 marks)**

(c)   Distinguish between factoring and invoice discounting, explaining the benefits of such ways of managing debtors.   **(5 marks)**

(d)   Define the terms 'price elasticity' and 'cross elasticity' of demand and briefly explain their relevance to product pricing decisions.   **(5 marks)**

(e)   Explain the meaning of the term 'venture capital'.   **(5 marks)**

(f)   What are the potential major effects of taxation on capital investment decisions?   **(5 marks)**

(Total: 20 marks)

Section C – TWO questions ONLY to be attempted.

4   Management accounting

(a)   Some writers have suggested that the purposes of management accounting systems are *costing* and *management control.*

Required:

Briefly discuss whether this satisfactorily describes the purposes of management accounting systems. **(6 marks)**

(b)   A company, which is engaged in retailing food and household products, has stores in many towns. These stores, whilst managed locally, report to a Head Office and are served from a few strategically located warehouses by the company's own transport fleet.

Required:

Discuss the management accounting information which is likely to be provided in such a company.   **(14 marks)**

(Total: 20 marks)

5   Bicycles

It is the quarter end at a UK company which sells bicycles throughout Europe. One model produced in a dedicated plant had a budgeted column of 20,000 units of production and sales for the quarter. The budgeted/standard manufacturing and selling costs, applicable to this one model, for the quarter are shown in Table 1 below:

Table 1

	Per unit £	Total £000
Manufacturing:		
Material	45	900
Labour and variable overhead	15	300
Fixed overhead		1,200
Total manufacturing cost		2,400
Selling:		
Variable overhead	15	300
Fixed overhead		340
Total selling overhead		640

1.   The fixed manufacturing overheads are recovered, at a rate per unit, based on the budgeted volume levels.

2.   Variable selling overheads are incurred in proportion to units sold.

3.   The standard selling price is £190 per unit.

For reporting purposes and identifying stock values the company operates a standard absorption costing system. For the quarter in question the production was 16.800 units, however sales were only 11,800 units.

In order to undertake some basic sales and marketing planning, costs are analysed into variable and fixed elements in order to compute the break-even point and profits at various sales volumes. The Sales Manager had calculated the break-even point as 1,339 units and for the 11,800 units sold in this quarter had predicted a loss. He was surprised therefore to see that the statement of actual profit/loss just produced for the quarter (Table 2) revealed a small profit as follows:

Table 2

Production 16.800
Sales   11.800

	£000		£000
Sales:			2,242
Manufacturing costs			
Standard cost of production			
16,800 units	2,016		
Less: increase in stock 5,000 units	600		
Cost of sales			1,416
Manufacturing margin			826
Less: Manufacturing Variances			
Fixed overhead volume	192		
Expenditure	48		240
			586
Selling Overheads			
Variable	138		
Fixed	376		514
Net profit			72

Required:

(a)   Using marginal costing:

(i)   Illustrate the calculation of the break-even point undertaken by the Sales Manager.

(ii)   Calculate the loss predicted by the Sales Manager based on the actual units sold of 11,800.

For part (a) use the budgeted/standard costs given for the quarter in Table 1.   **(4 marks)**

(b)   (i)   Demonstrate how the value of the manufacturing fixed overhead volume variance, shown in Table 2, has been computed and briefly explain its significance.   **(5 marks)**

(ii)   Calculate the expenditure and volume variances which apply to the selling overheads in this quarter.   **(3 marks)**

(c)   Reconcile the loss calculated in (a) (ii) with the profit for the quarter shown in Table 2 indicating all relevant differences. Briefly explain why an actual profit is revealed when a loss was anticipated by the Sales Manager.   **(8 marks)**
(Total: 20 marks)

6   Private hospital

A private hospital is organised into separate medical units which offer specialised nursing care (e.g. maternity unit, paediatric unit). Figures for the paediatric unit for the year to 31 May 2001 have just become available. For the year in question the paediatric unit charged patients £200 per patient day for nursing care and £4.4m in revenue was earned.

Costs of running the unit consist of variable costs, direct staffing costs and allocated fixed costs. The charges for variable costs such as catering and laundry are based on the number of patient days spent in hospital. Staffing costs are established from the personnel requirements applicable to particular levels of patient days. Charges for fixed costs such as security administration etc, are based on bed capacity, currently 80 beds.

The number of beds available to be occupied is regarded as bed capacity and this is agreed and held constant for the whole year. There was an agreement that a bed capacity of 80 beds would apply to the paediatric unit for the 365 days of the year to 31 May 2001.

The tables below show the variable, staffing and fixed costs applicable to the paediatric unit for the year to 31 May 2001.

Variable costs (based on patient days)	£
Catering	450,000
Laundry	150,000
Pharmacy	500,000
	1,100,000

Staffing costs

Each speciality recruits its own supervisors and assistants. The staffing requirements for the paediatric unit are based on the actual patient day, see the following table:

Patient Days per annum	**Supervisors**	**Nurses**	**Assistants**
Up to 20,500	4	10	20
20,500 to 23,000	4	13	24
Over 23,000	4	15	28

The annual costs of employment are: supervisors £22,000 each, nurses £16,000 each and assistants £12,000 each.

Fixed costs (based on bed capacity)	£
Administration	850,000
Security	80,000
Rent and property	720,000
	1,650,000

During the year to 31 May 2001 the paediatric unit operated at 100% occupancy (i.e. all 80 beds occupied) for 100 days of the year. In fact the demand on these days was for at least 20 beds more.

As a consequence of this, in the budget for the following year to 31 May 2002, an increase in the bed capacity has been agreed. 20 extra beds will be contracted for the whole of the year. It is assumed that the 100 beds will be fully occupied for 100 days, rather than being restricted to 80 beds on those days. An increase of 10% in employment costs for the year to 31 May 2002, due to wage rate rises, will occur for all personnel. The revenue per patient day, all other cost factors and the remaining occupancy will be the same as the year to 31 May 2001.

Required:

(a)   Determine for the year to 31 May 2001, the actual number of patient-days, the bed occupancy percentage, the net profit/loss and the break-even number(s) of patient days for the paediatric unit.   **(6 marks)**

(b)   Determine the budget for the year to 31 May 2002 showing the revised number of patient-days, the bed occupancy percentage, the net profit/loss and the number of patient-days required to achieve the same profit/loss as computed in (a) above.   **(5 marks)**

(c)   Comment on your findings from (a) and (b) offering advice to the management of the unit.   **(6 marks)**

(d)   A business or operating unit can have both financial and social objectives and at times these can be in conflict. Briefly explain and give an example.   **(3 marks)**
(Total: 20 marks)

Present Value Table

Present value of 1 i.e. $(1 + r)^{-n}$

Where   r = discount rate
        n = number of periods until payment

Discount rate (r)

Periods (n)	1%	2%	3%	4%	5%	6%	7%	8%	9%	10%	
1	0.990	0.980	0.971	0.962	0.952	0.943	0.935	0.926	0.917	0.909	1
2	0.980	0.961	0.943	0.925	0.907	0.890	0.873	0.857	0.842	0.826	2
3	0.971	0.942	0.915	0.889	0.864	0.840	0.816	0.794	0.772	0.751	3
4	0.961	0.924	0.888	0.855	0.823	0.792	0.763	0.735	0.708	0.683	4
5	0.951	0.906	0.863	0.822	0.784	0.747	0.713	0.681	0.650	0.621	5
6	0.942	0.888	0.837	0.790	0.746	0.705	0.666	0.630	0.596	0.564	6
7	0.933	0.871	0.813	0.760	0.711	0.665	0.623	0.583	0.547	0.513	7
8	0.923	0.853	0.789	0.731	0.677	0.627	0.582	0.540	0.502	0.467	8
9	0.941	0.837	0.766	0.703	0.645	0.592	0.544	0.500	0.460	0.424	9
10	0.905	0.820	0.744	0.676	0.614	0.558	0.508	0.463	0.422	0.386	10
11	0.896	0.804	0.722	0.650	0.585	0.527	0.475	0.429	0.388	0.305	11
12	0.887	0.788	0.701	0.625	0.557	0.497	0.444	0.397	0.356	0.319	12
13	0.879	0.773	0.681	0.601	0.530	0.469	0.415	0.368	0.326	0.290	13
14	0.870	0.758	0.661	0.1577	0.505	0.442	0.388	0.340	0.299	0.263	14
15	0.861	0.743	0.642	0.555	0.481	0.417	0.362	0.315	0.275	0.239	15

(n)	11%	12%	13%	14%	15%	16%	17%	18%	19%	20%	
1	0.901	0.893	0.885	0.877	0.870	0.862	0.855	0.847	0.840	0.833	1
2	0.812	0.797	0.783	0.769	0.756	0.743	0.731	0.718	0.706	0.694	2
3	0.731	0.712	0.693	0.675	0.658	0.641	0.624	0.609	0.593	0.579	3
4	0.659	0.636	0.613	0.592	0.572	0.552	0.534	0.516	0.499	0.482	4
5	0.593	0.567	0.543	0.519	0.497	0.476	0.456	0.437	0.419	0.402	5
6	0.535	0.507	0.480	0.456	0.432	0.410	0.390	0.370	0.352	0.335	6
7	0.482	0.452	0.425	0.400	0.376	0.354	0.333	0.314	0.296	0.279	7
8	0.434	0.404	0.379	0.351	0.327	0.305	0.285	0.266	0.249	0.233	8
9	0.391	0.361	0.333	0.308	0.284	0.263	0.243	0.225	0.209	0.194	9
10	0.352	0.322	0.295	0.270	0.247	0.227	0.208	0.191	0.176	0.162	10
11	0.317	0.287	0.261	0.237	0.215	0.195	0.178	0.162	0.148	0.135	11
12	0.286	0.257	0.231	0.208	0.187	0.168	0.152	0.137	0.124	0.112	12
13	0.258	0.229	0.204	0.182	0.163	0.145	0.130	0.116	0.104	0.093	13
14	0.232	0.205	0.181	0.160	0.141	0.125	0.111	0.099	0.088	0.078	14
15	0.209	0.183	0.160	0.140	0.123	0.108	0.095	0.084	0.074	0.065	15

Annuity Table

Present value of an annuity of 1 i.e $\dfrac{1-(1+r)^{-n}}{r}$

Where   r = discount rate
n = number of periods

Discount rate (r)

Periods (n)	1%	2%	3%	4%	5%	6%	7%	8%	9%	10%	
1	0.990	0.980	0.971	0.962	0.952	0.943	0.935	0.926	0.917	0.909	1
2	1.970	1.942	1.913	1.886	1.859	1.833	1.808	1.783	1.759	1.736	2
3	2.941	2.884	2.829	2.775	2.723	2.673	2.624	2.577	2.531	2.487	3
4	3.902	3.808	3.717	3.630	3.546	3.465	3.387	3.312	3.240	3.170	4
5	4.853	4.713	4.580	4.452	4.329	4.212	4.100	3.993	3.890	3.791	5
6	5.795	5.601	5.417	5.242	5.076	4.917	4.767	4.623	4.486	4.355	6
7	6.728	6.472	6.230	6.002	5.786	5.582	5.389	5.206	5.033	4.868	7
8	7.652	7.325	7.020	6.733	6.463	6.210	5.971	5.747	5.535	5.335	8
9	8.566	8.162	7.786	7.435	7.108	6.802	6.515	6.247	5.995	5.759	9
10	9.471	8.983	8.530	8.111	7.722	7.360	7.024	6.710	6.418	6.145	10
11	10.37	9.787	9.253	8.760	8.306	7.887	7.499	7.139	6.805	6.495	11
12	11.26	10.58	9.954	9.385	8.863	8.384	7.943	7.536	7.161	6.814	12
13	12.13	11.35	10.63	9.986	9.394	8.853	8.358	7.904	7.487	7.103	13
14	13.00	12.11	11.30	10.56	9.899	9.295	8.745	8.244	7.786	7.367	14
15	13.87	12.85	11.94	11.12	10.38	9.712	9.108	8.559	8.061	7.606	15

(n)	11%	12%	13%	14%	15%	16%	17%	18%	19%	20%	
1	0.901	0.893	0.885	0.877	0.870	0.862	0.855	0.847	0.840	0.833	1
2	1.713	1.690	1.668	1.647	1.626	1.605	1.585	1.566	1.547	1.528	2
3	2.444	2.402	2.361	2.322	2.283	2.246	2.210	2.174	2.140	2.106	3
4	3.102	3.037	2.974	2.914	2.855	2.798	2.743	2.690	2.639	2.589	4
5	3.696	3.605	3.517	3.433	3.352	3.274	3.199	3.127	3.058	2.991	5
6	4.231	4.111	3.998	3.889	3.784	3.685	3.589	3.498	3.410	3.326	6
7	4.712	4.564	4.423	4.288	4.160	4.039	3.922	3.812	3.706	3.605	7
8	5.146	4.968	4.799	4.639	4.487	4.344	4.207	4.078	3.954	3.837	8
9	5.537	5.328	5.132	4.946	4.772	4.607	4.451	4.303	4.163	4.031	9
10	5.889	5.650	5.426	5.216	5.019	4.833	4.659	4.494	4.339	4.192	10
11	6.207	5.938	5.687	5.453	5.234	5.029	4.836	4.656	4.486	4.327	11
12	6.482	6.194	5.918	5.660	5.421	5.197	4.988	4.793	4.611	4.439	12
13	6.750	6.424	6.122	5.842	5.583	5.342	5.118	4.910	4.715	4.533	13
14	6.982	6.628	6.302	6.002	5.724	5.468	5.229	5.008	4.802	4.611	14
15	7.191	6.811	6.462	6.142	5.847	5.575	5.324	5.092	4.876	4.675	15

June 2001 Answers

1   Kolb plc

(a)   Profit and loss account for the year ended 30 November 2000

	£m
Sales	120.0
Cost of sales	(105.0)
Operating profit	15.0
Interest charges	(1.28)
Pre-tax profit	13.72
Corporation Tax	(4.12)
Profits attributable to ordinary shareholders	9.6
Dividends	(3.75)
Retained earnings	5.85

Profit and loss account for the year ended 30 November 2000

	£m
Sales	156.0
Cost of sales	132.92
Operating profit	23.08
Interest charges	(1.28)
Pre-tax profit	21.80
Corporation Tax	(6.54)
Profits attributable to ordinary shareholders	15.26
Dividends	(4.13)
Retained earnings	11.13

Balance sheet as at 30 November 2001

	£m	£m	£m
Fixed assets			
Current assets:			
Stocks	26		
Debtors	6.5		
Cash	20.83	53.33	
Current liabilities:			
Trade creditors		(31.2)	
Net current assets			22.13
Total assets less current liabilities			62.13
Debentures (10%)			(8.0)
Bank loan (12%)			(4.0)
Net assets			50.13
Financed by:			
Issued share capital			8.0
(par value 50p)			42.13
Shareholders funds			50.13

(b)   The table below compares Kolb's ratios with those of its major competitor:

	Competitor	Kolb
Return on (long term) capital employed	15%	15/51 = 29%
Return on equity	12.8%	9.6/39 = 25%
Operating Profit Margin	10%	12.5% (given)
Current ratio	1:25:1	30/24 = 1.25:1
Acid test	1:1:1	10/24 = 0.4:1
Gearing (total debt/equity)	33%	12/39 = 31%
Interest cover	6.0	15/1.28 = 11.7
Dividend cover	3.0	9.6/3.75 = 2.56

Kolb's profitability, in terms of ROCE/ROE and the operating profit margin compares very favourably with that of its, major competitor. The ROCE might be inflated by the use of a historic cost base, insofar as assets have never been revalued, but although a revaluation might depress ROCE, the company appears attractive compared to its peers. The net profit margin of 12.5% is above that of the major competitor, suggesting a cost advantage either in production, distribution or administration. Alternatively, it may be that Kolb operates in a market niche with a strong brand name, and are able to charge premium prices. The greatest differential lies in the return on equity, which is almost twice that of the competitor. This seems to be a consequence of the higher operating profit margin, because even with the financial gearing for Kolb almost matching that of the competitor there is still a high level of interest cover.

Set against the apparently strong profitability is Kolb's current poor level of liquidity. The acid-test ratio is well below that of the competitor, but in moving to internet selling, liquidity should improve, as one would expect the cash collection to coincide with orders and so cash balances to be consequently larger. The forecast balance sheet for 30 November 2001, which shows a cash balance of over £20 million compared with just £5 million the preceding year, is indicative of increased liquidity. Re-calculating the acid-test ratio for November 2001, it works out at 0.88:1. This ratio is close to that of the major competitor, and suggest that the financial year ending November 2001 is a critical one for improving the liquidity of Kolb.

Present borrowings are all long term. The debenture is due for repayment within the next two years, but this is unlikely to put a strain on liquidity since the growth in sales serves to generate cash, and there is currently no demand for cash for capital investment purposes. The balance sheet for the year ended 30 November 2001 indicates that there is more than sufficient cash to redeem the debenture after just one year. Gearing is almost equal to that of the competitors, but Kolb retains a relatively high level of interest cover, which suggests that there is scope for additional borrowing if required.

(c)   (i)   Earnings for year ending 30 November 2001 : £15.26m
                 P E ratio: 8
                 Market Capitalisation = 8 x 15.26 = £122.08 million

                 There are currently 16 million shares in issue, as this gives a price per share of £122.08/16 = £7.63 per share.

        (ii)   Issue 2 million shares on a 1 for 8 basis
                 Already in issue 16 million, therefore total shares in issue post rights equals 18 million.
                 Issue price per share = 0.75 (£7.63) = £5.73 per share
                 This means the sum raised by the issue is £11.46 million.
                 Theoretical ex-rights price is therefore:
                 £122.08 + £11.46 million/18million = £7.42

        (iii)   In calculating the theoretical ex-rights price one of the assumptions made is that cash from the rights issue will be invested by Kolb in a project which yields a positive NPV, so that the issue will leave individual investors neither any worse nor any better off. A related assumption is therefore that the NPV generated will represent a rate of return equal to that of the existing business – in other words, the overall return on capital employed remains constant. In the case of Kolb plc, the theoretical ex-rights price of £7.42 therefore implies that the company will earn an NPV on the US investment which allows it to continue to generate an ROCE of 29%.

        (iv)   The share price might be higher than the theoretical ex-rights price for a number of reasons including:
                 -     an increase in the company's forecast earnings if the new Web site proves particularly successful at generating sales.
                 -     a high positive NPV for the investment
                 -     a rise in the projected ROCE in response to a successful joint venture agreement with a US company
                 -     a general rise in the stock market, or shares in the web based retail sector
                 -     a rise in the brand value of Kolb products, which leads in turn to increased sales volumes.

◇ FOULKS*lynch*

(v)   The rights issue will clearly work to reduce the gearing of Kolb to very low levels. The sum raised by the issue is almost equal to the current level of total debt. This may seem to be a good thing insofar as it appears to reduce the risk to shareholders, but it will also serve to slow down the rate of growth of returns to equity which are likely to accompany business expansion.

The cost of debt is generally accepted as being lower than the cost of equity, and so the weighted cost of capital of a moderately geared company tends to be below that of a low geared company. After the rights issue, the level of gearing in Kolb will be very low, so that by introducing a reasonable level of new borrowing it may be possible to reduce the cost of capital. The forecast balance sheet suggests that there is scope to do this, particularly as the company currently has no short term borrowing at all.

The lower cost of capital which would result from increased gearing would then serve to increase the profit attributable to shareholders thereby increasing the return on equity. It may be that the managers of Kolb are very risk averse, and it is for this reason that they have opted for low financial gearing. Even so, they should note that gearing can work to the benefit of shareholders in a company such as Kolb, where interest cover is high, and sales and profits are rising.

(d) (i)   From the profit and loss account for the year ended 30 November 2001, the post tax return on equity is equal to $15.26/50.13 \times 100 = 30.4\%$

The proportion of profits reinvested	$= (15.26 - 4.125)/15.26 \times 100 = 72.97\%$
From the formula	g $= rB$
	g $= (0.304)(0.7297)$
	$= 0.22$ or 22%

(ii)   Historically, the company has increased its dividends at a rate of 10% per year, and so a growth rate of 22% would represent a very substantial rate of increase. The problem with the Gordon Growth Model calculation is party that it is dependent upon just one set of results, which may/may not be representative of the longer term trends for the business. The financial year ended November 2001 is one of strong expansion for Kolb, and also one in which its cash generation is high, and no money is spent on capital investment. This may therefore by highly unrepresentative as a set of figures on which to base future dividend growth forecasts.

At the same time, the intention to move into the US market is likely to require substantial investment, which may well exceed the value of the cash raised via the rights issue. Dividends serve to drain cash from a business, and reduce the level of retained earnings. If Kolb is serious about gaining a foothold in large new overseas markets, it would be wise to preserve its cash. Maintaining the current growth rate of dividends of 10% should be adequate to keep the shareholders happy. Earnings per share are already high, and if the investors have confidence that their cash is being invested wisely, the stock market is unlikely to mark the shares down because dividends not increase by as much as 22% per year.

2   Sludgewater plc

(a)   The expected present value of the fines is equal to:
$EV = (0.3 \times £1.0m) = (0.5 \times £1.8m) + (0.2 \times £2.6m)$
$= £0.3m + £0.9m + £0.52m$
$= £1.72$ million

Calculation of the net present value of the investment requires computation of the capital cost plus incremental production costs as set out in the following table:

£M	YEAR				
	0	1	2	3	4
Equipment purchase	(4.0)				
European Union grant		1.0			
Increased production costs		(0.315)	(0.331)	(0.347)	
Tax saving at 30%			0.095	0.099	0.104
Writing down allowance	1.0	0.75	0.563	1.687	
Tax saving on WDA		0.3	0.225	0.169	0.506

Net cash flow	(4.0)	0.985	(0.011)	(0.079)	0.61
Discount factor @ 10%	1	0.909	0.826	0.751	0.683
Present value of cash flow	(4.0)	0.895	(0.009)	(0.059)	0.417
Net Present Value = (£2.756m)					

The negative NPV on the investment in spray painting equipment exceeds the present value of the fines which Sludgewater might expect to pay. It therefore seems that the project is not viable in financial terms and it is cheaper to risk payment of the fines, although the company must accept that to do so might risk them incurring the wrath of both shareholders and the environmental lobby.

MEMORANDUM

(b)   **Memo to:**   Sludgewater Board
       Subject :   Air pollution

On purely non-financial criteria it can be argued that our company has a moral and community responsibility to install anti-pollution equipment so long as the cost of installation does not jeopardise the long term survival of the company.

The figurers appended suggest that the project is not wealth creating for Sludgewater's shareholders because the expected saving in fines is below the expected cost of the project. The difficulty is that this conclusion is very dependent upon the current size of the fines payable, and if they were to rise substantially, then the optimal choice (in financial terms) may change. The difference between the expected value of the fines and the cost of the project is currently just over £1 million. This means that the fines would need to rise by nearly 60% (1/1.7 x 100) before the project becomes financially worthwhile. Changes in the size of the fines would be very difficult to predict as it is a political issue, but since the company is a persistent offender, and the green lobby is becoming more influential, it is not unreasonable to anticipate that the fines will rise in the future as a result of political pressure.

It would be advisable from a public relations perspective, for the Board to consider alternative and perhaps less expensive anti-pollution measures, and it is also possible that the market for this company's products might increase if it is perceived to be more environmentally friendly, and if customers are sensitive to this. It is even possible that the company's share price may benefit from managers of 'ethical' investment funds deciding to include Sludgewater shares in their portfolio.

In addition the company needs to think about its long term strategic objectives, and its stance on anti-pollution systems in relation to these objectives. The market positioning of the company over the longer term is likely to be affected by decisions made in the short term, and so even if not investing in the project makes short term financial sense, it may be more attractive from a long term viewpoint. It is also possible that technological and legal circumstances will change over time, and such changes need to be anticipated in current decisions.

3   Capital

Note: The answers provided are fuller than would be expected from the average candidate under exam conditions. Answers are provided in this degree of detail on the principle of offering guidance on the approach required, and the range of knowledge that would be expected from an excellent candidate.

(a)   The term sales and leaseback describes an arrangement whereby a firm sells an asset (usually freehold land or buildings) to a financial institution in return for an agreement to lease the asset back from the purchaser. The asset sale generates a cash sum which is transferred immediately to the vendor. The vendor then makes regular rental payments for the right to use the asset. It is usual for the rental period to be such that the purchaser receives back in rental an amount equal to the initial purchase price plus a premium but retains permanent ownership of the asset.

The advantage of such schemes is that they offer the opportunity for companies to convert highly valuable liquid assets into cash, which can then be used to fund capital investment or business expansion. The main disadvantage for the vendor is the fact that selling the asset means that they can no longer get the benefit of any future appreciation in the capital value of the asset. A further disadvantage is the reduction in the balance sheet value of assets which can be used as security against future borrowing, although it is also true that less borrowing will be required as a result of the cash injection from the sale and leaseback.

SSAP21 defines a finance lease as 'a lease that transfers substantially all the risks and rewards of ownership of an asset to the lessee'. To quality as a finance lease the present value of the minimum lease payments must amount to more than 90% of the fair value of the leased asset. This allows the lessor to recover the value of the asset. Once these costs have been recovered i.e. in the later years of the lease, the lease payments may be of nominal value only, and at this stage the lease can be cancelled without penalty. The lease is often in operation for the whole useful life of the asset.

The advantage of such an arrangement is that the finance lease acts as a source of medium term finance for the purchase of fixed assets, and allows for smaller incremental cash flows rather than a single large purchase payment. At the same time, lease rental payments are usually subject to some tax relief. In return, the lessee takes on the responsibilities of owner of the asset, and so must meet all maintenance, insurance and operation costs. Under the current UK tax rules, the disadvantage of leasing is that any capital allowances which may be available on the asset purchase accrue to the lessor and not the lessee. If, however, the lessee does not have the tax liability to utilise such allowances then leasing will be the preferred option. The detail of the tax rules is likely to vary from country to country and so the relative merits of leasing will vary accordingly.

(b)   Hard capital rationing occurs when a firm is unable to take advantage of financially viable investment opportunities due to restrictions which are external to the organisation. The restrictions may arise out of government regulations, the general economic climate or perhaps stock market conditions. For example a firm may wish to raise finance to invest in a project which shows a positive NPV, but be unable to do so because of depressed stock market makes raising finance difficult under current conditions.

Soft capital rationing arises when the restrictions on investment are a result of the company itself deciding to limit the level of capital expenditure. The capital budget serves as a means of control, and may be relaxed or tightened as desired. Segments of divisionalised companies often have their capital budgets imposed by the main board of directors.

A company may purposefully choose to restrict its capital expenditure for a number of reasons including:

(i)   Lack of management expertise to fully exploit all of the available investment opportunities.

(ii)   A deliberate policy of only utilising internal funds for capital expenditure. Hence the level of spending is restricted to the level of such funds available.

(iii) Senior management may prefer to focus attention on the best and most carefully thought out proposals. In this regard, self imposed capital rationing may be an exercise in quality control.

(c)   Factoring and invoice discounting are two ways in which a company can obtain speeding payment for credit sales. Both work to shorten the working capital cycle and in turn speed up the rate of cash flow into the business. This may then allow the company to reduce its dependency on alternative, possibly more expensive sources of short term finance such as a bank overdraft.

The factor takes responsibility for administration of the sales ledger and collection of the debts, and passes the remaining 20% of the debt to the client company once the invoices have been settled. Factoring is a service offered by financial institutions which will lend the firm around 80% of the value of its debtors once the invoice has been issued to the customer. The balance due is paid net of fees and charges, which are split into interest and administration charges. The service charge will vary between 0.5% - 2.5% of sales and the interest charges will typically be around 1-3% above base rate.

Factoring may be classes as with or without recourse. In the latter case any bad debts will be the responsibility of the factor, and an additional fee will be charged to compensate the factor for this additional risk.

Invoice discounting is used when a company wishes to retain the role of debt collector, but still needs to speed up the cash flow. Invoice discounting involves a financial institution purchasing selected invoices from the client as a discount. The interest cost of the service is reflected in the size of the discount charted. The administration of customer accounts remains with the client company, and the debt to the discounter is settled when customer payments are received.

(d)   Elasticity of demand measures the extent to which the demand for a product changes in response to a change in some other variable. Price elasticity of demand therefore measures the responsiveness of demand to a change in the price of the goods in question. If the change in demand is *more* than proportional to the change in price, then demand is said to be price elastic. Conversely, when demand changes *less than proportionally* to the change in price, it is described a price inelastic.

◈ FOULKS*lynch*

Cross elasticity is used to describe the sensitivity of demands for one product to a change in the price of another. For example, one could measure the impact of a rise in the price of red wine upon the sales of white wine or vice versa.

Management need to monitor very frequently and carefully all their products for price and cross elasticity. This would involve keeping an eye on competitors' pricing and the development of a pricing policy which ensures that a satisfactory contribution is generated and is flexible enough to respond to competitive changes. For example, if a competitor's substitute product is reduced in price the company need to know how they will react. Pricing cannot simply be done using cost-plus methods – it has to also take account of market demand and the level of competition.

(e)   Venture capital is a term generally used to describe equity funding which is provided for new or rapidly growing small business. The venture capitalist provides an injection of equity funds which supplements that put in place by the founding investors. This type of finance is offered by specialist institutions such as 3 (i)., who require management of fund applicants to produce a detailed business plan showing how the company will develop over the next few years. Venture capital funds do not usually expect to receive dividends on their investment, but instead look for substantial capital gain within a three to five year time scale. A large number of venture capital funds regain their initial investment via an initial public offering of the applicant company. For example, the venture capital firm may invest £2 million into a business via the purchase of a fixed equity share say 10%. If the company is then floated on the stock exchange five years later for a total value of £150 million, then the value of the tenure capitalist's stake has increased to £15 million. This investment can then be realised via direct sale of the shares in the market.

(f)   *Note:* This answer is based around current UK tax regulations.

Taxation can affect capital investment decisions in two key ways – firstly via the tax payable on the incremental cash flow arising from the investment and secondly via the application of writing down allowances. Any investment which yields a positive net present value will increase the worth of the business via an addition to profit either through higher sales or lower costs. The profit is subject to tax and so the additional tax burden reduces the value of the investment to the shareholders.

At the same time, for example, the current UK capital allowance regime allows companies to claim writing down allowances on investments in capital equipment. The current allowance rate is 25% calculated on a reducing balance. This allowance then reduces the amount of tax payable by the investing company. For example, if a company invested £2 million on which it was entitled to a 25% writing down allowance, then in the year of the investment the company could claim an allowance of £500,000. This would reduce the tax liability for that year, which is payable the following year. If tax is charged at 30% the cash value of the allowance in terms of the reduced tax payable is 30% of £500,00 i.e. £150,000.

The purpose of such allowances is, theoretically capital investment in the relief that such investments help to make industry more efficient and hence more competitive. Whether the allowances have this effect is debatable. A number of observers argue that the incentive would be more substantive if 100% first year allowance were implemented for all capital purchases in place of the current system.

The imposition of tax on the profits arising from capital investments has the general effect of reducing the net present value of the cash flows, thereby discouraging investment. Conversely, the granting of tax relief on debt finance, which may be used to fund such investments serves to cut the cost of capital, thereby encouraging capital investment. It is thus very difficult to disentangle the combined effect of revenue taxes, tax relief on borrowing and writing down allowances to determine whether the current tax regime encourages or discourages investment. It is likely that in reality the tax effect are peculiar to the individual company, as the tax liability and hence the opportunity to take advantage of any tax breaks that might be available, will be dependent upon individual circumstances.

4   Management accounting

(a)   The accuracy of the statement depends on the interpretation of the terms *costing* and *management control.* Costing can involve the ascertainment of costs, for example, of products, services, activities, machines, departments or divisions. Typical purposes of ascertaining these costs may be stock valuation, pricing, make or buy decisions or judgement of operating efficiency. For such purposes they may be full costs, variable costs or some permutation of decision-relevant costs. In this wide context it embraces much of the management accountant's work which may be part of a regular routine as in many standard costing systems or it may be part of an ad hoc reporting procedure.

Control in the enterprise implies the provision of information so that management may take some corrective action, where necessary, to bring events back on track. That is the regular reporting of events and deviations on an exception basis. This suggests the existence of a plan and desired course of action against which control may be exercised. The plan will have been specified by the longer-term objectives of the organisation and its strategy for attaining these objectives. This would be envisaged to take place within a framework of responsibility accounting and management by objectives including both financial and non-financial information.

In this light the terms costing and management control include the preparation of costs for various decision purposes and of information to support organisational planning and control activities. It does therefore, cover quite widely, the purpose of management accounting systems, though it doesn't make reference to drawing data from the external environment or the use of insights into competitor's activities which are increasingly occurring in the context of Strategic Management Accounting.

(b)   It will be the responsibility of the management accountant to serve the information needs of three management groups identified in the question – retail stores, transport and warehouse. Other functions not specifically mentioned could involve personnel and training, purchasing and marketing, some of the responsibility for the latter two being located centrally. We have no information regarding the extent to which this company undertakes these other functions so detailed comment will not occur though the sort of information would follow the pattern for the other functions described below.

Stores

Costing information would be the basis of setting minimum prices, making special offers and the range of mark up possibilities. Such decisions would be likely to apply to major lines and be based on predicted sales volumes and perceived minimum or break-even levels of demand for each store and the company as a whole. Any sales promotions by product manufacturers or competitive moves against other retailers would be taken into account. The extent to which individual stores had discretion to make pricing decisions would dictate the degree of detail available in stores or whether this information is maintained centrally. If this was a centralised function greater detail would be maintained at head office and the dictated policy would be confirmed by regular reports of gross margin by store and by major product group.

Retail store management would require regular reports on controllable costs (wages and some overheads) compared with a flexible budget. Some store costs may be fixed and hence not amenable to the use of a flexed budget. There should be scope however to manage staff levels to cope with busy and slack periods. Sales in total and by major product line should be monitored and compared with a budget and last year's sales. A monthly profit and loss summary should be provided which focuses on controllable profit with any head office cost allocations shown separately.

Stores would have responsibility for some parts of the company's working capital, for example, regular banking or takings for transmission to a central bank account and management of stock. Local stock levels and the rate and frequency of replenishment of major lines would also be the subject of regular reporting. Sales per square foot of floor space would be an example of a useful statistic for each store and major product line.

Transport

The responsibility of the transport fleet will be the supplying of stores efficiently and running the fleet as economically as possible. Cost reports on wages, vehicle repairs and other running costs in comparison with budget would be required. Statistics for measurement of vehicle use and mileage travelled in addition to data to select the most cost-effective delivery routes would be required. Some of this latter information would probably be located in the head office to enable some central direction of transport to take place.

Warehouse

Attention of the warehouse management must focus on efficient stock control. The right products must be delivered to store when required, yet they should not hold too much in stock as this ties up capital and products could eventually deteriorate. Some inputs for the mathematical models which help with stock management could fall within the remit of the management accountant. Reports therefore on stock levels and rate of stock turnover should be a priority in addition to the monitoring of costs. It is also likely that for some products, direct delivery from the supplier would be the practice and information to confirm the cost effectiveness of this practice should be maintained.

Head Office

The overall direction of the company will take place from the head office; this would involve senior management who would receive information on the performance of their functional areas in a more aggregated form and of a more strategic nature than at individual locations.

A centralised sales and marketing function governing price setting, advertising and sales promotion could be envisaged. In addition to summary sales statistics provided as routine to individual stores' management (see above), information from sources external to the company would be desirable, for example, covering market size or competitors' price levels. Additionally date to plot the longer-term activities such as market size, changing tastes, population trends and demographic statistics. This data would inform future development involving store extensions and the building of new stores as well as space management in stores. Some of this latter material will be generated by market researchers and may not be the remit of the management accountant alone.

5   Bicycles

(a)   (i)

$$\text{Break-even point} = \frac{\text{Fixed Costs}}{\text{Contribution per Unit}}$$

Fixed Costs = £1,200,000 + £340,000 = £1,540,000
Variable costs per unit = £45 + £15 + £15 (from Table 1) = £75

Hence Break-even point $= \dfrac{£1,540,000}{£190-£75} = \dfrac{£1,540,000}{£115}$

$= 13,391$ units

(ii)

		£000
Sales	11,800 units x £190	2,242
Variable costs	11,800 units x £75	885
		1,357
Fixed costs	11,800 units x £75	1,540
Loss		183

(b)   (i)   Manufacturing fixed overhead volume variance:

Budgeted volume	20,000 units
Actual volume	16,800 units
	3,200 units

Manufacturing fixed overhead rate (from Table 1):
$\dfrac{£1,200,000}{20,000} = $ £60 per unit

Volume variance (3,200 x £60)   £192,000

The volume variance is caused by the actual production level for the period falling below the volume that was used to compute the fixed overhead recovery rate, in this case the budgeted volume. It is an under-recovery of fixed overhead, which the company charged against the profits for the period. It occurs because an absorption costing system identifies fixed overhead costs with products based on a unit rate. It does not specifically represent an extra cots or a loss to the company as these fixed costs would be incurred anyway. But it acts as a basis of the reconciliation, of costs and profit, between the budgeted and actual volume of the period.

(iii)   Variable selling overhead:

		£000
Recovered/Flexible budget:		
11,800 x £15	=	177
Incurred		138
Expenditure variance		39 Fav.

Fixed selling overhead:

Recovered:		
11,800 x £17	=	200.6
Budget		340.0
Volume variance		139,4 Adv.
Budget		340
Incurred		376
Expenditure variance		36 Adv.

(c)

		£000
Predicted loss		183
Expenditure variances:		
Manufacturing	48A	
Variable sales	39F	
Fixed sales	36A	
Fixed overhead carried forward		
In stock value	300F	
		255F
Actual profit		72

An explanation of why an actual profit is revealed when a loss was anticipated by the sales manager is contained within the reconciliation above. To develop this explanation a little. The reconciliation is achieved when all the differences between the two statements are accounted for. This involves expenditure variances which were not in the budgeted cost statement but which were adjusted in the actual profit statement. It is not appropriate to adjust for volume variances (apart from any change in stock) as both statements are ultimately based on the actual fixed costs and these are the only costs to which volume variances apply.

Finally, and most significantly, a variable costing statement applies only variable manufacturing costs to stock values. An absorption costing statement, which the company uses for reporting actual results, values stock at full manufacturing costs. The production and sales levels for the period imply 5,000 units were added to stock, therefore a difference between the two stock values accounts for a difference in profit. The absorption costing statement is adjusted (relieved of cost) by fixed overhead carried forward in the increased stock value. That is 5,000 units at £60 per unit fixed overhead rate, £300,000. Thus the loss anticipated by the sales manager becomes a profit in the actual results reported.

6   Private hospital

(a)   For the year to 31 May 2001:

$$\text{Actual patient days} \quad \frac{£4.4m}{£200} \quad = \quad 22,000$$

$$\text{Bed Occupancy} \quad \frac{22,000}{29,200} \quad = \quad 75\%$$

Profit/(Loss)	£	£
Total revenue		4,400,000
Variable costs		1,100,000
		3,300,000
Personnel	4 x £22,000	
	13 x £16,000	
	24 x £12,000	584,000
Fixed charges		1,650,000
Profit		1,066,000

$$\text{Break-even point(s)} = \frac{\text{Fixed costs}}{\text{Contribution per patient day}}$$

Fixed costs consist of fixed charges and personnel costs for the bands of patient days shown in the question. The contribution per patient day is £150, being the charge per day of £200 less the variable cost of £50 per day.

Given the stepped nature of the staffing costs there are three break-even levels which can be calculated, two are shown below.
14,254 patient days (£1,650,000 + £488,000)£150 and
14,893 patient days (£1,650,000 + £584,000)/£150

Note: Two for the break-even points are shown above, the highest shown below for reference, is unlikely to apply for the year to May 2001 and therefore is not required a part of the answer to (a).

15,427 patient days (£1,650,000 + £664,000)/£150

(b) The changes for the year to 31 May 2002 are 20 extra beds occupied for 100 days. This has implications for bed capacity and for the patient days, and thus for the variable and fixed costs charged and the personnel employed.

Budget for year to 31 May 2002:
Revised patient days   22,000 + 100 x 20 = 24,000

$$\text{Bed occupancy} \quad \frac{24,000}{36,500} = 66\%$$

Revised profit/loss

		£
Total revenue		4,800,000
Variable costs		1,200,000
		3,600,000
Personnel	4 x £24,200	
	15 x £17,600	
	28,£13,200	730,400
Fixed charges	$\frac{100}{80}$ × £1,650,000	2,062,500
Profit		807,100

Required profit £1,066,000
Required contribution = R1,066,000 + £730,400 + £2,062,500 = £3,858,900
Required patient days = (£3,858,900/£150) = 25,72 days per year in 2002 to achieve the same profit as in 2001. This calculation uses the highest level of staffing costs.

(c) In the year to May 2001 the bed occupancy for 100 days was 100% (i.e. 8,000 patient days) and for the remaining 265 days it was 66% (22,000-8,000)/(265 days x 80 beds). Attempting to deal with the 100 days extra demand with 20 extra beds would reduce the overall occupancy from 75% to 66%. To cater for the 2,000 patient days demanded an extra number of potential patient days of 7,300 (365 x 20) were provided, this usage rate of 27% is a little unrealistic for this business. The extra fixed costs of bed capacity and extra costs of personnel (including the higher employment costs) exceed the extra contribution from patients by £258,900 which shows as a reduction in profit.

If the paediatric unit proceed to provide 2,000 extra patient days in this way, they will suffer a reduced profit of almost 25% when they have also covered the increased employment costs. They would have to achieve another 1,726 patient days per year, above the level anticipated for the year to May 2002, to attain the profit level reported in May 2001. They could accept the profit reduction in the interests of meeting their other objectives of patient and social welfare, but for a private sector company this seems unlikely. They would require a significant increase in patient occupancy to regain the profit position assuming no further changes to costs.

Possible alternative courses of action would be to account for bed occupancy differently, being more flexible and charging for part of a year. That may involve having beds available to move to areas of high demand as the occasion arises. Alternatively the hospital may decide to de-emphasise the net profit measure because of the influence of fixed costs, they could focus on contribution rather than profit. Achieving the 2,000 extra patient days would increase the contribution after personnel costs of £153,600. But this would have the disadvantage of not highlighting the efficient occupation of beds in this unit or, no doubt throughout the whole hospital, which may have adverse repercussions on overall profitability.

Attention to improved planning of bed occupation could offer improvements in terms of increasing overall occupancy. One option if not already undertaken, would be to prioritise demand for the paediatric unit when it has no empty beds available. This would involve treating the most urgent cases first, rather than first come first served, leaving less urgent cases until demand has fallen away during the remaining 265 days. This would not alter the fact that people were waiting for admission (or the size of the waiting list), though to the extent it was not adopted before, arguably it would improve the overall welfare of society.

(d)   Any business will have a variety of objectives. Some of these will be orientated towards financial aspects, for example, achieving sufficient profitability to enable an adequate return to shareholders or staying within a financial budget allocation of revenue. Social objectives involve provision of an adequate level of public health and welfare, safety and security education opportunities etc.

For many businesses there is likely to be a conflict between financial and social aspects. In other words greater financial return can be achieved only at the expense of poorer social provision of the reduced change of meeting social objectives. Alternatively, improved social provision is possible but the chance of achieving financial objectives may be compromised. This is where management judgement is often needed in balancing the trade-off between these objectives in any given situation.

In the provision of health care, improved quality of care or shorter waiting lists can be achieved if more public sector funding is provided or, in the private sector business, if a smaller profit is earned or higher prices are charged. In education likewise, one can always spend more to employ more teachers, reduce class sizes and improve education but this will add considerably to the costs incurred. The private sector will generally make provision only where it will achieve adequate financial return. Some aspects of social provision can be perceived to be so important that they are provided by the government because they are unlikely to be provided in entirety by a profit seeking business.

June 2001 Marking scheme

					Marks
1	(a)		Profit & loss a/c to Dec 2000	2	
			Profit & loss a/c to Dec 2001	2	
			Balance Sheet y/ended 31 Dec 2001	2	6
	(b)		Emphasis needs to be on discussion rather than calculation		
			Profitability: ROCE and ROE calculation	1	
			Comment on ROCE and margin	2	
			Liquidity: Current and acid test ratios	1	
			Comment	1	
			Gearing: Long-term:short-term debt mix	1	
			High interest cover and gearing ratio	1	
			Comment re redemption of debt	1	
					8
	(c)	(i)	Calculation of market capitalisation	2	
			Price per share	1	
					3
		(ii)	Issue price	1	
			Ex rights price peer share	1	
					2
		(iii)	1 mark per assumption with an extra mark where discussion is high quality up to maximum		3
		(iv)	1 mark per suggestion up to the maximum		3
		(v)	Lowered gearing + comment	2	
			Impact on WACC + comment	2	
			Impact on profit to equity + comment	2	
					6
	(d)	(i)	1 mark each for calculation of r and B		
			2 marks for final calculation	4	
		(ii)	1 mark per sensible comment, with extra mark for comment on problem of single year as a basis for calculation	5	
					9
			Total Maximum		**40**
2	(a)		Omission of consultants fee	1	
			EV fines	2	
			Production costs	1	
			Tax saving on higher costs	1	
			Writing down allowance	1	
			Tax on WDA	1	
			Net cash flow	1	
			Discount factor	1	
			Net present value	1	
			Discussion	2	
					12
	(b)		Memo format	1	
			Community responsibility	2	
			Significance of fine size	2	
			Possible changes in fines	1	
			Market effect of pollution avoidance	2	
					8
			Total Maximum		**20**

Marks

3	(a)	Sale and leaseback description	2
		Leasing description	3
			5
	(b)	Definitions (1 mark for each)	2
		Reasons for rationing – 1 mark each to max.	3
			5
	(c)	Definitions – 1 mark each	2
		Differences	1
		Benefits of each – 1 mark each	2
			5
	(d)	Definitions – 1 mark each	2
		Relevance to pricing decision, 1 mark per sensible comments	Max 3
			5
	(e)	Definition	1
		Link to specialist providers	1
		Investment for capital gain	1
		Alternative exit routes	1
		Overall quality of discussion	1
			5
	(f)	Twin impact – 1 mark each	2
		Shareholder impact of tax	1
		Explanation of WDA in reducing the net cost of investing	2
			5
		Total Maximum	**30**
4	(a)	Explain and develop costing	2
		Explain and develop control	2
		Other issues/evidence of judgement	2
			6
	(b)	2 marks for development of applied points on costing, control, strategy, non-financial measures etc., for each function mentioned and H/O	14
		Total Maximum	**20**
5	(a)	(i) BEP calculation	2
		(ii) Budgeted loss	2
			4
	(b)	(i) Variance calculation	2
		Explanation	3
			5
		(ii) Each variance 1 mark	3
	(c)	Expenditure variances	2
		Overheads in stock	2
		Achieving correct reconciliation	2
		Explanation	2
			8
		Total Maximum	**20**

				Marks
6	(a)	Patient days	1	
		Occupancy	1	
		Profit/loss	2	
		Break-even number(s)	2	
				6
	(b)	Patient days	1	
		Occupancy	1	
		Profit/loss	2	
		Required patient days	1	
				5
	(c)	Each developed point 2 marks		6
	(d)	Objectives	1	
		Conflict	1	
		Example	1	
				$\underline{3}$
		Total Maximum		$\underline{\underline{20}}$

Section 9

NEW SYLLABUS EXAMINATIONS

Pilot Paper 2001 Questions

Section A - This question is compulsory and MUST be attempted

1   Frantic Ltd

Frantic Ltd is a specialist car manufacturer and is a member of a group of companies that provides a range of automobile products and services. It is currently facing difficulties in the management of its working capital and the financial controller of Frantic Ltd is to investigate the situation with a view to optimising creditor payments, stock ordering and debtor discounts to ease projected cash flow problems.

Creditors

Creditors arise only for engine purchases. Engine suppliers have offered an early settlement discount of 15% if invoices are settled within one month of delivery. If the settlement discount is not taken, normal payment terms of two months from delivery apply.

Stock

Frantic has a budgeted production of 800 cars for the year. The most expensive bought-in component for the cars are engines. Other components are either made in-house or are minor items which are bought-in but which do not require special stock management. Engine purchase prices are subject to quantity discounts according to the following schedule:

Order quantity	Discount
0-49 units	0%
50-249 units	2%
above 249 units	3%

Other details are:
Engine price (before discounts): £1,300
Stock holding costs per annum
(as a percentage of engine costs): 22%
Delivery costs per order: £1,200
There is zero lead-time on engine orders.

Debtors

The cars are sold at £42,500 each and unit sales are equal to the units produced in each month. 50% of the cars are made to order and payment is on a cash on delivery basis. The remaining cars are sold to specialist retailers who take two months' credit. Frantic is considering offering the specialist retailers a 2% discount for payments made within one month of sale. It is expected that 75% of the retailers would take up the offer.

Other factors

A budget forecast is to be prepared for a six-month period. Other variable costs (including the other components) represent 65% of sales value and are payable immediately. Fixed costs are £18,000 per month for the first three months, rising to £22,000 per month thereafter. The first instalment of £3.2 million for a major re-tooling operation will be paid in month three of the budget forecast.

Assume that the opening bank overdraft is £25,000 and that there are creditors outstanding to the value of £97,500 which will be paid in the first month of the budget plan. It is expected that debtors payments of £1,062,500 will be received in each of the first two months.

The company uses its bank overdraft rate of 15% as its discount rate. Assume one month comprises 30 days, that no opening stock of engines is held and that production is evenly spread throughout the year.

Required:

(a)   Calculate:

(i)   if it is beneficial for Frantic to change from a two month payment period to a one month payment period for creditors   **(3 marks)**

(ii)   the optimal ordering policy for engines   **(6 marks)**

(iii)   if it is beneficial for Frantic to implement the 2% discount for debtors.   **(3 marks)**

(b)   On the basis of your answer to part (a), and the information given above, prepare the cash budget for Frantic for each of the next six months.   **(18 marks)**

(c)   Write a report to the Managing Director which identifies:

-    how cash flow problems can arise

-    the methods available for easing cash shortages

-    the techniques, besides cash budgeting, that could be used to monitor and manage cash resources

-    the benefits of centralising cash management in a treasury department for group companies.   **(20 marks)**

In all of your answers clearly state any assumptions you make.   **(Total: 50 marks)**

Section B - TWO questions ONLY to be attempted

2   Associated International Supplies Ltd

The following are summary financial statements for Associated International Supplies Ltd.

	1994 £'000	1999 £'000
Fixed Assets	115	410
Current Assets	650	1,000
Current Liabilities	513	982
Long Term Liabilities	42	158
Total	210	270
Capital and Reserves	210	270

	1994 £'000	1999 £'000
Sales	1,200	3,010
Cost of sales, expenses and interest	1,102	2,860
Profit before tax	98	150
Tax and distributions	33	133
Retained earnings	65	17

Notes

Cost of sales was £530,000 for 1994 and £1,330,000 for 1999.
Debtors are 50% of current assets and trade creditors are 25% of current liabilities for both years.

Required:

(a)   You are a consultant advising Associated International Supplies Ltd. Using suitable financial ratios, and paying particular attention to growth and liquidity, write a report on the significant changes faced by the company since 1994. The report should also comment on the capacity of the company to continue trading, together with any other factors considered appropriate.

An appendix to the report should be used to outline your calculations.   **(17 marks)**

(b)   Explain and evaluate the sources of finance available to small businesses for fixed assets.   **(8 marks)**
(Total: 25 marks)

3   Bread Products Ltd

Bread Products Ltd is considering the replacement policy for its industrial size ovens which are used as part of a production line that bakes bread. Given its heavy usage each oven has to be replaced frequently. The choice is between replacing every two years or every three years. Only one type of oven is used, each of which costs £24,500. Maintenance costs and resale values are as follows:

Year	Maintenance per annum £	Resale value £
1	500	
2	800	15,600
3	1,500	11,200

Original cost, maintenance costs and resale values are expressed in current prices. That is, for example, maintenance for a two year old oven would cost £800 for maintenance undertaken now. It is expected that maintenance costs will increase at 10% per annum and oven replacement cost and resale values at 5% per annum. The money discount rate is 15%.

Required:

(a)   Calculate the preferred replacement policy for the ovens in a choice between a two year or three year replacement cycle.   **(12 marks)**

(b)   Identify the limitations of Net Present Value techniques when applied generally to investment appraisal.
    (13 marks)
(Total: 25 marks)

4   Pan-Ocean Chemicals

Pan-Ocean Chemicals has one product which requires inputs from three types of material to produce batches of product Synthon. Standard cost details for a single batch are shown below:

	Materials			**Labour**	
Material type	Standard Kgs	Standard price per Kg (£)	Standard hours	Standard rate per hour (£)	
S1	8	0.3	1	5.00	
S2	5	0.5			
S3	3	0.4			

A standard loss of 10% of input is expected. Actual production was 15,408 kgs for the previous week. Details of the materials used were:

Actual material used (kg)

S1	8,284
S2	7,535
S3	3,334

Total labour cost for the week was £6,916 for 1,235 hours worked.

Required:

(a)   Calculate:

    (i)   total material mix, yield and usage variances   **(9 marks)**

    (ii)   labour rate and efficiency variances.   **(2 marks)**

(b)   Explain why the sum of the mix variances for materials measured in kg should be zero.   **(3 marks)**

(c)   Write a report to management which explains and interprets your results in part (a). The report should pay particular attention to:

-    explaining what is meant by mix and yield variances in respect of materials, and

-    possible reasons for all the results you have derived.   **(11 marks)**
    (Total: 25 marks)

5   ABC

(a)   Discuss the conditions under which the introduction of ABC is likely to be most effective, paying particular attention to:

-    product mix
-    the significance of overheads and the ABC method of charging costs
-    the availability of information collection procedures and resources, and
-    other appropriate factors.   **(17 marks)**

(b)   Explain why ABC might lead to a more accurate assessment of management performance than absorption costing.   **(8 marks)**
    (Total: 25 marks)

Pilot Paper 2001 Answers

1   *Frantic Ltd*

(a)   (i)   **Creditor policy**

The establishment of creditor payment policy involves a comparison of interest rates with the number of days credit in relation to the cash discount available.

Taking the discount yields a return of:

(discount %)/(100 − discount %) × (365/(final date − discount date)) = 1.5/98.5 × 365/(60-30) = 18.52% which is more than the discount rate the company uses and hence a one month payment policy is preferable.

Alternatively:

		No *Discount* £	*With* *Discount* £
Payment to supplier (per engine)		1,300.0	1,280.5
Return from investing £1,280.5 for (60 − 30) = 30 days: 1,280.5 × (30/365) × 15%		-	15.8
		1,300.0	1,296.3

Hence, taking the discount costs less.

This can be checked as: [(1,300 − 1,2805) × (365/30)]/1,280.5 = 18.52%.

(ii)   **Stock evaluation without early discounting**

Stock evaluation: production = 800 cars.

EOQ ignoring volume discounts = √[(2 × delivery costs × annual demand)/(holding costs per unit)] = √[(2 × 1,200 × 800)/(22% × 1,300)] = 81.93 or 82 whole units.

At this level a quantity discount would apply. Re-working the previous calculation with the quantity discount gives: = √[(2 × 1,200 × 800)/(22% × 1,300 × 98%)] = 82.76 or 83 whole units.

Hence the choice facing Frantic Ltd is between ordering 83 units or 250.

Unit evaluation for an order quantity of 83:

		£
Total purchase costs:	1,300 × 98% × 800 =	1,019,200
Holding costs:	0.5 × 83 × 1,300 x 98% × 22% =	11,631
Order costs:	(800/83) × 1200 =	11,566
Total annual costs:		1,042,397

Unit evaluation for an order quantity of 250:

		£
Total purchase costs:	$1,300 \times 97\% \times 800 =$	1,008,800
Holding costs:	$0.5 \times 250 \times 1300 \times 97\% \times 22\% =$	34,677
Order costs:	$(800/250) \times 1200 =$	3,840
Total annual costs:		1,047,317

An alternative answer relies on the basic EOQ calculation, adjusted for the appropriate discount, resulting in 83 units per order and then compares this with an ordering policy of 250 in the following incremental cost manner:

	£	£
Saving in purchase price $(1\% \times 800 \times 1,300) =$		10,400
Saving in ordering costs: $((800 \times 1,200)/83] – [(800 \times 1,200)/250] =$		7,726
Total cost savings		18,126
Holding costs at 250 (above):	34,677	
Holding costs at 83 (above):	11,631	
Additional holding costs:		23,046
Increased costs arising from ordering 250 units		4,920

Hence, the same conclusion is reached.

The optimal policy is therefore to order 83 engines at a time.

(iii) **Debtors**

Offering the discount implies a percentage cost of:

(discount %)/(100 – discount %) × (365/(final date – discount date)) = 2.0/98.0 × 365/(60 – 30) = 24.8%

This is more than the discount rate the company uses and is hence not worthwhile.

Alternatively, for every £100 worth of debtors:

	No Discount £	With Discount £
Receipt from debtor	100.0	98.0
Return from investing £98 for (60-30)=30 days; $98 \times (30/365) \times 15\%$	-	1.2
	100.0	99.2

This can be checked as: $[(100 – 98) \times (365/30)]1/98 = 24.8\%$.

Hence, it is not worthwhile to offer the discount.

(b)   As stated, the optimal policy is to order 83 engines at a time. This involves ordering 800/83 = 9.64 times per year. A production schedule can be drawn-up to assess when the orders would be made. If this is undertaken the following ordering schedule would result:

Month	1	2	3	4	5	6	7	8	9	10	11	12
Car production[1]	66.7	66.7	66.7	66.7	66.7	66.7	667	66.7	66.7	66.7	66.7	66.7
Orders placed	83	83	83	83	83		83	83	83	83		83
Stock at month-end	16	32	48	64	80	13	29	45	61	77	10	26

◆ FOULKS*lynch*

Thus, no orders are placed in the sixth month. This does not have any implications for the six month cash flow since creditors will be paid with one month delay (as determined by the answer to part (a)(i)).

Cash flow for first six months:

Month	1	2	3	4	5	6
Cash sales	1,416,667	1,416,667	1,416,667	1,416,667	1,416,667	1,416,667
Credit sales	1,062,500	1,062,500	1,416,667	1,416,667	1,416,667	1,416,667
Total income	**2,479,167**	**2,479,167**	**2,833,334**	**2,833,334**	**2,833,334**	**2,833,334**
Engine costs	97,500	106,281	106,281	106,281	106,281	106,281
Other expenses	1,841,667	1,841,667	1,841,667	1,841,667	1,841,667	1,841,667
Fixed costs	18,000	18,000	18,000	22,000	22,000	22,000
Capital costs			3,200,000			
Costs net of overdraft	**1,957,167**	**1,965,948**	**5,165,948**	**1,969,948**	**1,969,948**	**1,969,948**
Opening bank balance	−25,000	496,687	1,009,906	−1,322,708	−475,856	381,581
Overdraft costs	−313			−16,534	−5,949	
Closing bank balance	496,687	1,009,906	−1,322,708	−475,856	381,581	1,244,967

Notes:

(1)   Engine costs are $83 \times 98 - 5\% \times £1,300 = 106,281$ per month.

(2)   Other expenses are $65\% \times$ monthly sales $= 65\% \times (800/12) \times £42,500 = 1,841,667$.

(3)   Overdraft costs calculated as $(1/12) \times 15\% \times$ opening bank balance. Other bases of calculation acceptable such as average balances.

[1]Fractional production allowed and reflected in work in progress

(c)   **Report on cash budgeting**

Circulation: Managing Director and Senior Management Team
Author:
Date:

Introduction

This report addresses a number of key issues concerning Frantic's cash flow position and has four elements which are of immediate concern to Frantic.

How cash flow problems arise

It is important first to distinguish between profitability and cash availability. The key idea relates to insolvency since even profitable companies can face insolvency if cash positions are not properly managed.

Thus cash positions require management to avoid the difficulties associated with cash shortages. Cash shortages are likely to arise in a number of situations. The following is not an exhaustive list, but is likely to represent the most common. Cash flow problems can arise due to:

(i)   sustained losses in the business such that cash resources have been drawn-down;

(ii)   difficulties in dealing with inflating costs combined with an inability to raise sales prices proportionately;

(iii)   overtrading and inadequate financing of growth. This is very common with new businesses who are not able to finance working capital requirements sufficiently. Generally, such problems are associated with under-capitalised businesses and a lack of recognition that working capital requirements require a large base of long-term capital funding;

(iv)   seasonal trading against ongoing costs. This situation arises where income from sales is variable according to the time of year but fairly even monthly outgoings have to be met;

(v)   unplanned one-off large items of expenditure. This may arise, for example, as a result of a break down of a large piece of machinery; and

(vi)   poor credit management.

The importance and impact of each item will depend on a number of factors. Thus, losses may be sustained for a period depending on how large cash resources are, whether in the form of positive bank balances or the availability of overdraft facilities. Inflating costs above inflating sales prices is not sustainable in the long-run. The importance of this may depend on the capability of the business to implement cost savings, or to diversify markets where prices could be increased. Over trading is a problem of forecasting and planning for adequate long-term capital. The idea is that growth should be within available resources. Seasonal trading requires careful cash management and the extent to which cash resources can be smoothed over the year. Unplanned major items of expenditure may be important if alternative sources of finance are not available, such as leasing.

Methods of easing cash shortages

There is a variety of techniques which can potentially offset the effects of cash shortages. In the long-term, however, the adequacy of cash has to be addressed. Thus, for example, cash shortages may be alleviated by:

(i)   postponement of expenditure where feasible. This would not be feasible in the payment of staff wages, but might be in relation to replacing an old piece of equipment that is still working;

(ii)   accelerating inflows. For example, by more effective use of credit collection, better credit control, improved early payment incentives, or even the factoring of debt;

(iii)   sale of redundant assets either before or after any necessary re-organisation. This may involve the sale of a building where accommodation can be centralised. Other assets may be sold on a sale and lease-back basis, although careful consideration will have to be given to the net benefits arising from this; and

(iv)   re-negotiation of supplier terms or overdraft arrangements. In particular, bank debt may be mortgaged or secured to access lower rates. Suppliers may agree to lower prices or longer terms if negotiated agreements can be formalised such that a certain level of purchases are made over a period of time.

The importance of each item will depend on the degree of flexibility Frantic has in its financial structure and agreements. The room for manoeuvre may be limited but a thorough review of all possibilities is likely to yield at least a number of options. Furthermore, the impact of each potential response depends on how efficient Frantic has been in arranging its affairs in the first place. Finally, none of the items listed will have a sustained impact if the core problem is not identified and dealt-with.

Managing cash resources

There are a variety of methods which may be of use in managing resources. The particular tool chosen will depend on its reliability and appropriateness. Appropriateness, in turn, will be governed by the underlying assumptions of the technique employed. Some of the methods that may be used to managed cash resources are listed below:

(i)   Inventory approach to cash management. This method views cash in the same way as engine stock such that EOQ models may be employed. in such circumstances, cash is viewed as an asset with costs associated with it that should be minimised so as to determine what level of cash balances should be held. Thus, decreases or increases in cash balances can be determined according to planned growth, the time value of money and the costs of obtaining new funds.

(ii)   The Miller-Orr model recognises that cash balance requirements are likely to fluctuate and that active management is required in responding to these fluctuations. In particular, attention is paid to the variability (or variance) of cash flows, interest rates and the transaction costs of adjusting cash balances. It is the variability of cash balances that is crucial to understanding cash management since this will depend directly on understanding how Frantic's operations (fundamentally, sales and production) vary. For a volatile business, it is likely that large cash balances will need to be kept. Miller-Orr suggest a simple formula to estimate this although the formula itself is limited by the assumptions on which it rests.

(iii)   Probability approaches recognise a degree of uncertainty in predicting cash balances and allow for a range of outcomes to occur. If the assessment of such probabilities is accurate then cash resources can be put in place in readiness for the predicted events. The method is not wholly reliable in situations where the number of potential outcomes is small since unfeasible expected outcomes may be predicted by using a probability approach.

(iv)   Cash management is about managing surplus cash, also. The response of management should depend on whether the surplus is large and how long it is likely to exist. If the balance is large and is likely to remain then management have a duty to look for appropriate investment opportunities or else refund the investors with a special dividend, for example. Smaller cash balances can be actively managed via short term deposits.

A centralised treasury function

Treasury departments are normally a feature of larger companies than Frantic although it is perhaps beneficial to consider the benefits of such departments to assess what, if any, practices might reasonably be adopted. Essentially, treasury centralisation is an issue concerned with. economies of scale. The benefits of treasury departments are numerous and include:

(i)   consolidating bank accounts to create either a single account through which all cash resources are managed or a virtual single account with automatic offset between different accounts. Such an approach maximises deposit interest which is typically higher on larger cash balances for positive balances whilst minimising overdraft costs for negative balances.

(ii)   Borrowings can be arranged in bulk thus accessing lower rates.

(iii)   Foreign exchange management is improved. In the same way that cash balances are effectively consolidated then so can foreign exchange risk without the need to enter into expensive hedging agreements. Foreign exchange risk consolidation is a very common practice.

(iv)   Treasury expertise can be developed within a single department thus enhancing the quality of resource management generally.

(v)   Precautionary cash balances when centralised are likely to be lower than when considered on an individual account basis.

2   Associated International Supplies Ltd

(a)   Analysis of Company Position

Associated International Supplies Ltd

Circulation: Associated International Supplies Ltd (AIS Ltd.)
Author:
Date:

General appraisal

The first point to note is that the company would be regarded as small, by most standards, and therefore is likely to exhibit many of the problems typical of that sector. Generally, small companies which are characterised by strong growth also usually exhibit substantial borrowings in relation to equity funds. It is likely, therefore, that the appropriate mix of financing for the business becomes a critical issue in the appraisal of AIS Ltd.

Growth and liquidity

In the five year period from 1994 to 1999 sales for AIS have grown by 150%. The pressures of such growth in terms of supporting the business by adequate working capital can be substantial. Thus, in the same period we see that current assets have expanded by 53% and current liabilities by 91%. Whilst this aspect of the business will be dealt-with in more detail below it is worthwhile questioning at this stage whether sufficient funding for working capital is available to support the growth in sales.

Whilst there has been significant growth in sales during the period PBT as a percentage of sales has actually declined from 8% to about 5%. This must seriously call into question the management either of costs (operational or financial) or whether there is an inability to force price increases onto customers. Given the information available, the most likely source of this problem appears to relate to interest costs. Both current and long term liabilities have increased substantially (91% and 276%, respectively) against a background of barely increased equity funding. Debt funding (both long and short term) looks to have increased (see detail below) and this will have an associated interest burden. This has an importance in relation to the sustainability of the business.

Earnings retentions do not appear sufficient to fund business growth and hence it is clear that borrowings have been increased to deal with this problem. However, a balance must be kept in the business between its earnings capability and its capacity to service its debt commitments. Whilst PBT has increased by 53% over the period, retentions have declined by about 74%. This may be partly explained by an increased tax burden, but is obviously due mainly to excessive distributions. In other words, not enough funds are being retained in the business to support its growth or funded from increased equity issues.

The impact of excessive growth in relation to its funding base will have potentially a severe impact on liquidity. Net current assets are not seriously out of line if a ratio of current assets to current liabilities of unity is considered acceptable. However, when current assets are looked-at in relation to sales a different picture emerges. The ratio was 54% in 1994 and only 33% in 1999. This suggests, in combination with the other information, that stocks, debtors and cash resources might be insufficient in relation to sales. It might be argued that this reflects greater efficiency in current asset management which it does when debtor days are compared over the period (they declined from 99 to 60) but not in relation to creditor days which also declined (from 96 to 67 during the period). When working capital as a proportion of sales is measured we observe a decline from 11.4% in 1994 to 0.5% in 1999 which looks to be a reflection of reduced current asset investment and overdraft increases.

Because it is debt rather than equity funding that has grown, the business faces a potentially critical situation. We know that current assets are mainly comprised of stock and debtors (because the business has substantial borrowings it is unlikely to simultaneously have large cash balances) and that this is being funded by borrowing rather than retained earnings. The reason why this is the case is because the business is not generating adequate profits and it is distributing too much of post tax earnings. The outlook is for greater borrowing. The poor profit figures suggest that a critical point has been reached in terms of liquidity and solvency. This is reflected in debt/equity ratios which have increased from 2.19 in 1994 to 4.22 in 1999 (current and long term liabilities used as debt and capital and reserves used as equity). Unless a capital reorganisation can take place quickly, either through injected funds or conversion of debt into equity, the business is likely to become insolvent.

Company capacity to continue trading

Given the previous discussion it is unlikely that the business can continue in its current form. The trading performance is obviously very strong when measured in terms of its sales capacity and growth. This indicates a good customer base and the ability to service customer needs. The markets the company serves suggest a long term future for its product or service.

It is likely that the company's cost base will be overwhelmed by interest charges, which is resulting in reduced PBT/Sales ratios over the period in spite of significant sales growth. If that is the case, then it may well be that the underlying trading profitability is good. If it is not found to be good after further investigation then additional action may need to be taken. For example, if low profitability is due to aggressive pricing then an investigation into alternative marketing strategies may be appropriate. In addition, given the significant growth, it may now be timely to look at the customer base and withdraw service from those customers who are either unprofitable or otherwise difficult (late payers, for example). Product mix might be usefully assessed to focus on higher margin sales activities and to decrease effort on lower margin activities. A business plan describing the customer base and the strategy for greater profitability will underpin any bid for a reorganisation of AIS Ltd's finances.

Bank support is crucial to long term survival if the debt is in the form of bank related lending. Alternative sources of finance should also be considered, particularly in the form of equity which is required to re-balance the business.

Other factors

(i)   Venture capitalists may be interested in the business because of its significant growth but poorly structured finance. An equity injection would stabilise the business' finances.

(ii)   Future projections of growth might provide a clearer picture of how to respond to the business' situation.

(iii)   The maturity of the debt obligations would indicate any critical repayments that may be due.

(iv)   Comparisons with other businesses in the sector may provide some assurance as to the debt levels if high debt is a characteristic of the sector.

(v)   Investigation of possible renegotiation of the debt to ease the interest burden.

(vi)   Investigation of potential sale of the business or merger with a large partner with a view to securing a realistic equity base.

(vii)   Information on detailed trading results would enable an accurate assessment of the profitability of AIS Ltd.

(viii)   Working capital management needs to be investigated to assess if it is being efficiently organised.

Appendix to Report: Ratio calculations

Sales growth:	$(3,010 - 1.200)/1,200 = 150\%$
Current asset growth:	$(1,000 - 650)/650 = 53\%$
Current liability growth:	$(982 - 513)/513 = 91\%$
Long term liabilities growth:	$(158 - 42)/42 = 276\%$
PBT growth:	$(150 - 98)/98 = 53\%$
Retained earnings decline:	$(65 - 17)/65 = 74\%$

	1994	*1999*
PBT/Sales	$98/1,200 = 8\%$	$150/3,010 = 5\%$
Current Assets/ Current liabilities	$650/513 = 1.3$	$1,000/982 = 10$
Current Assets / Sales	$650/1,200 = 54\%$	$1,000/3,010 = 33\%$
Working capital/Sales	$(650-513)/1,200 = 11.4\%$	$(1,000-982)/982 = 0.5\%$
Debt/Equity	$(513 + 42)/253 = 2.19$	$(982 + 158)/270 = 4.22$
Debtors at 50% of current assets	£325,000	£500,000
Sales per day (365 days)	£3,287	£8,246
Debtor days	$325,000/3,287 = 99$	$500,000/8,246 = 61$
Creditors at 25% of current liabilities	£139,000	£245,000
Cost of sales per day (365 days)	£1,452	£3,643
Creditor days	$139,000/1,452 = 96$	$245,000/3,643 = 67$

(b)   General

Funds for fixed assets would normally be long term in nature in order to match asset use with funding maturity. Moreover, if the asset is a building or other major asset which has a secondary market value, then secured lending may be arranged where lower rates of interest are accessible. In particular, specific asset financing may be available (such as for fleet cars) which may represent an efficient source of funds. In general the purchase leasing option is available and represents a significant source of flexibility to the business. Fixed assets with secondary market values may also be subject to sale and leaseback arrangements.

Long-term sources of finance would typically be either equity funds (either injections or dividend retentions), bank debt or possible venture capital equity interests for small businesses. What would not be appropriate are debentures, convertibles, warrants, equity public issues, and listings (with the potential exception of a small company stock market like AIM).

The most significant barrier to secure external equity funding for small firms is the lack of liquidity or the inability to either find a market or buyer for the shares when the time arrives when the investor wishes to sell. The evidence is that small companies tend to have low gearing ratios when long-term debt finance to long-term finance plus equity is used as the measure of gearing. Moreover, a large proportion of the debt finance, in general, comes from overdrafts and short-term loans.

Sources of finance

No details are given concerning the nature of a business to comment on and hence only general recommendations can be made. Given that fixed asset finance is required then it is long term finance that is likely to be most appropriate. Below are listed some ideas of what might be most suitable:

(i)   If the fixed asset is substantial, such as a new building, or tooling for a new product, then the Alternative Investment Market may be suitable. AIM is directed at small and growing companies who do not qualify for the main stock market. The restrictions for admission are not that binding and may suit a company such as AIS Ltd. In particular, there are no eligibility criteria for new entrants in terms of size, profitability or existence. By listing on AIM, a company would address the market liquidity issue of equity investments for small firms.

(ii)   Venture capital may also be suitable. This would be desirable from the point of view that, whilst venture capitalists may take an equity participation, they are likely to liquidate their shareholders to the owners of the business and hence ownership dilution would not occur.

(iii)   Cash or dividend retentions. This would clearly take time for major asset purchases and may not be suitable for companies that face a funding shortfall in any case (the costs required in asset purchase may simply be too big for any realistic retention timescale).

(iv)   Entering a merger or partnership, or accessing 'Business Angel' funding.

(v)   Leasing the asset or arranging secured loans at lower interest rates.

(vi)   Possible mortgages for buildings or specialist financing for cars, for example (contracts, HP, leasing).

(vii)   Availability of government grants, European funding or other agency assistance.

3   Bread Products Ltd

(a)   There are a number of methods to answering this question and two are presented. The first problem is in deciding which broad approach to use. The broad approach which seems best is to inflate the cash flows at their different inflation rates and to discount at the money discount rate. Using this broad approach the lowest common multiple method would look like:

The lowest common multiple is $2 \times 3 = 6$ years. Hence the cash flows for each of the alternatives will be presented in these terms.

2 year cycle: (cash flows are inflated according to their individual inflation rates)

	0	1	2	3	4	5	6
Original cost	24,500		27,011		29,780		
Maintenance		550	968	666	1,171	805	1,417
Resale values			−17,199		−18,962		−20,905
Total	24,500	550	10,780	666	11,989	805	−19,488
Present values	24,500	478	8,151	438	6,856	400	−8,425
Net present value of costs	32,398						

3 year cycle: (cash flows are inflated according to their individual inflation rates)

	0	1	2	3	4	5	6
Original cost	24,500			28,362			
Maintenance		550	968	1,996	732	1,288	2,657
Resale values				−12,968			−15,012
Total	24,500	550	968	17,390	732	1,288	−12,355
Present values	24,500	478	732	11,434	418	640	−5,341
Net present value of costs	32,861						

Hence, a two-year replacement cycle is preferable since it represents the lowest cost.

Alternatively, an equivalent annual cost approach could be used:

2 year cycle: (cash flows are inflated according to their individual inflation rates)

	0	1	2
Original cost	24,500		
Maintenance		550	968
Resale values			−17,199
Total	24,500	550	−16,231
Present values	24,500	478	−12,273
Net present value of costs	12,705		

Equivalent annual cost = 12,705/(annuity factor at 15% for two years) = 12,705/1.626 = 7,813

3 year cycle: (cash flows are inflated according to their individual inflation rates)

	0	1	2	3
Original cost	24,500			
Maintenance		550	968	1,996
Resale values				−12,968
Total	24,500	550	968	−10,972
Present values	24,500	478	732	−7,214
Net present value of costs	18,496			

Equivalent annual cost = 18,496/(annuity factor at 15% for three years) = 18,496/2.283 = 8,101

Again, a two-year replacement cycle is preferable.

(b)   General limitations of Net Present Value when applied to investment appraisal

NPV is a commonly used technique employed in investment appraisal but is subject to a number of restrictive assumptions and limitations which call into question its general relevance. Nonetheless, if the assumptions and limitations are understood then its application is less likely to be undertaken in error.

Some of the difficulties with NPV are listed below:

(i)   NPV assumes that firms pursue an objective of maximising the wealth of their shareholders. This is questionable given the wider range of stakeholders who might have conflicting interests to those of the shareholders.

(ii)   NPV is largely redundant if organisations are not wealth maximising. For example, public sector organisations may wish to invest in capital assets but will use non-profit objectives as part of their assessment.

(iii)   NPV is potentially a difficult method to apply in the context of having to estimate what is the correct discount rate to use. This is particularly so when questions arise as to the incorporation of risk premia in the discount rate since an evaluation of the riskiness of the business, or of the project in particular, will have to be made and which may be difficult to discern. Alternative approaches to risk analysis, such as sensitivity and decision trees are, themselves, subject to fairly severe limitations.

(iv)   NPV assumes that cash surpluses can be reinvested at the discount rate. This is subject to other projects being available which produce at least a zero NPV at the chosen discount rate.

(v)   NPV can most easily cope with cash flows arising at period ends and is not a technique that is used easily when complicated, mid-period cash flows are present.

(vi)   NPV is not universally employed, especially in a small business environment. The available evidence suggests that businesses assess projects in a variety of ways (payback, IRR, accounting rate of return). The fact that such methods are used which are theoretically inferior to NPV calls into question the practical benefits of NPV and therefore hints at certain practical limitations.

(vii)   The conclusion from NPV analysis is the present value of the surplus cash generated from a project. If reported profits are important to businesses then it is possible that there may be a conflict between undertaking a positive NPV project and potentially adverse consequences on reported profits. This will particularly be the case for projects with long horizons, large initial investment and very delayed cash inflows. In such circumstances, businesses may prefer to use accounting measures of investment appraisal.

(viii) Managerial incentive schemes may not be consistent with NPV, particularly when long time horizons are involved. Thus managers may be rewarded on the basis of accounting profits in the short term and may be incentivised to act in accordance with these objectives and thus ignore positive NPV projects. This may be a problem of the incentive schemes and not of NPV; nonetheless, a potential conflict exists and represents a difficulty for NPV.

(ix)   NPV treats all time periods equally with the exception of discounting far cash flows more than near cash flows. In other words, NPV only accounts for the time value of money. To many businesses, distant horizons are less important than near horizons, if only because that is the environment in which they work. Other factors besides applying higher discount rates may work to reduce the impact of distant years. For example, in the long term, nearly all aspects of the business may change and hence a too-narrow focus on discounting means that N PV is of limited value and more so the further the time horizon considered.

(x)   NPV is of limited use in the face of non-quantifiable benefits or costs. NPV does not take account of non-financial information which may even be relevant to shareholders who want their wealth maximised. For example, issues of strategic benefit may arise against which it is difficult to immediately quantify the benefits but for which there are immediate costs. NPV would treat such a situation as an additional cost since it could not incorporate the indiscernible benefit.

4   Pan-Ocean Chemicals

(a)   (i)   **Direct materials mix variance:**

Standard cost per batch;
S1: $8 \times 0.3 = 2.4$
S2: $5 \times 0.5 = 2.5$
S3: $3 \times 0.4 = 1.2$
$$\overline{}$$
6.1 for 16kg
$$\overline{}$$

Actual usage in standard mix:
S1	9,576.5
S2	5,985.3
S3	3,591.3

Total   19,153.0

Standard cost of input per kg 6.1/16 = £0.38125
Input in standard mix = $19,153 \times 0.31825 = £7,302.1$
Mix variance: $7,586.3 – 7,302.1 = £284.2A$.

A more detailed calculation of the mix variance would involve:

	Actual usage in standard mix	Actual usage	Variance kg	Standard cost £	Variance £
S1	9,576.5	8,284	1,292.5 F	0.30	387.8 F
S2	5,985.3	7,535	1,549.7 A	0.50	774.9 A
S3	3,591.2	3,334	257.2 F	0.40	102.9 F
Total	19,153.0	19,153			284.2 A

Direct materials yield variance:

Standard output = 90% × 19,153 = 17,237.7kgs

A standard input per batch of 16kg of materials should yield: 90% × 16 = 14.4kg of output. Therefore, the standard cost per kg of output is (1/14.4) × 6.1 = £0.42361.

The yield variance = 0.42361(17,237.7 – 15,408.1) = £775.1A.

Materials usage variance:

Usage variance = 775.1A + 284.2A 1,059.3A

Proof of usage variance: actual production of 15,408kgs required input of (10/9) x 15,408 = 17,120 kgs which, in standard proportions, is:

S1	8,560	0.30	2,568
S2	5,350	0.50	2,675
S3	3,210	0.40	1,284
Total	17,120		6,527 (or 15,408 × 0.42361 = 6,527)

Actual proportions

S1	8,284	0.30	2,485.2
S2	7,535	0.50	3,767.5
S3	3,334	0.40	1,333.6
Total	19,153		7,586.3

Variance = 6,527 – 7,586.3 = 1,059.3A

(ii)   Standard labour cost = £5/14.4 = £0.3472 per kg

Rate variance: 6,916 – (1,235 × 5) = £741A

Efficiency variance (1,235 × 5) – (15,408 × 0.3472) = £825A

Total variance = 6,916 – (15,408 × 0.3472) = 825A + 741A = £1,566A.

(b)   The total mix variance measured in quantity is zero since the expected mix is based on the total quantity actually used and hence the difference between total expected and total actual is nil.

(c)   Analysis of variance for Pan-Ocean Chemicals

Circulation: Pan-Ocean Chemicals: Senior Management
Author:
Date:

General

The appendix to this report (results in part (a)) details mix, yield and usage variances for materials and rate and efficiency variances for labour over the last seven days. The purpose of this report is to explain what is meant by the analysis undertaken and to interpret the results derived.

Materials variances

Materials variances are normally categorised in four ways: usage, mix, yield and price. We are concerned only with mix and yield for the purposes of this report.

The three types of material used to produce Synthon (S1, S2 and S3) are not always used in the same proportions. Whilst it is the intention of the production team to use a constant, or standard, mix this is not always achieved. In practice, the proportions of input chemicals used can vary for many reasons, mostly associated with the physical properties of the chemicals which need not concern us here. To the extent that the standard mix is not used in the production of Synthon then mix variances arise which simply record to what extent the standard mix has not been followed.

Materials yield variances record the differences arising in what inputs should have been used for the output achieved against what inputs have actually been used. Essentially, yield variances are a description of how efficiently inputs have been used.

The adverse yield variance should give rise to some concern since such results indicate an inefficient use of inputs against what was expected. The adverse variance may have arisen, for example, because of a batch of poor quality input chemicals or because of inefficient working practices which have led to a significant degree of spoilage.

Labour variances

The labour rate variance has a simple interpretation in that it reflects changes in the hourly rate paid to workers during the year that are not reflected in the standard cost details. In the case of Pan Ocean, a wage increase from £5 per hour to £5.60 per hour took place. It is possible that the standard rate reflects an average of a variety of rates and that the variance arose because of an unexpected change of higher paid workers undertaking the tasks of lower paid workers. No information is given on the possible mix of rates of pay used.

The labour efficiency variance reflects an assessment of the difference in the time booked to a batch by workers from the standard allocation. In other words, the work undertaken on a batch over a weekly period was longer (because the variance was adverse) than that expected in the standard. This may have arisen because of inferior quality of input materials being used, or the introduction of new equipment or procedures.

Final comments

Variances of any type should be a signal for some sort of investigative action by management. This can be in terms of either looking to see how the variances have arisen or re-assessing the suitability of the standards that have been set; it must be accepted that the ruler by which materials and labour performance is being measured may not be an accurate one.

Recognition should also be given to the fact that new employees may have been deployed in which case there will be some learning curve effects. This would also arise in a situation where new chemicals are being used, or new processes to be learnt, such that – again – employees would not be fully familiar with their tasks.

5   ABC

(a)   Activity Based Costing (ABC) has been implemented across a range of organisations to enhance management information systems. The introduction of ABC changed the focus of cost accumulation from processes to activities. In this way, decision-relevant costs could be identified since management could, in principle, alter the activities undertaken. Traditional methods of product costing were often volume related (e.g. hours of labour used) but this did not develop with the growth in activities that had no relation to volume, or in multi-product businesses where there are complex production processes.

There are general conditions under which ABC are most likely to operate and these relate to the following factors:

(i)   where there is a requirement to apportion costs (e.g. in a multiproduct business)

(ii)   where there are significant overheads to apportion

(iii)   where the availability of sophisticated information retrieval systems allows management to track product costs as they pass through a production system.

Multiproduct businesses

The main issue is that there has to be at least two products in the business otherwise there are no costs to apportion between products. For a single product company, all the costs of the business are identifiable with the product and product probability is directly related to the profitability of the business as a whole.

However, ABC might still be useful in single product businesses when management decisions are required to determine the level of production. In such cases, optimum levels of output can be defined once costs can be split between fixed and variable elements. ABC will help identify variable costs as those that vary with the level of activities that incur costs. In principle, fixed costs are then those costs that do not vary with activity and hence it becomes possible to undertake profitability analysis in relation to activity levels.

Other advantages of ABC in multiproduct business relate to the accurate valuation of stock and facilitating the effective management of stock levels with multiple products. Allied to this is that there is reduced cross-subsidisation of products: with costs accurately identified with products it becomes easier for management to discern which products are profitable against those that are not.

The significance of overheads and the ABC method of charging costs

Since ABC is a cost apportionment system then it is principally beneficial when there is a high proportion of overhead costs to apportion to products. If a business incurs only direct costs, there is no issue for ABC to resolve.

ABC is based on the premise that it is activities that lead to costs being incurred and that costs should therefore be apportioned on the basis of the activities that different products consume. In this way management can better understand the behaviour of overheads as they relate to decisions.

ABC apportions costs by first identifying the activities that products are associated with. Cost drivers are then chosen that reflect the events that create costs when the activities are undertaken. The costs associated with each activity are then collected into cost pools where there are common cost drivers. Finally, products are allocated costs on the basis of the activities they use. In sum, if product overheads can be seen in terms of activities and activities can have costs associated with them, then the use of activities by a product can be costed.

Retrieval systems

A basic requirement for any cost allocation system is information availability. This is particularly so for ABC systems which rely heavily on activity information. Moreover, production systems are far more complex than in the days when traditional absorption costing was most effective. For example, manufacturing processes rely far more on quality control monitoring, inspection and set-up processes than they ever did and are not necessarily related to the volume of activity. With many products, and variants on products, the monitoring of costs itself becomes a large and complex process. With complexity inevitably follows greater support services, of which a major category would be computer support services.

In addition, ABC requires the monitoring of activities that have not involved monitoring previously. This raises issues of information capture and it is in new technology that answers to this are most likely to be found.

(b)   One of the key problems in assessing manager performance is in ensuring that costs are controllable and hence traceable to manager decisions. Manager performance will be unfairly assessed if non-controllable costs are incorrectly taken into account. ABC is often claimed to rest on a more accurate information base than absorption costing and hence the impact of management decisions is potentially more easily seen under ABC than it is under traditional volume-related absorption methods. Thus, it becomes possible to more closely align management decisions with their consequences and improve performance appraisal.

For example, in allocating and apportioning overheads the reapportionment of service department costs is reduced or eliminated under ABC. This is because ABC establishes separate cost pools for support activities and the costs of these activities are assigned to products directly on the basis of the appropriate driver. The accuracy of ABC in this context rests on the accurate identification of cost pools and cost drivers.

Also, ABC absorbs costs into products in a wider variety of ways than traditional absorption methods that rely mostly on labour and/or machine hours. In extending the range of absorption bases, ABC is able to more closely track costs to the causes of the costs which then links to management decisions.

The foregoing does not rule out accurate costing using traditional absorption methods, especially when a business has most of its costs varying with production volume. However, when overheads do not vary with output then other means of determining absorption rates, such as those based on cost drivers, are preferable. Thus, the scope for arbitrariness in manager performance appraisal is reduced.

Pilot Paper 2001 Marking Scheme

This marking scheme is given as a guide to markers in the context of the suggested answer. Scope is given to markers to award marks for alternative approaches to a question, including relevant comment, and where well reasoned conclusions are provided. This is particularly the case for essay based questions where there will often be more than one definitive solution.

				Marks	
1	(a)	(i)	Calculation of discount rate implied in the early settlement	2	
			Decision on payment period	1	
				—	3
		(ii)	Calculation of basic EOQ (ignoring discounts)	1	
			Evaluation of purchase costs with discounts	4	
			Decision on optimal policy	1	
				—	6
		(iii)	Calculation of discount rate implied in the early settlement	2	
			Decision on payment period	1	
				—	3
	(b)		Defining frequency of orders	1	
			Consideration of scheduling of orders	4	
			Preparation of cash budget in accordance with answer to part (a)	9	
			Identification of overdraft costs	4	
				—	18
	(c)		2 marks each for identification and elaborated examples of how cash problems arise (max 4)	4	
			2 marks each for identification and elaborated examples of easing cash shortages (max 4)	4	
			2 marks each for identification and elaborated examples of how cash resources may be managed (max 4)	4	
			2 marks each for identification and elaborated examples of the benefits of a treasury function (max 6)	6	
			Quality of presentation of report	2	
				—	20
					50
2	(a)		1 mark each for relevant ratios (max 6)	6	
			Analysis of company position	6	
			Comments on the capacity to continue trading	2	
			Other relevant factors	2	
			Quality of presentation of report	1	
				—	17
	(b)		2 marks each for identification of appropriate sources of finance		8
					25
3	(a)		Identification of appropriate cash flows for each alternative	4	
			Dealing correctly with inflated cash flows	2	
			Calculation of discounted cash flows	2	
			Calculation of optimal policies	4	
				—	12
	(b)		Up to 2 marks for each detailed limitations of NPV (1 mark each for limited responses)		13
					25

			Marks	
4	(a)	Materials usage variance	1	
		Materials mix variance	3	
		Materials yield variance	3	
		Labour rate variance	2	
		Labour efficiency variance	2	
			—	11
	(b)	Explanation of equivalence of total mix variances		3
	(c)	Explanation of mix and yield variances	5	
		Up to 2 marks each for identification of possible reasons for		
		the variances calculated in part (a)	6	
			—	11
				25
5	(a)	Comments on general conditions for ABC	1	
		2 marks each for detailed comments on overheads and the		
		methods ABC uses to allocate costs	7	
		Comments on the impact of ABC to multiproduct businesses	3	
		Comments on information retrieval systems	4	
		Quality and presentation of report	2	
			—	17
	(b)	General comments on performance evaluation	2	
		2 marks each for detailed comments on ABC and absorption costing	6	
			—	8
				25

December 2001 Questions

Section A –This is compulsory and MUST be attempted

1   Tower Railways plc

Tower Railways plc, which has a financial year-end of 31 December, operates a rail passenger service between the major cities in England. It is currently negotiating with the regulatory authorities about a five year extension and enhancement of its existing contract. Tower Railways has forecast passenger use over the next five year period to 31 December 2006 and, based on its proposed carriage capacity, has calculated the following figures:

Five year projections:

Number of carriages used on the line:	8
Maximum passengers per carriage:	55
Average occupancy rate:	60%
Average number of return journeys per day:	10
Average price per return trip:	£12
Number of days operating per year:	340

Contribution per unit (sales price less variable costs) is expected to remain at a constant 35% of price over the period. Additional fixed costs of £1m per annum will be incurred on the new project. The management accountant has suggested that, in addition, the existing fixed overhead apportionment be increased by £200,000 per annum to reflect the increased activities relating to this part of the business. If the contract is renewed, other services offered by Tower Railways will be reduced to enable capacity expansion on the new contract. This will involve the loss of a long-standing contract, which was expected to continue indefinitely, worth £250,000 in pre-tax cash inflows per annum.

One of the conditions of a successful new bid is that a minimum investment of £5m, in support equipment to enhance the existing service, is required at the start of the new contract on 31 December 2001. This equipment will no longer be needed to support the contract after four years and will be disposed of for £0.5m on 31 December 2005. Capital allowances are available for these transactions. A balancing charge or allowance would arise on disposal of the asset. The investment in this asset should be treated separately from any other asset investment for tax purposes (ignore any pooling requirements). Assume all tax payments and allowances arise at the end of the year in which the taxable transactions arise (in other words, not delayed). Assume that all operating cash inflows arise at the relevant year-end.

Other relevant information:

After tax discount rate per annum:	10%
Corporation tax rate:	30%
Writing down allowance:	25% per annum, reducing balance

Required:

(a)   Calculate separately the present value of the net operating cash flows (after payment of corporation tax and using annuities and perpetuities where appropriate), and the capital flows (investment, disposal and related tax flows). Assess if it is beneficial for Tower Railways to begin the new contract on 31 December 2001.

Express all calculations in this and other parts of the question to the nearest £1,000. State any assumptions you make.   **(18 marks)**

(b)   The Chairman of Tower Railways is concerned about the risk of the project, particularly with respect to the average price charged.

Calculate the sensitivity of the project in relation to the average price charged.   **(4 marks)**

Assume, in your answer that all other factors are as per you analysis in part (a).

(c)   On reviewing the initial proposal from your answer to part (a), the regulatory authorities are now insisting that further investment of £7m be made to ensure carriage availability to meet targets for the level of proposed service provision. This would not involve the purchase of additional carriages. Assume that by incorporating the additional £7m investment on top of the existing £5m, a total NPV at 31 December 2001 of £9.220m (negative) for the capital cash flows only will arise.

Required:

(i)   calculate the occupancy rate required to break even (that is, to produce a zero NPV);   **(4 marks)**

(ii)   calculate the length of the contract required to break even (that is, to produce a zero NPV);   **(4 marks)**

Assume, in your answers to each case, that all other factors are as per your analysis in part (a).

(d)   Write a report to the Chairman of Tower Railways, in your capacity as an external consultant, explaining:

(i)   what is meant by business risk;
(ii)   the methods of estimating business risk in the context of NPV; and
(iii)   the methods of reducing business risk.   **(20 marks)**
(Total: 50 marks)

Section B – TWO questions ONLY to be attempted

2   Standard costing

(a)   Outline the uses of standard costing and discuss the reasons why standards have to be reviewed.   **(13 marks)**

(b)   Standard costs are a detailed financial expression of organisational objectives. What non-financial objectives might organisations have? In your answer, identify any stakeholder group that may have a non-financial interest.
(12 marks)
(Total: 25 marks)

3   Parser Ltd

The managing director of Parser Ltd, a small business, is considering undertaking a one-off contract and has asked her inexperienced accountant to advise on what costs are likely to be incurred so that she can price at a profit. The following schedule has been prepared:

Costs per special order:

	Notes	£
Direct wages	1	28,500
Supervisor costs	2	11,500
General overheads	3	4,000
Machine depreciation	4	2,300
Machine overheads	5	18,000
Materials	6	34,000
		98,300

Notes

1   Direct wages comprise the wages of two employees, particularly skilled in the labour process for this job, who could be transferred from another department to undertake work on the special order. They are fully occupied in their usual department and sub-contracting staff would have to be brought in to undertake the work left behind. Sub-contracting costs would be £32,000 for the period of the work. Different sub-contractors who are skilled in the special order techniques are available to work on the special order and their costs would amount to £31,300.

2   A supervisor would have to work on the special order. The cost of £11,500 is comprised of £8,000 normal payments plus £3,500 additional bonus for working on the special order. Normal payments refer to the fixed salary of the supervisor. In addition, the supervisor would lose incentive payments in his normal work amounting to £2,500. It is not anticipated that any replacement costs relating to the supervisor's work on other jobs would arise.

3   General overheads comprise an apportionment of £3,000 plus an estimate of £1,000 incremental overheads.

4   Machine depreciation represents the normal period cost based on the duration of the contract. It is anticipated that £500 will be incurred in additional machine maintenance costs.

5   Machine overheads (for running costs such as electricity) are charged at £3 per hour. It is estimated that 6,000 hours will be needed for the special order. The machine has 4,000 hours available capacity. The further 2,000 hours required will mean an existing job is taken off the machine resulting in a lost contribution of £2 per hour.

6   Materials represent the purchase cost of 7,500 kg bought some time ago. The materials are no longer used and are unlikely to be wanted in the future except on the special order. The complete stock of materials (amounting to 10,000 kg), or part thereof, could be sold for £4.20 per kg. The replacement cost of material used would be £33,375.

Because the business does not have adequate funds to finance the special order, a bank overdraft amounting to £20,000 would be required for the project duration of three months. The overdraft would be repaid at the end of the period. The company uses a cost of capital of 20% to appraise projects. The bank's overdraft rate is 18%.

The managing director has heard that, for special orders such as this, relevant costing should be used that also incorporate opportunity costs. She has approached you to create a revised costing schedule based on relevant costing principles.

Required:

(a)   Briefly explain what is meant by opportunity cost.   (2 marks)

(b)   Adjust the schedule prepared by the accountant to a relevant cost basis, incorporating appropriate opportunity costs.   (11 marks)

(c)   Explain why very Small to Medium-sized Enterprises (SMEs), such as Parser Ltd, might face problems in obtaining appropriate sources of finance. In your answer pay particular attention to problems and issues associated with:

   (i)   uncertainty concerning the business;
   (ii)   assets available to offer as collateral or security; and
   (iii) potential sources of finance for very new SMEs excluding sources from capital markets.   (12 marks)
                                                                                              (Total: 25 marks)

4   Special Gift Supplies plc

Special Gift Supplies plc is a wholesale distributor of a variety of imported goods to a range of retail outlets. The company specialises in supplying ornaments, small works of art, high value furnishings (rugs, etc) and other items that the chief buyer for the company feels would have a market in the UK. In seeking to improve working capital management, the financial controller has gathered the following information.

	Months
Average period for which items are held in stock	3.5
Average debtors collection period	2.5
Average creditors payment period	2.0

Required:

(a)   Calculate Special Gift Supplies' funding requirements for working capital measured in terms of months.
                                                                                                      (2 marks)

(b)   In looking to reduce the working capital funding requirement, the financial controller of Special Gift Supplies is considering factoring credit sales. The company's annual turnover is £2.5m of which 90% are credit sales. Bad debts are typically 3% of credit sales. The offer from the factor is conditional on the following:

   1   The factor will take over the sales ledger of Special Gift Supplies completely.

   2   80% of the value of credit sales will be advanced immediately (as soon as sales are made to the customer) to Special Gift Supplies, the remaining 20% will be paid to the company one month later. The factor charges 15% per annum on credit sales for advancing funds in the manner suggested. The factor is normally able to reduce the debtors' collection period to one month.

   3   The factor offers a 'no recourse' facility whereby they take on the responsibility for dealing with bad debts. The factor is normally able to reduce bad debts to 2% of credit sales.

4   A charge for factoring services of 4% of credit sales will be made.

5   A one-off payment of £25,000 is payable to the factor.

The salary of the Sales Ledger Administrator (£12,500) would be saved under the proposals and overhead costs of the credit control department, amounting to £2,000 per annum, would have to be reallocated. Special Gift Supplies' cost of overdraft finance is 12% per annum. Special Gift Supplies pays its sales force on a commission only basis. The cost of this is 5% of credit sales and is payable immediately the sales are made. There is no intention to alter this arrangement under the factoring proposals.

Required:

Evaluate the proposal to factor the sales ledger by comparing Special Gift Supplies' existing debtor collection costs with those that would result from using the factor (assuming that the factor can reduce the debtors' collection period to one month).   **(8 marks)**

(c)   As an advisor to Special Gift Supplies plc, write a report to the financial controller that outlines:

(i)   how a credit control department might function;
(ii)   the benefits of factoring; and
(iii)   how the financing of working capital can be arranged in terms of short and long term sources of finance. In particular, make reference to:

- the financing of working capital or net current assets when short term sources of finances are exhausted; and

- the distinction between fluctuating and permanent current assets.   **(15 marks)**
                                                                                                              (Total: 25 marks)

5   All Premier Services plc

All Premier Services plc is a fee charging hospital that has two specialist wards, X and Y. A third ward, Z, is used for patients who are well enough to leave wards X and Y but who require a short period of hospital rest before being discharged. It is intended that ward Z will be only occupied by patients transferred from the other wards. Budgeted details relating to the wards are as follows (fixed and variable costs are for a complete week).

Ward:	X	Y	Z
Number of beds	60	40	45
Budgeted fee per bed per night (£)	225	200	170
Budgeted occupancy %	65	80	100

Budgeted costs:	£
Fixed overheads	127,300
Variable overheads	42,412

Fixed overheads are allocated to the wards on the basis of the number of beds available in each ward. Variable overheads are allocated to beds in proportion to the fees earned per ward.

Required:

(a)   (i)   Prepare a budgeted profit/loss statement (based on one week) for each of the wards and for the three wards combined. Calculate the total cost incurred per bed occupied per week (seven nights).   **(5 marks)**

       (ii)   A proposal has been put forward to increase the number of beds in ward Z to 75. This proposal would be expected to increase occupancy in wards X and Y to 80% and 95%, respectively. Budgeted occupancy in ward Z will remain at 100%. It is expected that total variable overheads would increase to £57,881 as a result.

               Evaluate this proposal on the same basis as your answer to part (a) (i).   **(5 marks)**

(b)   (i)   In making decision about expanding Ward Z, comment on the fact that it is only occupied by patients from wards X and Y.   **(2 marks)**

       (ii)   Briefly assess the relevance of the allocation bases for fixed and variable overheads.   **(3 marks)**

(c)   Describe the characteristics of a responsibility accounting system and discuss what factors exist in non-profit organisations that make responsibility accounting difficult to implement.   **(10 marks)**
                                                                                                              (Total: 25 marks)

December 2001 Answers

Section A

1   Tower Railways plc

(a)   **Data**

Discount rate (%)	10
Tax rate (%)	30
Variable cost proportion (%)	65
Occupancy rate (%)	60
No. of carriages	8
Passenger numbers per carriage	55
Number of trips	10
Average price per passenger (£)	12
Annual days travelling	340

CA Calculation Year to 31 December	31 Dec 01 £000	31 Dec 02 £000	31 Dec 03 £000	31 Dec 04 £000	31 Dec 05 £000	Total allowances £000
TWDV	5,000	3,750	2,812	2,109	1,582	
WDA	1,250	938	703	527		
Sale proceeds					500	
Balancing allowance					1,082	
Tax allowance	375	281	211	158	325	1,350
Capital projections						
Initial investment and proceeds	-5,000				500	
Capital allowances	375	281	211	158	325	
Net capital flows	-4,625	281	211	158	825	
Discount factor	1	0.909	0.826	0.751	0.683	
PV capital flows	-4,625	256	174	119	563	
NPV of capital flows	-3,513					

Projected revenue = $0.6 \times 8 \times 55 \times 10 \times 12 \times 340 = £10,771,200$

Annuity approach

Year	0	1-5
Projected revenue		10,771
Variable costs		-7,001
Additional fixed costs		-1,000
Incremental net revenues		2,770
Tax		-831
Post tax		1,939

◈ FOULKS*lynch*

Discount factor		3,791
PV revenue flows		7,351
NPV of revenue flows except perpetuity	7,351	
Perpetuity of lost flows net of tax	-1,750[1]	
NPV of capital flows	-3,513	
Total NVP	2,088	

Decision: Contract is worthwhile

Subject to rounding errors the extended approach produces the same answer.

[1] Perpetuity = $(250 \times (1-0.3))/0.1 = 1,750$

Basic approach

Year	31 Dec 01	31 Dec 02	31 Dec 03	31 Dec 04	31 Dec 05	31 Dec 06
Net operating cash flow projection						
Projected revenue		10,771	10,771	10,771	10,771	10,771
Variable costs		-7,001	-7,001	-7,001	-7,001	-7,001
Additional fixed costs		-1,000	-1,000	-1,000	-1,000	-1,000
Incremental net revenue		2,770	2,770	2,770	2,770	2,770
Tax		-831	-831	-831	-831	-831
Post tax revenues		1,939	1,939	1,939	1,939	1,939
Discount factor		0.909	0.826	0.751	0.683.	0.621
PV revenue flows		1,763	1,602	1,456	1,324	1,204
NPV of net operating flows except perpetuity	7,349					
Perpetuity of lost flows net of tax	-1,750					
Capital projections (See calculation above)	-3,513					
Total NPV	2,086					

Decision: Contract is worthwhile

(b)   It is quite possible to answer this and the next question by trial and error using the cash flow structures outlined. A quicker method is to use the structure of the cash flows to identify the relationship of price to the remaining variables. Thus if:

p	=	average price
cr	=	contribution rate = 0.35
oh	=	incidental overhead = 1,000
t	=	corporate tax rate = 0.3
A_n	=	annuity factor
r	=	occupancy rate

Total revenue p × occupancy rate × number of carriages × number of trips per day × number of days per year × number of passengers per carriage = $p \times 0.6 \times 8 \times 10 \times 340 \times 55 = 897.6p$. Thus profit can be defined as:

NVP = $A_n [(897.6p \times cr - oh)(1-t)]$ + Perpetuity + NPV capital flows = 0, for break even.

NVP = $3.791(897.6p \times 0.35 - 1,000)0.7 - 1,750 - 3,513 = 0$

897.6p $\times$ 0.35 – 1,000 = 5,263/(0.7 $\times$ 3.791) = 1,983

p = (1,983 + 1,000)/(0.35 $\times$ 897.6) = 9.50

Sensitivity is therefore:

(12 – 9.50)/12 = 20.83%

More succinctly, the same result can be derived via interpolation. A 10% change in contribution gives rise to a change in NPV of:

(10,771 – 7,001) $\times$ 0.1 $\times$ 0.7 $\times$ 3.791 = £1,000.444 or £1,000 to three figures.

To reduce NPV of this project to zero requires a (2,087/1,000) $\times$ 10% = 2 $\times$ 10% = 20% (approximate) change in price.

(c)   (i)   As before, total revenue = p $\times$ occupancy rate $\times$ number of carriages $\times$ number of trips per day $\times$ number of days per year $\times$ number of passengers per carriage = 12 $\times$ r $\times$ 8 $\times$ 10 $\times$ 340 $\times$ 55 = 17,952r. Thus profit can be defined as:

NPV = A_n ((17.952 r $\times$ cr – oh)(1 – t)) + Perpetuity + NPV capital flows = 0, for break even.

NPV = 3.791(17.952r $\times$ 0.35 – 1,000)0.7 – 1,750 – 9,220 = 0

3.791(17,952r $\times$ 0.35 – 1,000)0.7 = 10,970

17,952r $\times$ 0.35 – 1,000 = 10,970)(0.7 $\times$ 3.791)

r = (4,134 + 1,000/)(0.35 $\times$ 17.952) = 0.817 or 82%

(ii)   Profit can be defined as before:

NPV = A_n [(10,771 $\times$ cr – oh)(1-t) + Perpetuity + NPV capital flows = 0, for break even.

This time we can solve for A_n to find the length of the contract:

A_n (1,939) – 1,750 – 9,220 = 0

A_n (1,939) = 10,970

A_n = 10,970/1,939 = 5.658

Examining the annuity table under the 10% column for a figure closest to 5.658 we find the project length, expressed in whole years, should be at least 9 years long (at 9 years the annuity figure is 5.759).

(d)   **Report on Business Risk for Tower Railways plc**

Circulation: Chairman, Tower Railways

Author: A Student, AXY Consulting

Date: December 2001

Introduction

In the light of the possibility of an extension to the contract to services the main railway line this report makes an assessment of the background and specific risk relating to the project.

What is meant by business risk

1   *Basic description:* risk is related to the lack of certainty of future outcomes and is fundamentally related to decision making, such as the project proposed, in that business decisions are always taken against a background of risk. Because of that, it becomes important to understand the risk exposure that exists. At a basic level risk is positively associated with return in that the higher the return we expect from a project, the higher the degree of risk it is likely to be exposed to.

2   *Chance and Probability:* risk is associated with chance or probability in ways that allow us to quantify the degree of risk we face. This is particularly relevant to businesses that face variability in projected outcomes, for example, so that a fairly clear idea can be formed of the profit impact of risk. In the contract extension facing Tower Railways project outcome has been assessed using NPV techniques that assume cash flows are certain (without risk). However the cash flows are dependent on projections of future passenger occupancy, prices charged, implicit zero inflation, the relation of variable costs to sales,

discount rates, constant tax rates and so on. In fact every component of the calculation is subject to risk because we cannot be certain of ensuring that the figures we use will actually arise when the time comes or even at the time we project. Under such circumstances we can only estimate the most likely figures and the most likely times and accept that we may be wrong on either or both counts.

3   *Time:* risk is also related to the length of time the projections extend. There is an important distinction at this point between constant risk and increased exposure. For example, we may assume that passenger occupancy stays constant at 60% and we may feel that there is a risk associated with being wrong in this project by a factor of –1% or + 1% each year. Whilst risk might remain constant at + or -1% each year, it is feasible that after five years projected passenger occupancy could be less than 55% over 65%. Compounding effects of risk on risk over successive periods means that risk exposure grows without having to alter the risk percentage faced.

4   *Negative and Positive Variability:* another important point relates to risk being both a good or bad thing. Risk, in the context of NPV projections, relates to variability of returns, both positive and negative. Thus, while you may not welcome negative variability in income you would welcome it in relation to costs. Thus, risk is not only related to unwelcome outcomes, although it is often misperceived as such.

5   *Uncertainty:* risk can also arise but may be unforeseen. This is perhaps the most important aspect in that, whilst we may be able to anticipate variability in income, we may not anticipate fully the risk we are exposed to or the form it will take (variability in sales revenues may be more than we anticipate for example). This is the hardest aspect of risk to judge.

Methods of estimating the degree of business risk[2]

Because risk affects decisions in such a fundamental way, businesses attempt to estimate risk as a way of putting in place contingency plans and/or evaluating if the project is likely to produce a profitable outcome. This is usually incorporated into NPV decisions in a number of ways:

1   *Sensitivity Analysis:* this is one method which is widely used by which an assessment may be made of how responsive a project's NPV is to changes in its components. Thus, an idea may be gained of to what extent prices charged for a good or service have to reduce by before a zero NPV is produced. This technique can be applied to any cost, including initial capital costs, and also to the discount rate. Sensitivity is normally expressed as a percentage. Some of the difficulties associated with the techniques are as follows:

    –   the analysis can only deal with changes in one key factor at a time. It cannot deal with multiple changes in NPV components which may well arise.

    –   no idea is given in sensitivity analysis of the likelihood of occurrence of a key variable changing to the extent to produce a zero NPV. In other words, it measures the percentage change required to produce a catastrophic result, but does not indicate if this has a low, medium or high chance of occurring.

    –   as with any risk assessment, sensitivity analysis is only a guide. It cannot tell managers how important such a risk exposure is to the company. In order to assess this, the risk proclivity or otherwise of the managers needs to be determined. In other words, a high return/high risk company will want to be exposed to more risk than a low return/low risk company.

[2] *Tutorial note* discussions of CAPM and Certainty Equivalents may be included in this list. Whilst beyond the syllabus, appropriate references to these subjects will be rewarded.

2   *Probability analysis:* this approach attempts to use measures which indicate just how variable cash flows are. It addresses one of the key criticisms of the sensitivity approach in that it provides an idea of how much variability is likely whereas sensitivity analysis indicates the room for manoeuvre without an assessment of the likelihood that any such event will arise. Probability analysis is essentially a weighted average approach where the averages are determined by pre-set probabilities. By doing this, expected cash flows emerge based on the most likely outcomes. The degree of variability of the expected outcomes may be estimated from the standard deviation of the net present value. It is in this calculation that we at least get some idea of the degree of risk a project is exposed to, which can be expressed in terms of a range of NPVs. The important drawback of this approach is that a good idea of what probability weights to use must first be established. This can never be determined with 100% accuracy for project cash flows that arise in the future simply because the future is uncertain and so are the probabilities.

3   *Decision trees:* this is similar to a probability approach in that it relies on weighting future cash flows by probabilities to arrive at an overall average. The distinctive feature of decision trees is that certain cash flow outcomes can be made contingent on certain previous ones arising. Decision trees are most useful in expressing, in a systematic manner the different project outcomes that may emerge. Formally, the technique is no different to that of using compound probabilities and hence the criticisms of probabilities apply here also.

4   *Simulation models:* this method allows management to vary changes in the different cash flows simultaneously. As such it gives an idea of the variability in project cash flows overall by allowing changes in many of the outcomes. It can only give an idea since the number of changes allowed can be quite large and, when compounded together, the number of different combinations become unmanageable in terms of trying to interpret what is going on. The key advantage of this technique is that it allows an idea of the most likely range of project outcomes that could possible emerge. However, the technique requires many computations to be carried out.

Methods of reducing business risk

Risk can only be reduced to the extent that management can control events. Risks associated with uncontrolled events cannot be manipulated. There are a variety of ways the management can respond to risky situations:

–   undertake short payback projects. This is related to the fact that risk exposure increases with time because of its compounding effect even though the degree of risk may remain constant (this point is explained above).

–   avoid risky projects. If riskless projects are undertaken then only a risk free return could be expected. This may not satisfy shareholders.

–   ensure proper evaluations of risk are undertaken so that unnecessary exposure to risk is avoided.

–   employ risk avoidance project selection strategies. Management should not undertake high risk projects simultaneously, which might produce undesirable risk exposure to the business as a whole.

–   combine projects to diversify risk.

2   Standard costing

(a)   Standard costing has been employed for many years in situations where there is a significant degree of repetition in the production process or the service supplied. Repetition is a condition since standards presuppose that averages, as expected values, are accurate to a fair degree.

The main uses of standard costing relate to:

1   Valuation of stocks and costs of production for reporting purposes, either internally or for statutory reasons.

2   Providing an excellent management device which enables costs to be monitored, reviewed and controlled.

3   Enabling exception reporting through the use of variance analysis. Exception reporting allows management to exercise control with a lower degree of effort and less time than otherwise would be the case.

4   Assisting in the budgeting process. Standards, once established in a business, become the common language by which performance is discussed and measured.

5   Evaluating managerial performance.

6   Motivation of staff by setting standards at levels to which staff feel able to respond. In this respect, standards have been characterised as 'ideal', 'attainable', 'current' and 'basic' as a way of categorising the different ways standards may be viewed in terms of their motivational impact.

7   Improving efficiency. Standard setting is often viewed as a way of understanding the detail of a process through monitoring its important components. If standards are an accurate reflection of a process, then they can be used to highlight ways of improving efficiency and act as signals when the process becomes inefficient.

Once standards have been set they cannot be assumed to be accurate over long periods of time. Standards have to be reviewed to enable the benefits of standard costing to continue. In this respect, standards must change with the changing practices of an organisation. For example, in environments which continuously seek greater efficiency and reduced costs of production, standards have to change to reflect such improvements. In fact, under such circumstances, standards can very quickly become out of date. In order to review standards, they must be continually assessed to ensure that the basis of their calculation still applies. Moreover, other purposes of standards are undermined, if they are not continually reviewed. Thus, for example:

1   The motivational impact of standards may no longer be effective if standards are out of date.

2   Assessment of managerial performance becomes inaccurate.

3   Reporting procedures are undermined.

4   The credibility of standards in their role in assisting with the budget setting process is called into question.

5   The fate of standard costing as a management tool is put at risk if management do not trust the standards. Alternative mechanisms for management control inevitably emerge which may be undesirable, untested and lack organisational approval.

(b)   Financial statements of any sort are only an expression of organisational activities that can be measured. Many of the activities of an organisation cannot be easily measured, nor can its relations with various stakeholder groups who may have a non-financial interest in the organisation.

Non-finance objectives that may be difficult to measure or express in financial terms include:

1   welfare of employees and management

–   health

–   safety

–   leisure and other services

2   welfare in the broader community

–   minimisation of intrusion into the community (e.g. traffic)

3   the provision of a service for which no charge is made (e.g. public hospitals). Also including:

–   local or regional government services

–   housing

–   education

4   the effective supply of goods or services (in addition to costs/efficiency issued) such as:

–   product or service equality

–   ensuring product or service supply (e.g. vital services)

–   timelines

–   after sale support

–   customer or user satisfaction

5   fulfilment of product or services responsibilities: this is a very broad area and would cover many of the core activities of a business such as:

–   leadership in research and development

–   product development

–   maintenance of standards in goods or service provision

–   maintenance of good business and community relationships

–   employee training and support

6   support for community activities

7   minimisation of externalities (e.g. pollution)

8   fulfilment of statutory or regulatory responsibilities

Whilst it may be argued that many of the objectives expressed have an impact on profitability or costs, they only do so in an indirect manner. Moreover, as with most organisational activities, non-financial objectives crystallises into financial issues given enough time. Thus, for example, poor service provision will ultimately lead to loss of customers in a competitive environment.

The range of stakeholders that may have an interest in an organisation's activities are wide and, because organisations have to respond to stakeholder interests, the non-financial responsibilities and hence range of objectives, is extended. In this respect, stakeholders create for organisations a range of non-financial issues that have to be addressed. If organisations are responsive then these issues become part of the culture of an organisation and hence part of its broader purposes. Interest in the organisation's activities from a non-financial perspective can arise even if the stake holder has a financial relationship with the organisation. Thus, the stakeholders who may have an interest might include the following:

1   shareholders

2   suppliers and trade creditors

3   debt holders

4   customers

5   employees

6   pensioners and ex-employees

7   competitors

8   local community

9   broader national and international interests

10   government

11   regulatory authorities

12   tax authorities

13   special interest groups concerned with pollution, for example

Moreover, many of the stakeholders have common interests and hence stakeholders groupings can emerge.

3   Parser Ltd

(a)   Opportunity costs represent the value of the loss or sacrifice when choosing between scarce alternatives. Lack of scarcity implies zero opportunity cost.

(b)   Revised costs for special order:

	Notes	£
Subcontractor costs	1	31,300
Supervisor costs	2	1,000
General overheads	3	1,000
Machine maintenance	4	500
Machine overheads	5	22,000
Materials	6	31,500
Interest costs	7	900
		88,200

Notes

1   The choice lies between the two subcontractor costs that have to be employed because of the shortage of existing labour. The minimum cost is to have subcontractors employed who are skilled in the special process.

2   Only the difference between the bonus and the incentive payment represents an additional cost that arises due the special order. Fixed salary costs do not change.

3   Only incremental costs are relevant.

4   Depreciation is a period cost and is not related to the special order. Additional maintenance costs are relevan

5   The relevant costs are the variable overheads (£3 × 6,000 hours) that will be incurred, plus the displacement costs of £2 × 2,000 hours making a total of £22,000.

6   Since the materials are no longer used the replacement cost is irrelevant. The historic cost of £34,000 is a su cost. The relevant cost is the lost sale value of the stock used in the special order which is 7,500 kg × £4.20 kg = £31,500.

7   Full opportunity costing will also allow for imputed interest costs on the incremental loan. The correct intere rate is the overdraft rate since this represents the incremental cost the company will pay. Simple interest cha for three months are therefore: (3/12) × £20,000 × 18% = £900.

(c)   **Introduction**

SMEs contribute in a significant way to many economies in the world. Besides generating income, in often large proportions in relation to GNP across the world, they are frequently major employers and the sector which is most identified with new ideas and entrepreneurial spirit. It is these latter factors that help sustain and support growth rat many economies.

Despite this background of potential there is often associated with SMEs difficulties in accessing appropriate source finance. There are three main issues involved: uncertainty concerning the business, lack of assets available to offer collateral or security and the sources of finance for business start-ups or very new businesses.

Uncertainty concerning the business

It has been recognised in various studies that the problem of adequately financing SMEs is a problem of uncertainty defining characteristic of SMEs is the uncertainty surrounding their activities. However much owners or managers inform their banks of what they are doing there is always an element of uncertainly remaining that is not a feature of larger businesses. Larger businesses have grown from smaller businesses and have a track record – especially in ter of a long-term relationship with their bankers. Bankers can observe, over a period of time that the business is well-r that managers can manage its affairs and can therefore be trusted with handling bank loans in a proper way. New businesses, typically SMEs, obviously don't have this track record. The problem is even broader. Large businesses conduct most of their activities in public (e.g. subject to more external scrutiny) than do SMEs. Thus, if information public, there is less uncertainty. For example a larger business might be quoted on an exchange and therefore be sul to press scrutiny, exchange rules regarding the provision of certain of its activities, and has to publish accounts that been audited. Many SMEs do not have to have audits, certainly don't publish their accounts to a wide audience and press are not really interested in them.

Lack of assets available to offer as collateral security

If SMEs wish to access bank finance, for example, then banks will wish to address the information problem referred above. First, banks will screen loan applications to assess the underlying product or service, the management team, market addressed and, importantly, any collateral or security that can be offered. It is this last point which is of inte here. Besides investigating business plans, banks will look to see what security is available for any loan provided. phase is likely to involve an audit of the firm's assets and detailed explanation of any personal security offered by th directors and owner managers. Collateral is important because it can reduce the level of risk a bank is exposed to in granting a loan to a new business. In assessing a business plan and security, a bank would make assessment of the r of the business and any loan interest rate will reflect that risk. A key feature for accessing bank finance is therefore the assessment of risk from the information gathered and the security offered.

Potential sources of finance for very new businesses

Initial owner finance is nearly always the first source of finance for a business, whether from the owner or from fam connections. At this stage many of the assets may be intangible and thus external financing is an unrealistic prospec this stage or at least has been in the past. This is often referred to as the equity gap. With no organised market for

Business Angel Finance and which is otherwise difficult to set up there are limited means by which SMEs can find equity investors. Trade credit finance is important at this stage too, although it is nearly always very expensive if viewed in terms of lost early payment discounts. Also, it is inevitably very short term and very limited in duration (except that always taking 60 days to pay a creditor will obviously roll-over and become medium term financing. Business Angel Financing may be important and is represented by high net worth individuals or groups of individuals who invest directly in small businesses. It is possible, when a new business or its owner can offer adequate security, that a bank loan may be arranged. Another form of security that may underpin a bank loan is in the form of a guarantee from a reliable individual or other business with a banking track record.

4   Special Gift Supplies plc

(a)   The funding requirements for working capital is the sum of:

	Months
Stock holding period	3.5
Debtors collection period	2.5
Creditors payment period	(2.0)
Working capital funding period	4.0

Diagrammatically, the funding requirement may be represented as:

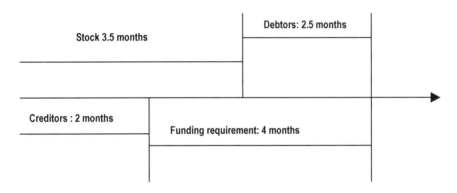

(b)   Annual sales: £2.5m

Credit sales: £2.5m × 90% = £2.25m

Factor will advance 80% of £2.25m = £1.8m. This is not adjusted for bad debts since the agreement is without recourse. Assuming sales are evenly spread, the factor will pay (2.25 – 1.8)/12 = £37,500 each month, in arrears by one month. Factors service charge is 4% × £2.25m = £90,000.

Commission charges payable to the sales force are ignored in the following calculations since they are common to both. The allocated overheads are also irrelevant for the evaluation. The factor's better record with bad debts is not part of the evaluation of the proposal in terms of the benefits to Special Gift Supplies.

Existing position:	£
Credit control salary	12,500
Bad debts 3% × £2.25m =	67,500
Annual funding costs for debtors (2.5/12) × 12% × £2.25m =	56,250
	136,250

Factor's offer:	£
Factor finance charge; £2.25m × 80% × 15% x (1/12) =	22,500
Unfactored funding costs at Special Gift Supplies cost of capital:	4,500
£2.25m × 20% × 12% × (1/12) =	
Factor service charge: 4% × £2.25m	90,000
One-off payment funding costs: at Special Gift Supplies cost	
of capital £25,000 × 12%	3,000
	120,000

Hence It Is Worthwhile To Factor The Debt

(c)   **Report on the credit control, factoring of debtors and the financing of working capital**

To: Financial Controller, Special Gift Supplies plc

From: A Student

Date: December 2001

Credit control

A good credit control department would exhibit a number of characteristics, some of which are included in the list below:

1   Preferably have a cash business relationship with customers to begin with

2   Obtain references for new customers and possibly visit their premises

3   Access the services of a credit rating agency

4   Only incrementally raise credit limits to that preferred by the customer

5   Maintain a history of transactions with each customer

6   Have documented procedures that explain to credit control employees credit limits and duration with clear action plans when these limits are breached

7   Create good reporting controls, such as aged list of debtors, and ensure the line of reporting is clear sothat senior management are aware of problem cases

8   Ensure the credit control reports form part of the monitoring of the working capital cycle as a whole so that imbalances do not arise

9   Access published information on customers, particularly through financial statements or through information services via credit or other agencies

10   Ensure all customers' credit limits are periodically reviewed

The benefits of factoring

A list of the benefits of factoring might include:

1   Access to flexible sources of finance. This is important for small businesses that experience rapid growth since the facility would normally grow with the business.

2   Sales ledger expertise. Factors can often bring a level of expertise to debtor management that small businesses may not have, either in skills or resources, thus making them more effective.

3   Factors can bring economies of scale to debtor management thus making them more efficient than a single small company could be.

4   The business can pay its own debts more promptly, thus ensuring continued supply of goods, for example and also in being able to access early payment discounts which may be substantial.

5   Stock levels may be optimally managed since they will be unencumbered by restrictions relating to payment difficulties. For example, it may be optimal for stock management purposes to reorder stock at lower, more expensive levels so that the whole of the stock related costs are minimised.

6   Debt factoring is a source of funds that ensure adequate financing for growing businesses. By facilitating this, one of the key issues involved in over trading is addressed.

7   Costs of sales ledger administration are avoided.

Financing of working capital

The financing of the components of working capital is not always undertaken on a completely maturity matched basis. That is, whilst working capital is regarded as net current assets that arguably should be funded by short term sources of finance, this is not always the case for two reasons. First, by construction, net current assets are funded by long term sources of finance to the extent that all short term sources of finance have been exhausted. This can be demonstrated from a characterisation of a typical balance sheet.

Fixed assets + net current assets – long term loans = capital and reserves

By simply re-arranging we see that:

Net current assets = capital and reserves + long term loans – fixed assets

That is, net current assets and funded by long term sources of finance not otherwise tied up in fixed assets. This amount will vary day to day because the components of working capital vary from day to day. However, to the extent that there exists positive net current assets, then adequate long term financing needs have to be considered.

Second, the liabilities component of working capital (trade creditors and bank overdrafts) represent sources of finance. As such, they are normally regarded as short term sources of finance. In reality for many businesses, there is likely to be a core of current assets that will always need funding: whilst the components of current assets will change on a day to day basis, their level – to an extent – will remain predictable. It is this predictable component that enables managers to utilise longer term sources of finance in the knowledge that the finance will always be required. The distinction is often made between fluctuating current assets and permanent current assets. To the extent that current assets are permanent, then they are more efficiently financed by longer term sources. This will help avoid the higher interest costs (implicit or explicit) in shorter term sources of finance. The distinction between fluctuating and permanent current assets is illustrated in the following diagram that indicates the relationship between asset variability and funding maturity.

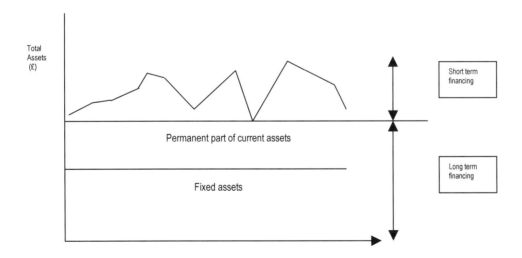

5   All Premier Services plc

(a)   (i)

	X	Y	Z
Number of beds	60	40	45
Fee per bed per night £	225	200	170
Assumed occupancy %	65	80	100
Occupied beds	39	32	45

Budgeted profit and loss statement per week

	X	Y	Z	Total
Income	61,425	44,800	53,550	159,775
Variable costs	16,305	11,892	14,215	42,412
Fixed costs	52,676	35,117	39,507	127,300
Total costs	**68,981**	**47,009**	**53,772**	**169,712**
Income less costs	-7,556	-2,209	-172	-9,937
Cost per occupied bed	1,769	1,469	1,194	

(ii)

	X	Y	Z
Number of beds	60	40	75
Fee per bed per night £	225	200	170
Assumed occupancy %	65	95	100
Occupied beds	48	38	75

Budgeted profit and loss statement per week

	X	Y	Z	Total
Income	75,600	53,200	89,250	218,050
Variable costs	20,068	14,122	23,691	57,881
Fixed costs	43,646	29,097	54,557	127,300
Total costs	**63,714**	**43,219**	**78,248**	**185,181**
Income less costs	11,886	9,982	11,002	32,869
Cost per occupied bed	1,327	1,137	1,043	

(b)   Ward Z patients from wards X and Y

The patients in ward z are existing patients and do not represent new admissions. For that reason, ward Z only exists a further outlet for wards X and Y. This implies a degree of dependency in operations. Decisions concerning ward Z cannot therefore be sepaprated from the decisions concerning X and Y. It may well be the case that, given the hospita private and presumably subject to competition, patients may choose All Premier Services because of the facilities offered in ward Z that might be available elsewhere.

The relevance of the allocation bases

Given that fixed overheads must be incurred irrespective of occupancy, then the fact that unoccupied beds are allocate costs irrespective of occupancy is probably the correct approach. On the other hand, variable overheads are allocate a fee earned per bed basis. The incorporation of fees into the allocation of variable overheads might reflect the fact t wards X and Y deal with patients with different medical conditions and costs. The fees charged by the hospital refle this fact. The adjustment for occupancy through the fees earned allocation base reflects the fact that variable overhea relate directly to resource use when beds are occupied. For this reason, it is probably an appropriate allocation base.

(c)   The characteristics of a responsibility accounting system imply a well organised system of budgetary control such that individuals are personally accountable for their budget centres and that there is a monitoring system which facilitates performance evaluation. The components of a well-organised system of control are:

1   a hierarchy of budget centres which mirror the lines of reporting within an organisation.

2   a defined purpose to the budget centre such that attached costs and revenues have an interpretation associated with the budget centre. Thus, if costs are rising in catering services and this is a budget centre, then a course of action can be devised which outlines alternatives to the way current catering facilities are delivered.

3   cost and revenues associated with a budget centre then become the responsibility of the budget holder to the extent that the budget holder can influence how the costs and revenues behave.

The difficulties associated with non-profit organisations are that the requirements for responsibility accounting are not easily met. For example, non-profit organisations:

1   often do not have clearly defined objectives or the objectives may be multiple. For example, local government offers a wide range of public services for which there are only fairly imprecise objectives. To the extent that objectives are unclear, then responsibility will be hard to define because there is no clear link between inputs and outputs (objectives).

2   many non-profit making organisations do not charge for their services and hence budget centres are then left monitoring rather that controlling costs. For example, hospital resources are consumed according to clinical decisions, but budget holders are often not medical staff.

3   value for money performance measures are sometimes used in the public sector that rely on measures relating to economy and efficiency. Whilst economy and efficiency may be measured in money terms, effectiveness may not be. Thus, non-financial objectives may be set off which may not be comparable between budget centres or to any overall objective.

4   public services are often characterised by a high level of fixed costs over which there is little discretion or room to change. Hence, responsibility is harder to define because change is difficult to implement.

December 2001 Marking scheme

				Marks	Marks
1	(a)		Calculation of capital allowance	3	
			Omission of apportionment overheads	1	
			Projected revenues	2	
			Variable costs	1	
			Incremental overheads	1	
			Tax on net revenues	1	
			NPV of revenues	1	
			NPV of lost contribution net of tax	2	
			Capital investment and disposal	1	
			Incorporation of capital allowances in cash flow	1	
			NPV of capital flows	1	
			Total NPV of new project	1	
			Use of correct discount factors	1	
			Investment decision	1	
					18
	(b)		Calculation of correct sensitivity		4
	(c)	(i)	Calculation of increase in occupancy	4	
		(ii)	Calculation of increase in contract length	4	
					8
	(d)		Up to 2 marks each for detailed points relating what is meant by risk	6	
			Up to 3 marks each for detailed points relating to estimating risk	12	
			Up to 2 marks each for detailed points relating to how to reduce risk	6	
			Presentation and quality of argument	2	
			Available	26	
			Total Maximum		20
					50
2	(a)		1 mark for each item referring to the use of standard costing	8	
			2 marks for each detailed item on why standards need reviewing	8	
			Available	16	
			Total Maximum		13

			Marks	Marks
(b)		Up to 2 marks for each detailed item on describing non-financial objectives	12	
		Up to 2 marks on role of stakeholders in shaping objectives	2	
		1 mark for identification of stakeholder	1	
		Available	15	
		Total Maximum		12
				25
3	(a)	Definition of opportunity cost		2
	(b)	Subcontractor costs	2	
		Supervisor costs	1	
		General overheads	1	
		Machine depreciation	1	
		Machine variable overheads	2	
		Materials	2	
		Interest costs	2	
				11
	(c)	Up to 2 marks each for detailed points relating to uncertainty	5	
		Up to 2 marks each for detailed points relating to collateral	5	
		Up to 2 marks each for detailed points relating sources of finance	5	
		Presentation and quality of argument	2	
		Available	17	
		Total Maximum		12
				25
4	(a)	Calculation of funding requirements in months		2
	(b)	Evaluation of existing position	2	
		Evaluation of factor's offer	4	
		Omission of overheads from evaluation	1	
		Omission of factor's bad debt record	1	
				8
	(c)	1 mark for each item characterising good credit control	5	
		1 mark for each benefit of factoring	5	
		Up to 2 marks for each detailed point on financing	6	
		Presentation and quality of argument	2	
		Available	18	
		Total Maximum		15
				25

◆ **FOULKS**lynch

5	(a)	(i)	Calculation of costs incurred per bed in each ward	5	
		(ii)	Calculation of costs incurred per bed in each ward	5	
				———	
					10
	(b)	(i)	Detailed comment that ward Z is serviced from wards X and Y	2	
		(ii)	Detailed comment of relevance of allocation bases	3	
				———	
					5
	(c)		Up to 2 marks each for detailed points on responsibility accounting.	6	
			Up to 2 marks each for detailed points on non-profit organisations	6	
			Presentation and quality of argument	2	
				———	
			Available	14	
			Total Maximum		10
					———
					25

Appendix
FORMULAE AND TABLES

Formulae

Linear regression

$r = [n\ \Sigma xy - \Sigma x \Sigma y\ ] / \sqrt{[n\ \Sigma x^2 - (\Sigma x)^2]\ [n\ \Sigma y^2 - (\Sigma y)^2]}$

If $y = a + bx$, $b = [n\ \Sigma xy - \Sigma x \Sigma y] / [n\Sigma x^2 - (\Sigma x)^2]$ and $= \Sigma y/n - b\Sigma x/n$

Economic order quantity

$EOQ = \sqrt{2C_0 D / C_H}$

Present Value Table

Present value of 1 i.e. $(1 + r)^{-n}$

Where r = discount rate

             n = number of periods until payment

Discount rates (r)

Periods (n)	1%	2%	3%	4%	5%	6%	7%	8%	9%	10%	
1	0.990	0.980	0.971	0.962	0.952	0.943	0.935	0.926	0.917	0.909	1
2	0.980	0.961	0.943	0.925	0.907	0.890	0.873	0.857	0.842	0.826	2
3	0.971	0.942	0.915	0.889	0.864	0.840	0.816	0.794	0.772	0.751	3
4	0.961	0.924	0.888	0.855	0.823	0.792	0.763	0.735	0.708	0.683	4
5	0.951	0.906	0.863	0.822	0.784	0.747	0.713	0.681	0.650	0.621	5
6	0.942	0.888	0.837	0.790	0.746	0.705	0.666	0.630	0.596	0.564	6
7	0.933	0.871	0.813	0.760	0.711	0.665	0.623	0.583	0.547	0.513	7
8	0/923	0.853	0.789	0.731	0.677	0.627	0.582	0.540	0.502	0.467	8
9	0.941	0.837	0.766	0.703	0.645	0.592	0.544	0.500	0.460	0.424	9
10	0.905	0.820	0.744	0.676	0.614	0.558	0.508	0.463	0.422	0.386	10
11	0.896	0.804	0.722	0.650	0.585	0.527	0.475	0.429	0.388	0.305	11
12	0.887	0.788	0.701	0.625	0.557	0.497	0.444	0.397	0.356	0.319	12
13	0.879	0.773	0.681	0.601	0.530	0.469	0.415	0.368	0.326	0.290	13
14	0.870	0.758	0.661	0.577	0.505	0.442	0.388	0.340	0.299	0.263	14
15	0.861	0.743	0.642	0.555	0.481	0.417	0.362	0.315	0.275	0.239	15

(n)	11%	12%	13%	14%	15%	16%	17%	18%	19%	20%	
1	0.901	0.893	0.885	0.877	0.870	0.862	0.855	0.847	0.840	0.833	1
2	0.812	0.797	0.783	0.769	0/756	0.743	0.731	0.718	0.706	0.694	2
3	0.731	0.712	0.693	0.675	0.658	0.641	0.624	0.609	0.593	0.579	3
4	0.659	0.636	0.613	0.592	0.572	0.552	0.534	0.516	0.499	0.482	4
5	0.593	0.567	0.543	0.519	0.497	0.476	0.456	0.437	0.419	0.402	5
6	0.535	0.507	0.480	0.456	0.432	0.410	0.390	0.370	0.352	0.335	6
7	0.482	0.452	0.425	0.400	0.376	0.354	0.333	0.314	0.296	0.279	7
8	0.434	0.404	0.376	0.351	0.327	0.305	0.285	0.266	0.249	0.233	8
9	0.391	0.361	0.333	0.308	0.284	0.263	0.243	0.225	0.209	0.194	9
10	0.352	0.322	0.295	0.270	0.247	0.227	0.208	0.191	0.176	0.162	10
11	0.317	0.287	0.261	0.237	0.215	0.195	0.178	0.162	0.148	0.135	11
12	0.286	0,257	0.231	0.208	0.187	0.168	0.152	0.137	0.124	0.112	12
13	0.258	0.229	0.204	0.182	0.163	0.145	0.130	0.116	0.104	0.093	13
14	0.232	0.205	0.181	0.160	0.141	0.125	0.111	0.099	0.088	0.078	14
15	0.209	0.183	0.160	0.140	0.123	0.108	0.095	0.084	0.074	0.065	15

◈ FOULKS*lynch*

Annuity Table

Present value of an annuity of 1 i.e. $\dfrac{1 - (1 + r)^{-n}}{r}$

Where r = discount rate

n = number of periods

Discount rate (r)

Periods (n)	1%	2%	3%	4%	5%	6%	7%	8%	9%	10%	
1	0.990	0.980	0.971	0.962	0.952	0.943	0.935	0.926	0.917	0.909	1
2	1.970	1.942	1.913	1.886	1.859	1.833	1.808	1.783	1.759	1.736	2
3	2.941	2.884	2.829	2.775	2.723	2.673	2.624	2.577	2.531	2.487	3
4	3.902	3.808	3.717	3.630	3.546	3.465	3.387	3.312	3.240	3.170	4
5	4.853	4.713	4.580	4.452	4.329	4.212	4.100	3.993	3.890	3.791	5
6	5.795	5.601	5.417	5.242	5.076	4.917	4.767	4.623	4.486	4.355	6
7	6.728	6.472	6.230	6.002	5.786	5.582	5.389	5.206	5.033	4.868	7
8	7.652	7.325	7.020	6.733	6.463	6.210	5.971	5.747	5.535	5.335	8
9	8.566	8.162	7.786	7.435	7.108	6.802	6.515	6.247	5.995	5.759	9
10	9.471	8.983	8.530	8.111	7.722	7.360	7.024	6.710	6.418	6.145	10
11	10.37	9.787	9.253	8.760	8.306	7.887	7.499	7.139	6.805	6.495	11
12	11.26	10.58	9.954	9.385	8.863	8.384	7.943	7.536	7.161	6.814	12
13	12.13	11.35	10.63	9.986	9.394	8.853	8.358	7.904	7.487	7.103	13
14	13.00	12.11	11.30	10.56	9.899	9.295	8.745	8.244	7.786	7.367	14
15	13.87	12.85	11.94	11.12	10.38	9.712	9.108	8.559	8.061	7.606	15

Periods (n)	11%	12%	13%	14%	15%	16%	17%	18%	19%	20%	
1	0.901	0.893	0.885	0.877	0.870	0.862	0.855	0.847	0.840	0.833	1
2	1.713	1.690	1.668	1.647	1.626	1.605	1.585	1.566	1.547	1.528	2
3	2.444	2.402	2.361	2.322	2.283	2.246	2.210	2.174	2.140	2.106	3
4	3.102	3.037	2.974	2.914	2.855	2.798	2.743	2.690	2.639	2.589	4
5	3.696	3.605	3.517	3.433	3.352	3.274	3.199	3.127	3.058	2.991	5
6	4.231	4.111	3.998	3.889	3.784	3.685	3.589	3.498	3.410	3.326	6
7	4.712	4.564	4.423	4.288	4.160	4.039	3.922	3.812	3.706	3.605	7
8	5.146	4.968	4.799	4.639	4.487	4.344	4.207	4.078	3.954	3.837	8
9	5.537	5.328	5.132	4.946	4.772	4.607	4.451	4.303	4.163	4.031	9
10	5.889	5.650	5.426	5.216	5.019	4.833	4.659	4.494	4.339	4.192	10
11	6.207	5.938	5.687	5.453	5.234	5.029	4.836	4.656	4.486	4.327	11
12	6.492	6.194	5.918	5.660	5.421	5.197	4.988	4.793	4.611	4.439	12
13	6.750	6.424	6.122	5.842	5.583	5.342	5.118	4.910	4.715	4.533	13
14	6.982	6.628	6.302	6.002	5.724	5.468	5.229	5.008	4.802	4.611	14
15	7.191	6.811	6.462	6.142	5.847	5.575	5.324	5.092	4.876	4.675	15

◈ FOULKS*lynch*

Official Publisher

FOULKS LYNCH
4 The Griffin Centre
Staines Road
Feltham
Middlesex, TW14 0HS
United Kingdom

For information and online ordering, please visit our website at:
www.foulkslynch.com

HOTLINES   Telephone: +44 (0) 20 8831 9990
Fax: +44 (0) 20 8831 9991
E-mail: info@foulkslynch.com

PRODUCT RANGE

We have been the **official publisher for ACCA** since 1995. Our publications cover all exams modules for the new syllabus which was first examined in December 2001.

Textbooks	£19.95	Interactive Online Courses	£150+VAT
Revision Series	£11.50	Tracks Audio Tapes	£7.95+VAT
Lynchpins	£6.25	Distance Learning Courses	£89.95

OTHER PUBLICATIONS FROM FOULKS LYNCH

We publish a wide range of study material in the accountancy field and specialise in texts for the following professional qualifications:

- **Association of Accounting Technicians (AAT)**
- **Certified Accounting Technicians (CAT)**
- **Chartered Institute of Management Accountants (CIMA)**

FOR FURTHER INFORMATION ON OUR PUBLICATIONS

I would like information on publications for: ACCA ❑   AAT ❑
CAT ❑   CIMA ❑

Please keep me updated on new publications: ❑   By E-mail ❑   By Post ❑

Your name...   Your email address................................
Your address:.......................................
....
....
....

Prices are correct at time of going to press and are subject to change